DATE DUE

~~DE 5'01~~			
~~DE 18 '02~~			
~~AG 10 '10~~			

DEMCO 38-296

AFRICAN-AMERICAN ENGLISH

African-American English: Structure, history, and use provides a timely, comprehensive, state-of-the-art survey of linguistic research. The main focus of the book is the linguistic features of African-American English, in particular the grammar, phonology, and lexicon. Further chapters explore the sociological, political, and educational issues connected with African-American English.

The editors are the leading experts in the field and along with other key figures, notably William Labov, Geneva Smitherman, and Walt Wolfram, they provide an authoritative, diverse guide to this topical subject area. Drawing on many contemporary references such as the Oakland School controversy and the rap of Mary J. Blige, the contributors reflect the state of current scholarship on African-American English, and actively dispel many misconceptions, address new questions, and explore new approaches.

The book is designed to serve as a text for the increasing number of courses on African-American English and as a convenient reference for students of linguistics, black studies, and anthropology at both undergraduate and postgraduate levels.

Salikoko S. Mufwene is Professor and Chair at the Department of Linguistics at the University of Chicago. **John R. Rickford** is Professor of Linguistics and **John Baugh** is Professor of Education and Linguistics, both are at Stanford University. **Guy Bailey** is Professor of English, Dean of Graduate Studies and Associate Provost for Research at the University of Texas.

AFRICAN-AMERICAN ENGLISH

Structure, history, and use

Edited by
Salikoko S. Mufwene, John R. Rickford,
Guy Bailey, and John Baugh

London and New York

First published 1998
by Routledge
11 New Fetter Lane, London EC4P 4EE

Simultaneously published in the USA and Canada
by Routledge
29 West 35th Street, New York, NY 10001

Typeset in Goudy by Keystroke, Jacaranda Lodge, Wolverhampton
Printed and bound in Great Britain by TJ International Ltd., Padstow, Cornwall

British Library Cataloguing in Publication Data
A catalogue record for this book is available from the British Library

Library of Congress Cataloguing in Publication Data
African-American English : structure, history, and use / edited by
Salikoko S. Mufwene . . . [et al.].
p.   cm.
ISBN 0–415–11732–1 (hardbound). – ISBN 0–415–11733–X (pbk.)
1. Afro-Americans–Language. 2. English language–Social aspects–
United Sates. 3. Black English. 4. Americanisms. I. Mufwene,
Salikoko S.
PE3102.N44A34   1998
427′.08996073–dc21   97–37628
CIP

ISBN 0–415–11733–X (Pbk)
ISBN 0–415–11732–1 (Hbk)

CONTENTS

CONTENTS

FIGURES AND TABLES

Figures

Tables

CONTRIBUTORS

Guy Bailey is Professor of English, Dean of Graduate Studies, and Associate Provost for Research at the University of Texas at San Antonio. He was recently Dean of Liberal Arts of the University of Nevada at Las Vegas. His research focuses on varieties of American English, mainly on language variation and change. He is co-editor of *Language Variety in the South* (1986) and *The Emergence of Black English* (1991).

John Baugh is Professor of Education and Linguistics at Stanford University. His main research interests are in the educational and policy applications of linguistics, including sociolinguistics, applied linguistics, phonetics, phonology, discourse analysis, historical linguistics, and dialectology. He is the author of *Black Street Speech* (1983) and co-editor of *Language in Use: Readings in Sociolinguistics* and *Towards a Social Science of Language: Papers in Honour of William Labov* (1997).

Lisa Green is an Assistant Professor in the Department of Linguistics at the University of Massachusetts at Amherst, on leave from the University of Texas at Austin. She teaches courses in syntactic theory and in the syntax and semantics of African-American English. She is the author of 'Remote Past and States in African American English', to appear in *American Speech*.

William Labov, the pre-eminent name in studies of AAVE, is Professor of Linguistics and Director of the Linguistics Laboratory at the University of Pennsylvania. Among his seminal publications on the subject matter are: *Language in the Inner City* and *Sociolinguistic Patterns* (1972), 'Objectivity and commitment in linguistic science', in *Language in Society* (1982), and 'Can reading failure be reversed?', in V. Gadsden and D. Wagner (eds), *Literacy Among African-American Youth: Issues in Learning, Teaching and Schooling* (1995).

Stefan Martin is a language arts teacher at Deer Park Middle School. He completed a Ph.D. in linguistics at the University of Maryland in 1992, with a dissertation titled 'Topics in the syntax of nonstandard English'.

Marcyliena Morgan is an Associate Professor of Anthropology at UCLA and Visiting Associate Professor at the Harvard Graduate School of Education. She is the editor of *Language and the Social Construction of Identity in Creole Situations* (1994) and author of several articles including: 'Redefining language in the inner city: Adolescents, media and urban space' (1996.) and 'Conversational signifying: Grammar and indirectness among African-American women', (in *Interaction and Grammar*, 1996).

Salikoko S. Mufwene is Professor and Chair at the Department of Linguistics at the University of Chicago. He works on the morphosyntax of primarily Gullah and has contributed critical essays on African-American English. He is associated with the "complementary hypothesis" of creole genesis and is currently working on an ethnographic-ecology approach to the subject matter as sketched in his 'The Founder Principle in creole genesis' (*Diachronica* 1996). He edited *Africanisms in Afro-American Language Varieties* (1993) and was Associate Editor of the *Journal of Pidgin and Creole Languages* (1989–1995).

John R. Rickford is Professor of Linguistics at Stanford University and current President of the Society for Pidgin and Creole Linguistics. He has been studying sociolinguistic variation in African-American vernacular English, Gullah, Guyanese, and other Caribbean English creoles since 1969. He is the author of numerous papers and author/editor of several books, including *Dimensions of a Creole Continuum* (1987), *Sociolinguistics and Pidgin-Creole Studies* (1987), and *Analyzing Variation in Language* (1987).

Geneva Smitherman is University Distinguished Professor of English and Director of the African American Language and Literacy Program at Michigan State University, at East Lansing. She was the chief advocate for the children in the 1979 "Ann Arbor Black English" King case. She has published or edited *Talkin and Testifyin: The Language of Black America* (1981), and *Black Talk: Words and Phrases from the Hood to the Amen Corner* (1993).

Arthur K. Spears is a Professor in the Linguistics and Anthropology Programs of The Graduate Center, The City University of New York (CUNY), and Chair of the Anthropology Department at the City College, CUNY. He has (co-)edited *The Structure and Status of Pidgins and Creoles* (1997) and *Race and Ideology: Language, Symbolism, and Popular Culture* (1998).

Erik Thomas is an Assistant Professor in the Department of English at North Carolina State University at Raleigh. His research has been on language variation, especially with regard to vowels of English. His publications include 'A comparison of variation patterns of variables among sixth-graders in an Ohio community' (In *Focus on the USA*, ed. E. W. Schneider, 1996), and 'The origin of Canadian raising in Ontario' (*Canadian Journal of Linguistics*, 1991).

Walt Wolfram is the William C. Friday Distinguished Professor at North Carolina State University, at Raleigh, where he directs the North Carolina Language and Life Project. The latest of his extensive publications on vernacular dialects of English include the following books which he has co-authored with his research associates: *American English: Dialects and variation* (1998), *Dialect Change and Maintenance on the Outer Banks* (1998), and *Hoi Toide on the Outer Banks* (1997).

ACKNOWLEDGEMENTS

We thank Lisa McNair-Dupree, Angela Rickford, and Sali Tagliamonte for feedback on the Introduction. Lisa has also been instrumental in the mechanics of preparing the manuscript for the publisher, converting the submissions from different electronic platforms to one, and reformatting all the manuscripts according to one style sheet. Delays in the production of the book would have increased without her timely intervention, and we are very grateful for her assistance.

We are also grateful to Routledge's editorial staff, especially Julia Harding, for their careful examination of the manuscript, which has certainly enhanced the quality of this volume.

The following individuals and institutions granted permission to reproduce copyright material:

Extracts from lyrics on *What's the 411?*, Mary J. Blige 1992, © Copyright by Bridgeport Music Inc., (BMI), Tony Do Fat Music, Jeffix Music Co, Great Walrus Ltd. and Fifth Floor Music Inc., All Rights Reserved. Used by permission.

Extract from "Imitation of Life" from the fall 1992 preview issue of *Vibe Magazine*, reproduced by permission of James Ledbetter.

Extract from "Very Special" on *Looks Like a Job for . . .* , Big Daddy Kane 1993, © Copyright by Fifth Floor Music Inc., All Rights Reserved. Used by permission.

Extract from "Fly Girl" on *Nature of a Sista*, Queen Latifah 1991, © Hal Leonard Corporation, All Rights Reserved. Used by permission. Words and music by Queen Latifah, Soul shock and Cutfather © 1991 EMI VIRGIN MUSIC, INC., CASADIDA MUSIC PUBLISHING, and TOMMY BOY MUSIC. All rights for CASADIDA MUSIC PUBLISHING controlled and administered by EMI VIRGIN MUSIC INC. All Rights Reserved. International copyright secured. Used by permission.

Extract from "Cop Killer", Ice T, reproduced by kind permission of Rythym Syndicate Music.

While the publishers and authors have made every effort to contact copyright holders of material used in this volume, they would be grateful to hear from any they were unable to contact.

INTRODUCTION

Salikoko S. Mufwene and John R. Rickford

For more than a quarter of a century, there has been no textbook on African-American vernacular English (AAVE) that represents the state of the art or is comprehensive enough to cover more than a few features traditionally associated with this vernacular, such as consonant cluster reduction, the absence of the copula, invariant or habitual *be*, time reference markers, and multiple negation. So this book should fill a need which has long been felt among linguists interested in this distinctive variety of American English. Education problems in the American public school systems have also underscored the need for educators and other citizens to have a reference work which can help them become better informed about AAVE's structural features, its history and lexicon, its use in discourse, and its relevance to the educational problems of African-American school children. The fury of polemics in the United States following the Oakland School Board's decision in December 1996 to make its teachers sensitive to the vernacular of African-American students has made it even more compelling to produce this kind of book. Although it does include analyses at a fairly technical and sophisticated level, much of this volume should remain accessible to teachers who have not had a class on AAVE. They should be able to turn to it to understand the systematic nature of AAVE, and the problems faced by a large proportion of African-American students in acquiring Standard English (SE).

This book responds to the twin demands of linguists and educators. We thought that a joint project, drawing on the strengths of many scholars, would come closest to satisfying the diverse interests of various instructors and students of AAVE. We have approached the project not only by discussing aspects of this vernacular which distinguish it from other varieties of English, but also by highlighting many aspects which it shares with some of them. This approach should help to dispel the misperception that AAVE consists only of deviations from other varieties of English spoken in North America, especially SE. At the same time, most of the chapters are written in such a way that the particular subsystem of AAVE that they cover will help readers realize that this vernacular has its own rules and regularities, like other living language varieties.

1

While contributors to this book extend the discussion of topics like AAVE's morphosyntax and history, which have been the foci of AAVE research for decades, they also broach others such as AAVE's phonology, lexicon, and pragmatics, which have received little or no attention in the linguistics literature, especially in recent years. It is hoped that this broadening of the scope of AAVE research will help to set the research agenda for the future. After all, if this vernacular is structurally self-contained, despite what it shares with other Englishes, there should be many more topics worthy of linguistic analysis than the few which the scholarship has covered to date.

Part I: Structure

We begin with "structure" partly because AAVE's grammatical features most clearly demonstrate that it is a structured and systematic variety, not the random or careless speech which many mistakenly assume it to be.

For years, the classic study of the structural features of AAVE was Fasold and Wolfram's (1970) article "Some linguistic features of Negro dialect," so it is fitting that Wolfram is also co-author of the updated survey of AAVE sentence structure in this volume. Stefan Martin and Walt Wolfram's "The sentence in African-American vernacular English" draws on recent Government Binding Theory to explicate what AAVE shares structurally with other varieties of English and where those typological similarities end. Their observation that surface differences often mask underlying similarities, while surface similarities often mask deeper differences, is a sobering thought to those who jump to facile comparisons. In addition to drawing our attention to classic AAVE features like multiple negation and negative inversion, they shed light on question formation, relative clauses, and double modals. Their data also raise interesting questions for other students of English syntax (after all, AAVE is a form of English!), such as: What are the necessary conditions for identifying a particular morpheme as a complementizer?

Lisa Green's "Aspect and predicate phrases in African-American vernacular English," like other chapters in this section, enriches the book by analyzing more than the kinds of structures that have typically been discussed in the literature and by relating the topics to current interests in theoretical syntax. Beginning with paradigms of verb forms which permit systematic comparison with other English varieties, Green highlights similarities and differences between AAVE and SE verb phrases, focusing on finite auxiliaries as well as on markers of tense and aspect like *be* and *BIN* which are legendary in the literature on AAVE. She starts with a primer for studying the verb phrase and gradually explores what may be identified as peculiarities of AAVE, articulating the meanings of aspectual auxiliaries. Readers of this chapter may want to explore further the question of what criteria make a particular item an auxiliary verb, a question which arises from a comparison of the facts she covers with those typically discussed in the syntax literature.

2

While Green extends the Martin and Wolfram overview of AAVE syntax by refining our view of the verb phrase, Salikoko Mufwene extends it by refining our view of the noun phrase. His chapter "The structure of the noun phrase in African-American vernacular English" is written in much the same style as are the preceding chapters on syntax, covering several aspects of this syntactic category. Among the topics he discusses are: What does the noun phrase consist of in AAVE? What are the strategies used in this vernacular to mark *plural* and *possession*? How is the distinction between *individuated* and *non-individuated* noun phrases expressed? How are relative clauses formed? Like other chapters in the volume, Mufwene's contribution covers both subsystems peculiar to AAVE and those that it shares with other varieties of English.

Part II: History

Forming a natural bridge between "structure" and "history" is Guy Bailey and Erik Thomas' chapter "Some aspects of African-American vernacular English phonology." The phonology of a language is of course an important part of the structure of any language, but the historical implications of Bailey and Thomas' study also make it relevant to the second, historical part of this volume. Since phonology has been such a neglected aspect of linguistic scholarship on AAVE in recent years, this chapter is particularly welcome. On the descriptive level, it covers a wide range of the vernacular's segmental features, distinguishing between those that are shared with most English varieties (including SE), those that are shared with other non-standard varieties (including Southern White speech), and those that are apparently unique to AAVE. The exposition is supplemented with revealing acoustic plots of the vowel systems of various individuals, Black and White. The chapter also has a significant historical overtone: the authors suggest when particular features may have emerged in the evolution of this variety, as they note which vowel features are suggestive of earlier creole connections and which are suggestive of twentieth-century innovation. Phonological features are rarely invoked in discussions of the creole origins of AAVE, and Bailey and Thomas' chapter will, we hope, help to reverse this trend and shed more light on this complex issue.

In his "Co-existent systems in African-American vernacular English" William Labov both widens the range of data on time reference and attempts to interpret these facts in terms of co-existent systems, each of which accounts for part of the data but not all. A general American-English system and a system more specific to AAVE are shown to co-exist with each other, an approach which makes it possible to highlight ways in which AAVE may be related, at least typologically, to Atlantic English creoles, while it shares part of its structures with other North American varieties of English. At the heart of Labov's chapter is his discussion of the "semantic efflorescence" of AAVE, represented by its significant, and apparently evolving, tense aspect markers, including *be*, *done*, *be done*, and stressed *BIN*. What places this chapter in the historical section of this book is its incidental discussion of the creole origins hypothesis, and its more detailed claim that these and other markers are "creations of the twentieth century." This is a controversial claim, which, like Labov's earlier suggestions that AAVE is currently diverging from other American vernaculars rather than converging with them, is likely to provoke considerable discussion.

John R. Rickford surveys a central historical question in the literature on AAVE in his chapter "The creole origins of African-American vernacular English: evidence from copula absence." He begins by explaining what it means to suggest that AAVE might have had creole influences or origins, and then identifies in detail the kinds of evidence that might be brought to bear on the issue. He then proceeds to examine quantitative evidence on copula absence – the most thoroughly studied feature of AAVE – from historical attestations, diaspora recordings, creole similarities, African language similarities, and English dialect differences, as these bear on the larger issue of prior creolization in AAVE. Although he concludes that "there is enough evidence in these data to suggest that AAVE did have some creole roots," he finds the data more complex and ambiguous than others have assumed, and he identifies several research questions that merit further investigation.

Part III: Use

This section begins with two chapters on the lexicon of AAVE, an area which has been severely neglected in our scholarship, but one which is often the subject of overt comment and discussion by native speakers and by members of the general public.

Geneva Smitherman's "Word from the hood: the lexicon of African-American vernacular English" makes the important point that distinctive AAVE lexicon cuts across social boundaries of all kinds within the African-American community, including sex, age, religion, social class, and region. While some elements certainly come from the domain of rap and hip hop, many AAVE words have arisen since the times of slavery, and the lexicon as a whole best captures the "commonality" of the African-American community. Among the subtopics which Smitherman covers are the evolution of terms for the race itself (from *African* to *Colored* to *negro* to *Negro* to *Black* to *African American*), and "cross over[s]" of words from the AAVE lexicon into varieties spoken by other Americans and peoples around the world – some of these have been co-opted for use in corporate advertising.

Arthur Spears' "African-American language use: ideology and so-called obscenity" is a daring chapter, as it takes up the scholarly analysis of uncensored speech which some find obscene or offensive. The very length of its introductory section highlights the sensitive nature of the material, as the author attempts to forewarn readers who might be offended and as he emphasizes that the words he discusses are not representative of his own speech or attitudes; they are nonetheless ones he hears daily. We too need to remind readers that the words Spears considers are used by some, but not all, speakers of AAVE. The two expressions on which he focuses are -ass words, such as *bitch-ass* and *jive-ass*, and the use of *nigga* (the "N word"). In both cases, he reveals regularities and provides insights about their grammar and use which might otherwise have been unnoticed, and in his conclusion he relates his discussion to larger issues concerning language evaluation and censorship. One of his main points is that different attitudes towards words of this type reveal class differences within the African-American community (this is the rupture side of the commonality Smitherman stresses), and betray the double-edged nature of African-American consciousness in the United States.

Marcyliena Morgan's "More than a mood or an attitude: discourse and verbal genres in African-American culture" covers a range of discourse and verbal genres used within the African-American community, including *signifying*, *playing the dozens*, *instigating*, *reading a person*, *reading dialect*, and *he-said-she-said* disputes. The discussion includes consideration of the kinds of *face* individuals try to project, the role of audience and interaction, and the kinds of indirect and direct speech which are cultivated and evaluated within the community. One virtue of Morgan's analysis is that it dispels the misconception, common in the early literature, that distinctive African-American speech events are the exclusive province of adolescent males. Not only does she skillfully distinguish between adolescent and adult usage, but she also draws most of her examples from the usage of African-American women, indicating which verbal strategies differ along gender lines.

The final chapter in this section is John Baugh's "Linguistics, education, and the law: educational reform for African-American language minority students," which is particularly relevant to Oakland's Ebonics proposal of 1996 and the fallout it provoked. One might wonder why it appears in this section, since it has to do neither with pragmatics nor vocabulary, the customary provinces of "use" and "usage." However, it does involve "use" in a larger sense, the use which educators and policy makers might make of the information about the systematic nature of AAVE provided in this book, and by linguists more generally. Among other things, Baugh distinguishes between the kinds of financial and educational assistance provided by Title I (students in poverty), Title VII (Limited English Proficiency students requiring bilingual education or English as a Second Language), and Special Education (cognitive and physical limitations) programs. He argues that speakers of AAVE, who are native speakers of English, but of a vernacular rather than standard variety, fall between the legal and educational cracks. He proposes a set of alternative categories and measures to remedy the situation.

Final remarks

Overall, the chapters of this book reflect more or less the state of current scholarship on AAVE. However, they do not simply summarize the state of the art. They also address new questions, explore new approaches, and sometimes apply current analytical frameworks in novel ways. The interest in matters of linguistic theory which some authors display have not eclipsed the primary interest of this book in disseminating facts about AAVE and the varying interpretations which different scholars have made of them. The chapters show that the same facts may be approached in more than one way. In fact, they indirectly invite the reader to take the same facts and try to approach them differently, to see whether we may understand them in ways that will shed new light on how language works. AAVE is relevant to the development of more than quantitative sociolinguistics, and it is as relevant to the development of theories of language structure and change as SE is.

Some chapters overlap in this book, especially Smitherman's, Spears', and Morgan's, as well as Green's, Labov's, and Martin and Wolfram's. They do not, however, merely repeat each other. We thought readers should benefit from their complementarity. The lack of consensus on some issues must be interpreted positively as reflecting limitations on what we know, which is true in almost all aspects of science qua quest for knowledge of reality around us. Again, we hope that readers consider this book an invitation to conduct their own research on aspects of AAVE of interest to them and to contribute to our ongoing understanding of this important variety.

The organization of the chapters is not intended to suggest any particular order in which topics must be read and discussed in a class on AAVE, nor to suggest any particular scale of importance. The chapters are typically self-contained, although knowledge of what was being written by other contributors has influenced what individual authors felt relevant to discuss, in order to reduce redundancies. Users of this book should thus feel free to start reading the book with any chapter that interests them. However, where topics have been identified by their grouping into sections as related, readers may benefit more from reading the essays in the order in which they are presented.

Some chapters will be most accessible to advanced college students who have had some linguistics, but not necessarily a lot. Where students have had no or little linguistics training, we hope that their teachers have, and that they can explain to the class what they should know in order to derive maximum benefit from the chapters. A useful strategy used by some of us has been to present and discuss relevant data first, before referring students to technical analyses and detailed references. Such introductory sessions may help some students understand the chapters better and lead them to participate more successfully in more advanced discussions. Of course, there are also several chapters, particularly those in the final section, which are fully accessible to readers with no, or little, linguistic background.

Finally, we hope that this book will interest its readers not only in AAVE but also, and more generally, in non-standard vernaculars. Except perhaps for work done in the research paradigm of quantitative sociolinguistics, our knowledge of the structures and other aspects of such varieties lags behind what is known about

Standard English. Yet all English varieties should contribute to the development of theories of English, just as all languages should bear on hypotheses about Language. May this book be considered a modest step in this direction.

Part I

STRUCTURE

1

THE SENTENCE IN AFRICAN-AMERICAN VERNACULAR ENGLISH

Stefan Martin and *Walt Wolfram*

1.1 Introduction

Speakers of other English dialects sometimes view the sentence structure of African-American vernacular English (AAVE) as distinct from the many varieties of English spoken in the United States and elsewhere. African Americans who speak AAVE may feel the same way, and some may even make this distinctiveness a point of ethnic pride. In the sense that each dialect of English is unique, those who believe that AAVE is *sui generis* are right. But the distinctiveness of AAVE does not particularly reside in the structure of its sentences. Basic utterance types – e.g., declarative, interrogative, and imperative sentences – are all formed in essentially the same way as they are in other dialects. Even where its sentence structure is notably different from most other dialects, AAVE is generally not unique: those syntactic structures purportedly found only in AAVE are in fact part of dialects spoken by other groups, especially but not limited to Anglo-American vernacular English speakers who live in the southern United States. Therefore, except where warranted, we will examine AAVE sentence structures without making any claims for their uniqueness.

When we say that AAVE shares its fundamental sentence structure with other varieties of English, we mean that the essential clause and phrase constituents within the sentence are the same. For example, the word order for AAVE canonical sentences (i.e., the most basic sentences) is subject-verb-object (SVO), just as it is in other varieties of English. Other languages use SVO too, but some use SOV or VSO word order part or all of the time.

As in other dialects of English, we also find that AAVE embeds or incorporates *finite clauses*, usually complementizer phrases (CP) in the main or matrix clause, as in (1a). AAVE also allows embedding of *infinitival (untensed) clauses* like (1b), and *small (verbless) clauses* (1c, d).[1]

11

(1) a. I think [_{CP} (that) the dog ate the meal]
    b. He told [_{IP} the students to be quiet]
    c. She saw [_{XP} the students working/alive/on the job]
    d. He called [_{XP} Bill a fool]

Although all embedded clause types are represented in AAVE syntax, some are not used as frequently as in other varieties. For example, a sentence with a clause structure, such as *I judge them to be the winners*, would not be found very frequently in AAVE or other vernaculars which typically use more informal language registers.

Finally, as in other varieties of English, the fundamental structure of AAVE phrases is head-first rather than head-last. That is, the central element or *head* of phrases is almost always on the left (in written English, or first in spoken language) rather than the right, like the verb *miss* in the verb phrase (VP) [[_V miss] [_{NP} the class]] or the preposition *by* in the preposition phrase (PP) [[_P by] [_{NP} the garden]].

1.2 Some conspicuous differences

Non-specialists and specialists alike have cited a number of AAVE features as evidence for the distinctiveness of AAVE sentence structure. But some of the most obvious traits do not involve differences in syntax but rather the lexical peculiarities of certain AAVE verbs. For example, consider the sentence in (2a).

(2) a. [_{IP} There [_{VP} go the pencil]]
    a'. [_{IP} There [_{VP} is the pencil]]

The structure of (2a), which is usually associated with younger AAVE speakers, is no different from Standard English (SE) (2a'), but the use of *go* is distinctive. In AAVE, it can denote the static location of an object. In other varieties of English, *go* is limited to objects which are beginning to move or act (e.g., *There goes the car, There goes Bill again*). Although this difference may be striking to speakers of other dialects because of its unfamiliarity, it is no more noteworthy than other semantic-lexical dialect differences observed in English. For example,

---

1 In this chapter we use theoretical notions from the Government Binding (GB) theoretical framework (Chomsky 1981). We have tried to minimize technical terms which may be unfamiliar to some readers, but some are necessary. Sentences, previously noted as S, are represented by *inflection phrase* (IP). Elements which are moved to the left of the subject raise to one of two positions inside a *complementizer phrase* (CP): *Comp* itself, which is now the head of CP; or to the *specifier* of CP (Spec CP). In the tradition of current syntactic analysis, the brackets [ ] are used to indicate a string of words that fit together as a constituent, such as a phrase or clause. The subscript within the brackets is used to indicate the phrase type. In this convention XP is used to indicate a range of phrase types.

the noun *soda*, depending on the regional variety, may or may not denote a drink which contains ice cream, but the word will almost always occupy the head position of a noun phrase (NP).

Sentence (3a) demonstrates another AAVE peculiarity, this one concerning the complementation of the verb *beat*.

(3) a. [$_{IP}$ The team [$_{VP}$ *beat*]]
     b. [$_{IP}$ The team [$_{VP}$ *won* easily]]
     c. [$_{IP}$ Alta Vista [$_{VP}$ *rules*]]

In many varieties of English, *beat* is always transitive – that is, it requires an overt direct object. However, in AAVE the object complement is not required in all uses. In its intransitive form *beat* is comparable to SE verb–adverb combinations like *win easily* (3b). This tendency to detransitivize verbs is not productive in AAVE, and it warrants no more comment than, for example, the appearance of intransitive verb *rule* in the current use of Anglo-American teenagers and young adults (3c). Certainly, AAVE has many verb forms that require overt objects, and the vast majority of verbs in AAVE match other English varieties in verb complement selection. Nonetheless, there are a limited number of cases in which the lexical verbs of AAVE may differ from other varieties.

The use of *ruded* in (4a) involves a *functional shift* peculiar to this item. This process transforms an adjective into a verb which takes an NP direct object and a locational prepositional phrase.

(4) a. The students [$_{VP}$ *ruded* them in line]
     b. Kim's lies [$_{VP}$ *soured* Stacey on the idea of a joint venture]

This use of *rude*, observed among young AAVE speakers in Baltimore, Maryland, is more regionally restricted than the uses of *go* and *beat*. We should expect this sort of regional lexical variation in AAVE, just as we do in other varieties which have wide geographic distribution. Moreover, as sentence (4b) shows, the shift of adjectives into verbs is a known tendency in other varieties of English.

1.3 Subtlety in patterning

While some conspicuous features have been used to argue for the syntactic distinctiveness of AAVE, these sometimes turn out to be isolated and unproductive lexical peculiarities, with little or no significance for the syntax of this variety. However, there are AAVE structures which at first look similar or identical to those in other varieties of English, but which in fact mask underlying differences. One of these is AAVE *béen* (5a), in which the form is stressed.

(5) a. The man *béen* married
    b. The man has *béen* married
    c. The man's *béen* married

At first glance, (5a) appears to be derived from the present perfect form of *be*, *has been*. We might assume that *has*, the full auxiliary verb (5b), is first contracted to *'s* (5c), then deleted (5a) through a phonological process common to vernacular varieties of English – e.g., *have/has* → *'ve/s* → Ø; *is* → *'s* → Ø, etc. (cf. Labov 1969). But this analysis cannot account for all instances of *béen* (Rickford 1975, 1977, as well as Chapters 2 and 5 of this volume). For example, *béen* can also occur in transitive VP constructions, e.g., (6a). If we reconstruct (6a) as we did (5a), the result is the ill-formed, or "ungrammatical" sentence (6b). Apparently, (6b) is not the underlying sentence for (6a). Instead, *béen* seems to be a distinct aspectual marker in the AAVE auxiliary paradigm denoting non-recent or 'remote past' time.

(6) a. The man [$_{VP}$ *béen* married [$_{NP}$ the woman]]
    b. * The man [$_{Infl}$ has [$_{VP}$ *béen* married [$_{NP}$ the woman]]]
    c. The woman *béen* married

The case for a distinct, AAVE-particular *béen* is further supported by differing interpretations which AAVE and Anglo-American English speakers assign to sentences like (6c) (Rickford 1975). The latter group typically understands that the sentence predicates something of a woman who was married but no longer is. AAVE speakers typically infer that the woman has been married a long time and still is – hardly a minor difference. Several other unique auxiliaries distinguish AAVE from mainstream varieties of English. Some of these are discussed in Chapters 2 and 5 of this volume. Another, double modals, will be discussed later in this chapter.

In the literature on AAVE, structures like (5a, 6a) are cited as examples of *camouflaging*, the phenomenon in which a vernacular form closely resembles a standard form while being different in structure or meaning (Spears 1982; Baugh 1984; Wolfram 1995). Sentence (7a) demonstrates another instance. "Indignant" *come* – called this because the *come* V +*ing* construction is used in AAVE solely to express speaker indignation – appears at first to behave like the *come* V+*ing* structures in other varieties, where it is used with verb combinations often indicating movement, as in (7b).

(7) a. They *come* talking that trash about him
    b. They came running when they heard the news

But Spears (1982) argues that "indignant" *come* is actually a semi-auxiliary verb which fulfills a unique semantic-pragmatic role in AAVE. Recognizing such potential differences in the structure and function of AAVE sentence constituents is certainly essential to an understanding of this variety.

AAVE *tell say* constructions (8a) are likewise camouflaged by their resemblance to a common narrative structure found in many other dialects (8b).

(8) a. They *tell* him *say*, "You better not go there"
    b. They told him, they said, "You'd better not go there"

But the AAVE *tell say* construction is distinctive. The verbs of this sentence type have a common subject, but it only appears once. And while *him* (the indirect object of *tell*) occurs between the two verbs in (8a, b), the AAVE verbs in (8a) are not conjoined (e.g. by *and*), nor are they typically separated by a pause.

Like *said* in (8b), the AAVE *say* (8a) marks the beginning of a quotation, as in the following example taken from an elderly resident of rural Mississippi. Here, *tell say* alternates with simple quotative *say*.

> once a white lady got up and *told* us *said*, "Now y'all colored people," she *say*, "I'm getting up to tell y'all that the government got something going," *say*, "and if you don't mind losing your home when you die, your peoples won't have nothing. But I want to let you know, hold your home." *Say*, "When they want to renew your home, don't do it."
>
> (Tape 4A: American English Speech Recording Collection, The Center for Applied Linguistics)[2]

Two related facts require us to consider whether *say* is a member of the complementizer class of words rather than a verb. First, we note that *tell say* does not co-occur with other complementizers, so that sentences such as (9a) are not permissible. It may also be noted that English does not permit doubly filled complementizer positions, so that it appears that *say* in AAVE might function as a kind of complementizer (e.g., *that*, *whether*, *what*) rather than a verb. But AAVE *say* also does not behave like other complementizers which can be fronted with their clauses. For example, compare the fronting of *whether* in (9b) with the ungrammaticality of fronting for *say* in (9c). We discuss this restriction on complementizers later in the chapter.

(9) a. * He told him [$_{CP}$ [$_C$ *say* that] [$_{IP}$ they ain't know what they were doing]]
    b.   Whether Bill is sick [$_{IP}$ John doesn't know *t*]
    c. * *Say* they ain't know what they were doing [$_{IP}$ He told them *t*]

---

2 The original interview was conducted by Natalie Maynor, who graciously permitted the Center for Applied Linguistics to include it in its collection of dialect recordings.

Instead, *tell say* seems to operate somewhat like a *serial verb construction*, in which two verbs operate together as a verbal unit (cf. Mufwene 1989). Thus, a seemingly unremarkable construction like *tell say* points to a unique feature of AAVE syntax. Although SE and other vernacular varieties sometimes combine two verbs in succession (10a), these constructions differ in important ways from serial *tell say*. For example, these SE combinations can occur alternatively with the conjunction (10b), whereas *tell say* constructions don't allow this (10c).

(10) a. Go get your mail
    b. Go and get your mail
    c. She *tell* him (*and) *say*, go get your mail

SE complex verbs may occur with imperatives (11a) or a modal (11b), neither of which have overt tense morphology, but tensed forms (11c, d) are not grammatical in SE. No comparable restriction holds for AAVE *tell say* (11e), which permit past tense morphology on *tell*.

(11) a. Go get your mail
    b. Can you go get your mail?
    c. * She goes gets her mail every day
    d. * She went got her mail
    e. She *told* him *say*, you ain't actin right

Thus we find no comparable serial construction in standard varieties of English, even though there exist some similar surface combinations of verbs.[3]

A final example demonstrates a different dimension of subtle difference in the structures of AAVE vis-à-vis other English varieties. Consider a structure such as *They call themselves dancing*. The meaning of this sentence is counterfactual

---

3 The serial verb construction is also of considerable significance with respect to the historical development of AAVE. While there are no truly comparable serial verb combinations for *tell* and *say* in standard varieties of English, serial verb constructions are fairly typical of the creole languages spoken in the African-American diaspora. In Atlantic creoles, for example, it is common for serial *say* to be used in ways similar to AAVE (Holm 1988: 185; Mufwene 1989, 1996). In these creole varieties, serial verb constructions are not limited to *say*. Usually there is a more expansive set of serial verbs that may include items such as serial *give* corresponding to *to* or *for* (e.g., *She buy a dress give me*, "She bought a dress for me," *She run go market*, "She ran to the market") and instrumentality (e.g., *He take knife cut the meat*, "He took the knife and cut the meat"). Because of the similarity, it is reasonable to attribute quotative *say* in AAVE to influence from a more broadly based creole continuum. While such an historical affinity may illuminate the historical source for this form, it is important to note that this is the only vestige of the more expansive serial verb pattern found in Atlantic-based creoles. If, in fact, it is a survival of earlier creole influence on AAVE, then its semantic-pragmatic role as a quotative is probably explained as another instance of structural camouflaging. Interestingly, no other classical types of verb serialization are found in AAVE. At best, then, this is an isolated, vestigial instance of verb serialization that may have survived in present-day AAVE.

in the sense that it implies that the person's actual behavior does not match the intended or "presentation" behavior. In this interpretation, the AAVE construction is parallel to the meaning of Standard English sentences such as *He calls himself a student* or *She calls herself nice*, which similarly carry a counter-factual reading. In other words, uttering a sentence such as *He calls himself a student* implies that there is, in fact, some question about his behaving like a real student. In this instance, the difference between AAVE and other varieties of English is found in the kind of verb complements permitted for the verb *call*. Most English dialects permit *call* to co-occur with noun phrases or adjective phrases, but not with V +*ing* constructions such as *dancing* or *acting real nice* in the sentence *He calls himself acting real nice*. In this instance, the shared semantic reading of the construction across dialects of English appears to camouflage the fact that the range of verb complements for *call* is more expansive in AAVE than in other dialects (Wolfram 1995).

Our presentation thus far should suffice to show that appearances sometimes may be misleading with respect to the sentence constituents of AAVE. In some cases, superficial, lexically-based differences between AAVE and other varieties have been assigned more popular significance than they merit in terms of their structural significance. At the same time, some more subtle but significant differences in AAVE sentence constituents have been overlooked because of their surface similarity to constructions in other varieties.

1.4 Some syntactic dimensions of AAVE

We now turn to the description and analysis of some characteristic AAVE sentences. Our profile is not exhaustive, but it indicates some typical AAVE syntactic phenomena. Most of these can be found in many other vernacular varieties as well. As we observed previously, the syntactic uniqueness of AAVE is revealed in the total range of structures available to AAVE speakers rather than unique syntactic structures *per se*.

1.4.1 Negative concord

1.4.1.1 Description

One of the most noticed characteristics of AAVE and many other varieties of English is the optional use of *negative concord*, also referred to as *multiple negation* and *pleonastic negation*. The essential characteristic of negative concord sentences is the use of two or more negative morphemes to communicate a single negation. In other words, if we were to represent the sentence in logical form, only one negative operator would appear. The negative morphemes most often negate an entire clause (12a, b, c), less frequently a smaller constituent such as an NP or a PP (12d). Standard English counterpart sentences (12a', b', c', d') must contain only one negative morpheme.

(12) a. He *ain't* got *no* car
    a'. He *doesn't* have a/any car
    b. *Nobody* round here *ain't never* heard of him (at all)
    b'. *Nobody* around here has ever heard of him (at all)
    c. *Nobody ain't* gonna spend *no* time going to *no* doctor[4]
    c'. *Nobody* is going to spend (any) time going to a/any doctor
    d. He went out into that storm *without no* coat or *nothing*
    d'. He went out into that storm *without* a/any coat or anything

Though some or all of the italicized words in (12a, b, c, d) could be heavily stressed when the speaker means to be quite emphatic, here they simply indicate the presence of negative morphemes. Where AAVE permits more than one such morpheme in a negative sentence, SE uses one and (optionally) one or more *negative polarity items* (NPIs) – that is, a quantifier word or phrase (e.g., *any, ever, a bit*) that occurs within the "scope" of the negative as in *She didn't want **any**/a **bit** of ice cream*.[5] With certain exceptions, NPIs are licensed only when they are in the scope of a negative element. Even without heavy stress on negative elements, concordant negatives and non-negative NPIs tend to add pragmatic emphasis to sentences.

The multiple negation of AAVE should not be confused with the "*logical*" *double negation* found in SE and most non-standard dialects. Unlike negative concord, logical double negation involves one negative element undoing another – a rare instance in which the prescriptive dictum "two negatives make an affirmative" actually obtains. Logical double negatives can always be distinguished from AAVE multiple negative sentences by their contrastive stress. That is, in logical double negative sentences, one of the negative words receives normal stress while the other receives heavier stress and often a rising tone. Thus AAVE (13a) conveys only one negation and can be paraphrased in SE as *I didn't say anything*. Standard English (13b), conveys two independent negations, the second of which is stressed. The meaning is that the speaker did in fact say something.

---

4 This type of sentence frequently occurs in inverted form, e.g., *Ain't nobody going to spend no time going to no doctor*. We will discuss this sentence type later in the chapter. For now, since nothing hinges on our choice of word order, we will use the uninverted form.

5 Scope is usually defined in current syntactic theory in terms of the technical notion of *c-command*. This notion refers to a hierarchical tree structure in which a node A c-commands another node, B, if the first category above A also dominates B. The tree configuration for this relationship would thus be as follows:

(13) a. I *ain't say nothing* – I just sat there
   b. I *didn't say **nothing*** – I just said it very softly

Moreover, unlike AAVE multiple negatives (which in some instances may use half a dozen negative morphemes to communicate one sentential negation), logical multiple negatives seldom if ever involve more than two negative morphemes undoing one another, perhaps because such sentences would be too difficult to process.

Researchers have noted that AAVE speakers tend to use more pleonastic negatives than Anglo-American speakers of vernacular dialects, but the grammar of AAVE does not require speakers to use these negatives in every possible location, just as speakers of other vernaculars or SE are not obligated to insert negative polarity items (NPIs) like *any* and *ever* at every possible opportunity. Alternation between NPIs and pleonastic negatives is possible in AAVE negative sentences, particularly among speakers whose language moves stylistically along a standard– non-standard dialect continuum. This is illustrated in a sentence such as (14), used by a twenty-five-year-old AAVE speaker from Florida (cf. also Labov 1972b: 785).

(14) *Ain't nobody ever* thought about picking up *nothing*

This mixed distribution of negative concord marking suggests that negative elements such as *nobody* and affirmative NPIs like *anybody* are morphological variants of each other (Martin 1996).

1.4.1.2 The distribution of multiple negative elements

Multiple negative elements can occur in many locations, both in the main clause and in embedded subordinate clauses. There is no particular position that must carry negative morphology in all instances of negative concord, but negation must occur in at least one position from which it can negate the sentence (15).

(15) a. *No way* you gonna get that outta here with *no half-ton truck*
   b. *Nobody don't* like that
   c. *Nobody ain't never* gonna make him take *nothing no more*
   d. Billy *can't see no* point in going *nowhere no more*
   e. Sheila *don't* like *nobody* with *no attitude*
   f. He *ain't no genius*
   g. *Nobody* saw *nothing* out there that looked like *no bear*

As indicated in (15), there are a variety of negation-triggering positions. Among the most common are preposed adverbials (15a), subject of the sentence (15b, c, g), auxiliary or modal verb (15b–f),[6] and predicate NPs: direct objects (15c, e), objects of prepositions (15a, e, g), and predicate nominals in equative sentences (15f). Noun phrases in any position may carry negation either by means of a negative determiner (e.g., *no car*) or by negative counterparts of non-negative NPIs. For example, *nobody* and *nothing* may be used respectively in place of *anybody* and *anything*. Adverbials (e.g., *ever, anywhere*) can also be marked redundantly for negation (e.g., *never, nowhere*). Generally, AAVE speakers prefer to place negation early in the sentence, often contracting *not* to *n't* and attaching the latter to the verb or modal in Infl (15b–f). But negation can also appear on the subject, bypass the verb, and recur in predicate positions (15f).

Concordant negatives can occur in the same clause in which negation is encoded, but they can also take up positions in embedded clauses (16a).

(16) a. [$_{IP}$ He *ain't* say [$_{CP}$ (that) *nobody* was eating with *no* college president]]

b. [$_{IP}$ *Nobody* was eating with *no* college president]

c. [$_{IP}$ He *didn't* say [$_{CP}$ that *anybody* was eating with *any* college president]]

These embedded negatives would ordinarily be able to negate the clause in which they occur (16b), but they are deprived of this ability by the presence of negation in the higher clause. In AAVE (16a), only the main clause is negated; the *no* which precedes *college president* does not contribute an independent negation, serving instead the same function as the non-negative NPI *any* in an SE sentence. Counterpart SE (16c) may not use the negative determiner *no* if only one negation is intended.

1.4.1.3 Where negation must appear in multiple negatives

One rule of negation observed by all English dialects is *negative attraction*, which requires that if an indefinite expression like *anyone* or *ever* occurs before a negated verb (e.g., as a subject or a preposed element like an adverb), the indefinite expression will "attract" (and "steal") the negative morpheme from the verb (Klima 1964; Labov 1972b). If two or more NPIs appear preverbally, the first one must be carry the negative morpheme. Thus AAVE (17a, b) and SE (17a', b') obey negative attraction and are grammatical, while their counterparts in (18) do not and therefore are not acceptable to respective speakers of AAVE and SE.

---

6 It is almost always the case that the first verb in a series of auxiliaries or modals receives the negative morphology, but see the discussion of double modals in Section 1.4.5.

(17) a. *Nobody* got no gas
   a'. *Nobody* has any gas
   b. *Never* say that to nobody
   b'. *Never* say that to anybody
(18) a. * Anybody *ain't* got no gas
   a'. * Anybody *doesn't* have any gas
   b. * Ever *don't* say that to nobody
   b'. * Ever *don't* say that to anybody

1.4.1.4 Where multiple negatives cannot appear

As with many other aspects of AAVE syntax, the restrictions on multiple negation are essentially the same as those in other vernacular dialects. Many restrictions are stated in terms of syntactic structure and rely on the syntactic concept *island*. Islands "isolate" whatever is inside them from the rest of the sentence. For example, islands prevent processes like the *movement* of Wh-expressions from occurring. Thus, if an English speaker tries to form a question by moving a Wh-expression from inside an embedded clause which has already fronted a Wh-term, the sentence will be ungrammatical (19). In sentence (19) the symbol t_i (technically, the "trace") indicates the position from which the element was moved; the subscript $_i$ matches it with its correspondent moved element. The ungrammaticality of a sentence such as (19) supports the argument that Wh-clauses are islands to movement in English (Ross 1967).

(19) * *What*$_i$ did the man [$_{CP}$ who bought t_i annoyed Sam]

Since multiple negation involves negative elements in different parts of the same sentence, we can surmise that islands will sometimes interfere with multiple negation. In other words, islands will sometimes prevent two or more negative elements from participating in a relationship that makes only one of the negatives "essential" and the others merely concordant. If multiple negation is blocked, two outcomes are possible: an ungrammatical sentence, or the obligatory interpretation of two separate negations where only one might be expected or intended.

To discuss the effect of islands on multiple negation, we now introduce the concept of *chain*. Chains are a formal way of relating two or more syntactic positions to one another. They are typically created by movement processes. Wh-questions (20a) and passive sentences (20b) demonstrate two common chain-forming operations. Both of these sentences move elements from inside the clause to a position outside the clause. In terms of the hierarchical tree representation of a sentence, these are "higher" positions in the structural tree diagram. We use subscripts to indicate the members of chains.

(20) a. [$_{CP}$ *What*$_i$ did [$_{IP}$ you see t_i]]?
   b. [$_{IP}$ *William*$_i$ [$_{VP}$ was kissed t_i by Mother Theresa]]

Though it is not clear that clausal negation involves movement,[7] it may be helpful to think of multiple negatives as forming a *chain*. Under this analysis, each negative is a link and the links are connected to one another. The negative chain is a single entity; there is in essence only one negation, even though its morphology extends throughout the sentence. But some structures do not allow a negative element within them to form a chain with a higher negative element. These structures are *islands* to the formation of *negative chains*.

For negative concord, the island group includes the structure we just presented – embedded Wh-clauses, which are generally assumed to be complementizer phrases (CPs). We see the effects of a Wh-island in (21a), which contains an embedded question. Here the *no* in the embedded clause cannot carry the same negation as *don't*; if the concordant negation is forced, the sentence is ungrammatical. Likewise, comparative clauses (which are usually considered Wh-islands, even though they do not contain an overt Wh-word) don't allow the negative elements they contain to be linked to negatives higher up in the sentence (21b).

(21) a. * She *don't*$_i$ remember [$_{CP}$ why Bill say he was going with him on *no*$_i$ vacation]

b. * Sally *ain't*$_i$ taller [$_{CP}$ than *nobody*$_i$ is][8]

c. I *ain't*$_i$ gonna marry [$_{NP}$ *no*$_i$/*any* man [$_{CP}$ (who/that) got *no*$_i$ money problems]]

d. I *ain't*$_i$ gonna marry [$_{NP}$ *no*$_i$/*any* man [$_{CP}$ (who/that) John *ain't*$_{*i/j}$ *never*$_{*i/j}$ met e[9]]]

In almost all cases, then, CPs with overt Wh-elements in their specifier positions are islands to the formation of negative chains. One exception is restrictive relative clauses, which allow the formation of negative chains across their borders, as long as the noun which governs the relative clause is overtly negative or a non-negative NPI (21c).

Another sort of island depends on a different aspect of clause structure – how clauses encode negation, and where negation is actually located within the

---

7 There are several analyses of negation in English and other languages which assume movement, among them Progovac (1994), Haegeman (1995), and Martin (1996).

8 It is important to make a distinction here between [*than nobody is*], which is a CP with a null Wh-word at the front, and *than nobody*, which is a prepositional phrase. The fact that the latter construction sounds much better to AAVE speakers may be due to two factors, and untangling them is difficult. First, many AAVE speakers would not likely use the CP structure, because it is part of a more formal register. Second, the fact that *than nobody* is a PP makes it governable by the root negative Infl, and therefore negative chains can extend into the PP. The CP, as expected, is an island to negative chain formation.

9 *e* stands for gaps of all kinds called "empty categories," especially when no movement of constituents is involved.

sentence. If the verb or modal of an AAVE embedded clause is marked with an overt negative morpheme, it usually cannot be part of a main-clause negative chain but instead must form its own chain, the result being two independent negations in the sentence (21d).

This is rather surprising, since many other positions (e.g., subject, object, adjunct) within an embedded clause can join a negative chain originating in a higher clause without negating the embedded clause. In AAVE (22a), we see that several positions within an embedded clause allow attachment of pleonastic negative morphology, and the reading (i.e., root clause negation only) is the same as SE (22a'), which uses NPIs in the same locations. But AAVE (22b) has a negated verb in the lower clause, and for most speakers this sentence has two separate negations in force, one in each clause, like Standard English (22b'). The resultant reading is a logical double negative, with one clausal negation undoing the other. In general, negated verbs produce negated sentences, and negative sentences are islands to the formation of negative chains which originate in higher clauses.

(22) a. [He *don't* think [$_{CP}$ *nothing* gonna happen to *nobody* because of *no* argument]]
   a'. [He *doesn't* think [$_{CP}$ that anything is going to happen to anybody because of any argument]]
   b. [He *don't*$_i$ think [Bill *ain't*$_j$ gonna bother *nobody*$_j$]]
   b'. [He *doesn't*$_i$ think [that Bill *isn't*$_j$ going to bother anybody]]

However, the ban on negative concord for verbs in embedded clauses is apparently not absolute in all varieties of AAVE, as demonstrated by the occasional appearance of sentences like (23a), reported in Labov (1972b: 773). The *e* in this sentence denotes a null complementizer which alternates with the overt complementizer *that*.

(23) a. [It *ain't*$_i$ no cat [*e can't*$_i$ get in no coop]]
   b. [There's *no* cat [that can get in any coop]]

While (23a) overtly negates the embedded modal *can*, the meaning intended by the young man who spoke the sentence is not two clausal negations but a single negative chain with the intended reading (23b). It is not clear how this type of sentence, in which a negative chain contains two verbs, should be accommodated in the grammar of AAVE negation. One approach that has recently been explored is a *parameter* on negative chain formation for various dialects that use multiple negation (Ladusaw 1991). One *setting* of this parameter would allow or even require a given position (e.g., VPs of embedded clauses) to participate in negative chain formation, while another setting would rule out negation on this position.

The exception of (23a) notwithstanding, what is so special about the verb, such that negating the verb of an embedded clause usually produces a separate negation? One ready explanation is that the verb is where sentential negation is represented in the phrase marker. In cases where negative morphology occurs not on the verb but on other elements, we can posit a specific structural relationship which must obtain between the verb and negative morphemes in order for sentential negation to occur.

1.4.1.5 Determining the "real" negative in multiple negative sentences

Multiple negative sentences contain two or more negative elements, and in many cases more than one of these elements is capable on its own of producing clausal negation. How then can we define the "real" negative in a sentence, as opposed to those which are pleonastic? This issue can be decided by using two criteria.

Generally, the *head* of the negative chain, or negative element which is responsible for negation, is the highest negative element in the tree, and it must, by itself, be capable of negating the clause or constituent. In (24a–c), *nobody*, *can't*, and *no*, respectively, are heads of negative chains.[10]

(24) a. *Nobody* don't want no lemonade
  b. You *can't* do nothing with no broken broom
  c. He got *no* patience for nothing
  d. [NP A man [CP who got no sense of humor]] *ain't* gonna win nothing around here
  e. [NP That picture of [CP a man with no fingers]] *ain't* gonna win no photography competition

In our search for the heads of negative chains, we must always rule out negatives which, though leftmost or highest in the derivational tree, are heads of separate chains, such as those in relative clauses embedded under subjects. These negatives are not within the scope (i.e., c-commanded by) the root negative head and thus cannot negate the main clause. In (24d), *no* is the leftmost negative in the sentence, but it is in a relative clause which modifies the subject of the sentence, and so this negative must be ruled out. The verb *ain't*, therefore, is the head of the negative chain. Likewise, the first negative in (24e),

---

10 While there are similarities, the reader should not confuse the notion *head of chain* with the notion *head of constituent*, discussed in the introduction to this chapter. Just to note one difference, heads of constituents *govern* their constituents. For example, a transitive verb is the head of a verb phrase (VP) and governs its complement, a noun phrase (NP) which is its object. The head of a negative chain, although it may be a lexical head, does not necessarily govern but rather binds the other members of its chain into a single unit as far as negation is concerned. Links in a negative chain can be much farther apart than the typical governing head is from its constituents.

no, is in a noun adjunct phrase and cannot negate anything but the noun *fingers*, its local constituent. Therefore, it is the head of its own (one-member) negative chain and is not associated with negation of the clause.

We have seen in the case of multiple negation that AAVE shares the majority of its structural aspects with many other dialects that allow more than one negative morpheme per negative sentence. The key differences between dialects like AAVE, which allow multiple negation, and those like SE, which do not, are expressed in the grammar as conditions on the formation of negative chains.

1.4.2 *"Negative inversion" sentences*

1.4.2.1 Existential sentences

Existential sentences announce the existence of persons, places, and things which have not already been established in a discourse. In most varieties of English, *there* is the expletive or "dummy" subject which occupies that position while not adding referential meaning to the sentence. The logical subject of existential sentences is the noun phrase which follows *there*, as in (25).

(25) a. *There's* [three women upstairs]
    b. *There's* [a plate in the cupboard]
    c. *There* [a corner of the building that all filled up with junk]

In some existential sentences, AAVE speakers use *it* or *they* in place of *there* as the expletive subject.

(26) a. *It/They* ain't nobody round here got nothing to say
    b. *It/They* ain't three people in the county ever heard of her
    c. *It's/They's* a woman in a dark suit applying for that new job

1.4.2.2 The Definiteness Restriction on existential sentences

As in other dialects of English, AAVE existential sentences must obey the *Definiteness Restriction* (Milsark 1974), which requires that the logical subject of the sentence (i.e., the entity whose existence or presence is being announced) be indefinite. In other words, the subject cannot denote a particular person, place, or thing which is already known to the speakers or which has already been introduced into the discourse. The sentences in (27) violate this restriction and are therefore ungrammatical.

(27) a. * *There/*It* [John upstairs in the bedroom]
    b. * *There/*It* [the big green plate in the cupboard]
    c. * *There/*It* [that corner of the building that all filled up with junk]

Of course, another reading is available in many of these sentences in which the speaker indicates the position of an object. But this is a distinct sentence type with its own intonation pattern – a strong stress on *there* is required. This reading is not related to existential sentences. Ruling out this alternative, all sentences like those in (27) are ungrammatical.

1.4.2.3 "Negative inversion" sentences as existential sentences

AAVE and some varieties of Anglo-American vernacular English spoken in the southern United States have a type of sentence which is clearly existential in intention but which does not have an overt dummy subject. This type is called the *negative inversion sentence*. These sentences are emphatic negative declaratives and should not be confused with yes/no questions.

(28) a. *Didn't* nobody laugh
b. *Ain't* nobody done nothing
c. *Ain't* a car in that lot got a speck of rust on it
d. *Can't no* man round here get enough money to buy their own farm
e. *Wouldn't* nobody help the poor man
f. *Couldn't* nobody in the place do more than they did
f. *Ain't* nobody done nothing

The most obvious fact about these sentences is the apparent movement in which the subject and auxiliary change places, so-called *subject–auxiliary inversion*. We find this process most often in question formation (see Section 1.4.3) and the fronting of negative elements for purposes of emphasis. *Did you go?* and *Under no circumstances will you go* are respective examples of these sentence types. In negative inversion sentences, the verb can be supporting *do* (28a), aspectual (28b) or linking *be* (28c), or a modal (28d–f). These sentences also observe the Definiteness Restriction we mentioned above.

As with those affirmative existential sentences which violate the Definiteness Restriction (27), the sentences in (29) are grammatical if they were interpreted as yes/no questions, but this alternative is easily distinguished from the one under discussion here by its differing intonation pattern and conversational use. While yes/no questions have rising intonation at the end of the sentence, negative inversion sentences exhibit a level or falling tone.

(29) a. * Didn't John laugh
b. * Can't that man down the road get enough money to buy they own farm
c. * Ain't the red car over there got no rust on it
d. * Wouldn't Sally and Jean help the poor man
e. * Couldn't my aunt from Chicago do more than she did
f. * Ain't the President done nothing

We should consider why, if inversion is the only process occurring in negative inversion sentences, they should obey the Definiteness Restriction. The most straightforward answer is that inversion does not occur. Rather, negative inversion sentences are *negative existential sentences*. While existential sentences announce or affirm the existence of an entity represented in an indefinite noun phrase (the logical subject of these sentences), negative inversion sentences negate existential propositions, denying the existence of a certain type of person, place, or thing. We see that if we place an expletive *there* or *it* to the left of (28c), repeated here as (30), the similarity is manifest. This is not to suggest that *there* or *it* can be inserted in this position in all AAVE negative inversion sentences, but to show that at least some of these sentences are the negative counterparts of affirmative existential sentences.

(30) (There/It) ain't no car in that lot got a speck of rust on it

If negative inversion sentences are in fact negative existential sentences, they should contain a grammatical subject position which is unfilled, either by phonetic non-realization or by deletion. Either way, this fact is remarkable in two respects: though some languages allow this, subjects generally cannot be null in English (31a). More specifically, AAVE affirmative existential sentences (like those in other English dialects) do not permit null expletive subjects (31c).

(31) a. * Went to the store
     b.   She went to the store
     c. * Three men in the office that want to see you
     d.   There's three men in the office that want to see you

Moreover, not all negative inversion sentences permit the insertion of an expletive subject.

(32) a. * There/It didn't nobody laugh
     b. * There/It can't no man round here get enough money to buy they own farm

Negative inversion sentences therefore remain something of a mystery, at least as far as their structure and the conditions on their distribution are concerned. We are likely dealing with more than one type of sentence, as suggested in recent work by Sells, Rickford, and Wasow (1996) and Weldon (1996). No doubt negative inversion sentences will be the subject of further research.

1.4.3 Question formation

We mentioned at the beginning of this chapter that AAVE is fundamentally identical to other English varieties in its formation of interrogative sentences.

Thus, yes/no questions (e.g., *Can you go to the show?*) and Wh-questions (e.g., *Where can you go?*) usually involve subject–auxiliary inversion. Sentences (33a, b) are interrogative versions of the declarative sentences in (34a, b).

(33) a. Can they go to the show?
     b. Have they seen the show?
(34) a. They can go to the show
     b. They have seen the show

The relevant phrase structures for the interrogative (33) and declarative (34) sentences are seen in (35a, b), respectively. These follow the subject–verb inversion process we mentioned above, technically involving the movement of an inflectional phrase (IP) to the complementizer phrase (CP). In this representation, categories designated by *e* are *empty categories*. These exist in the syntactic structure but have no phonological representation, i.e., they are not pronounced when a sentence is spoken. Empty categories can be generated by phrase structure, or they can be created when an element moves out of its original position in the sentence. Thus in (35a) Comp (C) is the empty head of the complementizer phrase, while in (35b) the empty category is created when the Infl category containing the auxiliary (here, *can*) moves to Comp.

(35) a. $[_{CP}$ can$_i$ $[_{IP}$ they $[_{Infl}$ $e_i]$ go to the show]]
     b. $[_{CP}$ $[_C$ $e]$ $[_{IP}$ they can go to the show]]

In Wh-questions, there are two movements. Infl moves to Comp as in (35b), but a Wh-term also raises from within the IP to the *specifier* (Spec) of CP at the beginning of the sentence. The Spec of CP occurs to the left of the complementizer head: $[_{CP}$ Spec [Comp] $[_{IP}$ Infl VP]]. Thus, a sentence such as (36b) is derived from the underlying (36a). Since there are two empty categories in this sentence, we have included subscript indices which link the empty categories to the moved elements.

(36) a. $[_{CP}$ $[_{Spec}$ $e]$ $[_C$ $e]$ $[_{IP}$ they will go to the show where]]
     b. $[_{CP}$ $[_{Spec}$ Where$_i$ $[_C$ will$_k$ $[_{IP}$ they e_k go to the show $e_i]$]]]

In embedded questions, often called *indirect questions*, the auxiliary verb in Infl does not raise to the Comp of the embedded clause. We see this in (37), where the embedded questions begin with complementizers *if* (37a) and *whether* (37b), but the modal *would* and supportive *do* remain in Infl. In other words, indirect questions do not typically undergo subject–auxiliary inversion.

(37) a. They asked her $[_{CP}$ if $[_{IP}$ she could go to the show]]
     b. They asked $[_{CP}$ whether $[_{IP}$ she showed up for work]]

While AAVE shares with other English varieties the vast majority of traits described for question formation, it differs in a few relatively minor ways (Burling 1973). Like other vernaculars, AAVE allows subject–auxiliary inversion in embedded questions. This inversion, however, only takes place when there is no overt complementizer realized, as in (38a). Sentences such as (38b), with inversion and an overt complementizer, are not grammatical in AAVE.

(38) a.   They asked [$_{CP}$ could [$_{IP}$ she e go to the show]]
     b. * They asked [$_{CP}$ if could [$_{IP}$ she e go to the show]]

This prohibition of an overt complementizer with inversion (38b) is related to a parameter of English syntax that forbids complementizers from containing two elements. If there already is an overt complementizer, the movement of another element into Comp constitutes a violation of this restriction. This has not always been the case in English; some earlier versions of English permitted doubly filled Comps. For example, Middle English sentences such as "Men shal wel knowe who that I am," written in 1485 by the earliest English printer, William Caxton, includes both *who* and *that* in the Comp (cited by Lightfoot 1979: 322).

AAVE generally shares the doubly filled Comp restriction with other current varieties of English, although Labov (1972a: 62) cites a case in which speakers produced structures similar to those in (38b). In a repetition task involving the complementizer *whether*, Labov found that about half of his AAVE-speaking subjects gave a response like that in (39b) to the sentence (39a).

(39) a.   I asked Alvin *whether he knows* how to play basketball
     b.   I asked Alvin *whether did he* know how to play basketball

From the standpoint of syntactic organization, it is interesting to note the relaxation of a minor parameter on Comp-filling demonstrated in such a response.

A second distinctive AAVE question pattern is the *non-inverted question*, such as those in (40a–e).

(40) a.   Who that is?
     b.   What that thing is?
     c.   Why she took that?
     d.   Where the kids went?
     e.   They took it?

AAVE is not alone in forming some direct questions with non-inverted order, but the kind of non-inverted question represented in (40a–e) is not found in standard varieties, nor is it found in comparable Anglo-American vernacular varieties.

29

In SE, a sentence such as (40e) might be uttered as an *echo question*, a sentence which repeats all or part of a sentence just uttered by another person. For example, (40e) in SE might be uttered as part of the kind of exchange found in (41). Of course, this response would have appropriate question intonation in its non-inverted form.

(41) *Speaker* A: They took that old beat up sofa
     Speaker B: They took it?
     Speaker A: They sure did

But AAVE sentences such as (40) can also occur as non-echo questions, thus setting them apart from their contextually restricted uses in standard varieties.

As seen in sentences (40a–d), the movement of a Wh-term to the front of the sentence may operate independently of subject–auxiliary inversion. In this respect, AAVE is different from standard varieties of English, where direct question formation necessarily involves both Wh-fronting and inversion. The potential independence of these movements produces a structural ambiguity for a sentence such as *What you doing?* SE can derive the sentence from an auxiliary deletion rule after inversion has taken place (42). In AAVE, because of the potential independence of inversion and Wh-fronting in direct questions, the question may also be derived from a non-inverted structure in which is is not phonetically realized or deleted (43).

(42) a. What're you doing?
     b. What you doing?
(43) a. What you are doing?
     b. What you *e* doing?

Non-inverted sentences such as those in (40a–e, 43b) have several structural constraints. Although non-inversion is possible when the subject NP is a pronoun or unexpanded NP, it is rare, if possible at all, with a *heavy NP*. A heavy NP is a very long noun phrase, such as one occurring with a relative clause (e.g., [$_{NP}$ *the person who likes to study syntax] read the article*). For example, sentences like (44a, b) are grammatical, but sentences like (44c, d), which contain heavy NPs, are questionable at best.

(44) a. Who [$_{NP}$ the woman is?]
     b. Where [$_{NP}$ she] is?
     c. *? Who [$_{NP}$ all the young women('s) best friends] is?
     d. *? Where [$_{NP}$ the woman doing all the work] is?

Furthermore, the use of non-inverted sentences seems to be favored with the copula (i.e., forms of *be*) as opposed to other verbs (i.e., *do* and modals); however, this is a variable constraint.

We conclude that non-inverted direct questions must be admitted as a part of AAVE syntax, but they are not a particularly productive pattern in the variety at this stage of its development. They seem restricted both structurally and socially, suggesting that they may exist as a vestigial retention from an earlier period when the non-inverted direct question was apparently a more productive and pervasive pattern for question formation. Non-inverted question production is, of course, a quite productive pattern in a wide range of creoles in the African-American diaspora (Holm 1988: 213). Chapters 5 and 6 of this volume provide readers with a more detailed discussion of the potential sources of AAVE's development.

1.4.4 Relative clause structures

AAVE speakers sometimes use the Wh-pronouns *who*, *where*, and *when* to introduce relative clauses, which complement or are adjoined to nouns naming, for example, persons (45a), places (45b), and times (45c). But more frequently, *that* is used for introducing relative clauses (45d–f). Either a Wh-relative pronoun or the complementizer *that* is used, never both, because of the ban on doubly filled Comps (45g).

(45) a. He the man [$_{CP}$ who go to college in New York]
    b. Sheila going to that place [$_{CP}$ where there's better pay]
    c. Bill remember the time [$_{CP}$ when everybody was here]
    d. He the man [$_{CP}$ that Charlie see every day]
    e. Sheila going to that place [$_{CP}$ that pay better]
    f. Bill remember the time [$_{CP}$ that everybody was eating crabs]
    g. * He the man [$_{CP}$ who that drive his car real slow]

As in most other varieties of English, some AAVE relative clauses can omit both *that* and the Wh-relative pronoun, leaving a bare relative clause. Most frequently, these are *object relative clauses*. That is, the head, italicized below, relates to an object position in the relative clause, designated below by *e*.

(46) a. Sheila the [$_{NP}$ *woman* [$_{CP}$ (that) Bill broke up with *e*]]
    b. Alan saw [$_{NP}$ a *car* [$_{CP}$ (that) Charlie sold *e*]]
    c. Walter [$_{NP}$ the *one* [$_{CP}$ (that) Sally gave the money to *e*]]

In (46a), *woman*, the head of the relative clause, is related to the object of the preposition *with*. In (46b), *car* is linked to the direct object of *sold*, and (46c)'s *one* is related to the indirect object of *give*.

However, this ability to delete relative pronouns and complementizers is limited to restrictive relative clauses, in which the relative clause restricts the meaning of the head noun, and the head noun governs the relative clause. As we noted above in the discussion on multiple negation (Section 1.4.1.4), restrictive relative clauses have a closer structural relationship with their head nouns than that established by non-restrictive relative clauses, which are opposed, more or less parenthetically, to their noun phrase. In the latter, the relative pronoun (and not the complementizer *that*) must be present (for structural differences, see (21c, d)). Non-restrictive relatives are more characteristic of formal registers of English and are not used by many AAVE speakers, but those speakers who have occasion to use this structure observe the restriction (47).

> (47) a.   Diane like French food, [which cost more than Chinese]
> b. * Diane like French food, [e cost more than Chinese]

A notable difference between AAVE and many other English vernaculars is AAVE speakers' ability to form bare *subject relative clauses* (cf. Smith 1969), in which the head noun is linked to the subject position inside the relative clause, as in examples (48a–c); parallel SE forms are (48a'–c'). In the AAVE examples the position to which the head noun is related is marked with an *e*.

> (48) a.   He [$_{NP}$ the man [$_{CP}$ *e* got all the old records]]
> a'.   He's [$_{NP}$ the man [$_{CP}$ who has all the old records]]
> b.   Wally [$_{NP}$ the teacher [$_{CP}$ *e* wanna retire next year]]
> b'.   Wally is [$_{NP}$ the teacher [$_{CP}$ who wants to retire next year]]
> c.   Jill like [$_{NP}$ that man [$_{CP}$ *e* met her mother last week]]
> c'.   Jill likes [$_{NP}$ that guy [$_{CP}$ who met her mother last week]]

Bare subject relative clauses tend to be favored with copula structures such as (48a) over other types of main verb sentences (48b, c), and they seem to be particularly prominent with existential sentences such as *There's/It's a teacher brought some food for the party*. We see, then, that AAVE differs from other varieties of English not in the permissibility of Wh- and *that* deletion, but in the structural context of its application.

1.4.5 Double modals

AAVE is one of the English dialects that may use more than one modal auxiliary in a clause (Di Paolo 1989; Butters 1991; Mishoe and Montgomery 1994; Battistella 1995). In this regard, AAVE is identical to southern Anglo-American vernacular varieties. Sentences such as (49a–f) are representative, and incidentally, they rank among the most-noticed sentence types of AAVE. But unlike phenomena which look syntactic but which are merely lexical, there is evidence of structural distinctiveness in double modals.

> (49) a.   He *might could* do the work
> b.   She *may can* do the work

  c. They *should can* stay out here
  d. They *should oughta* go
  e. They *might should oughta* do it
  f. They *useta could* do it

Although *might could* is the most commonly occurring double modal, a number of productive combinations are possible (49b–f), even the occasional triple modal (49e). At the same time, not all possible combinations occur (e.g., **should could* and **may would* do not occur), so apparently there are some lexically based restrictions on the permissible combinations and sequencing of modals. For example, while the sequence *might could* occurs very frequently, the sequence *could might* is quite rare and unattested in most studies of AAVE, as is a combination such as *will must*. The tense-bearing capability of double modals stands out by comparison with the usual auxiliary–main verb combinations of more standard varieties of English. In SE and in many vernaculars, the modal carries tense and is followed by a tenseless main verb (50).

  (50) a. He might could *go*
       b.* He might could *goes*

In AAVE, both modals may carry the same tense (e.g., *might could, may can*) or can mix tenses (e.g., *might can, may could*), although tense matching is the preferred pattern (Di Paolo 1989). The possibility of marking tense at more than one point within a clause is somewhat unusual for English sentences, although this is apparently not the only case of double tense marking within a clause (cf. Chaski 1995).

It might be tempting simply to consider double modals as mere lexical peculiarities or idiom chunks, with no significant internal syntactic structure, but there are several reasons for analyzing them syntactically. Some internal structure for double modals must be recognized in order to account for the way they behave with respect to syntactic processes such as inversion, tag-question formation, adverbial placement, and negation (Battistella 1995). For example, in inversion (51) and tagging (52) the second modal of *might could* is raised.

  (51) [$_{CP}$ Could [$_{IP}$ we might *e* do it now?]]
  (52) She might could go to the show, couldn't she?

This pattern suggests that *could* is in some sense the "true" modal. In (51), *could* is the tensed constituent that moves in the subject–auxiliary inversion typical of question formation, and in (52) it is only *could* that appears in the tag version of the modal. Given sentences like these, which involve the movement of an auxiliary and tense, it seems that *could* operates as an authentic modal constituent, while *might* more closely resembles an adverbial specifier.

33

The syntactic processes of negative placement and parenthetical and adverb placement, however, suggest that the status of the modals in a double modal combination is not so clear cut. For example, negated auxiliaries in English usually place the negative after the auxiliary carrying tense (the first auxiliary when more than one auxiliary occurs), as in *I couldn't have gone*. In the case of *might could*, the negative may occur after *might* (53a), but it may also follow *could* (53b); however, the former is preferred. There are even rare instances where negation can occur on both (Di Paolo 1989).

(53) a. I *might not* could go to the show
     b. I might *could not* go to the show

Furthermore, adverbs and parentheticals can occur between the modals as in (54a, b).

(54) a. I *might just could* go to the show
     b. *I might, I think, could* go to the show

Syntactic factors such as those illustrated in sentences (51–54) show that double modal combinations cannot be treated as single lexical items without any internal syntactic structure; instead, they are made up of separable constituents which must be considered in the overall syntactic configuration of the sentence.

As noted, however, the internal structure of double modals does not fit neatly into the most obvious options for categorization, either the category auxiliary (Infl) or adverb. On the one hand, a simple classification of *might* as an adverb like *possibly*, *perhaps*, or *supposedly* (i.e., *He might could go to the show* as the structural equivalent to *He possibly could go to the show*) does not suffice. Both members of the double modal combination may carry tense (although they do not have equal constraints on their tense-bearing functions), and the possibilities for moving the adverb *might* do not neatly match the movement of other adverbs in this set. For example, adverbs such as *possibly* can be moved to the right of the modal (55a), but *might* cannot do this (55b).

(55) a.   She could *possibly* go to the show
     b. * She could *might* go to the show

At the same time, we see in the diagnostic processes of inversion and tagging that the modal *might* does not behave like a typical tense-carrying auxiliary. Thus, the empirical descriptive evidence suggests a kind of intermediate status for the modal *might* in *might could*. Battistella (1995) suggests that *might* be treated as a kind of adverbial modal that modifies *could*, the head modal of the clause. By classifying the spurious modal as a type of tertiary syntactic element along with demonstratives, classifiers, quantifiers, and degree words, Battistella unifies double modals with general principles of phrase structure.

Although a consensus on the internal structure of double modals in AAVE has not yet emerged, the descriptive facts pose an intriguing challenge for modern syntactic theoreticians in their attempts to match universal principles of syntactic organization with the sometimes elusive empirical data represented in vernacular varieties such as AAVE.

1.5 Conclusion

In this chapter, we have noted that AAVE shares the vast majority of basic sentence types with other vernacular varieties as well as Standard English. We have also observed several structures which are AAVE-specific. Some cases of apparent cross-dialectal similarity turn out to camouflage differences, while, at the same time, some transparent differences do not represent fundamental distinctions in the sentence structure of AAVE, but lexical peculiarities across dialects. Linguists and other students of AAVE thus face two challenges: they must look past superficial aspects of the dialect to find those features common to a number of English varieties, and they must study apparent similarities which mask underlying differences across dialects. If these challenges are met, we can provide a broader basis for claims about English than exists currently, and we can provide accurate descriptions of those structures which belong to AAVE alone.

References

Battistella, Edwin (1995) "The syntax of the double modal." *Linguistica Atlantica* 17: 19–44.

Baugh, John (1984) "Steady: Progressive aspect in Black English Vernacular." *American Speech* 59: 1–12.

Burling, Robbins (1973) *English in Black and White*. New York: Holt, Rinehart, and Winston.

Butters, Ronald (1991) "Multiple modals in United States Black English: Synchronic and diachronic aspects." In *Verb Phrase Patterns in Black English and Creole*, Walter F. Edwards and Donald Winford (eds.). Detroit: Wayne State University, pp. 165–178.

Chaski, Carole E. (1995) "The future pluperfect: Double tenses in American English AUX." *American Speech* 70: 3–20.

Chomsky, Noam (1981) *Lectures on Government and Binding*. Dordrecht, Netherlands: Foris.

Di Paolo, Marianna (1989) "Double modals as single lexical items." *American Speech* 64: 195–224.

Haegeman, Liliane (1995) *The Syntax of Negation*. Cambridge: Cambridge University Press.

Holm, John (1988) *Pidgins and Creoles*. Cambridge: Cambridge University Press.

Klima, Edward S. (1964) "Negation in English." In *The Structure of Language: Readings in the Philosophy of Language*, Jerry A. Fodor and Jerrold J. Katz (eds.). Englewood Cliffs, NJ: Prentice-Hall.

Labov, William (1969) "Contraction, deletion, and inherent variability of the English copula." *Language* 45: 715–759.

—— (1972a) *Language in the Inner City: Studies in the Black English Vernacular.* Philadelphia: University of Pennsylvania Press.

—— (1972b) "Negative attraction and negative concord in English grammar." *Language* 48: 773–818.

Ladusaw, William (1991) "Interpreting negative concord structures," manuscript, University of California Santa Cruz.

Lightfoot, David (1979) *Principles of Diachronic Syntax.* Cambridge: Cambridge University Press.

Martin, Stefan (1996) "Neg-criterion extensions: Negative concord across relative clause boundaries in nonstandard English." Paper presented at Linguistic Society of America annual convention, 7 January 1996.

Milsark, Gary (1974) "Existential Sentences in English," unpublished dissertation, MIT, Cambridge, MA.

Mishoe, Margaret and Michael Montgomery (1994) "The pragmatics of multiple in modal variation in North and South Carolina." *American Speech* 69: 3–29.

Mufwene, Salikoko S. (1989) "Equivocal structures in some Gullah complex sentences." *American Speech* 64: 304–326.

—— (1996) "Creolization and grammaticization: What creolistics could contribute to research on grammaticization." In *Changing Meanings, Changing Functions*, Philip Baker and Anand Syea (eds.). London: University of Westminster Press, pp. 5–28.

Progovac, Ljiljana (1994) *Negative and Positive Polarity: A Binding Approach.* Cambridge: Cambridge University Press.

Rickford, John (1975) "Carrying the new wave into syntax: The case of Black English *been.*" In *Analyzing Variation in the Form and Use of Language*, Ralph W. Fasold and Roger W. Shuy (eds.). Washington, DC: Georgetown University Press, pp. 162–183.

—— (1977) "The question of prior creolization in Black English." In *Pidgin and Creole Linguistics*, Albert Valdman (ed.). Bloomington, IN: Indiana University Press.

Ross, John R. (1967) "Constraints on variables in syntax," dissertation, MIT, Cambridge, MA. Published 1983 as *Infinite Syntax!* New York: Garland.

Sells, Peter, John Rickford, and Thomas Wasow (1996) "Variation in negative inversion in AAVE: An optimality theoretic approach." In *Sociolinguistic Variation: Data, Theory, and Analysis*, Jennifer Arnold, Renee Blake, Brad Davidson, Scott Schwenter, and Julie Solomon (eds.). Stanford, CA: CSLI Publications, pp. 161–176.

Smith, Riley (1969) "Interrelatedness of certain deviant grammatical structures in Negro nonstandard dialects." *Journal of English Linguistics* 3: 82–88.

Spears, Arthur (1982) "The semi-auxiliary *come* in Black English Vernacular." *Language* 58: 850–872.

Weldon, Tracey (1996) "Another look at negative inversion in African American Vernacular English: An HPSG account." Paper presented to the Triangle Linguistics Club, February 1996.

Wolfram, Walt (1995) "On the sociolinguistic significance of obscure dialect structures: NP_i *call* NP_i Ving in African American Vernacular English." *American Speech* 69: 339–360.

2

ASPECT AND PREDICATE PHRASES IN AFRICAN-AMERICAN VERNACULAR ENGLISH

Lisa Green

2.1 Introduction

One of the goals of research in African-American vernacular English (AAVE) has been to provide a description of the properties of the verbal elements in its system. Verbal forms have been a central focus of study in this variety of English basically because they show marked differences from forms in other varieties. The purpose of this chapter is to present a discussion of AAVE verb forms in general and to provide an analysis of the internal structure of phrases in which they are generated. The overall aim is to present an analysis which will give some insight into the way the verbal system in AAVE functions as a part of the grammar.

This chapter is divided into two parts. Section 2.1 consists of three subsections which provide an overview of the types of phrases that occur in AAVE and give a general description of verb forms in the system. Section 2.1.1 provides an introduction to the types of phrases and compares them to their counterparts in Standard American English (SAE). Section 2.1.2 focuses on verb forms which occur in some phrases, explaining the patterns which arise in various paradigms. Section 2.1.3, the final subsection in 2.1, continues the discussion of these verb forms, paying attention particularly to the interaction between aspect and past morphology.

Section 2.2 offers a more detailed discussion of the internal structure of phrases in AAVE. The first major subsection, Section 2.2.1, distinguishes finite auxiliaries and aspectual markers. The members of the class of finite auxiliaries are characterized by their properties in questions and negation, and the members of the class of aspectual markers are characterized by the meaning they denote. Section 2.2.2 presents a structure in which finite auxiliaries, on the one hand, and nonfinite auxiliaries, on the other, are generated as separate projections.

Section 2.3.3 considers aspectual markers and tests for constituency, and Section 2.3.4 discusses aspectual markers as they occur with a range of predicate phrases.

Auxiliaries *be* (and main verb *be*), *do*, and *have* will be written with initial capital letters (*Be*, *Do*, and *Have*) to avoid confusion with aspectual markers in AAVE.

2.2 Overview of types of phrases and verb forms

2.2.1 Structure of phrases in AAVE

Sentences in AAVE may contain the following types of phrases: verb phrase (VP), noun phrase (NP), adjective phrase (AdjP), prepositional phrase (PP), and adverb phrase (AdvP). These phrases are exemplified in the italicized segments of the sentences below:

(1) They $_{VP}$*walking to school.*
(2) The lady in the red coat $_{NP}$*the teacher* for this class.
(3) They thought the little boy was $_{AdjP}$*quiet.*
(4) All the newspapers $_{PP}$*in the recycling bin.*
(5) The student was $_{AdvP}$*already there.*

These italicised phrases are exactly the same kinds of phrases which occur in SAE and other varieties of English. The major difference here is that the verb *Be* does not necessarily occur on the surface, as shown in (1), (2), and (4). This is a complicated and interesting topic, which has been discussed at great length in the literature.[1] The following VPs also occur in AAVE, showing that the verbs which are generated in them have the same subcategorization frames as in corresponding phrases in SAE:

(6) The baby $_{VP}[_V$*slept*].
(7) The teacher $_{VP}[_V$*gave* $_{NP}$*the test*].
(8) Dee $_{VP}[_V$*went* $_{PP}$*to the store*].
(9) She can $_{VP}[_V$*put* $_{NP}$*the rope* $_{PP}$*in the trunk*].

---

1 Copula absence has been a controversial and widely researched topic in AAVE. Labov (1969) discusses the phonological process of copula and auxiliary *be* deletion in varieties of English. Baugh (1980) and Holm (1984) re-examine some of the earlier analyses of copula absence in AAVE. More recent studies such as Rickford *et al.* (1991) provide an overview of research on this topic as well as new data coming to bear on the analysis. Mufwene (1992) raises important questions about the interpretation of claims about the data which have been used in arguments about the status of *be* in AAVE.

The verb *slept* in (6) is intransitive and does not take an object NP, while the verb *gave* in (7) subcategorizes for a direct object NP. *Went* selects a PP, as shown in (8), and the verb *put* (9) selects an NP and a PP. The properties of the verbs here are identical to their properties in SAE. However, as this chapter unfolds, it will be shown that other verbal elements which are homophonous with verbal forms in SAE have selectional requirements which are quite different from the requirements of the superficially identical forms in SAE.

Sentences in AAVE can also consist of aspectual phrases (AspPs), which can occur with the following phrases: VP, NP, AdjP, PP, AdvP, and other AspPs. The aspectual marker *be* occurs with these different phrases in the examples below:

(10) She always [$_{AspP}$be $_{NP}$a clown $_{PP}$on Halloween].
  'She always dresses as/portrays a clown on Halloween.'
(11) I think those buses [$_{AspP}$be $_{AdjP}$blue].
  'I think those buses are always/usually blue.'
(12) The children [$_{AspP}$be $_{PP}$at school $_{CP}$when I get home].
  'The children are usually at school when I get home.'
(13) He can't find his mail because it [$_{AspP}$be $_{AdvP}$here].
  'He can't find his mail because it is always/usually here.'
(14) They [$_{AspP}$be $_{AspP}$done $_{VP}$left $_{CP}$when I get there].
  'They have usually already left by the time I get there.'

(CP stands for complementizer phrase.) The SAE equivalents of the sentences in (10–14) are given in single quotation marks, but a discussion of the meaning of these aspectual markers and the meanings of sentences in which these markers occur will be presented in Section 2.3.

Throughout this discussion of phrases in AAVE, I follow a basic X-bar theoretic model, so the structure of phrases is taken to be the following:

(15)
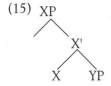

The diagram in (15) is a general representation of the internal structure of phrases. Given the structure, X heads the phrase XP and takes a complement YP. The head is important in that it makes the phrase a particular type. For example, the verb is the head of a VP, and the noun is the head of an NP.

In the following tree diagram, AspP and VP are used in the instantiation of the structure in (15).

(16)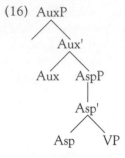

(AuxP stands for auxiliary phrase. The AspP is headed by Asp, the position in which aspectual markers occur.)

Some differences between phrases in AAVE and those in SAE are in phrases containing verbal predicates in the two systems. I will present some verb paradigms to illustrate the types of patterns that are relevant here. It will be shown that in some cases, the verb sequences resemble forms in SAE, with the exception that AAVE constructions may not consist of the different forms of auxiliary elements which are used in the corresponding SAE sequences. In addition, AAVE uses verbal elements differently than SAE does. The comparison shows that AAVE is not a set of random deviations from SAE, while the data show that AAVE is rule-governed in its verb sequences.

2.2.2 Verb paradigms

The following paradigms (17–28) and (30–41) represent the types of verb forms which are marked for tense and aspect in AAVE. The plural forms (*we, you, they*) are not given because the corresponding verb forms are not inflected for number; singular and plural verb forms are identical in many cases: *he/they eat*.[2]

    (17) Present tense:
        a. I/you/he eat/run
        b. I/you/he DO eat/run
        c. I/you/he don't eat/run
    (18) Past tense:
        a. I/you/he ate/ran
        b. I/you/he DID eat/run
        c. I/you/he didn't eat/run

---

2 The auxiliaries which are in capitals are emphatic or stressed forms. It is important to note that the level of stress may vary, so the auxiliaries written in capitals can represent an auxiliary which is lightly or heavily stressed.

(The form *run* may also occur in some past environments. Schneider (1989: 106) notes that "uninflected *run* is clearly dominant in the past tense." His data are based on verb forms which are argued to represent earlier stages of African-American English.)

(19) Preterite *had*:
  I/you/he had ate
(20) Future tense:
  a. I'ə/you'ə/he'ə eat/run[3]
  b. I/you/he WILL eat/run
  c. I/you/he won't eat/run
(21) Present progressive:
  a. I'm eating/running
  b. You/he eating/running
  c. It's eating/running
  d. We/y'all/they eating/running
  e. I AM eating/running
  f. You (and all other persons) IS eating/running
  g. I/you/he ain't eating/running
  h. I'm/you/he not eating/running
(22) Past progressive:
  a. I/you/he was eating/running
  b. I/you/he WAS eating/running
  c. I/you/he wadn't (wasn't) eating/running
(23) Future progressive:
  a. I'ə/you'ə/he'ə be eating/running
  b. I/you/he WILL be eating/running
  c. I/you/he won't be eating/running
(24) Present perfect:
  a. I/you/he ate/ran
  b. I/you/he HAVE ate/ran
  c. I/you/he ain't/haven't ate/ran
(25) Past perfect:
  a. I/you/he had ate/ran
  b. I/you/he HAD ate/ran
  c. I/you/he hadn't ate/ran

(It may be the case that the forms *eaten* and *run* occur in some environments,

---

3 The symbol 'ə' indicates vocalization of *l* in AAVE. The vocalization of *l* and *r* in AAVE is a common process. See Labov (1972) for a review. This symbol will also be used for contracted *Have* (or in environments in which contracted *Have* can occur; cf. (28)).

but this matter is probably more thoroughly discussed in variation and style shifting studies.)

(26) Present perfect progressive:
  a. I/you/he been eating/running
  b. I/you/he HAVE been eating/running
  c. I/you/he ain't/haven't been eating/running
(27) Past perfect progressive:
  a. I/you/he had been eating/running
  b. I/you/he HAD been eating/running
  c. I/you/he hadn't been eating/running
(28) Modal perfect:
  a. I/you/he should'ə been eating/running
  b. I/you/he shouldn('t)'ə been eating/running

The forms in (17–28) are similar to their counterparts in SAE, but there are some differences, which will be highlighted here.[4]

Given that this chapter is an attempt to represent that form of AAVE which is most different from SAE, more focus is placed on the cases in which a single verb form is used with all persons, and less emphasis is placed on variation in the system. As shown in (17), the first person form of the verb may be used with all persons, so *eat* (17) occurs with singular *I*, *you*, and *he* as well as with plural *we*, *y'all*, and *they*. Likewise *DO* in (17b) occurs with singular *I*, *you*, and *he* and with plural *we*, *y'all*, and *they*. AAVE also differs from SAE with respect to the forms of the copula and auxiliary *Be*. As shown in some sequences in (21), forms of *Be* do not necessarily occur on the surface (*You running* and *He running*). Also in (21), sequences such as *I'm running* and *It's running* show that there are environments in which *Be* does occur on the surface. DeBose and Faraclas (1993) propose an analysis in which the forms *I'm* and *it's* are variants of *I* and *it*, respectively, and are not contracted forms of *I am* and *it is*. As such, it is unnecessary to analyze some forms in AAVE as instances of the retained copula and others as instances of the deleted copula. Notice, in addition, that the third person singular form of the auxiliary (*is*) is used with all persons (except first person singular): *you, he, we, they IS running*. This is the same pattern which occurs with *eat* and *Do*, as explained above in reference to (17). Another property which is revealed in the paradigms is that there are two ways in which the *Be* sequences (21) can be negated. On the one hand, negation may be represented by the form *ain't*, as in *He ain't eating*, and, on the other, it may be marked by the bare form *not*, as in *He not eating*. Note that in the latter case, no form of *Be* surfaces.

4 I have overlooked some facts about the sound patterns of AAVE in different regions in the United States. Some of these patterns are discussed in Labov (1972), Burling (1973), Wolfram and Fasold (1974), and Dandy (1991).

Another observation which can be made here is that the past form is used in past and past participial contexts; therefore, the past form *ate* occurs in the simple past (18) as well as in the present perfect (24) and past perfect (25). The forms in (24a) are also worth noting in that they show that *Have* does not occur in what might be taken to be regular present perfect environments. Note, however, that the simple past and present perfect can be distinguished in stressed environments because the auxiliaries *Did* and *Have*, respectively, surface in those cases. As shown in (24b), the auxiliary *Have* occurs in present perfect sequences in emphatic environments. This is not a property which is unique to the auxiliary *Have*, because *Do* and *Be* also surface in emphatic environments (17) and (21), respectively. Likewise forms of these auxiliaries also occur in environments in which they host negation. The modal *will* and the auxiliary *had* surface in future and past perfect environments, respectively. The final element which will be noted here is preterite *had*. This auxiliary, which occurs in simple past environments, has been discussed in Rickford and Rafal (1996). Although preterite *had* has been argued to be used by pre-adolescents and adolescents, it has also been observed in the speech of young adults. Consider the following sentence:

I had got sick when I went to the fair.
'I got sick after going to the fair.'

The simple past is indicated by the sequence *had* + V, the pluperfect in SAE. In the sentence, having gone to the fair precedes having gotten sick, so *had* in its use here does not set the getting sick event at some point prior to the time at which the going to the fair event took place. As such, this is not an instance of the pluperfect, rather it indicates the preterite meaning.

In addition to the verbal sequences in (17–28), forms such as those in (29a–e) also occur in AAVE. Throughout this chapter, these uses of *be*, *BIN*,[5] and *dən* will be referred to as aspectual uses of the verb forms:

(29) a. I *be* sleeping when they call.
      'I am always/usually sleeping/asleep when they call.'
   b. Bruce *BIN* playing the guitar.
      'Bruce has been playing the guitar for a long time.'
   c. They *BIN* washed the dishes.
      'They washed the dishes a long time ago.'
   d. They *dən* washed the dishes.
      'They have already washed the dishes.'
   e. The children *be dən* ate by the time I get there.
      'The children have usually already eaten by the time I get there.'

---

5 I adopt Rickford's (1975) notation of *been*: *BIN*. He also uses a stress mark (*BÍN*), which I omit here.

f. Hello, I came to talk to Bruce. He not here; he *BIN dən* gone.
   'He's not here; he left a long time ago.'

(The difference between (29f) and *He dən gone* is that in (29f) the going event occurred in the remote past. The difference between *He BIN dən gone* and *He BIN gone* is less straightforward and will not be discussed here.)

In the following paradigms, the aspectual markers and following verb forms with which they occur are highlighted.[6]

(30) Habitual:
   a. I/you/he *be eating/running*
      'I am usually eating/running'
   b. I/you/he DO be eating/running
      'I AM always/usually eating/running'
   c. I/you/he don't be eating/running
      'I am not always/usually eating/running'
(31) Remote past:
   a. I/you/he *BIN eating/running*
      'I have been eating/running for a long time'
   b. I/you/he HAVE BIN eating/running
   c. I/you/he ain't/haven't BIN eating/running
(32) Remote past:
   a. I/you/he *BIN ate/ran*
      'I ate/ran a long time ago'
   b. I/you/he HAVE BIN ate/ran
   c. I/you/he ain't/haven't BIN ate/ran
(33) Remote past perfect:
   a. I/you/he had *BIN ate/ran*
      'I had eaten/run a long time ago'
   b. I/you/he hadn't BIN ate/ran
(34) Resultant state:
   a. I/you/he *dən ate/ran*
      'I have already eaten/run'
   b. I/you/he HAVE dən ate/ran
   c. I/you/he ain't/haven't dən ate/ran
(35) Past perfect resultant state:
   a. I/you/he had *dən ate/ran*
      'I had already eaten/run'
   b. I/you/he hadn't dən ate/ran

6 The plural forms of the pronouns are not given because the aspectual markers do not bear any agreement features.

(36) Modal resultant state:
 I/you/he should'ə *dən ate/ran*
 'I should have already eaten/run'
(37) Remote past resultant state:
 a. I/you/he *BIN dən ate/ran*
  'I finished eating/running a long time ago'
 b. I/you/he HAVE BIN dən ate/ran
 c. I/you/he ain't/haven't BIN dən ate/ran
(38) Remote past perfect resultant state:
 I/you/he had *BIN dən ate/ran*
 'I had already eaten/run a long time ago'
(39) Habitual resultant state:
 a. I/you/he *be dən ate/ran*
  'I have usually already eaten/run'
 b. I/you/he DO be dən ate/ran
 c. I/you/he don't be dən ate/ran
(40) Future resultant state:
 a. I/you/he'ə *be dən ate/ran*
  'I will have already eaten/run'
 b. I/you/he WILL be dən ate/ran
 c. I/you/he won't be dən ate/ran
(41) Modal resultant state:
 a. I/you/he might *be dən ate/ran*
  'I might have already eaten/run'
 b. I/you/he might not be dən ate/ran

The labels heading the paradigms in (30–41) are basically given to indicate the type of meaning which is associated with the markers. They are not intended as absolute names of the verb forms, so they may vary from one discussion of AAVE to another.

The first point to note about aspectual markers in (30–41) is that they denote meaning, which can give the following phrase a certain interpretation. For example, *eating* in (30a) has a reading in which the event occurs on different occasions. A semantic analysis is important in that it can help to explain the meaning denoted by these markers, and it can also account for the grammatical combinations, such as *be dən* and *BIN dən*. In addition, such an analysis can be helpful in explaining the range of meanings which can be expressed by the elements in the verbal system in AAVE. One case in point here is that a semantic analysis of the marker *be* (30) shows that the AAVE system has a way of marking habituality which is not available in SAE. In AAVE, aspectual *be* signals the recurrence of a process or state of affairs (Green 1993; Mufwene, in press), whereas in SAE, simple present tense constructions and a combination of adverbials are used in such ways as to express this meaning. In fact AAVE can make a distinction between a general property (*Bruce smokes*) and a usual occurrence of an eventuality (*Bruce be smoking*). Such a distinction is made, but it is sometimes difficult to state without presenting a semantic discussion, which goes beyond the scope of this chapter. The subtle meaning difference between *Them shoes expensive* ('Those shoes are expensive') and *Them shoes be expensive* ('Those shoes are always expensive') is basically due to the element of "time" or "occasion" associated with the latter sentence. While it seems to be the case that being expensive is a property of the shoes in both sentences, the *be* sentence expresses more than this property. This sentence can be uttered to mean 'Every time I see those shoes in the stores, I find that they are expensive.'

A thorough semantic analysis will not be given here, but I will summarize the meaning of the aspectual markers.[7] Aspectual *be* denotes the recurrence of a process or state; therefore, the 'sleeping' in (29a) occurs on particular occasions. As shown in the sentences in (10–14), aspectual *be* also occurs with NPs, AdjPs, PPs, AdvPs, and AspPs. In each construction, it has the same function that it has in (29a). In (10) the state of being a clown recurs, and in (12) the children are at school on different occasions. In (13) the mail is here from time to time, and in (14) *be* is used to denote the recurrence of having already left by some particular time. Note that *be* occurs with the marker *dən* in (14). At first glance, the use of *be* in sentence (11) appears to be slightly different from the others in that it does not refer to an activity or state which can occur on different occasions. For all practical purposes, the buses do not change colors, so the sequence *be blue* does not mean that the buses are one color, say, blue on one occasion, yellow on another, and green on even another occasion. Fasold (1972) refers to such use of *be* as distributive, because, as he puts it, the entity denoted by the subject is interpreted as being distributed over time.

The analysis in this chapter is that the NP *the buses* (11) denotes a type, and different tokens of this type can exist simultaneously in different places. Although 'blue' here is a predicate which describes the more or less permanent state of the color of the buses, *be* can still occur with it, resulting in the meaning that the buses of a particular type are usually or always blue. Those occasions on which there are buses of this particular type indicate the instantiations that *be* picks out. The examples (10–14) show that *be* can occur with a range of predicate types; the marker denotes habitual or temporal meaning in the sequence in which it occurs with an activity or state. A number of other complicated issues are related to the semantics of aspectual *be*, but they go beyond the scope of this chapter.

Returning to the sentences in (29), we observe that the marker *BIN* indicates that the initial point of an eventuality or the entire eventuality is in the remote past. The 'playing' in (29b) started at some point in the remote past and

---

7 For a detailed semantic analysis of aspectual markers, see Green (1993). Relevant to this subject matter is also Dayton (1996), which was not accessible while this chapter was being written (the Editors).

continues up to the moment of utterance. In this case, the initial point of the eventuality is in the remote past. This sentence can have two readings: (1) state reading: 'Bruce started to play the guitar an hour ago, and he has not stopped' and (2) habit(ual) reading: 'Bruce's habit of playing the guitar started ten years ago, so he plays the guitar from time to time.' In (29c) the 'washing' event was completed at some point in the remote past, so the entire eventuality is situated in the remote past. This is in contrast with (29b), in which the only part of the eventuality that is situated in the remote past is the beginning. In all of these cases, the remote past is subjective; it can be used in reference to a time period starting fifteen minutes ago or one starting fifteen years ago. In some sense, it can be argued to refer to a time period which is longer than normal for performing the activity, or it can be used to affirm that a state has indeed held for some period of time.

The marker *dən* has been characterized as denoting the perfective (Dillard 1972; Baugh 1983) and perfect (Mufwene 1992).[8] Perfective aspect, as it has been discussed in Comrie (1976: 4) "looks at the situation from outside, without necessarily distinguishing any of the internal structure of the situation." Comrie underscores the point that the "whole of the situation is presented as a single unanalysable whole, with the beginning, middle, and end rolled up into one" (p. 3). He notes that "the use of 'completed', however, puts too much emphasis on the termination, whereas the use of the perfective puts no more emphasis, necessarily, on the end of a situation than on any part of the situation, rather all parts of the siutation are presented as a single whole" (p. 18).

Dən has also been defined as a completive marker, which indicates that an eventuality is over (Green 1993). It is clear that *dən* has the perfective meaning that Comrie discusses and that other researchers note, and it can also be shown that, in some readings, the marker also denotes completion. As there are no separate markers in AAVE for the perfective and completive, *dən* is used in both environments. Consider its uses in (42a–c) in which the sentences are ambiguous. They can refer to the whole event or to the fact that the event is over:

(42) a. Bruce *dən* lost his wallet.
          'Bruce just lost his wallet.'
          Literally: 'It has just been realized that Bruce has lost his wallet.'
      b. Look! I *dən* cooked a turkey!
          'I just cooked a turkey.'
          Literally: 'I have just cooked a turkey. Look at the finished product!'
      c. Don't talk to me like that – after I *dən* bought all these groceries.
          'Don't talk to me like that – after I have just bought all of these groceries.'

8 Edwards (1991) provides a thorough discussion of *dən* in Guyanese Creole in AAVE.

Literally: 'Don't be so disrespectful and inconsiderate. After all, I have been kind enough to buy groceries.'

The meaning of the sentences in (42a–c) is also compatible with the perfect, which indicates the "continuing relevance of a previous situation" (Comrie 1976: 56). As explained in Green (1993), the event in dən constructions has culminated; it is in its resultant state, a condition which continues to hold up to the present.[9] Dən is thus compatible with the perfect in a number of ways; they both share the characteristic of indicating present relevance. As a result, dən can occur in perfect environments. For example, the marker is compatible with adverbs that refer to a time including the present:

(43) a. I dən saw him today/this month/this year/??recently.
b. I have seen him today/this month/this year/recently.

Another parallel is that like the perfect, dən is excluded from occurring with adverbials that indicate past time:

(44) a. * I dən went back to visit two months ago.
(cf. * I have gone back to visit two months ago.)
b. * I dən went back to visit last weekend.
(cf. * I have gone back to visit last weekend.)
c. * I dən went back to visit yesterday.
(cf. * I have gone back to visit yesterday.)

Notice, however, that, as the sentences in (46) suggest, the uses of dən and the perfect do not always coincide:

(45) His sister has been an invalid all her life. (Quirk et al. 1972: 91)
(46) a. * His sister dən been an invalid all her life.
(This sentence is grammatical with the following reading: 'She dən been an invalid all her life, but now you want to try to help her.'
Literally: 'How dare you offer your help now (ten years too late). She's been an invalid all her life!')
b. * She dən knew that all her life.
(cf. She has known that all her life.)
c. * She dən wanted to do that all her life.
(cf. She has wanted to do that all her life.)

9 Green (1993) adopts Parsons' (1990) use of resultant state to capture the present relevance of an event that has taken place. For example, the eating event in dən ate is said to be in its resultant state.

These sentences are ungrammatical because *dən*, which refers to an eventuality that is over, is incompatible with states. The expressed eventualities in *dən* constructions must have ended in the past, but in the ungrammatical sentences in (46) above, they extend up to the present; states continue to hold. In summary, *dən* constructions are compatible with a range of meanings. To a great extent, the context or nature of the situation will determine which meaning is intended.

Turning our attention back to the examples in (29) (and the paradigm in (34)), we observe that in (29d) *dən* refers to an event, such as 'having washed' which is over. The sentences in (29e, f) are included to show that markers can combine. The meaning of the *be dən* sequence in (29e) is compositional in that it consists of both habitual (denoted by *be*) and resultant state (denoted by *dən*) meanings. Generally speaking, the meaning of the sentence in (29e) is that it is usually the case that the children have already eaten by the time I get there.[10] In the sentence in (29f), *BIN dən* denotes a remote past (and resultant state).

As shown in (29) and the paradigms in (30–41), aspectual markers are not inflected for person and number. In addition, the data in (30–41) also show that certain co-occurrence restrictions are placed on the elements preceding and following the aspectual markers. For example, the auxiliary *Do* occurs with *be* and *be done* in stressed environments, (30b) and (39b), respectively, and the auxiliary *Have* occurs with *BIN* (31b, 32b) and *dən* (34b) in stressed environments. Notice that with respect to the following elements, aspectual *be* takes a verb in the *-ing* form (30) (*be eating/running*), and *BIN* takes a verb in the *-ing* form (31) (*BIN eating/running*) as well as one in the *-ed* form (32) (*BIN ate/ran*), depending on the meaning. The marker *dən* requires the following verb to be in the *-ed* form, so *dən* (34), *BIN dən* (37, 38), and *be dən* (39, 40) take a verb form such as *ate/ran*.

---

10 It is probably misleading to refer to *be dən* as a separate aspectual marker given that the sequence simply shows that *be* can combine with *dən*. There are at least two other *be dən* sequences in AAVE. One sequence can be characterized by its property of relating some future time to an event that is in its resultant state:

    a. They'll probably be *dən* growed out that by then.
    'They will probably have grown out of that by then.' (Green 1993: 161)

The other *be dən* sequence is similar to conditionals in SAE:

    b. Boy I make any kind of move, this boy *be dən* shot me.
    'If I move, then this boy will shoot me.' (Green 1993: 162)

The marker *BIN* can also combine with *dən* (*BIN dən*) to indicate that the resultant state started to hold in the remote past completive:

    Bruce *BIN dən* left.
    'Bruce left a long time ago.'

The paradigms above show that the forms of the auxiliary *Be* in (21) and the markers *be* in (30) and *BIN* in (31) can take VP predicates. These markers can also take the following predicates, as shown below: NP (a), AdjP (b, b'), PP (c), and AdvP (d). The constructions in (47) illustrate the basic, morphosyntactically unmarked pattern.

(47) a. She Ø the person you need to see.
      'She's the person you need to see.'
  b. That ribbon Ø blue.
      'That ribbon's blue.'
  c. The car Ø in the garage.
      'The car's in the garage.'
  d. I think Mark Ø here.
      'I think Mark's here.'

(48) a. She always *be* a clown on Halloween.
      'She always dresses as/portrays a clown on Halloween.'
  b. I think those buses *be* blue.
      'I think those buses are always/usually blue.'
  b'. Her eyes *be* red.
      'Her eyes are always/usually red.'
  c. The children *be* at school when I get home.
      'The children are always/usually at school when I get home.'
  d. He can't find his mail because it *be* here.
      'He can't find his mail because it is always here.'

(49) a. Mr Jones *BIN* a preacher.
      'Mr Jones has been a preacher for a long time.'
  b. That two story house *BIN* white.
      'That two story house has been white for a long time.'
  c. That dress *BIN* in the closet.
      'That dress has been in the closet for a long time.'
  d. His mail *BIN* here.
      'His mail has been here for a long time.'

The following section will continue the discussion of properties of verbal elements in AAVE.

2.2.3 Past morphology in AAVE

As noted in Section 2.2, there is generally no distinction between the forms used for simple past and past participle forms in AAVE; for the most part, the same form is used in both contexts.[11] An exception is the main verb *was*, which is used only as the past form. In some cases, the chosen form is the simple past (50), and in others, it is the past participle (51).

(50) a. I *ate* yesterday.
  b. I HAVE already *ate*.
(51) a. Bruce *drunk* the chocolate milk last night.
  b. Bruce HAVE *drunk* chocolate milk before.

The past participle form of the following verbs surfaces in past and past participial environments: *drink* (*drunk*), *ring* (*rung*), *see* (*seen*), *sink* (*sunk*), and *sing* (*sung*). Some examples of aspectual constructions, which are presented below, give us an idea of how such verb forms are used.

In most cases, the main verb forms in *BIN* constructions bears simple past morphology, as in (52a–c). There are, however, some instances in which the verb form in these constructions is in the past participle form, as shown with *BIN gone* (52d).

(52) a. The mirror *BIN broke*.
    'The mirror has been broken for a long time.'
    'The mirror broke a long time ago.'
  b. His pants *BIN tore*.
    'His pants have been torn for a long time.'
    'His pants tore a long time ago.'
  c. The soup *BIN cooked*.
    'The soup has been cooked for a long time.'
  d. That stew *BIN gone*.
    'That stew has been gone for a long time.'

All the verbs in (52) have adjectival readings ('has been V-*ed* for a long time'). In these readings, what is denoted by the participle is predicated of the subject NP, so in (52a) *broke* describes the state of the mirror. The verbs *broke* (52a) and *tore* (52b) also have a more verbal use, in which the reading is 'V-*ed* a long time ago.'

Simple past morphology (and the past participle form *gone*) is also used in the predicates following *dən*. Consider the *dən* sequences in (53):

(53) a. The mirror *dən broke*.
    'The mirror has (just) broken.'
  b. His pants *dən tore*.
    'His pants have (just) torn.'
  c. The chef *dən cooked* the food.
    'The chef has (already) cooked the food.'

11 Other non-standard dialects of English also use a single form for the simple past and past participle. Christian *et al.* (1987: 91) report that in Appalachian and Ozark English "for some verbs which have distinct preterite and past participle forms, one of the two may be extended to serve both functions."

d. Sue *dən ate* the cake.
   'Sue has (already) eaten the cake.'
e. The students *dən went, gone/left* already.
   'The students have (already) gone/left.'
f. The students *dən went/gone* to class.
   'The students have (already) gone to class.'

Thus far the discussion of past morphology in aspectual sequences has been restricted to the markers *BIN* and *dən*. There should also be environments in which the past tense form of the verb in its adjectival use occurs with aspectual *be* because, as has been shown above (48b, b'), the marker takes adjectival complements. The question here is whether the type of verbal and adjectival readings associated with *BIN* and *dən* sequences are also available with aspectual *be*. The sentences in (54), in which *be* sequences have both verbal and adjectival readings, show that the answer to this question is affirmative:

(54) a. Half of them things *be showed* on tv don't be happening.
        'Half of the things that are shown on tv don't usually happen.'
        Literally: 'Most of the stories that are featured on talk shows do not happen in real life.'
     b. Breakfast *be cooked* at 8 o'clock.
        'Breakfast is usually cooked at 8 o'clock.'
        Two readings are possible here:
        1. 'It is the case that someone usually cooks breakfast at 8 o'clock.'
        2. 'Breakfast is usually already cooked by 8 o'clock.'
     c. They *be gone* when I get there.
        'They are usually gone when I get there.'
        (cf. They *be done* gone when I get there. 'They have usually already left when I get there.')

Sentence (54a) has a verbal reading, in which case the focus is on the 'showing' event. Similarly the sequence in (54b) has a verbal reading (as in 1), but it also has an adjectival reading (as in 2) in environments in which *cooked* modifies the state of the breakfast. The sentence in (54c) also has an adjectival reading.

This section has provided an overview of past morphology in AAVE. The data have shown that, in most cases, one form is used in both simple past and past participial contexts. Finally, this section has also discussed cases in which aspectual V-*ed* sequences have verbal and adjectival readings. The first part of this chapter has given a general overview of the types of phrases which occur in AAVE. Section 2.3 focuses on the internal structure of these phrases.

2.3 Finite auxiliaries and aspectual markers

2.3.1 *Distinguishing finite auxiliaries and aspectual markers*

The data which have been discussed in Section 2.2 show that VP, NP, AdjP, PP, and AdvP occur in AAVE just as they do in SAE. The differences that we have seen so far between AAVE and SAE are differences in the verbal elements within these respective phrases. For example, there are some differences between surface structures of copula/auxiliary *Be* constructions in AAVE and SAE, and there are some differences in the selection of past morphology in the two systems as well. A final difference is that AAVE has a range of aspectual markers which are not used in SAE. In the discussion of the structure of phrases in AAVE, we will pay particular attention to AspP, the category in which these aspectual markers are generated, and phrases which occur with them.

The following abbreviated structure (55) accounts for the range of sentences and sequences which have been presented above:

(55) CP

```
CP
 \
  C'
 / \
C   TP
    |
    T'
   / \
  T   NegP
     / \
   Neg  AuxP
        |
        Aux'
       / \
     Aux  AspP
          |
          Asp'
         / \
       Asp  XP
```

As represented in the structure in (55), auxiliaries *Be*, *Do*, and *Have* and aspectual markers *be*, *BIN*, and *done* are generated in different positions. The auxiliaries *Be*, *Do*, and *Have* are base-generated in Aux, head of the auxiliary phrase (AuxP), and aspectual markers *be*, *BIN*, and *dən* are base-generated in the aspect phrase (AspP). In Section 2.2.2, paradigms were presented to show that AAVE uses both auxiliaries and aspectual markers, which have different distributions. Section 2.3.2 will provide evidence for the type of structure in

(55), which shows that there is a position "Aux" for finite auxiliaries and a position "Asp" for aspectual markers. The categories (CP, TP, and NegP) above AuxP are required for other parts of the sentence, and they will be mentioned in Sections 2.3.3 and 2.3.4.

2.3.2 Auxiliaries: a case for two types

The purpose of this section is to show that AAVE has a set of finite auxiliaries and a set of non-finite auxiliaries. The first type, finite auxiliaries *Be*, *Do*, and *Have* in AAVE, have the more traditional properties which have been linked to auxiliaries, and these properties will be outlined in Section 2.3.2.1. On the other hand, the second type, non-finite auxiliaries or aspectual markers (as they are labeled in this chapter) *be*, *BIN*, and *dǝn* denote aspectual properties. In the following discussion, finite auxiliaries and aspectual markers will be distinguished. The distinction between the two classes may also be made by labeling one class non-aspectual auxiliaries (i.e., finite auxiliaries) and the other aspectual auxiliaries (i.e., non-finite auxiliaries). I make the finite/non-finite distinction and ultimately refer to the classes as finite auxiliaries and aspectual markers.

2.3.2.1 Finite auxiliaries

A number of analyses in SAE have been set forth to account for the order of auxiliaries and the affixes which are required to occur with them. In early transformational grammar, auxiliaries were generated by the phrase structure rule AUX → Tense (Modal) (*have* + *en*) (*be* + *ing*), which characterizes tense, modality, and aspect elements as being generated under the AUX node and as occurring in a specific linear order. In addition, auxiliaries have been defined by a set of criteria. (The criteria are not without their problems, but they will not be discussed here.) These criteria or diagnostics are summarized in Palmer (1987), and they are also noted, critiqued, and evaluated in other studies of auxiliaries (Akmajian *et al.* 1979; McCawley 1988; Warner 1993). Auxiliaries occur in negation (56a), subject–auxiliary inversion (56b), V'-ellipsis (56c), and emphatic affirmation (56d), as exemplified in the examples below:

(56) a. They *don't* know the answers.
b. *Do* they know the answers?
c. The students know the answers, and the coaches *do*, too.
d. They *DO* know the answers.

Main verbs do not exhibit these properties; the corresponding sentences are ungrammatical when main verbs are used in the environments in which auxiliaries occur in (56).

(57) a. * They *known't* the answers.
     b. * *Know* they the answers.
     c. * The students know the answers, and the coaches *know*, too.
     d. * They Know the answers.

(The intended reading of (57d) is that of emphatic affirmation.) Much attention has been given to the elements *Have* and *Be* in the literature in that they
share properties with auxiliaries on the one hand and main verbs on the other.
For example, the main verb *Be* in *Bruce is here* occurs in the environments of
auxiliaries in the sentences in (56) above. The verb *is* is inverted in *Is Bruce
here?*

Subsequent analyses have been proposed to account for the order of these
auxiliary elements, their interaction with Tense and Agreement, and the differences between auxiliaries and main verbs. For example, in Pollock (1989) and
Chomsky (1991), both auxiliaries *Have* and *Be* and main verbs are generated
in the VP, but auxiliaries are distinguished by agreement features and their
raising properties. Modals are generated under Tense because they do not show
agreement for person and number; they do not bear agreement features. Under
the analysis, modals are base-generated in Tense to avoid movement through
agreement phrase (AgrP), where they would acquire agreement features. The
verbs *Be* and *Have* bear agreement features, so they raise to Agr (as indicated by
the arrow):

(58)

TP
   T'
  T NegP
modals
     AgrP
      Agr'
    Agr VP
        V'
      V

Notice that if modals were generated in the VP, they would be in a position to
move to Agr, as indicated by the arrow, and acquire agreement features as in
**She cans*. In more current analyses, the properties of verbs and auxiliaries are
distinguished by the strength of their tense and agreement features.

The analysis of auxiliaries, aspectual markers, and main verbs in this chapter is similar to some of the previous analyses in that it also takes the approach of distinguishing the properties which characterize these verbal elements. Auxiliaries in AAVE can be distinguished basically by the same type of properties which have been exemplified above (in 56a–d). They can invert in yes–no questions, host negation, and occur in V'-ellipsis and VP-fronting constructions. In addition they can delete in yes–no questions. The sentences below provide examples of auxiliaries in emphatic affirmation, auxiliary deletion, inversion, and negation constructions. V'-ellipsis and VP-fronting will be discussed in Section 2.3.4:

(59) a.   Becky *IS* watching the basketball game.
     a'.   Becky Ø watching the basketball game.
     b.   *Is* Becky watching the basketball game?
     b'.   Ø Becky watching the basketball game?
     c.   Becky *ain't* watching the basketball game.
     c'.   Becky Ø not watching the basketball game.

(60) a.   Becky *DO* be watching the basketball games.
     a'.   Becky Ø be watching the basketball games.
     b.   *Do* Becky be watching the basketball games?
     b'.   Ø Becky be watching the basketball games?
     c.   Becky *don't* be watching the basketball games.

(61) a.   Becky *HAVE BIN* watching the basketball games.
     a'.   Becky Ø BIN watching the basketball games.
     b.   *Have* Becky BIN watching the basketball games?
     b'.   Ø Becky BIN watching the basketball games?
     c.   Becky *ain't* /*haven't* BIN watching the basketball games.[12]

(62) a.   Becky *HAVE* dən, watched the basketball games.[13]
     a'.   Becky Ø dən watched the basketball games.
     b.   ? *Have* Becky dən watched the basketball games?
     b'.   Ø Becky dən watched the basketball games?
     c.   Becky *ain't*/?*haven't* dən watched the basketball games.

(63) a.   Becky *DO* be dən watched the basketball games when I get there.
     a'.   Becky Ø be dən watched the basketball games?
     b.   *Do* Becky be dən watched the basketball games?
     b'.   Becky be dən watched the basketball games?
     c.   Becky *don't* be dən watched the basketball games.

---

12   *Ain't* can be used as a negation marker in a number of environments in AAVE. In this sentence, it is used as *haven't*. It can also be used in environments where *didn't* occurs, as in the following:

He ain'(t) ate that.
'He didn't eat that.'

13   Some older speakers may use *is* instead of *have* here.

The sentences in (59–63) show that auxiliaries *Be* (generally realized as *Is*), *Do*, and *Have* receive a pitch accent in emphatic environments (a), move to the front of sentences in questions (b), delete in questions (b'), and host negation (c). The (a') sentences are included to show that the declarative can also occur without the stressed form of the auxiliary. In (59c) *ain't* is taken to be a negated form of the auxiliary *Be*. It should also be noted that *ain't* can be used in environments in which *haven't* occurs (61c, 62c). Another side point here is that *Have* is not as acceptable in (62c) as it is in (61c).

Now that some properties of auxiliaries have been reviewed, the characteristics of aspectual markers will be discussed.

2.3.2.2 Non-finite auxiliaries: aspectual markers

A number of syntactic tests can be used to distinguish aspectual markers from auxiliaries. Consider the following sentences, which show that aspectual markers cannot occur in the positions occupied by finite auxiliaries:

(64) a.   Becky *be* watching the basketball games.
    b.   Do Becky *be* watching the basketball games?
    b'. * *Be* Becky watching the basketball games?
    c.   Becky don't *be* watching the basketball games.
    c'. * Becky *be not/ben't* watching the basketball games?

(65) a.   Becky *BIN* watching the basketball games.
    b.   Have Becky *BIN* watching the basketball games?
    b'. * *BIN* Becky watching the basketball games?
    c.   Becky ain't/haven't *BIN* watching the basketball games.
    c'. * Becky *BIN not/BIN't* watching the basketball games?

(66) a.   Becky *dən* finished watching the basketball games.
    b. ? Have Becky *dən* finished watching the basketball games?
    b'. * *Dən* Becky finished watching the basketball games?
    c.   Becky ain't/haven't finished watching the basketball games.
    c'. * Becky *dən not/dən't* finished watching the basketball games?

(67) a.   Becky *be dən* watched the basketball games when I get there.
    b.   Do Becky *be dən* watched the basketball games?
    b'. * *Be dən* Becky watched the basketball games?
    b''. * *Be* Becky *dən* watched the basketball games?
    c.   Becky don't *be dən* watched the basketball games.
    c'. * Becky *ben't dən* watched the basketball games?
    c''. * Becky *be dən't* watched the basketball games.

The (b, b', b'') sentences in (64–67) show that the aspectual markers cannot invert in yes–no questions, and the (c, c', c'') sentences (in 64–67) show that the aspectual markers cannot host negation. The aspectual markers, which are non-finite, denote aspectual meaning in the sentences in which they occur; they are not characterized by properties which are associated with the finite auxiliary elements discussed in the previous section. In summary, the sentences in (64–67) show that aspectual markers actually pattern differently from finite auxiliaries. They are similar to non-finite auxiliaries in that they do not exhibit the properties of the auxiliaries discussed above.

In the following section, we return to the structure in (55) for a discussion of auxiliary–aspectual sequences. The structure will reflect the distinction which is made between the two types of auxiliaries, finite auxiliaries on the one the hand and non-finite auxiliaries or aspectual markers on the other.

2.3.3 The category AspP

The structure below illustrates the categories AuxP and AspP in (55) above:

(68)

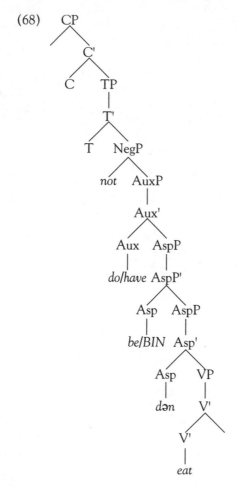

Given this structure, finite auxiliaries such as *Do* and *Have* are base-generated in Aux (which is head of AuxP). These finite auxiliaries can raise through Tense and move to C, as in the sentences in (60–63). Auxiliaries which move to C invert in yes–no questions. Likewise they can form an amalgamation with the negative element *not*, which would result in the negated auxiliaries in the (c) sentences in (60–63).

Aspect is represented independently in the syntactic category AspP, which is headed by Asp. This seems to be along the correct lines since there is grammaticalization of these markers as separate elements (*be* for habitual, *BIN* for remote past, *dən* for an event that is over, i.e., in its resultant state). Note here that there are two distinct positions for aspectual markers for cases in which the sequence of two aspectual elements (e.g., *be dən* and *BIN dən*) is generated. Given the structure, the following sequences can be generated: *Do be eating*, *Do be dən ate*, *Have BIN eating*, *Have BIN ate*, *Have BIN dən ate*, *Have dən ate*.

Some structural and featural distinctions can be made between Aux, the category for finite auxiliaries, and Asp, the category for non-finite auxiliaries. Asp is argued to project its features onto Aux, which leads to agreement or feature sharing between the two. As such, the finite auxiliary which occurs with the aspectual marker will always be one that has the features of the aspectual element. In the case of aspectual *be*, the feature [+habitual] is projected from the head Asp in AspP to Aux in AuxP. As a result, the Aux (*Do*) acquires the feature [+habitual]. The feature sharing between the two types of elements explains why certain auxiliaries occur with certain aspectual markers.

Members of the category Asp have expressly verbal features, and they, on the one hand, share characteristics with auxiliaries and, on the other, share characteristics with main verbs. These aspectual markers are like other auxiliaries, finite and non-finite alike, in that they require main verbs which follow them to select specific affixes: *be V-ing*, *BIN V-ing/-ed*, *dən V-ed*.

One major property that these markers share with main verbs is that they, too, are "supported" by auxiliaries in questions and negative constructions.[14] We have explained this property in part by saying that aspectual markers are non-finite and must occur with finite auxiliaries in some environments. Another shared property is that aspectual markers can undergo processes such as V'-deletion or V'-ellipsis, which apply to verbs. (Some examples of V'-deletion are given in the next section.) Finally, aspectual markers are non-finite, but main verbs can be finite in some environments and non-finite in others. For example, the verb 'read' in 'I read the paper yesterday' is finite.

---

14 Main verbs require *do*-support in some environments. In sentences such as the following, *do* is argued to be inserted to rescue the stranded tense feature:

Does Bruce run?

The next section will look more closely at the category Asp and V'-ellipsis and VP-fronting.

2.3.4 The category AspP and two tests for constituency

Tests such as V'-ellipsis and VP-fronting have been used to show how sequences of auxiliaries and main verbs are grouped in English. More specifically, these tests have been used to show that auxiliaries and main verbs do not form a constituent. The following examples of VP-ellipsis from Warner (1993) show that auxiliary elements such as modals and *Have* can be stranded, not grouping with the main verb in the VP:

(69) a. John may come on Tuesday, but I don't think Paul will ____.
  b. John may come on Tuesday.
     Well, I don't think Paul will ____.
  c. Paul has written to his grandmother, and I suppose Robert may have too, even if Charlie ____.
  d. Paul will bring Mary because he should ____.

According to Warner (1993: 5), "Auxiliaries both finite and nonfinite may appear in elliptical constructions without their normal complement, where the sense of the complement is to be retrieved from the linguistic context of the utterance."

Napoli (1993) (and earlier works such as Akmajian *et al.* 1979) provides examples of VP-fronting as a test for constituency in SAE.

(70) Bill said he'd buy lunch and *buy lunch* he {did/may . . . }.

(Napoli 1993: 422)

This is another example that the auxiliary is in its own phrase and not in the VP. Although Akmajian *et al.* (1979: 23, 28) use VP-fronting to discuss a topic much broader than constituency, their examples in (71) serve to illustrate the point that auxiliary elements can be left behind while the VP undergoes some process.[15]

(71) a. They all said that Harry had to get his PhD, and get his PhD he must ____.
  b. He claimed he could take first place, and taken first place he has ____.
  c. He swore he would sail across the Pacific, and sailing across the Pacific he is ____.

---

15 We have not discussed the issue of whether there is some restriction on the auxiliaries which can be stranded. This is discussed in Akmajian *et al.* (1979) and Warner (1993), but it goes beyond the scope of this chapter.

    d. He vowed he would get even some day, and getting even he has been ____.

    e. They all said that John was being obnoxious before I arrived, and being obnoxious he was ____.

    f. They all said that John was being followed, and being followed he was ____.

As has been shown in the paradigms in (17–28), AAVE also makes use of a set of finite auxiliaries, which can invert in yes–no questions and host negation. They can also occur in V'-ellipsis (72) and VP-fronting (73) constructions:

(72) a. Becky might go to the movie, and Bruce *might*, too.

      b. Bruce 'ə leave at 9 o'clock, and I *will*, too.

(73) a. Becky said that she would speak to the teacher, and speak to the teacher she *did*.

      b. Bruce said that he was gon' pass the test, and pass the test he *did*.

Now consider ellipsis in (74) in which the aspectual markers, non-finite auxiliaries, are used in elliptical constructions. These sentences are less than acceptable:

(74) a. Becky be watching the basketball games, and Bruce do/*be, too.

      a'. ?? Becky be watching the basketball games, and Bruce do be, too.[16]

      b. Becky BIN watching the basketball games, and Bruce have/*BIN, too.

      b'. * Becky BIN watching the basketball games, and Bruce have *BIN*, too.

      c. Becky dən watched the basketball games, and Bruce have/*dən, too.

      c'. * Becky dən watched the basketball games, and Bruce have *dən*, too.

The stranding of these non-finite auxiliaries in VP-fronting results in the same type of ungrammatical sentences in (75).

(75) a. The teacher think the students be playing in class, and *be* playing in class they do.

      a'. * The teacher think the students be playing in class, and playing in class they *be*.

      a''. ?? The teacher think the students be playing in class, and playing in class they do *be*.

---

16 Given my intuitions, this sentence is not as ungrammatical as the sentences in (64b') and (64c'). See also the sentences in (63). It is clear, however, that the sentence is not completely acceptable. See also the sentence in (64a).

b. The teacher think the students BIN playing in class, and *BIN* playing in class they have.

b'. * The teacher think the students BIN playing in class, and playing in class they *BIN*.

b''. * The teacher think the students BIN playing in class, and playing in class they have *BIN*.

c. ? The teacher think the students dən trashed the class, and *dən* trashed the class they have.[17]

c'. * The teacher think the students dən trashed the class, and trashed the class they *dən*.

c''. * The teacher think the students dən trashed the class, and trashed the class they have *dən*.

The sentences in (74a, b, c) show that aspectual markers cannot be stranded and thus do not support V'-ellipsis. The sentences in (74a', b', c') show that these aspectual elements do not form a constituent with finite auxiliaries. Consider the ungrammatical results in these sentences in which the aspectual markers are not deleted along with the VP. These same facts are supported by the sentences in (73). In (75a, b, c) the aspectual markers are fronted along with the VP, but in (75a', b', c') they are stranded, resulting in ungrammatical sentences. The sentences in (75 a'', b'', c'') are included to show that the structure cannot be rescued by a finite auxiliary. That is to say that it is clear that the source of the ungrammaticality is the stranding of the aspectual marker.

At this point, there is one possibility which has not been explored: AspP is actually a part of the VP. Such an analysis would certainly account for the ellipsis and fronting facts which have just been illustrated with aspectual markers. If these markers were analyzed as being a part of the VP, then there would be an explanation for the ungrammatical sentences in (74) and (75) resulting from aspectual marker stranding. The explanation would be that they cannot be left behind because they form a unit with the VP. In addition, such an analysis would be in accord with the affixal and meaning facts explained earlier. In other words, as part of the VP, aspectual markers would share features with it. This account is appealing in some respects, but the facts can be accounted for by analyzing AspP as it has been analyzed thus far, as a separate phrase. This will become clear once we explore the range of phrases with which aspectual markers can occur.

Aspectual markers have been represented as being generated in a separate phrase, AspP, and they have been shown to share some characteristics with finite auxiliaries on the one hand and main verbs on the other. These non-finite aspectual elements are, in some ways, different from non-finite auxiliaries

---

17 Given the analysis, this sentence should be completely grammatical.

in SAE. In AAVE the markers cannot occur in phrase-final position in V'-ellipsis and VP-fronting constructions, but in SAE non-finite auxiliaries can occur in elliptical constructions, as shown in the examples from Akmajian *et al.* (1979: 25):

(76) a. John would be a good doctor, and Bill would be ____, too.
   b. John could be arrested by the police, and Bill could be ____, too.

It should also be noted that there is no restriction in this environment on the occurrence of phrase-final non-finite *Be* and *Have* in AAVE:

(77) a. Bruce must'ə been working, and Sue must'ə been, too.
   b. Bruce must'ə left, and Sue must'ə, too.

(ə here is the contracted form of *have*. *Been* here should not be confused with *BIN*.) The sentences suggest that the restriction that is placed on the occurrence of aspectual markers in sentences such as (74a', b') does not apply to the non-finite *Be* and *Have* forms here.

2.3.4.1 Summary

Now that we have presented a description of the environments in which finite auxiliaries and aspectual markers occur, we can provide a summary of their properties:

(78)
Operation	Finite auxiliary	Asp marker
Yes–no question	yes	no
Negation	yes	no
V'-ellipsis	yes	no
VP-fronting	yes	no

In summary, finite auxiliaries can move to the front of the sentence in yes–no questions, host negation, and be stranded in V'-ellipsis and VP-fronting environments, whereas aspectual markers cannot. In addition it was noted that aspectual markers can be distinguished from main verbs. The first difference is that aspectual markers are always non-finite, but main verbs, when they are the only verb in the string, are finite. The second difference is that aspectual markers can occur with main verbs, but main verbs do not co-ocur. These differences are summarized below:

(79)
Property	Main verb	Asp marker
Can be finite	yes	no
Occurs with main verb	no	yes

Aspectual markers, which have verbal features, are generated in AspP, and project their features onto the Aux node. As such, auxiliaries which occur with aspectual markers bear the features of the aspectual elements. Aspectual markers also enter a feature-sharing relationship with the verbs which follow them. For example, verbs which occur with aspectual *be* bear the *-ing* suffix. Note that aspectual *be* can also occur in passive constructions, in which case the following verb takes past morphology. See the discussion in Section 2.2.3.

The following section explains why the alternative analysis, base-generating aspectual markers as a part of the VP, is not pursued in this study. In addition, it discusses predicate phrases (PredP) in AAVE.

2.3.5 Aspect and predicate phrases

The discussion so far has focused on aspectual markers and following VPs. One reason for arguing against the analysis in which aspectual markers are specifiers of VP (that is, base-generated within VP) is that these markers also occur with other phrases, as shown with *be* and *BIN* in the sentences in (48) and (49), repeated here as (80) and (81):

(80) a. She always *be* a clown on Halloween.
  'She always dresses as/portrays a clown on Halloween.'
 b. I think those buses *be* blue.
  'I think those buses are always/usually blue.'
 b'. Her eyes *be* red.
  'Her eyes are always/usually red.'
 c. The children *be* at school when I get home.
  'The children are usually at school when I get home.'
 d. He can't find his mail because it *be* here.
  'He can't find his mail because it is always here.'
(81) a. Mr Jones *BIN* a preacher.
  'Mr Jones has been a preacher for a long time.'
 b. That two story house *BIN* white.
  'That two story house has been white for a long time.'
 c. That dress *BIN* in the closet.
  'That dress has been in the closet for a long time.'
 d. His mail *BIN* here.
  'His mail has been here for a long time.'

In (80) and (81), there is no VP of which the aspectual elements can be specifiers. Under the specifier analysis, aspectual markers would be generated as follows:

(82)

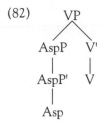

In the sentences in (80) and (81) in which there are no VP's, the markers *be* and *BIN* head AspP and assign meaning in these constructions. For example, when aspectual *be* occurs with an NP as in (80a), it indicates that the property of the following NP holds of the subject NP on particular occasions.

The diagram in (82) shows that Asp can occur with a range of PredPs (NP, AdjP, PP, AdvP), including but not limited to VP:

(83)

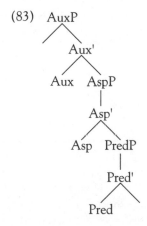

The aspectual sequence in (80a) can be generated in the structure in (82), in which case the PredP could be the NP *a clown*. In this particular sentence, the state of being a clown is a state which holds of the subject NP on occasions which are on Halloween. The analysis can be extended to the sentences in (81), in which *BIN* denotes the remote past meaning in the sentence. More specifically in (81c), it is the case that for a long time, the dress has been in the state of being in the closet, so having been in the closet for a long time is a state which holds of the dress.

The claim here about the aspectual elements in (80) and (81) is that they are generated in AspP, and the phrases following them are generated in the PredP.

(84) a. The children be at school.
       b. The children $_{AspP}$be $_{PP}$at school.

(85) a. That dress BIN in the closet.
      b. That dress $_{AspP}$BIN $_{PP}$in the closet.

Aspectual markers are not taken as main verbs here, although they may have properties which are characteristic of main verbs. This is an interesting issue, which remains to be pursued.

2.4 Summary

This chapter gives a general overview of aspectual markers and following phrases in AAVE. The following types of phrases can function as predicate phrases in the language system: VP, NP, AdjP, PP, and AdvP. The data presented in Section 2.2 of this chapter provide examples of the environments in which phrases occur and the range of phrases which can occur with aspectual markers. In addition, Section 2.2 provides an inventory of verb paradigms in AAVE and a discussion of the way the forms differ from those in SAE. The discussion notes that verb sequences in AAVE may differ from those in SAE with respect to morphology in past and past participial contexts. In addition, it also notes that the preterite *had* is used in simple past contexts.

The discussion in Section 2.2 proceeds with a description of aspectual sequences in AAVE, summarizing the type of meaning they contribute to the phrases in which they occur. The data show that when aspectual markers occur with verbs, they must bear certain morphology, such that they are in their *-ing* or *-ed*, *-en* forms. AAVE differs from SAE in that it makes use of such aspectual markers.

The focus in Section 2.3 is on generating aspectual sequences. AAVE is argued to distinguish finite auxiliaries and non-finite auxiliaries (aspectual markers). Finite auxiliaries invert in yes–no questions, host negation, and occur in V'-ellipsis and VP-fronting constructions, whereas aspectual markers do not. This difference is reflected in the structure in that finite auxiliaries are generated in AuxP, while aspectual markers are generated in AspP. Some similarities and differences between aspectual markers and main verbs are also mentioned in the discussion. The chapter ends with a statement about the different predicate phrases with which *be* and *BIN* can occur.

References

Akmajian, Adrian, Susan M. Steele, and Thomas Wasow (1979) "The category AUX in Universal Grammar." *Linguistic Inquiry* 10: 1–64.

Baugh, John (1980) "A re-examination of the Black English copula." In *Locating Language in Time and Space*, William Labov (ed.). New York: Academic Press.

—— (1983). *Black Street Speech: Its History, Structure, and Survival.* Austin: University of Texas Press.

Burling, Robbins (1973) *English in Black and White.* New York: Holt, Rinehart, & Winston.

Chomsky, Noam (1991) "Some notes on economy of derivation and representation." In *Principles and Parameters in Comparative Grammar*, Robert Freidin (ed.). Cambridge: The MIT Press.

Christian, Donna, Walt Wolfram, and Nanjo Dube (1987) *Variation and Change in Geographically Isolated Communities: Appalachian English and Ozark English*. Tuscaloosa: University of Alabama Press.

Comrie, Bernard (1976) *Aspect: An Introduction to the Study of Verbal Aspect and Related Problems*. Cambridge: Cambridge University Press.

Dandy, Evelyn B. (1991) *Black Communications: Breaking Down the Barriers*. Chicago: African American Images.

Dayton, Elizabeth (1996) "Grammatical categories of the verb in African-American vernacular English," unpublished PhD dissertation, University of Pennsylvania, Philadelphia.

DeBose, Charles and Nicholas Faraclas (1993) "An Africanist approach to the linguistic study of Black English: Getting to the roots of the tense-aspect-modality and copula systems in Afro-American." In *Africanisms in Afro-American Language Varieties*, Salikoko S. Mufwene (ed.). Athens: University of Georgia Press.

Dillard, J. L. (1972) *Black English: Its History and Usage in the United States*. New York: Random House.

Edwards, Walter F. (1991) "A comparative description of Guyanese Creole and Black English preverbal aspect *don*." In *Verb Phrase Patterns in Black English and Creole*, Walter F. Edwards and Donald Winford (eds.). Detroit: Wayne State University Press.

Fasold, Ralph W. (1972) *Tense Marking in Black English: A Linguistic and Social Analysis*. Arlington: Center for Applied Linguistics.

Green, Lisa J. (1993) "Topics in African American English: The verb system analysis," unpublished PhD dissertatioin, University of Massachusetts, MA.

—— (1994) "A unified account of auxiliaries in African American English." Paper presented at the Chicago Linguistic Society, April 1994.

Holm, John (1984) "Variability of the copula in Black English and its Creole kin." *American Speech* 59: 291–309.

Labov, William (1969) "Contraction, deletion, and inherent variability of the English copula. *Language* 45: 715–776.

—— (1972) *Language in the Inner City: Studies in the Black English Vernacular*. Philadelphia: University of Pennsylvania Press.

McCawley, James D. (1988) *The Syntactic Phenomena of English*. Chicago: University of Chicago Press.

Mufwene, Salikoko S. (1992) "Ideology and facts on African American English." *Pragmatics* 2: 141–166.

—— (1994) "On the status of auxiliary verbs in Gullah." *American Speech* 69: 58–70.

—— (in press) "African-American English." In *The Cambridge History of the English Language*. Volume 6: *History of American English*, John Algeo (ed.).

Napoli, Donna Jo (1993) *Syntax: Theory and Problems*. New York: Oxford University Press.

Palmer, F. R. (1987) *The English Verb*. 2nd edition. New York: Longman.

Parsons, Terence (1990) *Events in the Semantics of English: A Study in the Subatomic Semantics*. Cambridge: The MIT Press.

Pollock, J.-Y. (1989) "Verb movement, Universal Grammar, and the structure of IP." *Linguistic Inquiry* 20: 365–424.

Quirk, Randolph, Sidney Greenbaum, Geoffrey Leech, and Jan Svartvik (1972) *A Grammar of Contemporary English*. London: Longman Group Limited.

Rickford, John R. (1975) "Carrying the New Wave into syntax: The case of Black English *been*." In *Variation in the Form and Use of Language*, Ralph W. Fasold (ed.). Washington, DC: Georgetown University Press.

Rickford, John R., Arnetha Ball, Renee Blake, Raina Jackson, and Nomi Martin (1991) "Rappin' on the copula coffin: Theoretical and methodological issues in the analysis of copula variation in African-American Vernacular English." *Language Variation and Change* 3: 103–132.

Rickford, John R. and Christine Theberge Rafal (1996) "Preterite *had* + V-*ed* in the narratives of African American adolescents." *American Speech* 71: 227–254.

Schneider, Edgar (1989) *American Earlier Black English: Morphological and Syntactic Variables*. Alabama: University of Alabama Press.

Warner, Anthony (1993) *English Auxiliaries: Structure and History*. Cambridge: Cambridge University Press.

Wolfram, Walter A. and Ralph W. Fasold (1974) *Social Dialects in American English*. Englewood Cliffs: Prentice-Hall.

3

THE STRUCTURE OF THE NOUN PHRASE IN AFRICAN-AMERICAN VERNACULAR ENGLISH

Salikoko S. Mufwene

3.1 Introduction

The noun phrase (NP) is a phrase which is typically headed semantically by a noun in the sense that this is the component without which we would not be speaking of a noun phrase in the first place. The category NP is assigned to constructions such as *a man, the smart girl,* and *the guy that ran away*. It also includes one-word constituents with only a noun or a pronoun, as in *Jane plays tennis* and *He dated her*. In addition, it applies to some less prototypical, many-word NPs in which the head is neither a noun nor a personal pronoun but what is basically an interrogative pronoun, a *wh*-word, *what* in the following example: *what you see is what you get*. Such NPs without a head noun are called "headless relative clauses." They are less prototypical because they lack some of the charac-teristics typically associated with an NP. For instance, they cannot combine with a determiner (e.g., article or demonstrative), which specifies the mode of reference (definite or indefinite). Neither can they combine with an attributive adjective or a prepositional phrase (PP) modifying the head.[1] The examples in (1) illustrate how typical NPs and the non-typical NPs differ in regard to these respects. Here, as in the rest of the chapter, the relevant items are underlined.

---

1 Note that proper names are not an exception to this statement, although those that name indi-viduals tend to be used without an article or a modifying phrase. There are several cases where proper names behave like common nouns, as in the following examples:

  (a) *A disappointed Gerald Ford* left the White House.
  (b) *That's the Judith you told me about*.

Aside from names such as *the White House*, we should also consider team names, such as *the Bears*, which typically occur with a definite article and in the plural.

(1) a.   *God created (a) man/(*a) him.*[2]
     b.   *(*A) he was a (good) student.*
     b'. **Good what you see is what you get.*
     b''. *(*The) what you see is what you get.*
     c.   *Boys with flowers went out with the girl with the long dress.*
     c'. **They with flowers went out with *her with the long dress.*

This chapter is intended to highlight aspects of the structure of the NP in African-American vernacular English (AAVE) that make it different from other varieties of English. To focus on only these aspects might give the false impression that AAVE must differ from other varieties of English in (several) other ways too. We will therefore note what is not (so) different in order to give a less incomplete and less distorted picture of AAVE's system.

3.2 Structure of the NP

Although we will dwell on features that distinguish AAVE from other varieties of English, we must bear in mind that with regard to the NP, it resembles them more than Gullah and other English creoles which developed between the seventeenth and the nineteenth centuries.[3] For instance, unlike English creoles, AAVE does not have the option of expressing generic reference through a non-individuated noun or nominal, i.e., a noun or nominal typically in the singular

---

2 The asterisk means that the construction (combination of words to make a larger phrase, including sentences in some cases) is ill-formed. Between parentheses, it means that only the construction with the optional constituent (bracketed by the parentheses) is ill-formed; the alternative without it is otherwise well-formed. Slashes separate alternative constituents. The one marked with an asterisk is the one which may produce, or produces, ill-formedness. Example (1a) summarizes the following alternatives:

   (a) *God created man.*
   (b) *God created a man.* (This gives an interpretation that is different from what is stated in the Bible.)
   (c) *God created him.*
   (d) * *God created a him.* (The combination *a him* is what produces ill-formedness.)

3 This is not to suggest that AAVE may not be called a creole. Using this label depends on criteria on which creolists themselves do not seem to agree. Even those who, based on considerations consistent with structural distance from the lexifier, like to characterize AAVE as a semicreole, rather than a full-fledged one, do not seem to have invoked convincing criteria. One of the problems is that it is artificial to try to define a language variety by structural criteria that distinguish it from others. Natural languages are typically not defined; they are identified by association with their speakers (Mufwene 1997). For instance, German is the language typically spoken by the Germans, English is the language originally spoken by the English (formerly by the Angles), etc. The fact that the rest of English is not monolithic and that some of its other varieties share some of the same features associated with AAVE makes it fruitless to apply a structural yardstick.

form and without a determiner or quantifier (see below) but having generic reference in the present case.[4] Thus, it does not have a nominal construction that is structurally equivalent to the Gullah and Jamaican Creole examples in (2):

(2) a. *All e do is chase ooman.* (Gullah)
   All he does is chase <u>women</u>.
   b. *Daag no nyam daag.* (Jamaican, Cleary, n.d.)
   <u>A dog</u> does not eat dog (meat).
   <u>Dogs</u> do not eat dog (meat).

Barring those cases where a plural or a possessive marker is omitted (see below), non-individuated NPs in AAVE have the same kinds of interpretation as in other varieties of English, referring to substance, matter, or the relevant activities in an institution, among other things, as illustrated in (3):

(3) a. *He don eat fruit/fruits.*
   He doesn't eat <u>fruit</u>/fruits.
   b. *She go(es) to church/the church.*
   She goes to <u>church</u>/the church.
   c. *Tha(t)'s the chicken/chicken's leg.*
   That's the <u>chicken</u>/chicken's leg.
   d. *The kid got asthma/AIDS.*
   The kid('s) got <u>asthma</u>/<u>AIDS</u>.

AAVE has the same kinds of inconsistencies as other varieties of English regarding the morphosyntactic reflexes of the individuated/non-individuated contrast. The inconsistencies are illustrated by the examples in (4), in which an NP with a definite article, rather than one without an article or a quantifier (more typical of non-individuated NPs)[5] is used to refer not to a specific and already identified place but to a kind of place and to the activity associated with it. In other words, despite their formal features (notably the article), the NPs in (4) are interpreted like the non-individuated NPs in (3), rather than like their individuated alternatives (*fruits, the church,* and *chicken*):[6]

---

4 Further details are provided in Mufwene (1984, 1986), the second of which provides an explicit contrastive summary of English with the creoles' system.
5 According to Mufwene (1984, 1986), non-individuated NPs refer to the substance or the condition of being what is denoted by the NP. They may thus not be specified as definite or indefinite, a distinction which applies only to individuated NPs.
6 Note that the final S in *AIDS* is not a plural marker (the word being an acronym for *acquired immune deficiency syndrome*), although there are inconsistencies in the plural forms of non-individuated nouns such as *dregs* and *groceries*. Regarding the examples in (4), I am ignoring those situations where one may be referring to a definite and specific market or grocery store that has been previously identified in the discourse or may be assumed to be known to the addressee in the discourse context.

(4) a. *Joe run to <u>the market</u>/<u>the grocery store</u>.*
    Joe ran to <u>the market</u>/<u>the grocery store</u>.
  b. *Jawanda got <u>the flu</u>/<u>the measle(s)</u>.*
    Jawanda got <u>the flu</u>/<u>the measles</u>.

In British English, people do in fact speak of *going to market*, by analogy to the *going to church* kind of construction. Inconsistencies in all varieties of English are further illustrated by constructions such as *I heard it on <u>the radio</u>* and *I read it in <u>the news</u>* versus *I saw him on <u>television</u>*. By analogy to the former type, it is not unusual to also hear *on <u>the TV</u>* in AAVE, as in, for instance, American White Southern English.

Like all other varieties of English, AAVE allows its more prototypical NPs to be delimited sometimes with, and sometimes without, a determiner, depending on the intended meaning, as may be partly determined from the examples in (3). It also has nouns that are typically used without an article and are called **mass nouns**, for instance, *water, beer, food,* and *hair*. Such nouns call for a special interpretation (in terms of reference rather than denotational meaning) when used as individuated nouns (Mufwene 1984, 1986) – with an indefinite article or a numeral quantifier. Thus, *two beer(s)* refers to two standard units of beer, bottle or glass, depending on where the substance is served. In *She saw <u>a hair</u> in her food*, the word *hair* is used to refer to a strand of hair, whereas in *that's <u>a food</u> he don like*, the word *food* is used to refer to a kind of food.

Likewise, AAVE also has nouns which are typically used with a determiner in the singular and may combine with an indefinite article or a numeral quantifier, without calling for a special interpretation. They are said to be **countable**, and also call for a special referential interpretation when used on the pattern of mass nouns, either in the non-individuated delimitation (i.e., without a determiner, and typically in the singular form) or with a non-numeral quantifier such as *much* and *little*. For instance, *car* and *girl/woman* have special reference to the condition of being a car or a woman/girl in *A Cadillac's <u>too much car</u> for me* and *Juanita's <u>too much woman/girl</u> for my boy*.

Many other nouns, however, alternate between mass (non-individuated) and countable (individuated) usage without suggesting such drastic changes in referential meaning, for instance *television, church, school, chicken,* and *cake*. Some contexts seem to prefer one pattern and others the other. On the other hand, some other nouns show more than changes in referential meaning through such mass-use and countable-use alternations. The word *company*, for instance, means different things, depending on whether it is used as a mass or a count noun, as in *Tasha has <u>company</u>* and *Tasha has/owns <u>a company</u>*. Such is the case also with the word *class*, as in *Larry did it with <u>class</u>* and *Larry did it in <u>his class</u>* or *Larry is from <u>another (social) class</u>*. As in other varieties of English, much remains to be explained beyond the usual distinction between mass and countable nouns.

Like other varieties of English, too, AAVE distinguishes between **proper** and **common** nouns. Keeping in mind the above observations about the countable/

mass distinction, nouns may switch easily between common-noun and proper-name uses. "Toasts"[7] and other popular oral literature narratives contain several examples of common nouns or nominals used as proper names, e.g., *Mr Lion, Mr Devil, Brother Fox, Old Marsta, Ole Massa, Massa/Master,* and *Miz Bimbo Bottom.*[8] It is also noteworthy that in long narratives, several common nouns which have definite reference and have previously been used in a discourse, are often repeated without an article, on the pattern of proper names, e.g., *Preacher, Deacon, Dude, Brother, Sister,* and *Police.*[9] All these examples have been found in uses other than the vocative; they typically have third person reference and some of them have been attested in the possessive function, as in <u>Massa's</u> best wine. In regular vernacular one hears pet names or nicknames such as *Preacher, Deacon, Baby, Turtle, Homeboy, Big Red, Motor, Li'l Brother, Sugar, Low Bel', Jelly Roll* (now out of fashion), and *Lady,* although proper-name uses of adjectives are more common, e.g., *Tiny* and *Sweetie.*

Conversely, proper names may have common-noun uses, as in *He pulled a <u>Smith & Wesson</u> from his pocket, Billy wearing <u>Calvin Klein</u>,* and *If you want my opinion, that's <u>some mean Peter</u> there.*

AAVE also distinguishes between nouns and **pronouns**. The latter may be divided into several kinds: (1) **personal pronouns** such as *I* and *you*; (2) **interrogative pronouns** such as *who, what,* and *where*; (3) **relative pronouns**, which have the same form as interrogative pronouns (see p. 76); and (4) **indefinite pronouns** such as *somebody, something,* and *somewhere.* Personal pronouns change forms, some more, or less, than others, depending on whether they are subject, possessive, or objects of a verb or preposition. They may be listed as in Table 3.1.

The pronoun *he* might be heard in the possessive function, but it is rather rare, compared to Gullah, where it is the most common possessive variant. The pronunciation of *they, their,* and *them* with [d] is variable, though common. They are also pronounced sometimes with the interdental fricative [ð], as in the standard and other varieties of English. *Them* is also often reduced to *em,* as in *take em home.* It frequently assumes the form *nem* in the associative plural *and them* (see below), as in <u>Felicia an' them</u> done gone (Felicia and her friends/family/associates have/had gone (already)).

This **associative plural** strategy, which AAVE shares with English creoles, rather than with other varieties of English,[10] is also often reduced to *nem,* as in *Felicia nem.* I suppose that after the independent *them > em* reduction and the

---

7 *Toasts* are epics that celebrate weak animal characters (representing the underprivileged in society) or street heroes, such as pimps.

8 *Massa* and related forms are more typically used as honorifics, but there are some narratives in which they are used not only as referential honorifics but also as proper names.

9 Examples of such uses abound in Dance (1978).

10 Guy Bailey (p.c., 1996) informs me that the associative plural is also used among Whites in the American South. He speculates that this usage may reflect influence from African-American speech.

Table 3.1 AAVE personal pronouns

	Subject	Possessive	Object
1SG	*I*	*my*	*me*
2SG	*you*	*your* [yo:]	*you*
3SGM	*he*	*his*	*(h)im*
3SGF	*she*	*(h)er*	*(h)er*
3SGN	*(h)it*	*its*	*(h)it*
1PL	*we*	*our* [aʷ]	*us*
2PL	*you/yall*	*your/yall's*	*you/yall*
3PL	*they* [deʸ]	*their* [dɛ:]	*them* [dɛm]

reduction of *and* to *an'* pronounced [ən], the two words blend into one and a resyllabification in the form of [ə-nɛm] (with stress on the second syllable), rather than [ən-ɛm], makes possible the optional omission of the schwa, on the same pattern as in the alternations *about* ~ *'bout* and *allow* ~ *'llow*, which also all bear their stress on the second syllable for the full form. Words starting with a schwa followed by a stressed syllable typically drop the unstressed syllable (with the schwa), as in non-standard American White Southern English.

The rest of this chapter will focus on NPs that are headed by a **countable** common noun, where some differences have typically been observed between AAVE and other varieties of English. Before we get to differences, let us note here that basically the same rules govern the constituent structure of the NP, with the determiner coming first, as in *this/the/a/my boy*, then the adjectival or nominal modifier, as in *the tall girl* and *this wall plug*. The noun may be modified further on the right by a prepositional phrase, as in *the woman with the long dress*, or by a relative clause, as in *the story what you tell me* ('the story that/which you told me'). From a strictly syntactic point of view, i.e., regarding the sequence and hierarchical organization of constituents, the structure of the NP is as in other varieties of English, including the alternation of words from different lexical categories in the same syntactic positions. The **determiner** position may be assumed by an article (definite or indefinite), a demonstrative (*this, that, these, those*, or *them/dem*[11]), or a possessive. The possessive may be a possessive pronoun (any of the alternatives listed in Table 3.1) or a noun phrase in the possessive function, as in *Sonya('s) sister* and *my ole/old man('s) car*. The possessive marker *'s* is often not pronounced, subject to some phonological conditions, i.e., depending on whether the noun to which it is attached ends in a vowel or a consonant and whether the head noun, which follows, starts with a vowel or a consonant. It is most often omitted between two consonants (one at the end of the word to which it is expected to be attached, the other at the start of the head

---

11 *Them/dem* is actually more complex: it is often used without or with a weak demonstrative meaning, and interpreted as a marker of definiteness and plural. I will say more on this below.

noun). It is omitted least often between two vowels. Baugh (1983: 94) observes that these "internal linguistic constraints play a relatively minor role in whether or not suffix /-s/ is used, especially when compared with the verb *to be* or the absence of /-t/ and /-d/." It appears that a greater role is played by the kind of speech event that the speaker is engaged in. "Speech between familiars" is most likely to trigger the omission of the markers (pp. 95–97).

In any case, the dominant interpretation in the literature since Labov (1969) is that this variable behavior may be accounted for, as in the case of nominal plural (see below) and the copula, in terms of a phonological deletion rule. That is, there is a possessive marker at some underlying level of analysis but this marker is deleted, subject to the phonological conditions summarized above, in the syntactic surface structure, where phonological rules apply.

An alternative account which has not been ruled out to my satisfaction is that in the underlying level there would just be an abstract specification for possession, without any marker; during the derivation, the speaker would have the option of applying alternative morphosyntactic rules to reflect this relation. They may rely on word order alone, as in Gullah and several other English creoles, or on both word order and morphological marking, as in other varieties of English. The application of the morphological marking rule – let us call it an insertion rule – would be subject to the same phonological conditions, amounting to preferred or non-preferred phonological environments for marking the possessive.

Deciding whether there is no possessive marker in a construction because it has been deleted, or because it has not been inserted, depends in part on whether the analyst assumes that the grammar of a language is a communally monolithic system in which all speakers apply identical sets of rules (Mufwene 1992) and on whether it is necessary to posit underlying representations that contain the same kinds of forms that are perceived in an utterance (i.e., surface structure forms). The decision also depends on how psychologically real analysts claim their derivations to be, for instance whether they assume that hypothetical strategies do the same things as the mind does but are not necessarily identical to actual mental processes, or whether they claim the derivations to be identical to those mental processes. This matter will not be pursued here. Suffice it to note that possessive constructions in AAVE often do not contain a possessive marker. Whether or not the absence of the marker reflects the application of the same rule in all speakers is a separate question that we cannot answer here. Whether the facts are explained by a deletion rule or by an insertion alternative, they do not change and AAVE diverges somewhat from other varieties of English with regard to marking the possessive, as the marker is omitted at a rate not attested in other varieties.[12]

---

12 Note that, consistent with my assumption that grammars are not monolithic at the communal level (Mufwene 1992), it is possible that some speakers do apply the deletion rule – although I

However, one must bear in mind that the absence of the possessive marker is variable. So the difference from other varieties of English is not categorical. Variability also means more than one thing here, since no difference is usually made between inter- and intra-individual variation. There are speakers who tend to stick to one pattern only, while most speakers alternate between the two and will let one or the other dominate, depending on pragmatic conditions such as whether they are at home talking with family or friends, or whether they are talking to strangers in a formal setting.

Going back to the structure of the NP, after the determiner, the **modifier** position may be assumed either by a modifying noun, as in *the wall plug*, or by an adjective, as in *the cute girl*. Adjectives behave very much as in other varieties of English, especially the non-standard ones, in which the comparative and superlative are often formed with *more* and *most* even where the suffixal alternatives with -*er* and -*est* would be the only, or par excellence, choices in Standard English. Thus *Toya's the most smart woman I know* is as good as *Toya's the smartes(t) woman I know*. In closing this topic it is probably useful to note that the comparative with *less* is rare in AAVE, which has been underscored by Orr's (1987) title *Twice as less*.

When we compare AAVE with other varieties of English, what perhaps deserves the most attention regarding post-nominal modifiers are **relative clauses**, most elaborately studied to date by Smith (1973). Noteworthy in this construction are the following features: (1) the relative pronouns *who*, *which*, and especially *whose* are typically not used;[13] (2) relative clauses are typically introduced by the null complementizer (e.g., *everything Ø Larry talked about yesterday*), by the complementizer *that* (e.g., *everything that Larry talked about yesterday*), sometimes by *what*, which also behaves more like a complementizer than like a relative pronoun (e.g., *everything what Larry talked about* versus **everything about what Larry talked*), or in some cases by the complementizer (*for*) *to* when the clause is infinitival (e.g., *something (for Felicia) to write with*); (3) the

---

find no compelling motivation for the account – and that others apply the insertion alternative proposed here. One particular consideration that may be assumed to support the deletion account is the independent fact of consonant "cluster simplification," as in *ghos' buster* and *nex' guy*. However, the fact that for some speakers the plural of *ghos'* is actually *ghosses* but not *ghosts* suggests that the /t/ sound is not part of the word in the first place (and that even the apostrophe used in the eye dialect representations *ghos'* and *nex'* to suggest omission of a sound is misleading). For then, the "cluster simplification" has applied not at the level of speech but etymologically in the structure of the word.

13 In the cases that would involve a possessive relative pronoun, namely, *whose*, subordination is generally avoided. Thus, corresponding to Standard English constructions such as *I talked to the man whose daughter you met yesterday*, one often hears a paratactic sequence such as *Remember the girl/woman (that) you met yesterday? I talked to her father*. Avoidance of relative clauses in such cases may be typical of all non-standard varieties of English. Relative clauses with *of which*, as in *the magazine on the cover of which I saw your picture*, are not used either. Such constructions are more common in educated (written) varieties.

null complementizer is allowed even when the relative NP – then gapped – is a subject, as in (5):

(5) *That's the man Ø come here the other day*.

It goes without saying that, as relative pronouns are avoided, constructions such as *everything that Larry talked about yesterday* have no alternative with a fronted preposition, according to the pied-piping convention that applies optionally in Standard English, e.g., *everything about which Larry talked yesterday*. On the other hand, the forms *who*, *what*, and *where* normally begin headless relative clauses, as in:

(6) a. *That's who you said come 'ere the other day*.
   b. *That's what I hear 'round 'ere*.
   c. *Is that where you live*?

One of the most commonly discussed aspects of AAVE is the variable absence of the PLURAL marker on the head noun where it would be required in other varieties of English. Because of its phonological similarity to the variable absence of the possessive *'s* and of the third person singular agreement marker on the verb in the simple present tense, the absence of the nominal plural marker has generally been explained since Labov (1969) in terms of deletion of the marker by a low-level phonological rule. That is, the marker is assumed to be present at the syntactic level but disappears variably, according to some phonological conditions, at the phonological level of the derivation. Baugh (1983: 93) goes as far as suggesting that they are the same phenomenon, as he speaks of "suffix /-s/ consist[ing] of three different functions, each occurring at the ends of words . . . The information that /-s/ conveys is therefore vulnerable to omission, because it adds nothing to the content of the sentence, from a logical point of view."

To be sure, like the subject–verb agreement marker of the present tense third person singular, the possessive marker may be considered redundant, because the order of possessive and head noun already specifies the POSSESSION relation. As for the nominal plural marker, it is not always redundant; the suffix {-S} is often the only marker of plurality in the NP, as in, for instance, *I got the caps*.

In any case, the classic phonological conditions are as stated above for the possessive. Discussing Gullah, Rickford (1986, 1990) argues that the phonological factors/conditions have primacy over semantic factors, such as the presence of a numeral quantifier. (He may assume the pragmatic factors emphasized by Baugh to be an established fact.) His position does not entail that semantic factors play no role at all, because, as Baugh (1983) shows, in controlled behavior, when speakers of AAVE interact with outsiders to their communities, only the absence of subject–verb agreement – which may be said to play a purely formal function with no semantic justification at all – is almost favored for absence. It has a probability value of .417 (which is still significant although in quantitative analysis values of less than .5 are considered as "disfavoring" a particular variant), as opposed to .249 for the absence of the possessive marker and .345 for the absence of the plural marker. Summarizing several studies of *plural* in AAVE, Schneider (1989: 156) observes:

> To give a few examples, in Wolfram's study (1969: 143–146), the plural *-s* is missing in the lower working class in 5.8 percent of all possible cases and in 10.8 percent of all tokens after NUM [a numeral]. . . . In the data by Labov *et al.* (1968, 1: 161–62), the deletion rate varies within a range of 4 to 30 percent, according to style and linguistic environment, and in Baugh's study (1983), it is 17.3 percent. Thus Labov's conclusion has to be accepted:

> > we are convinced that there is far more interest in the problem of the plural than the case deserves;[14] that NNE [Negro Nonstandard English] plural is quite intact, and that the small amount of disturbance is the result of (a) phonological processes of consonant cluster simplification, (b) several individual items that have zero plurals in NNE, and (c) a few individual speakers who show much less regularity in plural inflections than the norm for NNE (Labov *et al.* 1968, 1: 163).

Overall, studies of different {-S} markers show that the proportion of absence of third person singular suffix on the verb in the present tense is much higher (though the phenomenon varies from speaker to speaker) than the proportion of the absence of nominal plural {-S}. The proportion of the omission of the possessive marker falls in between, sometimes close enough to that of the third person singular marker in in-group speech, at least according to the following probability values from Baugh (1983: 95): .753 for third person singular, .611 for possessive, and .173 for nominal plural. (This is shown most recently in the relative frequencies of each variable reported for Old, Middle Aged, and Teenage speakers in Rickford 1992, Table 1.) Schneider (1989) presents very good summaries of statistical analyses, which show among other things that the nominal plural marker should not be confused with the possessive marker and the third person singular marker on the verb in the present tense, although they share phonological constraints.

Poplack and Tagliamonte (1994) show that the set of semantic factors determining the absence of the plural marker {-S}, even in white non-standard

---

14 The plural is discussed in this chapter because the goal is to describe not only those features which distinguish AAVE from other varieties of English but also those which it shares with them.

vernaculars, is very complex. Among other things, nouns of weight and measure seem to figure prominently in contexts in which the plural marker is absent, especially when they combine with a quantifier. Having compared White-Nova Scotian English with African-Nova Scotian English, which is very similar to AAVE, they observe: "the precise detail of the conditioning of plural -s deletion in white[-]Nova Scotian English could not be replicated in either African-Nova Scotian English or our other early black English varieties. But the other side of the coin is that the main lines of variability in plural marking are all there" (p. 253). The last sentence of this quotation bears not only on the question of whether or not AAVE started as a creole but also on the fact that much of the literature has compared features of AAVE, a non-standard vernacular, with those of Standard English, thus misrepresenting the extent to which AAVE and creoles are restructured relative to their non-standard and structurally non-monolithic lexifiers.

As accurate as the above observations are, no convincing case has been made against the alternative of an insertion rule, which would assign a phonological shape to an abstract syntactic specification of plural, subject to the same phonological conditions. That is, the nominal PLURAL specification could be pronounced just in those phonological environments which have been assumed not to favor "deletion" and it could be interpreted to surface as Ø just in those environments which have been assumed to favor "deletion." The phonological favoring and disfavoring factors remain otherwise the same. Again, this is an issue that is tied with one's assumptions about how sentences are "derived," especially how grammatical markers such as for nominal plural are specified in the underlying structure.

It would be misguided to interpret the above syntactic-phonological facts as evidence for assuming that PLURAL is an optional category in AAVE. The above phenomenon has to do with marking PLURAL morphosyntactically, not with its semantic role in the grammar of the language variety. We are dealing in fact with variable ways of expressing it, which include also the option of using a *dem* in the determiner position of definite NPs, as in *dem boys* 'the boys; those boys.' The determiner *dem* is not subject to variable insertion or deletion and may cooccur with the suffix {S}. Neither is its function the same as that of the plural suffix {S}, as it marks both PLURAL and DEFINITE/DISTAL DEMONSTRATIVE; the suffix marks only PLURAL and applies even to indefinite NPs.

As noted above, *dem* is also used postnominally, in definite NPs, even with proper names, to mark the ASSOCIATIVE PLURAL, which translates as 'and family,' 'and friend,' and 'and company,' depending on the case, with the purpose of identifying individuals typically associated with the referent of the head noun. Examples of this construction, typically restricted to NPs referring to humans (Cunningham 1970; Rickford 1986) are: *Larry (an') dem/The boy nem lef already when I got here.* The counterpart of *an' (d)em/nem* for non-humans is *an' thing(s)*, as *he don' like coffee an' thing(s).* The postnominal, associative plural *dem* does not cooccur with the prenominal, basic plural marker *dem*.

There is nothing to report about **quantifiers** that would make AAVE different from other varieties of English. There is a distinction in this vernacular between numeral and non-numeral quantifiers, and among the latter some are sub-categorized for individuated (countable) noun uses only, as in *We brought many/few ropes*, and some for non-individuated (mass) uses only, as in *I don' have much rope left*. There are as many issues involved in the syntactic analysis of quantifiers in AAVE as in other varieties of English, as they do not all belong in the same lexical category and are therefore not subject to the same combinatorial constraints, as shown in McCawley (1988). For instance, numeral quantifiers, such as *one*, *two*, and *three*, may combine with, and follow, the determiner, as may the non-numeral quantifiers *many* and *numerous*; however, the non-numerals *several* and *most* cannot. One hears things such as *I have met some of her many friends* but not *I have met *some of her most friends*. And some quantifiers such as *a number* behave syntactically like NPs with a post-nominal modifier introduced by *of*, with the difference that this modifier is the semantic head of the larger NP, as in *a number of her friends play volley ball*. On the other hand, there are some constructions that are simply not as clear, for instance, *many of his friends like Sandra*. The lexical status of *many* is not clear, though it may be claimed to be an adjective in *her many friends*. That of *most* is even less clear in *most of her friends*.

3.3 Conclusions

The NP in AAVE is in several respects like the NP in other non-standard varieties of English, though it shows some frequency differences from them. It shares with them features such as the complementizer-like use of *what* in relative clauses, the gapping of the subject relative NP in relative clauses starting with a null complementizer, and the use of *dem* in the determiner position to mark both definiteness and PLURAL. In some respects, it shows similarities to Atlantic English creoles, such as in the use of the associative plural and the omission of the possessive marker. As shown above, surface similarity with other varieties of English or with Atlantic creoles is not necessarily evidence that the same rules apply in all these varieties. Future research will have to consider more language-internal evidence to decide whether alternative accounts are ipso facto mutually exclusive or what account is more adequate.

References

Baugh, John (1983) *Black Street Speech: Its History, Structure, and Survival*. Austin: University of Texas Press.

Cunningham, Irma Aloyce Ewing (1970) "A Syntactic Analysis of Sea Island Creole ('Gullah')," unpublished PhD dissertation, University of Michigan, Ann Arbor.

Dance, Daryl Cumber (1978) *Shuckin' and Jivin': Folklore from Contemporary Black Americans*. Bloomington: Indiana University Press.

Labov, William (1969) "Contraction, deletion, and inherent variability of the copula." *Language* 45: 715–762.

Labov, William, Paul Cohen, Clarence Robins, and John Lewis (1968) *A Study of the Non-Standard English of Negro and Puerto Rican Speakers in New York City.* Cooperative Research Project 3288. Vol. 1: *Phonological and Grammatical Analysis.* Vol. 2: *The Use of Language in the Speech Community.* New York: Columbia University.

McCawley, James D. (1988) *The Syntactic Phenomena of English.* Chicago: University of Chicago Press.

Mufwene, Salikoko S. (1984) "The count/mass distinction and the English lexicon." In *Papers from the Parasession on Lexical Semantics*, David Testen, Veena Mishra, and Joe Drogo (eds.). Chicago Linguistic Society, pp. 200–221.

—— (1986) "Number delimitation in Gullah." *American Speech* 61: 33–60.

—— (1992) "Why grammars are not monolithic." In *The Joy of Grammar: A Festschrift in Honor of James D. McCawley*, Diane Brentari, Gary N. Larson, and Lynn A. MacLeod (eds). Amsterdam: John Benjamins, pp. 225–250.

—— (1997) "Jargons, pidgins, creoles, and koinés: What are they?" In *Pidgins and Creoles: Structure and Status*, Arthur Spears and Donald Winford (eds.). Amsterdam: John Benjamins, pp. 34–69.

Orr, Eleanor W. (1987) *Twice as Less: Black English and the Performance of Black Students in Mathematics and Science.* New York: Norton.

Poplack, Shana and Sali Tagliamonte (1994) "-S or nothing: Marking the plural in the African-American diaspora." *American Speech* 69: 227–259.

Rickford, John (1986) "Some principles for the study of black and white speech in the South." In *Language Variety in the South: Perspectives in Black and White*, Michael Montgomery and Guy Bailey (eds.). Tuscaloosa: University of Alabama Press.

—— (1990) "Number delimitation in Gullah: A response to Mufwene." *American Speech* 65: 148–163.

—— (1992) "Grammatical variation and divergence in Vernacular Black English." In *Internal and External Factors in Syntactic Change*, Marinel Gerritsen and Dieter Stein (eds.). Berlin and New York: Mouton de Gruyter, pp. 175–200.

Schneider, Edgar W. (1989) *American Earlier Black English: Morphological and Syntactic Variables.* Tuscaloosa: University of Alabama Press.

Smith, Riley B. (1973) "Interrelatedness of certain deviant grammatical structures in Negro non-standard dialects." In *Black Language Reader*, Robert H. Bentley and Samuel D. Crawford (eds.). Glenview, IL: Scott, Foresman, pp. 90–96.

Wolfram, Walter A. (1969) *A Sociolinguistic Description of Detroit Negro Speech.* Washington, DC: Center for Applied Linguistics.

Part II

HISTORY

4

SOME ASPECTS OF AFRICAN-AMERICAN VERNACULAR ENGLISH PHONOLOGY

Guy Bailey and *Erik Thomas*

4.1 The importance of AAVE phonology

In many ways phonology is the neglected stepchild of research on African-American vernacular English (AAVE). Even the most cursory review of the literature will show that morphology and syntax have long been the primary focus of work on AAVE (see Montgomery and Bailey 1986, and Bailey, Maynor, and Cukor-Avila 1991 for overviews of this literature). Two factors seem to account for the focus on morphology and syntax: the most distinctive features of AAVE, at least at first glance, are grammatical (e.g., zero copula, habitual *be*, and remote time *been*) and the issues that have driven research on AAVE (e.g., debates about the uniqueness of AAVE, its origins, and its current path of development) have hinged primarily on arguments about grammatical features.

The focus on morphology and syntax does not mean that linguists regard AAVE phonology as unimportant, however. In fact, during the late 1960s and early 1970s linguists saw the phonological differences between AAVE and white varieties of English as crucial to the reading difficulties and standardized test biases faced by African-American children. A series of studies, undertaken primarily in response to these educational problems, documented many of the features of AAVE phonology (see, for instance, Baratz and Shuy 1969; Wolfram 1969; Fasold and Wolfram 1970; Labov 1972; Luelsdorff 1975). More recently, researchers in speech and language pathology have examined the role that AAVE phonological features play in the assignment of a disproportionately high percentage of African Americans to special education classes and to speech-language therapy (Wolfram 1994; Stockman 1996). Such assignments are often made on the basis of dialect differences rather than pathologies; they not only stigmatize African-American children unfairly, but they also fail to address real problems that these children face. Finally, work on subjective reactions to

AAVE and on language and discrimination has shown that phonology plays a crucial role in ethnic identification and hence in discrimination based on language (Tucker and Lambert 1966; Bailey and Maynor 1989; Kerr-Mattox 1990; Baugh 1996). In fact, some work suggests that phonology alone is sufficient for ethnic identification (Graff *et al.* 1986; Bailey and Maynor 1989; Thomas and Bailey, forthcoming), and indeed that intonation alone may suffice (Rickford 1977: 205).

Thus, while research on AAVE phonology is relatively sparse, the research which does exist demonstrates that an understanding of the subject is crucial for attacking the educational and social problems which confront speakers of AAVE. It also provides an extensive inventory of features and a place to begin assessing the role of phonology in AAVE.

4.2 Some well-known features of AAVE phonology

Table 4.1, which is based on Wolfram (1994) and Stockman (1996), lists many of the features that have been documented in studies of AAVE phonology. There are a number of ways of examining these features, but one of the most useful is to look at their uniqueness to AAVE. As Table 4.1 indicates, from this perspective there are four types of AAVE phonological features.

(1) Some processes, such as final consonant cluster reduction and the deletion of reduplicated syllables, occur in all or most varieties of English but seem either to be more frequent in AAVE or to occur in a wider range of contexts (items one through four on Table 4.1). Consonant cluster reduction is perhaps the best example of this phenomenon. In a phrase like *first time*, when the cluster is followed by an obstruent with the same place of articulation, the final consonant in the cluster is almost always lost in most varieties of English, producing *firs' time*. It is also likely to be lost when the cluster is followed by an obstruent with a different place of articulation – as in *first girl*, for example, yielding *firs' girl*. Reduction is much less likely if the word following the consonant cluster begins in a vowel (as in *first apple*) or if the final consonant in the cluster marks past tense (as in *walked*).[1] In other words, both the following sound and the morphological status of the final consonant affect consonant cluster reduction – i.e., there are both phonological and grammatical constraints on the process. These constraints seem to be universal in that they affect all varieties of English, but their relative effects differ from one variety to another. Wolfram (1991) indicates that in Standard English the influence of the following consonant is more important than the morphological status of the final consonant but that in Southern AAVE (and also in Southern white

---

1 The effect of a following pause differs from one dialect to another. In Southern AAVE, a following pause has an effect more like that of a following consonant than a following vowel.

vernaculars) these constraints are reversed: the /t/ in *first apple* is more likely to be lost than the /t/ in *walked quickly*. Southern AAVE, then, differs from non-Southern varieties both in the overall frequency with which consonant cluster reduction occurs and in the ordering of constraints on the process; it differs from other Southern varieties in the frequency of the process.[2]

(2) Some processes, such as the substitution of /d/ for /ð/ initially (as in *dese* for *these*) and of /f,v/ for /θ,ð/ medially and finally (as in *mouf* for *mouth*, *brover* for *brother*), occur in some other non-standard dialects, but not in standard varieties (see items 5–8 on Table 4.1). Again, these features seem especially frequent in AAVE, but little comparative data is available. Two other points should be made here. First, many of the non-standard varieties that have these processes have no historical connection to AAVE. For instance, the substitution of /d/ for /ð/ in words like *these* and *those* also occurs in the working-class vernacular of New York City (see Labov 1966), but any connections between that vernacular and AAVE occurred long after the substitution of /d/ for /ð/ emerged in both varieties. The process may have different sources in each vernacular, may have arisen independently in each of them, or may have been inherited independently from colonial sources from which the two varieties developed, following different trajectories. In any event, this substitution does not reflect the influence of New York City speech on AAVE or vice versa. Second, the constraints on most of these features are unclear. For instance, in our data from the Brazos Valley in Texas, some AAVE speakers pronounce the word *with* variously as [wɪt], [wɪd], [wɪf], and [wɪv] (e.g., as in *the boy she came with*). The voiced variants generally occur when the following sound is voiced, the voiceless ones when the following sound is voiceless or *with* is phrase-final. However, the factors that lead to the use of the labiovelar as opposed to the alveolar variants or vice versa are not clear.

(3) Those items in the shaded area of Table 4.1 represent general features of Southern American English (SAE) phonology. Most of these carry little social stigma in the South, but outside of the region they do. As a result, African-American children outside of the South who have these features are often assigned to speech therapy. Three points should be made about this group of features.

First, items 9–13 are old-fashioned features of Southern phonology that are rapidly disappearing in white speech. For instance, although [æks] for [æsk] was not uncommon in earlier white folk speech, data collected for the Linguistic Atlas of the Gulf States (LAGS) suggests that it has almost completely

---

2 Wolfram notes that one Southern variety, Appalachian English, patterns with Standard English in regard to the ordering of constraints. Wolfram's figures for Northern AAVE suggest a greater effect of the following sound than in Southern AAVE, but the morphological status of the final consonant remains a strong influence too.

Table 4.1 Frequently cited features of AAVE phonology

	Feature	Examples	Scope
1	final consonant cluster reduction (loss of 2nd consonant)	cold → col_ [coul]; hand → han_ [hæn]	most Eng. varieties; more frequent in AAVE
2	unstressed syllable deletion (initial and medical syllables)	about → 'bout [baut]; government → gov'ment [gʌvmənt]	most Eng. varieties; more frequent in AAVE
3	haplology (deletion of reduplicated syllable)	Mississippi → [mɪsɪpi]; general → [dʒɛnɹɫ]	most Eng. varieties
4	vocalization of postvocalic /l/	bell → [bɛɤ]; pool → [puɤ]	many Eng. varieties
5	loss of /r/ after consonants (after /θ/ and in unstressed syllables)	throw → [θou]; professor → [pəfɛsə]	other non-standard varieties, esp. in the South
6	labialization of interdental fricatives	bath → [bæf]; baths → [bævz]	other non-standard varieties, esp. in the South
7	syllable-initial fricative stopping (especially with voiced fricatives)	those → [douz]; these → [diz]	other non-standard varieties, esp. in Northern cities
8	stopping of voiceless interdental fricatives (especially contiguous to nasals)	tenth → [tɪnt]; with → [wɪt]	other non-standard varieties
9	metathesis of final /s/+stop	ask → [æks]; grasp → [græps]	old-fashioned Southern white speech
10	vocalization or loss of intersyllabic /r/	hurry → [hʌɹi]; furrow → [fʌɤ]	old-fashioned Southern white speech
11	vocalization or stressed syllabic /r/	bird → [b3d]; burr → [b3]	old-fashioned Southern white speech
12	vocalization of postvocalic /r/	four → [foə], [fou]; ford → [foəd]	older Southern white speech
13	vocalization of unstressed syllabic /r/	father → [fɑðə]; never → [nɛvə]	older Southern white speech
14	glide reduction of /ai/ [ɑɪ → ɑ] before voiced obstruents and finally	tied → [tɑːd]; tie → [tɑɪ]	Southern white speech

Table 4.1 continued

Feature	Examples	Scope
15	glide reduction of /ɔɪ/ [ɔɪ → ɔə] before /l/	oil → [ɔəɬ]; boil → [bɔəɬ]	Southern white speech
16	merger of /ɛ/ and /ɪ/ before nasals	pen → [pɪn]; Wednesday → [wɪnzdi]	Southern white speech
17	merger of tense and lax front vowels before /l/	bale → [bɛəɬ]; feel → [fɪəɬ]	Southern white speech (possibly elsewhere)
18	fricative stopping before nasals	isn't → [ɪdn̩]; wasn't → [wʌdn̩]	Southern white speech
19	front stressing of initial syllables	police → [pouˈlis]; Detroit → [diːrɔɪt]	Southern white speech
20	reduction of final nasal to vowel nasality	man → [mæ̃]	apparently unique to AAVE
21	final consonant deletion (especially affects nasals)	five → fɪ_ [faː]; fine → fɪ_ [faː]	apparently unique to AAVE
22	final stop devoicing (without shortening of preceding segment)	bad → [bæt]	apparently unique to AAVE
23	coarticulated glottal stop with devoiced final stop	bad → [bæt?]	apparently unique to AAVE
24	loss of /j/ after consonants	computer → [kəmpurə]; Houston → [hustn̩]	apparently unique to AAVE
25	substitution of /k/ for /t/ in /str/ clusters	street → [skrit]; stream → [skrim]	apparently unique to AAVE

Sources: Wolfram (1994), Stockman (1996).

disappeared among younger whites.[3] The situation regarding features 10–13 is more complex. Although Southern speech has long been regarded as "r-less," it is important to recognize that "r-lessness" potentially comprises four different phonological environments (see Figure 4.1). These include postvocalic /r/, as in *four* and *fourth*; stressed syllabic /r/, as in *fur*, *bird*, and *burr*; unstressed syllabic /r/, as in *father*; and intersyllabic /r/, as in *furrow*, *hurry*, and *borrow*. In each of these environments, /r/ was vocalized to some extent in earlier black and white speech (see Bailey 1997). Over the last seventy-five years, however, constricted /r/ has expanded rapidly in all environments in white speech, as Table 4.2 suggests. As Table 4.3 indicates, constricted /r/ seems to be expanding in AAVE as well, although its spread is progressing at a slower rate than in white speech. Using LAGS data, Lambert (1995) confirms and elaborates these findings. She shows that while AAVE is becoming more "r-full," younger AAVE speakers are still more "r-less" than older whites.

Second, items 14–17 do not appear or are rare in the earliest records for both AAVE and Southern white vernaculars. However, all four features begin to appear during the last quarter of the nineteenth century and thereafter expand rapidly in both black and white speech. The most thoroughly documented of these features is the merger of /ɛ/ and /ɪ/ before nasals (a process that makes *pen* sound like *pin*). Brown (1991) uses both linguistic atlas records and written documents to show that this feature was not very widespread in SAE before 1875. She also shows that during the last quarter of the nineteenth century

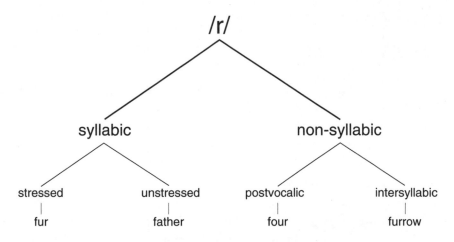

Figure 4.1 Environments where unconstricted /r/ can appear

3 Those who have seen any of the recent documentaries on the assassination of John F. Kennedy may remember Lee Harvey Oswald, upon being asked by a member of the press if he had assassinated the President, saying, "the first time I heard that was when the newspaper people in the hall [ækst] me that."

Table 4.2 Expansion of constricted /r/ in South Alabama white speech (percentage of constricted forms in the speech of five females from the same family)

Date of birth	Number of tokens	Overall rate of constriction	Stressed syllabic	Post-vocalic	Unstressed syllabic
1890	1162	3	2	0	0
1911	725	12	49	2	2
1930	829	41	99	48	2
1953	700	78	100	77	62
1970	320	98	100	100	95

Table 4.3 Expansion of constricted /r/ in AAVE and white vernacular English in Texas (percentage of constricted forms in three environments for two age groups)

Ethnic/age group	Stressed syllabic	Postvocalic	Unstressed syllabic
African American			
Older	16	5	0
Younger	20	11	4
White			
Older	31	17	0
Younger	100	93	71

the merger began to expand rapidly until by the 1930s it had gone virtually to completion in both AAVE and white speech in the South. It is not clear whether these features first emerged in AAVE, in white vernaculars, or simultaneously in both. What is clear, though, is that they are features that became widespread in both varieties only after 1875.

Third, the fact that features 9–19 also occur in Southern white speech does not necessarily mean that they reflect the influence of white speech on AAVE. In fact, Feagin (1997) argues that "r-lessness" in white speech reflects the influence of AAVE, and, as noted above, it is not clear in which variety the nineteenth-century innovations appeared first. Rather, these features simply reflect the fact that AAVE shared much of its history with Southern white vernaculars.

(4) Features 20–25 seem to be largely restricted to AAVE.[4] None of these processes has been studied in much detail, although Wolfram (1994) lists some of the constraints that affect (a) the reduction of final nasals to vowel nasality (coronal consonants are more likely to be reduced to vowel nasality than are non-coronal ones, and a following pause or consonant favors reduction) and (b)

---

4 Although the devoicing of final /d/ occurs in Southern white vernaculars too, as Fasold (1981) points out, the devoiced /d/ in AAVE is different because it is also glottalized.

the deletion of final consonants (nasals are more likely to be deleted than non-nasals, and a following consonant promotes deletion). The origins and histories of these features are unclear. In fact, we do not even know whether or not these six features occurred in earlier AAVE.

Three additional points should be made about the features in Table 4.1. First, the high frequency of processes such as consonant cluster reduction leads to the question of whether or not the underlying representations of some words in AAVE differ from those in other dialects. The lack of phonological conditioning in consonant cluster reduction, the presence of plural forms such as *desses* [dɛsɨs] for *desks*, and the problems that some adolescents have with classroom correction tests (see Labov 1972) suggest that at least some younger AAVE speakers may have different underlying representations of words with final consonant clusters, but the evidence for this is far from conclusive. The vocalization of /r/ presents a different kind of problem. The vocalization of stressed syllabic /r/ in words like *heard* and *her* leads to the pronunciations [h3d] and [h3ː], but the stressed syllabics are easily analyzable as /ər/. Likewise, in unstressed syllabics and in most postsyllabic environments, the reflex of vocalized /r/ is [ə], clearly an allophone of /r/. However, when postvocalic /r/ is "vocalized" after /o/ and /ɔ/, there is sometimes no phonetic reflex of /r/. Thus words like *four* can be pronounced as either [foə] or [fou]. In the second case it is not clear that /r/ is part of the underlying representation, especially for some older AAVE speakers who have only the latter pronunciation. This same situation obtains for inter-syllabic /r/. As with consonant cluster reduction, no consensus exists on the underlying representation of these forms.

Second, many of the features in Table 4.1 are variable, rather than categorical, processes and are sensitive to the surrounding phonological environment, as the discussion of consonant cluster reduction and the vocalization of /r/ above suggests. Although the factors that constrain the processes listed in Table 4.1 are not known in every case, most of the processes are clearly variable. In fact, the only ones that do not seem to be variable are the shortening of the glide in /aɪ/ before voiced obstruents (e.g., in words like *ride* and *rise*), the shortening of the glide in /ɔɪ/ (in words like *boil* and *boy*), and the merger of /ɛ/ and /ɪ/ before nasals (which makes words like *pen* and *pin* homophones).

Third, with the exception of the glide shortenings in /ai/ and /ɔi/ and the mergers of /ɛ/ and /ɪ/ before nasals and of tense and lax front vowels, all of the features in Table 4.1 involve consonants. Recent research, however, suggests that the vowel system may be a more important locus for addressing some of the fundamental questions about the history of AAVE and its relation to other American dialects.

4.3 The AAVE vowel system

In one respect there is nothing remarkable about the AAVE vowel system. The same set of vowel phonemes that characterize SAE (and many other American dialects) characterize AAVE, and the partial vowel mergers and glide shortenings that appear in AAVE (see Table 4.1 above) also appear in SAE. However, in a seminal article on the configurations of vowel space that differentiate American dialects, Labov (1991) argued that most varieties of English follow one of the three major patterns in their organization of vowel space. The first two patterns involve "chain shifts," or systematic rotations of vowel positions, while the third hinges on the merger of /ɔ/ and /ɑ/ (the low back vowel merger) in words like *caught* and *cot*. Figure 4.2 illustrates the first pattern of chain shifting, which Labov calls the Northern Cities Chain Shift. Among its features are (1) tensing and raising of /æ/ (in words like *bad*) to mid and even high ranges; (2) lowering of /ɪ/ and /ɛ/ (in words like *bit* and *bet*); and (3) preservation of the distinction between /ɔ/ and /ɑ/. Figure 4.3 illustrates the second pattern, the "Southern Shift." Among its features are (1) the lowering of /e/ in words like *day* and (2) the fronting of the back vowels /u/ and /ʊ/ in words like *boot* and *book*.[5] The third pattern involves no rotations of vowels; its major feature is the low back vowel merger mentioned above. Labov argues that AAVE fits none of these patterns and in fact constitutes a "fourth dialect." The work of Thomas and Bailey (1993; 1994; forthcoming) confirms Labov's observations about the uniqueness of the AAVE vowel system and provides an overview of its evolution.

In order to examine the AAVE vowel system, Thomas and Bailey assemble a database of mechanical recordings from African Americans whose dates of birth range from 1844 to 1984, along with recordings from a comparable group of

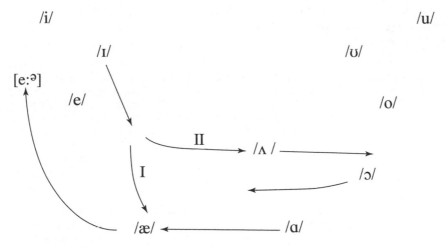

Figure 4.2 Vowel rotations in the Northern Cities Chain Shift
Source: Labov (1991).

5 In some varieties of Southern speech /o/ is also fronted; in other varieties it is both fronted and lowered, as in Figures 4.17 and 4.18 below.

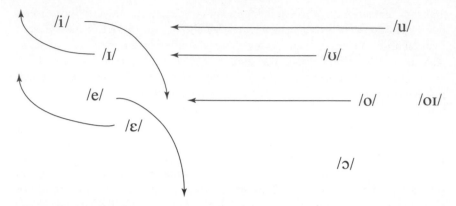

Figure 4.3 Vowel rotations in the Southern Shift
Source: Labov (1991).

whites whose dates of birth cover roughly the same period.[6] They then analyze
the recordings spectrographically and plot the results of their vowel measurements on an F1/F2 grid.[7] The plots below, taken from the work of Thomas
and Bailey, provide a graphic illustration of the evolution of the AAVE vowel
system.

Figures 4.4 and 4.5 are vowel plots of two African Americans born in the
middle of the nineteenth century. The most striking features of their vowel
systems are /e/ and /o/, which are either monophthongal or have very short
offglides. This same pattern appears in all extant recordings made with African

6 The recordings of African Americans born before 1865 come from the Archive of Folk Song in
   the Library of Congress. Bailey, Maynor, and Cukor-Avila (1991) describe the contents of these
   recordings and provide transcriptions of them. Other recordings come from the Brazos Valley
   Survey (see Bailey and Maynor 1985), the Springville Project (see Cukor-Avila and Bailey 1996;
   Cukor-Avila 1995), and a Phonological Survey of Texas (see Bailey and Bernstein 1989). The
   recordings with whites born after 1865 come from the same sources as the ones with African
   Americans; the recordings made with whites born before 1875 come from a variety of sources. We
   wish to thank John Rickford for making available the recording of the Guyanese speaker analyzed
   here and Larry Beason for providing the one from Grenada.
7 The spectrographic analysis was done on a Kay Sona-Graph Model 5500, with signal input at a
   level of 45 db with high frequency shaping and lowpass filtering at 4 khz. In the spectrograms,
   100-point transforms were used for male speakers and 75-point transforms for females. Upon
   examination of the spectrograms on a viewing screen, power spectra were taken in the middle of
   the vocoid for monophthongs and at points 25 ms from the beginning or end of the vocoid for
   diphthongs. In the power spectra, 512-point transforms were used. The wide-band spectrograms
   allowed the vowel formants to be seen clearly, while the narrow band power spectra allowed the
   harmonics to be seen clearly. Instead of the ranges plotted by Labov *et al.* (1972), mean values of
   vowel measurements (shown as reference points) were plotted on F1/F2 grids because reference
   points make it easier to show offglides, and, as this paper shows, offglides are crucial in the history
   of the AAVE vowel system.

Americans born during the middle of the nineteenth century. A comparison with similar white vowel systems (see Figures 4.6 and 4.7), however, suggests that /e/ and /o/ were both diphthongal in mid-nineteenth century white varieties. As Thomas and Bailey (forthcoming) show, evidence from the Linguistic Atlas of the Middle and South Atlantic States (LAMSAS) confirms these patterns: in LAMSAS, monophthongal /e/ and /o/ are largely restricted to AAVE.[8]

Further comparison of Figures 4.4 and 4.5 with Figures 4.6 and 4.7 suggests both additional differences between the mid-nineteenth-century AAVE and white vowel systems, and also differences between mid-nineteenth-century and current AAVE. As Figures 4.4 and 4.5 show, early AAVE had fully backed /u/ and /ʊ/ and non-fronted onsets of /au/, unlike white vowel systems (see Figures 4.6 and 4.7). Although these features are preserved in later AAVE, early AAVE did not have the shortened glides in /ai/ before voiced obstruents that characterize current varieties (see the discussion below).

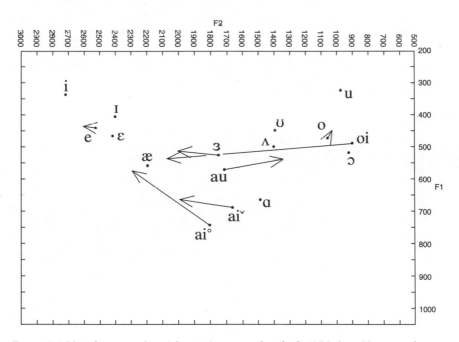

Figure 4.4 Vowel system of an African-American female, b.1856, from Hempstead, Texas

8 When monophthongs do appear in white speech in LAMSAS, they generally occur in the old plantation areas that have large African-American populations, something which suggests the influence of black speech on white speech rather than vice versa. The German area of northern Maryland is the only Southern non-plantation area where monophthongs appear regularly (see Thomas and Bailey, forthcoming).

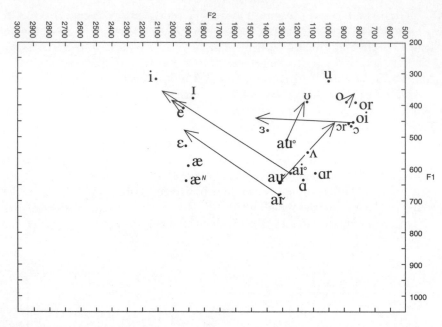

Figure 4.5 Vowel system of an African-American male, b.1848, from Charlottesville, Virginia

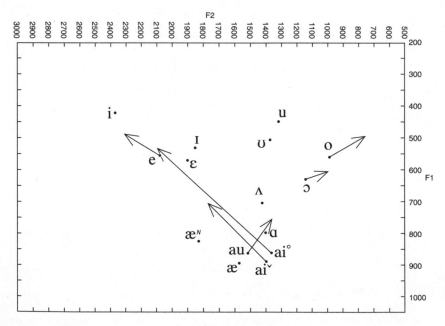

Figure 4.6 Vowel system of a white male, b.1847, from Dallas, Texas (b. in White County, Arkansas)

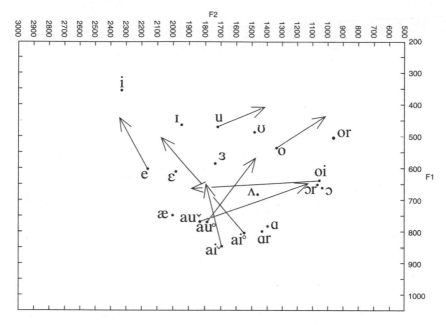

Figure 4.7 Vowel system of a white male, b.1846, from southeast Virginia

The differences between mid-nineteenth-century AAVE and Southern white vernaculars, of course, raise questions about the sources of the AAVE vowel features. An examination of the vowel systems of Caribbean creoles provides some interesting clues here. Several of the features of the earlier AAVE vowel system that do not appear in comparable white vernaculars have parallels in these creoles (Thomas and Bailey, forthcoming). As Figures 4.8, 4.9, and 4.10 indicate, Gullah and the creoles spoken in Grenada and Guyana all have monophthongal /e/ and /o/, non-front onsets of /au/, and fully back /u/ and /ʊ/. Of course a number of characteristics of these creoles are not reflected in AAVE (e.g., the lack of a distinction between /æ/ and /ɑ/ in Guyanese), but the presence of all of the distinctive characteristics of the early AAVE vowel system in all three creoles, along with their infrequent occurrence in white speech, suggests that their presence in AAVE reflects a shared heritage with the creoles. Thomas and Bailey (forthcoming) indicate that monophthongal /e/ and /o/ may ultimately have their origins in West African languages, but the evidence at this point is suggestive rather than definitive.

By the end of the nineteenth century, diphthongal variants of /e/ and /o/ had begun to replace monophthongs in AAVE, as the vowel systems represented in Figures 4.11 and 4.12 suggest. However, other distinctive features of the earlier AAVE vowel system remain (e.g., non-front onsets of /au/ and fully back vowels) and two other features begin to emerge as well. These include the shortening of the offglide of /ai/ before voiced obstruents and the raising of /æ/

97

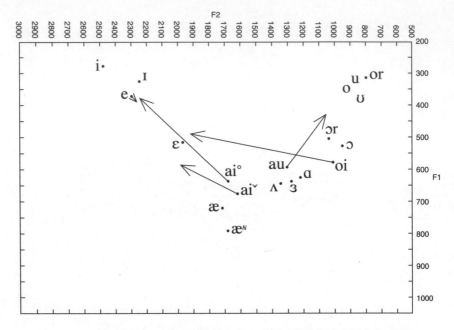

Figure 4.8 Vowel system of an African-American male (a Gullah speaker), b.1844, from Skidaway Island, Georgia

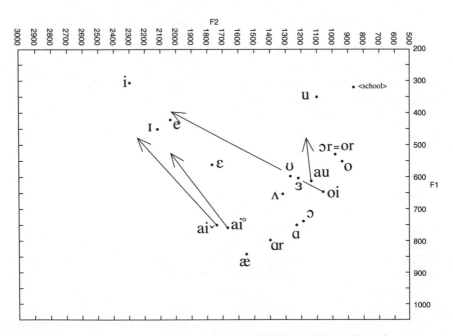

Figure 4.9 Vowel system of an African-American male, b.1918, from Grenada

98

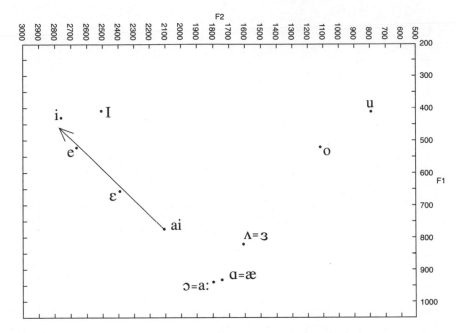

Figure 4.10 Vowel system of an African-American female, b.1933, from Guyana

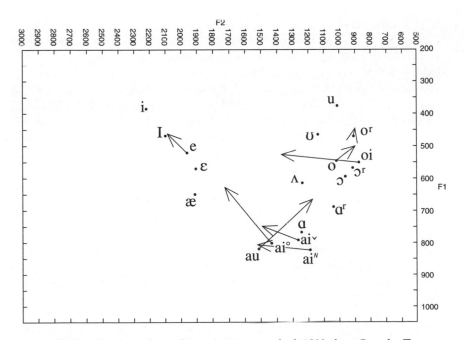

Figure 4.11 Vowel system of an African-American male, b.1892, from Ganado, Texas

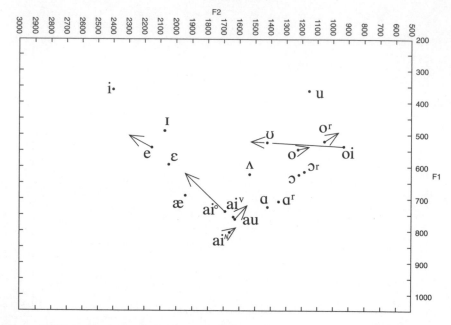

Figure 4.12 Vowel system of an African-American male, b.1912, from Springville, Texas

to mid-front position (again, see Figures 4.11 and 4.12). As Figures 4.13 and 4.14 show, the first of these features is clearly shared by Southern white vernaculars. While Figure 4.13 also suggests some raising of /æ/, our evidence indicates that any /æ/ raising that did develop in white vernaculars was short lived: twentieth-century records show little evidence of raised /æ/. Of course raised /æ/ does occur in many Northern cities as part of the Northern Cities Chain Shift (see Figure 4.2 above), but raised /æ/ in AAVE does not seem to be part of a chain shift, and late-nineteenth-century AAVE had little connection with the vernaculars of Northern Cities. Until World War I, nine out of ten African Americans lived in the South. Both glide-shortened /ai/ and raised /æ/, then, are clearly innovations in AAVE: neither early recordings of AAVE speakers nor our recordings of Caribbean creole speakers show evidence of these features (nor, for that matter, do our recordings of earlier white speakers either).

A comparison of Figures 4.11 and 4.12 with Figures 4.13 and 4.14 illustrates another emerging difference between AAVE and Southern white vernaculars as well. Figures 4.13 and 4.14 show the beginnings of the "Southern Shift," one the three major configurations of vowel space identified by Labov (1991), in white vernaculars. (See Figure 4.3 above for an overview of the Southern Shift.) Figures 4.13 and 4.14 suggest that by the last decade of the nineteenth century, both /u/ and /ʊ/ had become fronted to central position in many white

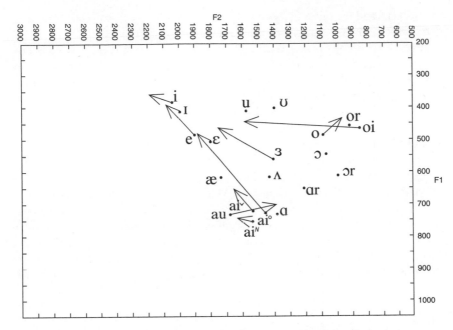

Figure 4.13 Vowel system of a white male, b.1894, from Chappell Hill, Texas

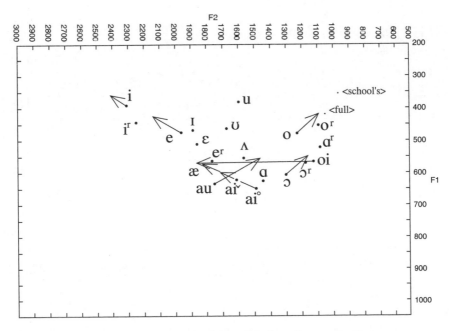

Figure 4.14 Vowel system of a white female, b.1907, from Springville, Texas

vernaculars and the onset of /au/ had begun moving to the front position as well. The vowel plots of the two African Americans born around the turn of the century (Figures 4.11 and 4.12) show no evidence of these innovations. However, as indicated above, AAVE and Southern white vernaculars do share a series of conditioned vowel mergers that began during the last quarter of the nineteenth-century. These include (1) the merger of /ɛ/ and /ɪ/ before nasals (so that *pen* and *pin* both sound like the latter); (2) the merger of tense and lax front vowels before /l/ (so that in the pairs *feel/fill* and *bale/bell* both members sound like the latter member), and (3) the merger of /ɔ/ and /o/ before /r/ (so that *horse* and *hoarse* both sound like the latter).[9] The reorganization of vowel space, though, appears only in white speech.

More than a half a century later AAVE still showed little evidence of this reorganization of vowel space. In Figures 4.15 and 4.16, which provide vowel systems of two African Americans born after 1960, all of the back vowels remain back, the onset of /au/ remains a central vowel, and /e/ is only marginally lower than /ɛ/. In Southern white vernaculars, however, the reorganization of vowel space progressed rapidly so that by the middle of the twentieth century, the

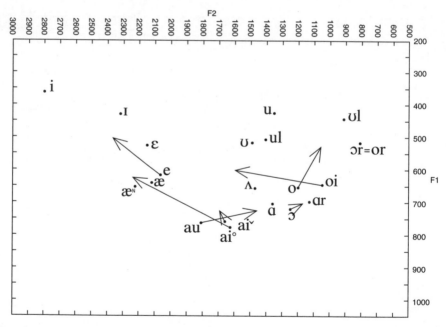

Figure 4.15 Vowel system of an African-American female, b.1961, from Springville, Texas

9 See Bailey, Wikle, and Sand (1991) and Thomas and Bailey (1992) for evidence on these mergers.

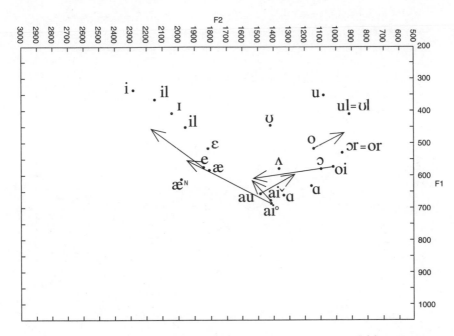

Figure 4.16 Vowel system of an African-American male, b.1969, from Silsbee, Texas

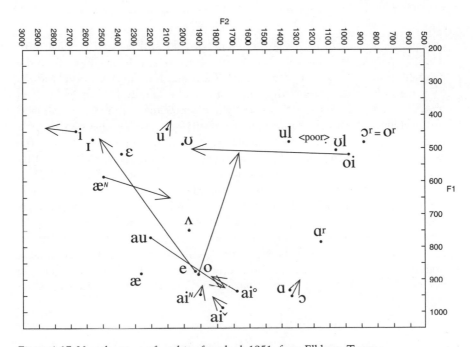

Figure 4.17 Vowel system of a white female, b.1951, from Elkhart, Texas

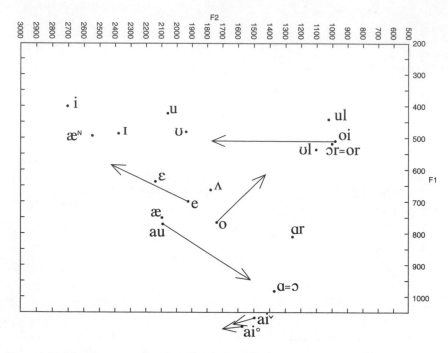

Figure 4.18 Vowel system of a white female, b.1955, from Grand Prairie, Texas

onset of /e/ was often as low as /æ/, and both /u/ and /ʊ/ had become front rounded vowels, as Figures 4.17 and 4.18 show. These figures also show the centralization and lowering of the onset of /o/, another Southern Shift feature. By the middle of the twentieth century, then, the Southern Shift had moved virtually to completion in Southern white vernaculars, but AAVE showed little evidence of this reorganization of vowel space. AAVE also showed little evidence of two other developments in Southern white vernaculars: the expansion of glide-shortened /ai/ into voiceless environments, something that characterizes many white vernaculars in Texas (see Figures 4.17 and 4.18) and the merger of /ɔ/ and /ɑ/, a relatively new sound change that is expanding rapidly in Texas (see Figure 4.18). Thus while AAVE and Southern white vernaculars share a set of conditioned vowel mergers that arose in the last decades of the nineteenth century, the use of vowel space in these two vernaculars remains quite distinct, as Table 4.4 shows. Some of the differences reflect the unique origins of AAVE, but others reflect innovations in white speech that did not develop in AAVE or innovations in AAVE that never spread to white vernaculars.

Table 4.4 Relationship between the vowel systems of present-day AAVE and Southern white vernaculars

Feature	AAVE	SWV	Emergence
Non-front onsets of /au/	+	−	before 1860
"Back" back vowels	+	−	before 1860
Merger of /ɛ/ and /ɪ/ before nasals	+	+	1875–1940
Glide-shortened /ai/ before voiced obstruents	+	+	1875–1940
Merger of tense and lax vowels before /l/	+	+	1900–1940
Merger of /ɔ/ and /o/ before /r/	+	+	1900–1940
Onset of /e/ as low as /æ/	−	+	after 1900
Onset of /o/ lowered and fronted	−	+	after 1900
Glide shortened /ai/ before voiceless obstruents	−	+	after 1900
Merger of /ɔ/ and /ɑ/	−	+	after 1945

4.4 The importance of vowel differences

While the vowel differences outlined above may seem esoteric, especially in comparison with morphosyntactic features such as habitual *be*, remote *been*, and *be done*, they are in fact crucial both for addressing social problems faced by African Americans and for understanding the evolution of AAVE. As indicated above, research on language and discrimination indicates that phonology alone may be sufficient for ethnic identification. Based on their experiments and those reported on in Haley (1990), Bailey and Maynor (1989) suggest that vowel differences provide many of the phonological cues that listeners use in ethnic identification. An examination of the vowel system of the speaker most often misidentified in Bailey and Maynor's experiments (see Figure 4.19) is quite suggestive in this respect. Unlike most other African Americans whose vowel systems we have analyzed, this informant has fronted /u/ and /ʊ/, fronted onsets of /au/, and non-raised /æ/ – all vowel features associated with white vernaculars. Since the passages that subjects in Bailey and Maynor's experiments were responding to were controlled for lexical and grammatical content, vowel differences such as these must have played an important role in identifications. Understanding them will thus be crucial in addressing problems of language and discrimination.

Reconstructing the history of AAVE is perhaps the most difficult problem that researchers who study that variety face. The dearth of early texts means that the contexts which might yield infrequent morphosyntactic forms such as remote *been* are extremely rare. Without adequate diachronic texts, claims about the linguistic history of AAVE are guesswork at best. The vowel system provides more solid ground for historical reconstruction: even very brief recorded texts provide evidence on most vowels. Using the vowel developments outlined above as a framework (Tables 4.4 and 4.5 summarize these), it is possible to make some tentative generalizations about the history of AAVE.

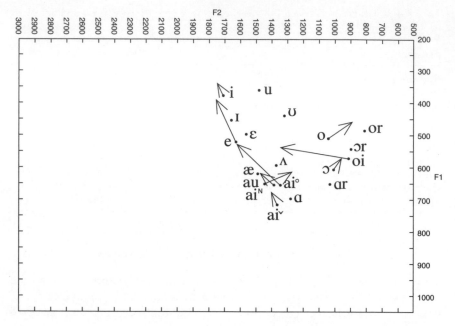

Figure 4.19 Vowel system of an African-American male, b.1922, from Leona, Texas

As Table 4.5 shows, some of the distinctive characteristics of the AAVE vowel system are a consequence of its unique origins, origins that reflect some sort of shared history with Caribbean anglophone creoles.[10] Although some of the earlier AAVE features that most clearly tie AAVE to its creole relatives have disappeared (e.g., monophthongal /e/ and /o/), other features (e.g., non-front onsets of /au/ and fully back vowels) persevere. The unique origins of AAVE, however, do not account for all of the distinctive characteristics of the vowel system. During the last quarter of the nineteenth century and first decades of the twentieth century, a number of innovations emerged in AAVE. Some of these are shared with Southern white vernaculars (e.g., glide shortening in /ai/ before voiced obstruents and a series of conditioned vowel mergers), while others (e.g., the raising of /æ/) appear only in AAVE. AAVE does not share more recent innovations that developed in Southern white vernaculars (e.g., the radical reorganization of vowel space which began to emerge around the turn of the century). The changes in white vernaculars serve to accentuate and widen differences that already existed between these vernaculars and AAVE. The AAVE vowel system, then, suggests a history marked by unique origins,

10 As Thomas and Bailey (forthcoming) point out, exactly what this shared history comprises is not clear. We need far more evidence on the vowel systems of both Caribbean creoles and West African languages before we can begin to sort this history out.

Table 4.5 Evolution of the AAVE vowel system

Feature	Pre 1875	1875–1900	After 1900
Monophthongal /e/ and /o/	+	+/–	–
Central onsets of /au/	+	+	+
"Back" back vowels	+	+	+
Raised /æ/	–	–/+	+
Glide-shortened /ai/ ____ voiced	–	–/+	+
Merger of /ɛ/ and /ɪ/ before nasals	–	–/+	+
Merger of tense/lax vowels ____ /l/	–	–/+	+
Merger of /ɔ/ and /o/ before /r/	–	–/+	+

shared history, and independent development – the same kinds of things that characterize the histories of most languages.

4.5 Conclusion

Although phonology is the subsystem of AAVE that has received the least amount of attention, it is clearly not the least important. Because phonological features are often used to assign children who speak AAVE to special education and speech therapy and because phonological features are often the cues that listeners respond to in language discrimination, phonology is a key to addressing some of the most intransigent social problems that confront African Americans. Because the vowel system provides a more solid basis for diachronic analysis than most morphosyntactic features do, phonology is integral to an understanding of the origins question and the issue of the current path of development of AAVE. Its role in addressing all of these issues makes phonology an ideal locus for future research on AAVE.

References

Bailey, Guy (1997) "When did Southern American English begin?" In *Englishes Around the World*, Edgar Schneider (ed.). Amsterdam: John Benjamins, pp. 255–275.

Bailey, Guy and Cynthia Bernstein (1989) "Methodology of a phonological survey of Texas." *Journal of English Linguistics* 22: 6–16.

Bailey, Guy and Natalie Maynor (1985) "The present tense of *be* in Southern Black folk speech." *American Speech* 60: 195–213.

—— (1989) "The divergence controversy." *American Speech* 64: 12–39.

Bailey, Guy, Natalie Maynor, and Patricia Cukor-Avila (eds) (1991) *The Emergence of Black English: Texts and Commentary*. Amsterdam: John Benjamins.

Bailey, Guy, Tom Wikle, and Lori Sand (1991) "The linguistic landscape of Texas." *North American Culture* 7: 21–48.

Baratz, Joan C. and Roger W. Shuy (1969) *Teaching Black Children to Read*. Washington, DC: Center for Applied Linguistics.

Baugh, John (1996) "Perceptions within a variable paradigm: Black and white racial detection and identification based on speech. In *Focus on the USA*, Edgar Schneider (ed.). Amsterdam: John Benjamins, pp. 169–182.

Brown, Vivian (1991) "Evolution of the merger of /ɛ/ and /ɪ/ before nasals in Tennessee." *American Speech* 66: 303–315.

Cukor-Avila, Patricia (1995) "The evolution of AAVE in a rural Texas community: An ethnolinguistic study," unpublished dissertation, University of Michigan, Ann Arbor.

Cukor-Avila, Patricia, and Guy Bailey (1995) "An approach to sociolinguistic fieldwork." *English World-Wide* 16: 1–36.

—— (1996) "The spread of urban AAVE: A case study." In *Sociolinguistic Variation: Data, Theory, and Analysis*, Jennifer Arnold, Renee Blake, Brad Davidson, Scott Schwerter, and Julie Solomon (eds.). Stanford: CSLI, pp. 469–485.

Fasold, Ralph W. (1981) "The relationship between black and white English in the South." *American Speech* 56: 163–189.

Fasold, Ralph and Walt Wolfram (1970) "Some linguistics features of Negro dialect." In *Teaching Standard English in the Inner City*, Ralph W. Fasold and Roger W. Shuy (eds.). Washington, DC: Center for Applied Linguistics, pp. 41–86.

Feagin, Crawford (1997) "The African contribution to Southern States English." In *Language Variety in the South Revisited*, Cynthia Bernstein, Thomas Nunnally, and Robin Sabino (eds.). Tuscaloosa: University of Alabama Press, pp. 123–139.

Graff, David, William Labov, and Wendell A. Harris (1986) "Testing listeners' reactions to phonological markers of ethnic identity: A new method for sociolinguistic research." In *Diversity and Diachrony*, David Sankoff (ed.). Amsterdam: John Benjamins, pp. 45–58.

Haley, Ken (1990) "Some complexities in speech identification." *SECOL Review* 14: 101–113.

Kerr-Mattox, Beverley (1990) "Language attitudes of teachers and prospective teachers towards black and white speakers," unpublished thesis, Texas A&M University, College Station.

Labov, William (1966) *The Social Stratification of English in New York City*. Washington, DC: Center for Applied Linguistics.

—— (1972) *Language in the Inner City: Studies in the Black English Vernacular*. Philadelphia: University of Pennsylvania Press.

—— (1991) "The three dialects of English." In *New Ways of Analyzing Sound Change*, Penelope Eckert (ed.). New York: Academic Press, pp. 1–44.

Labov, William, Malcah Yaeger, and Richard Steiner (1972) *A Quantitative Study of Sound Change in Progress*. Philadelphia: US Regional Survey.

Lambert, Sage (1995) "The r-ful truth of the matter: An analysis of the constriction of /r/ in Mississippi and Louisiana," unpublished thesis, University of Memphis, Memphis, TN.

Luelsdorff, Phillip A. (1975) *A Segmental Phonology of Black English*. The Hague: Mouton.

Montgomery, Michael B. and Guy Bailey (eds.) (1986) *Language Variety in the South: Perspectives in Black and White*. Tuscaloosa: University of Alabama Press.

Rickford, John R. (1977) "The question of prior creolization of Black English." In *Pidgin and Creole Linguistics*, Albert Valdman (ed.). Bloomington: Indiana University Press, pp. 190–221.

Stockman, Ida J. (1996) "Phonological development and disorders in African American children." In *Communication Development and Disorders in African American Children*,

Alan G. Kamhi, Karen E. Pollock, and Joyce L. Harris (eds.). Baltimore: Paul H. Brookes, pp. 117–153.

Thomas, Erik and Guy Bailey (1992) "A case of competing mergers and their resolution." *SECOL Review* 17: 179–200.

—— (1993) "The evolution of some Southern American vowel systems." Paper presented at the Southeastern Conference on Linguistics, Auburn, AL.

—— (1994) "The fourth dialect." Paper presented at NWAVE 23, Stanford University.

—— (forthcoming) "Parallels between vowel subsystems of African American Vernacular English and Caribbean Anglophone Creoles." *Journal of Pidgin and Creole Languages*.

Tucker, G. Richard and Wallace E. Lambert (1966) "White and Negro listeners' reactions to various American English dialects. *Social Forces* 47: 463–468.

Wolfram, Walter A. (1969) A *Sociolinguistic Description of Detroit Negro Speech*. Washington, DC: Center for Applied Linguistics.

Wolfram, Walt (1991) *Dialects and American English*. Englewood Cliffs, NJ: Prentice Hall.

—— 1994. "The phonology of a sociocultural variety: The case of African American vernacular English." In *Child Phonology: Characteristics, Assessment, and Intervention with Special Populations*, J. Bernthal and N. Bankston (eds.). New York: Thieme.

5

CO-EXISTENT SYSTEMS IN AFRICAN-AMERICAN VERNACULAR ENGLISH

William Labov

5.1 Introduction

This contribution to the study of African-American vernacular English (AAVE) is an interpretation of the special linguistic features of this dialect in the light of its co-existence with other co-territorial dialects of English. It begins with a review of the idea that AAVE can be seen as a system in itself, analyzed without reference to other dialects, which has been a repeated theme of research in this area from the very beginnings to the present day. Although it must be admitted that this monolithic approach has often produced descriptions that are far removed from linguistic and social reality, it has also been a continued source of insights, bringing to our attention striking differences between AAVE and other dialects that would otherwise have been overlooked. In fact, the analysis I am presenting here is heavily indebted to two linguists who have attempted to extract an invariant core that is unique to AAVE, in the earliest and the most recent contribution to the study of this dialect. One source is the work of Beryl Bailey, who brought to AAVE the insights from her description of Jamaican Creole English, drawn from her internalized knowledge as a native speaker. The recognition of my indebtedness to her work was the original motivation for this chapter. The other source is the monumental study of the tense and aspect system of AAVE by Elizabeth Dayton, begun in the 1970s and only recently brought to completion. Dayton's meticulously transcribed observations are the product of many years of participation in the daily life of a Philadelphia African-American community. Her data on the tense and aspect particles of AAVE, carefully noted in the midst of the social interactions that produced it, is roughly ten times as extensive as all the combined observations of all other researchers. In the original version of this chapter, written five years ago, I drew upon a number of handouts from unpublished papers that Dayton had given throughout the years. In revising this chapter, I have not attempted to re-incorporate the massive amount of data and extensive analyses of her 1996 dissertation. I hope that the point of view developed here will continue to be useful in the years to come, when the linguistic community has begun to assimilate Dayton's data and her analysis of the AAVE system.

5.2 The heritage of Beryl Bailey

My first acquaintance with the issues raised in this chapter came through my close association with Beryl Bailey, who was a fellow student with me at Columbia. Both of our dissertations were directed by Uriel Weinreich, who encouraged us to apply the tools of linguistics to the language of every-day life, and to set aside the barriers between linguistic analysis and dialectology. Beryl came from a school teacher's family and a school teacher's world. For many Jamaicans, that means cleaving to the standards and norms of school teachers, and never looking back at the life and language of ordinary people. Beryl wrote in the introduction to her thesis that she wanted to

> explode once and for all the notion which persists among teachers of
> English in Jamaica, that the "dialect" is not a language: and further that
> it has no bearing on the problem of the teaching of English.

She began work on Jamaican Creole English (JCE) in 1956, made several return trips to Jamaica, and produced a language guide to Jamaica to help train Peace Corps volunteers. Her dissertation, Jamaican Creole Syntax, appeared in 1966 and was the first comprehensive description of a creole's syntax. It is also an important point of reference for the structure of AAVE in the US. To get some insight into Bailey's style, and the tradition she came from, one might simply cite her dedication:

> to the memory of my
> great-grandfather
> Henry Loftman
> whose passion for the
> rudiments of English grammar
> earned him the nickname
> "syntax."

5.2.1 Bailey's view of AAVE

Bailey's approach to AAVE is exemplified in her first paper on the topic, "A new perspective in Negro English dialectology" (1965). Her insights into the nature of the dialect were motivated in part by her reaction against the dialectological view of AAVE as a collection of mistakes or deviations from Standard English. Outside of the school setting, Beryl was not a field worker, and her whole article was based on an examination of the speech of the narrator in one novel, The Cool World. She apologized for this fact in words that are worth citing:

(1) I was compelled to modify the orthodox procedures and even, at times, to adopt some completely unorthodox ones. The first problem that I had to face was that of abstracting a hypothetical dialect which could reasonably be regarded as featuring the main elements of the deep structure. This may sound like hocus-pocus, but indeed a good deal of linguistics is. A hocus-pocus procedure which yields the linguistic facts is surely preferable to a scientifically rigorous one which murders those facts.

Bailey's main theme is that AAVE must be understood as an independent structure in its own right. The most remarkable result of her analysis is the following set of three phrase structure rules for non-verbal predications:

(2) English predications

$$P \rightarrow be + \left\{ \begin{array}{l} \text{Adj} \\ \text{Nom} \\ \text{Loc} \end{array} \right\}$$

(3) Jamaican Creole predications

$$P \rightarrow \left\{ \begin{array}{l} \emptyset + \text{Adj} \\ a + \text{Nom} \\ (de) + \text{Loc} \end{array} \right\}$$

(4) *Cool World* predications

$$P \rightarrow \emptyset + \left\{ \begin{array}{l} \text{Adj} \\ \text{Nom} \\ \text{Loc} \end{array} \right\}$$

It should be clear that Bailey anticipated in this juxtaposition the long discussion of the AAVE copula to follow. The separation of the copula from the progressive auxiliary has since been recognized as a useful strategy (G. Bailey and N. Maynor 1989). Her abstraction from the *Cool World* data of a grammar with categorical absence of the copula did not prove to be characteristic of AAVE, but this type of structure has recently re-appeared in John Singler's (1991) description of the mesolect in Liberia.[1] Most importantly, she identified a family resemblance between AAVE and JCE which was the basis of most of the research that followed.

---

1 Later developments showed that Bailey's Jamaican Creole copula rule may have been more relevant than she thought to the structure of modern AAVE, but this required the study of variable contraction and deletion before the different grammatical environments. The argument that this variation can be explained by the Jamaican treatment of the copula has been extensively developed by Holm (1984) and Baugh (1980). If the complete zeroing out of the copula that Singler found in some Liberian speakers is a typical mesolectal stage, it is not clear how the

5.3 The recognition of separate systems

Though Bailey did not study every-day speech in JCE or AAVE, she was well aware of variation that did not fit within the rules of her grammar. Following the logic of her basic methodology given in (1), she assigned the variation of every-day speech automatically to interference from another language (or dialect), which one might call Standard English or Jamaican Standard English. This approach to the resolution of variation has been put forward frequently from the very beginning of studies of variation and change. It has been suggested as a way of handling the variation of constricted and non-constricted /r/ in New York City, or the variation of fricatives, affricates, and stops for the interdentals *dh* and *th*. The resolution into separate dialects is in fact the limiting case of the general solution to the problem of variation. One begins with a surface variation, say between [kɑərd] and [kɑːᵊd], or between *He's tired* and *He tired*. The analytical task is to discover what this surface variation reflects in the organization of the grammar: mere phonetic variability, variation in a more abstract phonological rule, the variable insertion of a morpheme, the alternation of allomorphs, variation in the syntactic parsing or syntactic movements, or in many cases the combined effects of morphological and phonological variation (Guy 1981). The limiting possibility is that the surface variation is caused by the alternating use of two separate systems, each comprising in itself a complete and coherent grammar. The crucial question for the general study of variation is to decide what kind of evidence bears on the assignment of variation to what level, and what kind of evidence could justify the recognition of distinct systems, not simply competing rules.

The issue of where variability is located in the grammar has been given a new impetus by Mufwene (1992: 233), in a general argument for the recognition of heterogeneity in linguistic systems. In discussing the AAVE copula, he attributes the variation found in the actual realization of Bailey's rule (4) not to phonological contraction or morphological insertion, but to a fundamental difference in the basic phrase structure rules of the grammar:

(5) Unlike standard English, [Black English] allows both S → NP VP and S → NP PredP as alternative surface combinatoric rules in its non-elliptical clauses. . . . Those speakers producing copula-less sentences more frequently may be assumed to subscribe predominantly to the S → NP PredP rules and the others to the S → NP VP rule. There is undoubtedly individual variation among BE

influence of the basilectal differentiation of the copula could determine modern AAVE structure. Winford (1992) shows that this is only one possible scenario of development, and demonstrates close parallels between the treatment of the copula in AAVE and the mesolectal Trinidadian English Creole.

speakers regarding whether the second rule is favored when the PredP is headed by an adjective or by a preposition.[2]

In arguing for such an assignment, and against contraction and deletion rules, Mufwene refers only to one set of constraints: the following grammatical environment. But even if Mufwene's concept of a heterogeneous grammar should not apply to the variation of finite *be* – which I will view here as a part of the general English component of AAVE – I will argue that the situation is fundamentally as he describes it: the grammar is characterized by two sets of non-overlapping and structurally inconsistent rules. Both contraction and deletion are favored by subject pronouns as against full noun phrases, reflecting a long-standing pattern in the history of English (G. Bailey, Maynor and Cukor-Avila 1989). More importantly, contraction and deletion are inversely affected by the phonological form of the subject: vowel-final subjects favor contraction and consonant-final subjects favor deletion, as one would predict from the unmarked status of CVC syllables.[3] Phonological constraints of this type indicate that the object being acted on is in place at a higher level of abstraction, and that its alternation with zero is controlled by a phonological rule (Labov 1987). But if Mufwene's suggestion does not apply to the variation of finite *be* – which as we will see is a member of the general English component of AAVE – we will find other areas of the grammar where it does apply.

The major topic of this chapter – the tense and aspect systems of AAVE and other American dialects (OAD) – will show many differences that reflect a higher level variation comparable to that suggested by Mufwene. The questions to be addressed will concern contrasts like *He be tired* vs. *He tired*. There has never been any reason to believe that this is the result of a low level rule of phonological deletion of *be*. The issue is whether these two forms differ only by the optional choice of the aspect marker *be*, or whether the choice of invariant *be* vs. finite *be* reflects an alternation at a higher level that involves layered sets of rules.

The discussion to follow will pursue the suggestion of Labov (1971) that the recognition of a linguistic system as a separate entity depends upon the strict co-occurrence of sets of rules. In the simplest schema (6), a community may

---

2 As the last sentence of this quotation shows, Mufwene's proposals involve variation at the level of individual speakers as well as the assignment of variation to relatively abstract syntactic rules. We are concerned here only with the latter aspect of his analysis. As far as individual variation is concerned, I have not been able to locate evidence to support the existence of stable individual idiolects which are not based on communities defined socially or geographically (Labov 1975).

3 This effect has been replicated in a number of studies, culminating in Rickford *et al.* (1991). In the East Palo Alto data, contraction consistently shows the favoring effect of a preceding vowel. When deletion is analyzed as operating on the pool of contracted items, the effect reverses, though not when no connection between deletion and contraction is assumed (Tables 3–6).

show variation involving two rules, A and B, which may apply or not apply in four different possible arrangements for various subgroups:

(6)   {1}   {2}   {3}   {4}

	{1}	{2}	{3}	{4}
Rule A applies	yes	yes	no	no
Rule B applies	yes	no	yes	no

If all four possibilities occur (i.e., if the two rules occur in all combinations), then the choice of A is independent of the choice of B, and there is no evidence for a separate system. We can recognize two separate and independent variable rules (A, B). But if we find only possibilities {1} and {4} and never {2} and {3} (i.e., if rules A and B are constrained to co-occur or not occur at all), then we can say that rules A and B are in some way dependent on each other or upon some more abstract choice. In this sense, they are linked systematically and form part of a (possibly larger) separate system. It is just such linking or co-occurrence of properties that we will search for in re-opening the question of co-existent systems in AAVE.

5.4 The current consensus on AAVE

Given the active state of research on AAVE, and the impending impact of Dayton's work, any attempt to state a general consensus can only be momentarily successful; the following brief account is my own attempt to update the effort of Labov (1982) in this respect.[4] For this purpose it will be useful to compare AAVE with OAD. While there is considerable variation within this range of "other dialects," particularly within the Southern states, it can still be argued that they share many features in common and are differentiated as a whole from AAVE.[5] The term AAVE or African-American vernacular English will be used to refer to

---

4 For the study of the phonology and morphological patterns, and syntax of AAVE, I will be drawing principally on Labov et al. (1968); Wolfram (1969, 1974); Fasold (1972); Baugh (1983); Rickford et al. (1991); Rickford & McNair-Knox (1994). Evidence on the tense and aspect system of AAVE will be drawn from Labov et al. (1968); Fickett (1970); Fasold (1972); Rickford (1973, 1980, 1986); Dunlap (1977); Bailey and Maynor (1985, 1987, 1989); Bernstein (1988); Myhill (1988); and above all from the papers and dissertation of Elizabeth Dayton. For evidence on earlier stages of AAVE and its development, I will be relying upon Poplack and Sankoff (1987), Poplack and Tagliamonte (1989, 1991); Bailey et al. (1989); Singler (1991), Montgomery et al. (1993). For the relations between Caribbean creoles and AAVE, I will be drawing upon Edwards and Winford (1991), For an overview of the history of work on AAVE, see Labov (1982), the Introduction to Montgomery and Bailey (1986) and G. Bailey (1993).
5 OAD includes standard broadcast or classroom English, which is commonly used as a base for comparison with AAVE. It does not include Hawaiian Creole English, since its structure is far more different from OAD than AAVE is. Nor does it include the range of dialects spoken by Hispanic Americans. In general, the varieties subsumed under OAD are used by speakers on the mainstream side of the line that sharply divides American speech communities along racial lines.

what was earlier called the Black English Vernacular, as defined by Baugh (1983): the uniform grammar used by African Americans who have minimal contact with other dialects typically in contexts where only speakers of that vernacular are present.

It is logical to group the findings that relate AAVE to OAD into three sets. One set shows a great area of similarity between AAVE and OAD; another set shows discrete and categorical absence in AAVE of certain elements of OAD; the third finds elements of AAVE that do not exist in OAD. In short, the common, the negative, and the positive.

The common area is by far the largest. The most striking features of AAVE syntax are shared by white Southern states' white dialects: negative concord, negative inversion, lack of inversion in embedded questions, double modals (Labov *et al.* 1968; Wolfram 1974; Boertien 1979; Feagin 1979; Di Paolo 1989; Martin and Wolfram, this volume). AAVE and OAD share most categorical rules, and for variable rules, differ only quantitatively, not qualitatively. In the noun phrase, there are no significant differences in the expression of person or number, and the category of possession is intact.[6] AAVE and OAD show no differences in the forms or semantics of the past tense, or the general present, and only small formal differences in the future. The past perfect can be used in the same way as in OAD, but as has become increasingly clear, it is also extended to serve as a simple preterit (Labov *et al.* 1968; Cukor-Avila 1995; Dayton 1996; Rickford and Rafal 1996).

AAVE also uses the same basic set of aspects as OAD: the progressive *be + ing* and the present perfect *have + en*. The only observable difference in the use of the progressive is some differentiation in the constraint on its use with stative verbs. In AAVE, the present perfect has an uncertain status in the positive, but is used consistently in negative sentences.

AAVE shares with OAD the basic categories of mood (indicative, imperative, subjunctive), the same modals, and voice (active, passive, middle, causative), with only slight differences in form.

The second set of findings is concentrated in morphology, and those areas of syntax that intersect with morphology. The possessive morpheme in attributive position is absent. There is no third singular /s/ in AAVE and no subject–verb agreement, except for the copula.[7]

---

6 The -s of the plural is somewhat more consistent in AAVE than in OAD, since the zero plurals of *deer*, *fish*, *sheep*, etc. are regularized. The -s of the attributive possessive is absent, but in the absolute form it is consistent and regularized to yield *mines* as well as *hers*.

7 Despite the fact that verbal -s shows up in third singular position with a higher frequency than in other positions, the absence of subject–verb concord at the most fundamental level is shown by a number of criteria. In group sessions, vernacular speakers approach 0 percent use. No studies have found phonological conditioning of the verbal -s. In more careful styles, hyper-correct -s appears in many irregular positions besides finite verb marking for other persons and numbers.

The third set of findings concerns a series of auxiliary particles found in AAVE but not in OAD: *be, done, be done, been done, been, steady, come*. The semantics and syntax of those particles show only small overlap with elements found in OAD.[8]

There are several recognized ways of bringing these three sets of observations to bear on the present-day relations of AAVE and OAD.

(a) AAVE and OAD can be seen as separate languages or dialects, and variation as code-switching between them. This is the position of Beryl Bailey cited in (1) on p. 112.

(b) AAVE and OAD can be seen as systems that are distinct but interdependent. This is the notion of co-existent systems introduced by Fries and Pike (1949), who used it to characterize a phonological subset that had entered the language with Spanish loan words. In this concept, one of the two systems may not be a complete or independent entity, capable of generating a complete range of utterances, but merely a sub-set that is used to supplement or combine with the other. This concept has been further refined by the various senses of "non-monolithic" developed in Mufwene (1992).

(c) AAVE can be seen as a mesolectal stage in the upper part of a creole continuum, in which the standard variety of OAD is the acrolect (Bickerton 1975). In such a continuum, there may be an implicational scale that will rule out {3} in (6) above, but not {2}. Thus not all combinations of rules are permitted, but there is no strict co-occurrence rule that links rule A automatically to rule B.

(d) AAVE can be viewed as a de-creolized dialect of English with the many persistent creole-like features embedded in it. Descriptions of AAVE written from this perspective (Stewart 1971; Dillard 1972) did not as a rule consider variation, but followed implicitly the line of (a) above.[9]

One might argue for a more sophisticated combination of (b), (c), and (d), combining synchronic and diachronic perspectives (Rickford, p.c.). The hypothesis to be advanced here is focused directly on (b), the recognition of co-existent systems. It is proposed that AAVE consists of two distinct components: the General English (GE) component, which is similar to the grammar of OAD, and the African-American (AA) component. These two components are not tightly integrated with each other, but follow internal patterns of strict

---

8 In the case of *done*, it will appear that Southern white dialects show the basic use with a *perfect* meaning, but the semantics are considerably elaborated in AAVE.

9 A more refined view of the creole character in AAVE is not inconsistent with the idea (b) that AAVE and OAD are distinct but interdependent systems. Creole influence in the early development of AAVE does not imply that its later history is simply one of de-creolization (Winford 1993).

co-occurrence. On the other hand, they are not completely independent structures. On the one hand, GE is a fairly complete set of syntactic, morphological, and phonological structures, which can function independently. Through the GE component, speakers of AAVE have access to much the same grammatical and lexical machinery as speakers of OAD and use it for much the same range of grammatical functions. On the other hand, the AA component allows speakers of AAVE to construct sentence types that are not available in OAD. The AA component is not a complete grammar, but a subset of grammatical and lexical forms that are used in combination with much but not all of the grammatical inventory of GE in ways that will be explored below. In the end, we will see that the distinct positive features of AAVE in this AA component are free to develop a specialized semantics that is used primarily in highly affective, socially marked interactions.[10] Thus the AA component may be seen as an addition to the GE component, in some ways complementing the OAD elements that have been subtracted from or were never present in AAVE. The GE component then serves as a set of default values for AAVE: when no AA element is supplied, the GE component is used. The AA component is concentrated largely in a set of aspectual particles and their semantic structures.

5.5 The African-American components of the tense–aspect system

I will now examine briefly the development of the AA aspectual particles, following the work of recent scholars who have described with some precision their distributions, use, and meanings within the social context of the vernacular African-American community. I will be drawing heavily on the long-term participant observation of John Baugh in Los Angeles and Elizabeth Dayton in Philadelphia. These grammatical particles cannot be studied in the same way as the closed sets of the GE component: they are marked elements whose non-occurrence is not easily quantifiable, and their use is concentrated in the kind of face-to-face interaction which requires direct observation by the participant–observer.[11]

---

10 That is not to say that all uses of the specific AAVE grammatical particles are engaged in this highly affective semantics. As Rickford has pointed out (p.c.), this would be a serious error.
11 Baugh worked for four years as a lifeguard at a swimming pool in the African-American community of Pacoima, a suburb of Los Angeles. He eventually succeeded in recording interviews of a number of key individuals in four different social situations, but also made many linguistic observations directly in the course of his work. Dayton lived for four years in a section of Philadelphia that was almost entirely African-American, and participated in family and friendship networks of people who had no other direct contacts with whites. None of her linguistic observations was recorded on tape, but they were written down on paper with the surrounding circumstances as soon as possible after they occurred.

These particles – *be, been, done, come, steady* – are all invariant forms, which are placed before the main verb of the sentence in the positions reserved for modals or aspectual markers in OAD. They are clearly grammaticalized markers and distinct from the homonymous main verbs or adverbs in several respects that are typical results of grammaticalization.[12] In these respects, they are typologically similar to the tense and aspect particles of Caribbean creoles: Jamaican *a/de, (b)en, done*; Haitian *ap, pe, te* (Lefebvre *et al.* 1982; Spears 1990). As we will see, they do not participate in any of the syntactic operations associated with INFL: auxiliary inversion, negative placement, tag questions, or cliticization on the subject. In these respects, the AA particles share properties with the Afro-Caribbean grammars of creole languages, and it was only natural for linguists following the Beryl Bailey tradition to see them as the direct continuation or the inheritance of a similar creole grammar spoken on the American mainland in the eighteenth and nineteenth centuries (Stewart 1967, 1971; Dillard 1972). However, the relation of BEV (Black English Vernacular, as it was then called) to creole grammars of the Caribbean appears in a very different light as the result of a number of the findings of recent research (Dunlap 1977; G. Bailey and N. Maynor 1987, 1989; Poplack and Sankoff 1987; Myhill 1988, 1991; Poplack and Tagliamonte 1989, 1991; Edwards 1991; Montgomery *et al.* 1993). These various sources give varying degrees of support to the main thesis of G. Bailey and N. Maynor, which can be summed up in two statements:

(a) The particular form/meaning combinations of the AAVE particles are quite different from those found in the Caribbean.
(b) The grammar used by African Americans in the South in the nineteenth century did not show these patterns, but rather a grammar much closer to that of OAD.

The general conclusion that is emerging from studies of the history of AAVE is that many important features of the modern dialect are creations of the twentieth century and not an inheritance of the nineteenth. The creole affinities of AAVE and the creole-like structural properties that we do observe are not to be accounted for by direct transmission, but by the more subtle process of substrate influence and by parallel drift or development. This view of the situation is presented as the best working hypothesis to date, certainly not one that is established beyond challenge. If we accept for the moment that AAVE has diverged in many respects from OAD in recent decades, and is continuing to diverge, we tend to draw different conclusions about the structure of the dialect.

---

12 They show the five principles of grammaticalization set out in Hopper (1991): layering, divergence, specialization, persistence, and de-categorization.

5.5.1 Non-finite be

The particle *be* is the most frequent and the most salient of the AA elements in AAVE. Its morphology is clear: it always appears as /biy/ (and occasionally with an /s/ suffix[13]). It shows three syntactic properties that distinguish it sharply from GE auxiliary elements:

(a) It does not accept negative affixation (*ben't* or *be not*). Instead, the negative particle precedes *be* and requires *do*-support (*don't be . . .*).
(b) It does not form tag questions (*. . . , be he?*).
(c) It does not participate in auxiliary inversion (*Be he doing that?*).

These three properties will be referred to as the *non-finite* syntax of *be*, a set of properties shared by all of the AA particles to be discussed below. This non-finite syntax of AA particles is the chief evidence to be advanced for the heterogeneous character of AAVE, since the central mechanisms of GE auxiliary syntax are missing, and with them much of the motivation for attributing the same structures to sentences with AA auxiliaries as to those with GE auxiliaries.

Further evidence for the non-finite character of *be* and other AA particles is found in their semantic behavior. Dayton has demonstrated that the AA particles *be, done, be done* are free of any limitation to past, present, or future time. It is well known that *be* occurs in future contexts; in early work, these were set aside as indicating possible deletion of contracted *will*:

(7) When June come, I *be* outta school and outta work. (Dayton 1996)

Similarly, contexts with past habitual behavior were set aside as indicating a possible deletion of contracted *would*, as in the second case of *be* in (8):

(8) When they used to tell us that the nipples *be* pink on pregnant women, we *be* laughin'; we were laughin' 'cause it don't *be* like that. (Dayton 1996)

However, Dayton gives many examples of such forms following noun phrases ending in consonants, where contraction is not possible, as in (9):

(9) When my son was young, the women *be* givin' him money. (Dayton 1996)

These and many other sentences all lead to the conclusion that non-finite *be* carries no tense information. Most sentences with *be* do co-occur with verbs

---

13 Though various suggestions have been made for a functional or semantic interpretation of *bes* vs. *be*, no clear evidence to support this view has emerged.

referring to present situations, since that follows from its aspectual characterization of 'habitual' behavior, but there is no bar to it appearing in any temporal context. The same argument will be repeated for all AA particles.

The non-finite syntax and semantics of AA auxiliaries might indicate continuity with or affinity with the Afro-Caribbean mesolectal grammars that share these properties. The evidence for discontinuity and divergence rests upon the particular combination of form and meaning involved. The central meaning of 'habitual' was recognized for non-finite *be* very early in studies of AAVE (Stewart 1967; Labov *et al.* 1968; Fasold 1972), and there is little disagreement about this. There has however never been any clear agreement on whether non-finite *be* is opposed to finite *be* as a privative opposition. If this were the case, "He talking about you" would mean 'at the moment' and could not mean 'habitually.' We often find a free alternation of non-finite *be* and finite *is/am/are*. For example, from the adolescent Jets in New York City:

(10) Like – . . . she *be* standin' with her hand in her pocket, and her friend is standin' there, and a man *is* messin' with her friend. (member of the Jets, 16; Labov *et al.* 1968)

When it was first realized that non-finite *be* had a habitual meaning, it was natural to connect this with the 'habitual' or 'iterative' aspect of Caribbean creoles.[14] However, comparatively few creoles have a specialized marker for habituals. Some use the same non-punctual marker to indicate both progressive and habitual, while others merge the habitual and the future (Taylor 1977; Holm 1988). Some English creoles show a specifically habitual marker *doz* in the present and *useto* in the past: in Trinidad (Winford 1992), Guyana (Rickford 1980), Barbados (Burrowes and Allsop 1983), Mosquito Coast Creole English (Holm 1988). Invariant *be* is rare in the Caribbean, but it is a common feature of Hiberno-English and other English dialects, sometimes in combination with *do* as *do be* or *does be*, but also alone. The 'habitual' meaning makes a direct link with the Irish habitual copula, or "consuetudinal *be*." Evidence on the origin of the invariant *be* form is not conclusive in either direction, and may indicate a convergence of several forms of contact. Rickford (1980) demonstrates a route by which Gullah *doz be* gave rise to a reduced *be* form, and Rickford (1986) sums up the evidence for early contact of black speakers with Irish laborers.

In any case, the historical origins of non-finite *be* are not as relevant to the main theme of this chapter, the current trajectory of AAVE, as the intricate

---

14 While most general treatments of aspect distinguish sharply between habitual and iterative, there is a tendency in Creole studies to associate iterative with habitual without further comment (e.g., Bickerton 1975: 6; Holm 1988: 157). As a result, early observations about BEV non-finite *be* tended to refer to both semantic features, though, as shown below, Dayton finds that the iterative expressions co-occur with *done*, not *be*.

semantic development of this particle in recent times. The semantic range reported by studies of the vernacular over the past twenty years is quite different from anything reported so far for Caribbean *a* or *de*. To begin with, it is now clear that the association of iterative and habitual, common in describing Caribbean creole grammars, was mistaken. Dayton has conclusively demonstrated that there is complementary distribution in this respect between *be* and *done*. Adverbs that indicate indefinite, habitual behavior like *always*, *all the time*, *every*, *sometimes*, and *steady* co-occur regularly with non-finite *be* in AAVE.

> (11) When you don't *be* talkin' about someone else all the time. (member of the Jets, 16; Labov *et al.* 1968)

On the other hand, adverbs that indicate iterated behavior like *twice* and *five times* co-occur with *done* (see below). The differences are almost categorical in Dayton's extensive data.

This specialization of the meaning of *be* is only one indication of the idiosyncratic semantic development found in AAVE. From the first observations of *be*, it was clear that there are some utterances that do not fit into the category of 'habitual.'

> (12) So you know it all *don't be* on her; it *be* half on me and half on her. (12-year-old girl, in Chicago, 1965)

While (12) might be interpreted as habitual behavior, it was not intended as such; rather, it dealt with the attribution of blame for a particular incident. Such utterances almost always indicate a durative state of affairs, usually accompanied by an intensive quality. This is particularly evident in (13), said by a woman in the University of Pennsylvania hospital to another woman in a conversation of an intensely religious character:

> (13) Her Father *be* your Father.

The steady state character of (13) is also found in (14), called out by a man leaning out of a truck in West Philadelphia to a woman on the sidewalk:

> (14) Hey baby, this *be* Heywood!

A fair number of such utterances collected over the years indicate that non-finite *be* has developed the capacity to refer to extended steady states, usually indicating a higher state of reality than normally predicated. This affective quality can be thought of as the super-real, or *surrealis*, as contrasted with the irrealis category that unites futures and modals as referring to a state of affairs that is less than real.[15] This surrealis feature is found in a number of AA elements, as will be evident in the discussion to follow. However, it should be noted that such highly affective utterances form only a part of the uses of invariant *be* that fail to show habitual or durative aspect. For this reason, Dayton argues that the semantic core of invariant *be* is stativity, opposed in this respect to *done* within the aspectual system.

Before these special semantic developments of the non-finite *be* occurred, one might suppose that there was a simple habitual, perhaps a habitual/iterative category that was the modern continuation of an Anglo-Irish or Caribbean category. This supposition is difficult to maintain, however, in the light of the evidence presented by Bailey and Maynor that the habitual feature of non-finite *be* is a development of recent times, following the great migration of southern rural blacks to urban centers (G. Bailey and N. Maynor 1985, 1987, 1989; G. Bailey 1993). Their repeated studies show that "children and teen-agers, especially those with urban connections, generally use [non-finite *be*] +V+*ing* to mark durative/habitual actions while the older adults never do" (G. Bailey 1993: 303). In the earlier pattern, reflected in the narratives of ex-slaves as well, non-finite *be* appears to have been an alternate of finite *be*, with similar syntactic and semantic distribution. The work of Rickford and his associates in East Palo Alto shows a similar recent increase in the frequency of non-finite *be* and its habitual pattern (Rickford and McNair-Knox 1994). Rickford (1992) argues that the change is primarily a quantitative one: that the sentences cited from older rural speakers show evidence of the habitual feature. However, G. Bailey (1993) demonstrates that the growth of habitual *be* + *ing* is a qualitative break: that use of invariant *be* + *ing* to mark habitual aspect is found among *all* urban speakers born after 1944 and rural speakers with strong urban ties born after 1944, while none of the speakers born before 1944 uses this feature. This demonstration that habitual *be* is a creation of the second half of the twentieth century is typical of the many findings of sociolinguistics which completely reverse previous expectations. Despite the many objections that have been raised by those who support the older conception, the evidence brought to bear in G. Bailey (1993) is overwhelming; seldom has the case for abrupt linguistic change been more decisively argued.[16]

Thus the recent history of the first of the AA particles, non-finite *be*, provides

15 This was reflected in the greeting that became quite common in the early 1980s, *What it be like?*
16 The change of the normative pattern for tautosyllabic /r/ in New York City showed a similar abrupt character; Labov (1966) shows that 100 percent of those who were below 40 in 1963 showed positive evaluation of (r), while those over 40 gave almost random responses. World War II is implicated as a punctuating event in both cases, but the timing is different. The change in New York City affected those who were under 21 in 1944, while the growth of habitual *be* is found only among those who were born in 1944. Given that the population movements created by the war were instrumental, this difference follows logically, since the new (r) norm affects superposed dialects, learned later in life, while invariant *be* is a feature of the vernacular learned in early childhood.

a sharp challenge to our understanding of the nature of modern AAVE. The farther we come from a common origin with the Caribbean creole populations, the more similarity we find to creole grammars in the tense and aspect system. But this similarity is not the precise correlation of forms and meanings that constitutes the essential evidence for historical linguistics. Rather it is a typological similarity of the sort that provides relatively weak evidence for historical reconstruction. This puzzling situation recurs in the study of other AA elements of the dialect.

5.5.2 Perfect done

AAVE has always possessed the perfect particle, *done*, which is found both in white Southern states English and in Caribbean creoles. In AAVE, *done* precedes a verb that makes reference to an action completed in the recent past. If that is a telic verb, which implies a change of state, *done* will indicate that the action is completed. Thus in (15) and (16), the verb *use* must mean 'use up' in combination with *done*:

> (15) You don't have it 'cause you *done* used it in your younger age. (isolated individual, 15, South Harlem, 1966)
> (16) It don't make no difference, 'cause they *done* used all the good ones by now. (Baugh 1983)

The second common semantic feature of the perfect – relevance to the present – is usually implicit. But in both (15) and (16) current relevance is foregrounded, since *done* is attached to a subordinate clause of causation which explicitly states that this event is a cause of the event of the main clause. In (17), this connection is implicit: *so* might be inserted before *le's run*.

> (17) We *done* got this far; le's run! (member of the Oscar Brothers, 15, South Harlem, 1966)

When *done* modifies a punctual verb like *tell*, the sense of 'completion' is neutralized; one does not 'completely tell' someone something. It is then equivalent to 'occurrence in the recent past, with effects on the present', and can be translated as 'already.' Indeed, *done* commonly co-occurs with *already*. (18) and (19) were spoken by the same person on the same occasion.

> (18) I *done* told you on that.
> (19) I *done* told you already. (member of the Jets, 13, South Harlem, 1966)

Among adults, one often finds *done* alternating with the GE present perfect *have* + *en*, showing that for some AAVE speakers this GE form can be an equivalent to the present perfect. The meaning of 'effect on the present' characteristic of the present perfect then emerges, not only for *tell* in (20) but also for *get wet* in (21), which can accept the meaning of 'completive.'

(20) But you *done* tol' em, you don't realize you d – you *have* told 'em that. (South Harlem, 39, 1967)

(21) Buff, I *done* got wet twice goin' to the store. (What?) I *have* gotten wet twice; that's how hard it's rainin'. (Dayton 1996)

When *done* is used with iterative adverbs like *twice*, the 'completed' meaning can be suspended for each individual event; in (21), the speaker need not have gotten thoroughly wet and dried out each time. The 'completeness' of the action is translated into its iterative character; it is not so much the completeness of the action as the high degree of change of state that has an effect on the action.

This use of *done* with *twice* illustrates an important development which Dayton discovered in the semantics of this particle. As mentioned above, *done* co-occurs with iterative adverbs like *twice, five times*, but *be* does not. Thus it is reasonable to oppose AAVE *done* to *be* as [+definite] to [–definite].

In AAVE, as in many languages of the world, perfect aspect develops an 'intensive' meaning. In (22), *done* shows the stereotypical use of intensive *done* where the sense of 'completion' is pushed into the background.

(22) Well, we useta get into trouble and . . . y'know . . . like . . . if Pop'd catch us, he say, "Boy – you *done* done it now." (Baugh 1983)

Done is frequently used with other verbs that do not easily accept the notion of 'completed.' The verb *win* is such a punctual act; (23) does not gracefully accept a translation with *completely*.

(23) After I *done* won all that money. (member of the T-Birds, 12, South Harlem, 1965)

In (24) , the action of *get the works* is in itself completive, and *done* is best seen as carrying an 'intensive' meaning. From the speaker of (18) and (19):

(24) After you knock the guy down, he *done* got the works, you know he gon' try to sneak you. (member of the Jets, 13, South Harlem, 1966)

We find in addition that AAVE has developed new uses of *done* which cannot be characterized as either a 'completed' meaning or 'intensive'. *Done* can precede a verb that refers to a socially defined act that cannot *be done* completely or intensively:

(25) He *done* slept with Francine and he *done* slept with Darlene . . . and he supposed to be a good friend of Henry. (Darlene's husband, from W. Philadelphia)

Sleeping with someone is an action that is defined by society as either done or not done: it can't be done partially or completely, intensively or moderately, so the meaning of *done* is not transparent in this case. A similar problem is found in (26), which also concerns a man who was cheating on his wife. In this case, *done* is used as a modifier of the socially punctual action of going to work.

(26) So he went to where she was . . . and got the nerve to lie to me . . . talking 'bout he *done* went to work. (Baugh 1983)

What is the meaning of *done* in (25) and (26)? Speakers of AAVE generally agree that *done* here resonates with the sense of moral indignation and can be translated by the phrase 'had the nerve to,' which appears explicitly in the matrix sentence in (26). This interpretation also applies directly to (25). But in (26), moral indignation is not directed to the act of going to work but to lying about going to work; we then have to assume that *done* is associated with the higher verb *talk* in the underlying form, and has been lowered to its present position before *went*.

Whenever we find such extended meanings of a grammatical particle, we must consider the possibility that they are "contextually pragmatic interpretations" (Winford, p.c.), and not meanings within the grammatical system. There is no general criterion for deciding when a particular interpretation has been grammaticalized and is now a part of the fundamental meaning of the particle. However, we must be prepared to describe, at least informally, the rules of interpretation that take us from 'completed' or 'intensive' to 'moral indignation.' I do not know of any pragmatic analysis that would carry the *done* of (25) from 'intensive' to 'morally undesirable' rather than to 'thoroughly,' 'magnificently,' or 'spectacularly.' One might say that the presence anywhere in the context of moral disapproval, no matter how generally derived, will select the 'moral indignation' sense of *done*. If such a rule operated generally on any particle meaning 'completed' or 'intensive' it would produce such an interpretation from "he told her he already went to the office" or "he told her he really went to the office." In the absence of any evidence for such a rule, we must assign 'moral indignation' as one of the selectable elements of the meaning of *done* in AAVE.

Since *done* is used in Caribbean English-based creoles as well as in AAVE, we can benefit from the opportunity to contrast the syntax and semantics of the particle in AAVE with those of a particular Caribbean community. Edwards (1991) provides a penetrating and insightful review of the semantics of *done* in Guyana, based on his own recordings in 1974 and a review of the literature.[17]

126

He recognizes the arguments of Feagin (1979) and Wolfram and Christian (1976) that AAVE *done* is related to the *done* of white Southern states English. But he maintains that the semantic similarities of the Guyanese and AAVE form lead to the conclusion that "preverbal *done* is a decreolized variant of Caribbean creole preverbal *don*" (p. 253). He provides a set of observed sentences that show Guyanese *don* translatable as 'already,' referring to a state of affairs in effect prior to the moment of speaking, and still in effect at the moment of speaking, as in (27):

(27) Bai taim mi lef de fu kom hee som a dem *don* marid.
'By the time I left there to come here some of them were already married.'

(28) Dem *don* gat di koolii-man rom.
'They already have the Indian man's rum.'

Another type can be glossed as 'be finished.'

(29) Somtaim wen you *don* wok yu go an bai a dringk.
'Sometimes when you [are] finished working you go and buy a drink.'

Edwards' overall portrait of the semantics of Guyanese *don* shows a marker of perfect aspect that embodies location in the past, completion, and current relevance. In these respects, it resembles AAVE *done*. But Edwards also points out many features of Guyanese *don* that are quite different.

- Guyanese *don* occurs with statives as well as non-statives; sentences of type (27–28) occur with statives, sentences of type (29) with non-statives. But AAVE *done* occurs only with non-stative verbs.
- Guyanese *don* also functions as a non-stative main verb with the meaning of 'finish'; though some of these sentences are equivalent to AAVE forms with deleted copula, others cannot be so translated.

(30) Yu kyan *don* baut trii, akaadin to hau yu plant.
'You can be finished around three, according to how you plant.'

When main verb *don* combines with preverbal *don*, we get the following:

(31) He *don* don.
'He is/has already finished.'

(32) Mi bin *don* don wen Jaan kom.
'I had already finished when John came.'

---

17 This is the *done* that occurs with moderate stress, not the unstressed *done* that occurs in Guyanese Creole.

Though these are formally similar to AAVE (22), the meanings are quite different. While (31) and (32) show aspectual particles, dealing with contour in time, (22) displays a modal meaning, best translated as 'really' rather than 'already.'

- Guyanese *don* receives stress, in some cases less than the main verb, in others, like (31–32), more than the main verb. AAVE *done* is always unstressed, frequently reduced to [dn] or a nasal flap.

Edwards puts into question the status of Guyanese *don* as an auxiliary, arguing that it has many properties of a main verb, and concludes that it may best be regarded as a serial verb. Below we will see reasons to question the status of AAVE *done* as an auxiliary, but for completely opposing reasons: it might well be classed as an adverb rather than an auxiliary. Edwards views these differences as changes that have taken place since the transition from the Caribbean to the mainland.

> (33) [AAVE *done*] has lost its strong stress, has become more integrated into the auxiliary system of [AAVE], and has followed the paths of cliticization and grammaticalization similar to that followed by *i*, *em* and *baimbai* in Tok Pisin.
>
> (Edwards 1991: 253)

Edwards' treatment also contains a rich set of observations of AAVE *done* from Detroit, made by himself and the Rev. Fido Giles. In these extracts we can see the semantic features that were recognized as parallel to those of Caribbean creoles, but also the new semantic features that are not reported from the Caribbean. One set shows the meaning of 'recent event affecting the present,' co-occurring with or translated by 'already':

> (34) He already *done* tried to kill me.
> (35) This dude *done* already tried to kill me.
> (36) He *done* turned the corner.

Other sentences are best translated as 'completely,' where past location is backgrounded, and the thoroughness of the action is what affects the present. This sense of completeness may be quantitative:

> (37) These children *done* ate all the candy.

or more often, qualitative, in the sense of 'the highest degree of the state'; that is, 'intensive':

> (38) You *done* made me mad.
> (39) These people *done* gone crazy.

But other sentences do not easily translate as either 'already' or 'completely' or 'intensive.' Typical of these are sentences with *tell*:

(40) This motherfucker *done* told me I gotta go.

Here the completion of the act of telling is not the relevant predication, nor its location in the recent past. The term *motherfucker* echoes the sense of 'moral indignation' which illustrates the similarity with (25) and (26).

Though every perfect has the potential for being used as an intensive, the extension to a modal of moral indignation in (25), (26), and (40) does not seem characteristic of Caribbean grammars.[18] One of Edwards' most insightful observations is the contrast between the emotional character of the AAVE examples and the lack of this in the Guyanese examples. His Guyanese sentences range over the full range of every-day life situations; a few are emotional but many are matter of fact. Edwards notes that in his own, and in Baugh's data, most of the examples were negative in force. He speculates that "preverbal *done* in [AAVE] serves the pragmatic function of signalling disapproval from the speaker's viewpoint." Myhill (1988, 1991) comes to the same conclusion on several AAVE particles: that they serve to communicate disapproval. Before we can assign this meaning to *done* without reservation, it would be necessary to find out what proportion of the interview or recorded materials expresses disapproval, sarcasm, envy, and exasperation and what proportion expresses more positive feelings. One might conclude, as with the two following particles, that this negative discourse matrix provides the raw material out of which the new grammatical meanings are forged. The semantic bleaching characteristic of grammaticalization will usually reduce such rich discourse context to more abstract features like 'intensive,' 'sequential,' or 'inevitable.'

In sum, Edwards' analysis of the Guyanese situation shows how AAVE *done* has followed a different syntactic trajectory from Guyanese *don*, and his observations in the United States have confirmed our view of the rich semantic development that has carried the dialect further away from its Caribbean relative.[19]

18 The difference between the Caribbean *don* and this AAVE use is shown in the reaction of one Guyanese woman who said that she understood (26) to mean that the man said he went to work and had returned: that is, the process of going to work had been completed. No African-American speaker has provided this interpretation.

19 Other treatments of Caribbean *done* show the same pattern of similarities and differences from the AAVE development. See Herzfeld (1983) for Limon and Panamanian Creole and Shepherd (1981) for Antiguan Creole.

5.5.3 *Sequential* be done

AAVE also shows the combination of *be* and *done* as *be done*. This can frequently be translated as equivalent to the GE future perfect, equivalent to 'will have done.' This is explicit in the alternation of *be done* with *will be done* as in the contracted form *I'll be done* . . . As an equivalent of the future perfect, it is not simply an aspect marker but a combination of tense and aspect which indicates both completion and location in the future. The future perfect is attached to the first of two successive events in the future, and asserts that the first action will occur and be completed before the second. This relationship is prototypically indicated by the phrase *by the time*.

(41) My ice cream's gonna *be done* melted by the time we get there. (25-year-old woman; Dayton 1996)

(42) So they can *be done* ate their lunch by the time they get there. (30-year-old woman at vacation summer school; Dayton 1996)

(43) I should *be done* lost 70 pounds by the time we get there. (25-year-old woman; Dayton 1996)

(44) 'Cause I'll *be done* put – stuck so many holes in him he'll wish he wouldna said it. (member of the Jets, 16; Labov *et al.* 1968)

(45) We *be done* washed all the cars by the time JoJo gets back with the cigarettes. (at a church car-wash; Baugh 1980)

The semantic interpretation of (41–45) is shown in Figure 5.1. Along the time line, the time of speaking is indicated by "0," and two events in the future by "A" and "B." When *be done* is attached to the first of the two future events, it indicates that this event will be completed before the second one occurs. Like the GE future perfect, this gives information on location in future time as well as the completed character of the first event.

The formal relationship with *will have + en* is strengthened by the fact that *be done* is followed by a past participle form. In a number of cases, the regular *-ed* form is neutralized by the following context, but whenever there is a vowel following, or an irregular past, we find the past form of the participle realized. We do not find forms like *We be done wash all the cars* . . .

A first indication that AA *be done* is not equivalent to GE *will have* comes from utterances that are not located in the future. Both (46) and (47) are not located at any particular time, and refer to a general condition, so that translations with *will have* are misleading.

(46) They *be done* spent my money before I even get a look at it. (Baugh 1983)

(47) It stink in there. You *be done* spit up before you order. (of a Chinese restaurant; Dayton 1996)

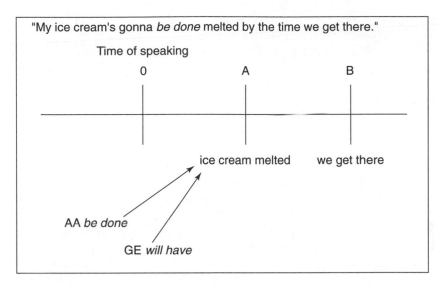

Figure 5.1 AA *be done* as a future perfect tense, attached to the first of two future events

A number of examples show that AAVE *be done* is distinct from the GE future perfect in that it does not locate events in the future; in fact, it is free of any reference to absolute location in time. In both (48) and (49), the first event is firmly located in the past, the second in the present.

(48) Here I am talkin' shit. You *be done* slapped me by now.
   ('you would have usually walked away from me by now'; Dayton 1996)
(49) I coulda *be done* ran up the steps by now. (Dayton 1996)

A radically different meaning of *be done* appears in (50), one first discovered by Baugh (1980). Here the aspect marker is attached to the second of two events, and it cannot be translated by the GE future perfect.

(50) I'll *be done* killed that motherfucker if he tries to lay a hand on my kid again. (Baugh 1980)

The interpretation of this utterance depends upon an understanding of the exact circumstances in which it was said. During the summer, a number of young men called "Cool Aids" were employed at the pool to keep order. One of them had apparently restrained one of the boys swimming at the pool in a way that his father thought was too rough. He was very angry, and came to the pool for a confrontation. (50) was his summary statement of the situation. Here *be done* is attached to the second of two events that follow the time of speaking, as shown in Figure 5.2.

131

This is a new use which developed in AAVE. The meaning that can best be assigned to it combines relative location in time with 'inevitable result,' and might then be termed a *future resultative*. It is then a member of the modal system rather than the aspect system, since it deals with the degree of reality attributed to an event. Dayton traces its development as a separate sense of *be done* in a large number of examples. Most of them, like (50), are threats or warnings. Dayton points out that although *be done* does not in itself carry the meaning of a threat, the speech act of threatening is the discourse matrix from which this meaning has arisen.

(51) He [a nephew] knows best not to talk back to me 'cause I *be done* slapped the little knock kneed thing upside the head. (19-year-old woman; Dayton 1996)

(52) Get outta my way or I'll *be done* slid you in the face! (to a dog, barking; 25-year-old woman; Dayton 1996)

(53) Don't do that 'cause you *be done* messed up your clothes! (to cousins 4, 5, 6 running up and down steps; 27-year-old woman; Dayton 1996)

Among the observations of AAVE made by Rev. Giles, reported by Edwards (1991), there are three examples of *be done*. Two are single clauses that do not provide enough context to assign them to the types of Figures 5.1 or 5.2. The third gives more context:

(54) Stop it dammit before I *be done* lay down my religion.

This sentence is plainly a threat that the speaker will abandon his usual peaceful conduct and become violent. The aspect marker *be done* is assigned to the second of two events. Though Edwards states that "this construction is used in [AAVE] as a future perfective," a translation with *will have* will not do. This example, recorded from Detroit, reinforces the observations made in Los Angeles, New York, and Philadelphia which indicate that the resultative construction is quite frequent in AAVE use, and demonstrates again the homogeneity of AAVE throughout the United States.

The typical future location of the two events may reflect the historical origins of *be done* and its connection with threats and warnings. But Dayton points out that like other AA elements, *be done* resultative does not essentially carry tense information, and it can be used to refer to inevitable consequence in past, present, or future. We find *be done* used in observations about general conditions, as in (55):

(55) I don't pay them no attention, child. If you pay them attention, you *be done* went batty. (Dayton 1996)

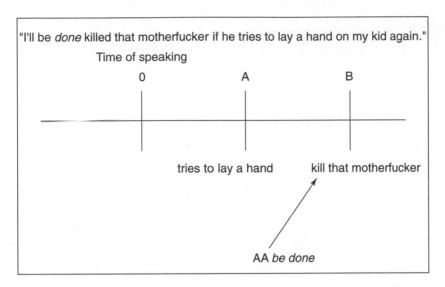

Figure 5.2 AA *be done* as a resultative aspect, attached to the second of two future events

In (56) and (57), the first event is not located in the future, but in the general present, while the second is an event that will follow in the future.

> (56) I don't want no silver dollars in my possession because I *be done* dropped them in the machines. (25-year-old woman; Dayton 1996)
> (57) If you love your enemy, they *be done* eat you alive in this society. (Dayton 1996)

If this is the case, this second *be done* should be termed simply the *resultative*. Its relation to its origin in the future perfect is signaled by the fact that the past form of the participle is still retained although the semantics do not focus on the completion or terminal state of the second event to which *be done* is attached.

The resultative *be done* is also free of any reference to a specific location in time in relation to the moment of speaking. (58) shows *be done* attached to the second of two events. Both are contrary-to-fact conditions; the first fact that is hypothetically contradicted is clearly located in the past, while the consequent holds generally for all succeeding times.

> (58) If she wasn't spaded, she'd *be done* got pregnant 'cause she gets out. (Dayton 1996)

A full account of *be done* in Dayton's data must deal with the extension of this form to cases where only a single event is involved, but the sense of 'inevitability' or 'high probability that the event did or will occur' remains. In some ways, this extension of *be done* is parallel to the extension of *be* to 'intensive steady state.' In (59), *be done* expresses the inevitability of both events; in (60) of a series of events; in (61), of a single event which has already occurred.

> (59) I'm gonna *be done* hafta went back and finished in eight years. (30-year-old woman; Dayton 1996)
> (60) The readin' of the announcements, all that's gonna *be done* done. (40-year-old woman; Dayton 1996)
> (61) A: Where's Mike?
> B: He *be done* left. (36-year-old woman; Dayton 1996)

A complete account of *be done* must also consider its compositional character. Do the individual meanings of *be* and *done* survive in the combination, and can this combination be used to derive its meaning? First, it is apparent that the 'habitual' meaning of *be* does not appear in *be done*, which normally refers to a single event, not an indefinite series of events. Mufwene (p.c., 1997) points out that the use of *be* in *be done* need not carry the semantics of 'habitual' *be*, but simply represent the non-finite form of *be* dictated by AAVE syntax, combining with *done* as a required non-finite copula. Indeed, Dayton (1996) shows many examples where the meaning of invariant *be* must be less specific than 'habitual,' with a core meaning of stativity, and Green (this volume) suggests that *be* in *be done* constructions is often habitual. The crucial question then is whether the semantics of *done* can be derived from the independent *done* that appears with adverbial syntax.

We have seen that the 'completive' feature of *done* does survive in the future perfect *be done*, but not in the resultative *be done*. The intensive meaning of *done* does appear in both uses of *be done*, and particularly in the resultative, but since we also find this feature in *be*, it may be a parallel development rather than one inherited from *done*. The feature of moral indignation, which we found to be the only semantic characteristic for some uses of *done*, is often found with *be done* in combination with other meanings, but never alone, and it may be regarded as a general characteristic of this type of discourse rather than one specific to *be done*.

I have referred here to "two uses" of *be done* rather than two different aspectual particles. They are in complementary distribution rather than contrast, since the interpretation depends on whether *be done* is attached to the first or second of two successive events. The general interpretation is that of a sequence of two events, one completed before the other begins, and we may therefore refer to *sequential be done* in AAVE.

5.5.4 Non-recent perfective **been**

In the development of the African-American component of AAVE, one can follow the trajectory of a number of particles from basic grammatical functions found in many languages of the world to a set of highly marked meanings specific to AAVE, distinct from the descriptions we now have of tense, mood, and aspect in the languages of the Caribbean, West Africa, or elsewhere. Typical of this trajectory is *been*, which began as an unstressed, past or anterior pre-verbal particle.[20] The particle being defined here is not the unstressed *been*, but instead a stressed, low-tone *been*, with three semantic components:

{1}   a condition referred to was true in the past
{2}   it has *been* true for a comparatively long time (non-recent)
{3}   it is still true.

All three semantic components are prominent in utterances such as:

(62) They *been* called the cops, and they're still not here. (Baugh 1983)
(63) She *been* told him she needed the money. (Baugh 1983)

This use of *been* always precedes a preterit form of the verb, which in itself may be considered to carry the past tense information {1}. Semantic features {2} and {3} are information conveyed by *been* itself. When the form with *-ed* is ambiguously a participle or a preterit verb, then *been* itself can be heard as equiv-alent to GE *has been* with the *'s* (contracted *has*) deleted. This is apparently the interpretation made most commonly by whites of expressions such as

(64) She *been* married.

Rickford (1973) investigated the interpretations of (64) by blacks and whites through the question "Is she still married?" The characteristic white response was "No," since *has been* without a temporal modifier of duration implies the completion of the action. The majority of blacks responded "Yes," consistent with {3} above. In this situation, *been* is said to be *camouflaged* (Spears 1982). However, the simple cases of (62) and (63), and the great majority of other instances of *been* to follow, are unambiguously AA elements. The special AA character of *been* is particularly evident where it precedes *be + ing*

(65) I *been* been knowing Russell. (Baugh 1983)

20 Unstressed *been* appears to be quite different from stressed *been*. Rickford (1973) found almost unanimous agreement on the semantic features of stressed *been*, but no agreement at all on the unstressed particle. During his research in West Philadelphia, Rickford observed over 200 examples of unstressed *been* in natural speech, as against 66 stressed *been*. Most of the unstressed particles appeared to function as English present perfects, and could be interpreted as reduced forms of the OAD *have + been* (*I been playing cards since I was four*). The present discussion therefore deals only with the aspectual marker stressed *been*, which is unique to AAVE.

In other cases, *been* may follow *have* (or its equivalent), but cannot be interpreted as a form of *have been* because it is followed by an active preterit form
with the same agent and a different patient, as in *They shoulda been realized that.*
The GE interpretation is possible *for they shoulda been told*, or *they shoulda been
instructed.*

The semantic feature of an extended period of time {2} is frequently the
foregrounded aspect of the meaning. In (66), *been* is used first by A to assert that
people have left.[21] B asks for confirmation, using the perfect adjective *already* to
convey doubt that their leaving is complete at the present time A responds with
a re-assertion of *been*, which here contrasts the 'non-recent' sense of *been* with
the 'recent' sense of *already*.

> (66) A: They *been* left.
> B: They left *already?*
> A: They *been* left. (Dayton 1996)

The term 'non-recent' is simply the negation of the idea that the event is 'new,'
or 'hot news' in the sense that it can be reported as a current observation.
Dayton points out that *been* is frequently used for cases where a very short period
of physical time is psychologically (or socially) long. Stressed *been* can be used
to assert that the speaker has quit a game or made a move in a game directly
after he or she has done so.

> (67) A: You gonna quit?
> B: I *been* quit. (member of the Jets, 16, South Harlem)

One consequence of Dayton's long-term participant-observation is that we can
observe the discourse matrix in which the current semantics of *been* have arisen.
A very common use of *been* occurs after A notices that B has a new possession.
Such observation can play the role of a pre-request for a loan, given the fact that
B has just displayed that he or she has resources available. Here the use of *been*
signals (by semantic feature {2}) that the situation observed is not new; that the
acquisition has been made some time ago. The inference that new resources are
available is negated.

> (68) A: New glasses, Ron?
> B: I *been* had 'em, man. (Dayton 1996)
> (69) A: Are those new earrings?
> B: I *been* had 'em. (Dayton 1996)

---

21 Here the action of leaving is presented as completed, but the sense {3}, that the situation is still
true, holds for the condition that results from the action. This is a common situation with change
of state verbs, both accomplishment and achievement verbs.

Again, it is important to note that the frequency of such a discourse context does not imply that it represents the *meaning* of been, but that the current meaning has developed in that context, just as the resultative *be done* arose in the context of threats and warnings. Stressed *been* is of course used in many contexts where no loan is expected or no new resources are involved.

(70) A: That's a new coat, Eddie?
     B: I *been* had that for weeks. (15-year-old boy to WL, West Philadelphia, 1978)
(71) A: This is Bill.
     B: I *been* know your name. (6-year-old to WL, West Philadelphia, 1979)
(72) A: Is Donna woke?
     B: She *been* woke. (Dayton 1996)
(73) A: Look how fat she's gettin'.
     B: I *been* fat. (Dayton 1996)

There is often a further social connotation of *been* that is similar to the use of *done* to register moral indignation. When someone has just made an observation that they think reports a recent state of affairs, which is actually not recent, the denial can carry a criticism of that person's competence as an observer of the social scene. In (74), C uses *been* to assert that this state of affairs has *been* true for such a long time that if A was a competent member of the group, he or she should have known it.

(74) A: . . . 'cause CW is our vice president [of the group].
     B: You mean y'all *finally* realize that?
     C: They shoulda *been* realized that. (Dayton 1996)

5.6 An overall view of the recent development of the AA component

The recent development of the AA component is sketched in Figure 5.3. At top are shown the GE tense and aspect elements. Below these are the elements reported for early stages of AAVE that can be considered to have been inherited from a creole-like grammar, aligned with the GE element that mostly closely corresponds to them. The first row of AAVE elements is assigned the characteristic semantics of creole systems. Anterior unstressed *been* corresponds roughly to the GE past, invariant *be* to the general present copula, perfect *done* to present perfect *have + ed* and future perfect *be done* to future perfect *will have +ed*.

Figure 5.3 shows the following developments:

• Anterior *been* has developed to the non-recent perfective stressed *been*.

137

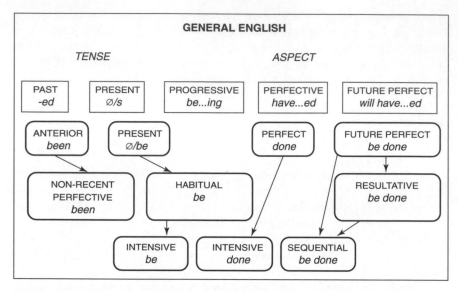

Figure 5.3 An overall view of the development of AAVE in the twentieth century

- General present invariant *be* has developed to habitual *be* and then added the sense of 'intensive steady state.'
- Perfect *done* with the meaning of 'completive' has added the sense of 'intensive' *done*, and then the modal sense of 'moral indignation.'
- Future perfect *be done* has added the 'resultative' sense, which may be combined with the future perfect as a single 'sequential' use of *be done*.

This is not intended as a complete view of the AA components of AAVE; I have not included in this picture the role of the modal *come* in the grammar (Spears 1982), nor the combined form *been done* (Dayton, in progress), nor the grammaticalized adverb *steady* (Baugh 1983). However, the trajectories shown by the four AA elements discussed here should provide a basis for the fundamental argument to be presented: that AAVE contains two parallel systems with different functional and formal properties.

5.7 Evidence for co-existent systems in AAVE

In Section 5.3 we considered the simplest possible approach to the resolution of variation: to assign each variant to an invariant rule of a separate language or dialect. This analytical device is attractive in that it reduces many different kinds of variation to a single kind: the choice of system A or system B at a given point in the utterance. But at the same time, it removes the variation from any further linguistic analysis based on system-internal relations. All variation would then be a form of *code-switching*, where the system is assumed to be intact, and analytical problems are reduced to finding the set of possible choice points for switching.

The same situation would prevail for the case of co-existent systems, unless we can constrain in some way the choice of one system or the other. What kinds of evidence would tend to support or reject the establishment of two separate systems? The argument of Fries and Pike (1949) depends upon the lack of integration of Spanish borrowings into the phonology of the original language: in other words, the symmetry and simplicity of the phonology can best be maintained by assigning the new elements to a separate, co-existent system. Four conditions that favor the recognition of co-existent systems can be identified:

I   *The segregation of variants*
    The variants of linguistic variables are not evenly distributed across texts or situations, but concentrated in long runs of the same value, so that extended stretches of speech show one value rather than the other.
II *Heterogeneity of constraints*
    Variables at the same level of linguistic structure are constrained by radically different types of linguistic factors.
III *Absence of phonological conditioning*
    A variant alternates with zero or with another variant without any evidence of phonological conditioning.
IV *Strict co-occurrence*
    Rules show strict co-occurrence, so that one never applies without the other.

Conversely, one can say that the intimate mixing of variants, parallelism of constraints, the presence of phonological conditioning, and the absence of strict co-occurrence favors the recognition of a single system. Before elucidating the application of these conditions to the recognition of co-existent systems, it will be helpful to state what is meant by the term *system*. That concept is in fact defined by Condition IV, where systematicity and co-occurrence are co-extensive. A *minimal system* is then a simple combination of two rules, which show the behavior indicated in (6) above. The recognition of a systematic relation here is equivalent to inserting a node in the set of branching rule-decisions that eliminates the separate decisions to choose rule A or rule B. For such a specification to be meaningful, A and B must be potentially independent, and not linked by a bleeding or feeding relationship (blocking or prompting the application of the next rule). The clearest cases of such small subsystems are found in place names which have two competing pronunciations drawn originally from two different languages. Thus the town of *Saint Lambert* in Quebec is usually pronounced in English as [sẽnt'lɛ̃mbərt], but local residents may also use in English the French pronunciation [sælã'bɛr]. No intermediate combinations are possible: [sẽntlã'bɛr], [sæ'lɛ̃mbərt], [sẽntlɛ̃m'bɛr] are never heard. Here seven features of pronunciation are combined in two co-occurring sets. Once the decision to use the French pronunciation is taken, no further decision points are available. The assignment of the combined variants to the choice of the French subsystem or the English subsystem is obviously an efficient form of description. Furthermore, it captures a generalization about the language that would be difficult to recognize if one did not have available the rules of French pronunciation.[22]

Condition I is the simplest and most obvious condition for the recognition of co-existent systems. If speakers are capable of segregating the values of a number of variables according to the context or topic, the simplest way to describe their behavior is to say that a given style, dialect, or language has one set of variants, and another has a different set. We can then say that in one situation, a person speaks French; in another, English. The popular approach to the use of AAVE applies this intuitively: "I can speak Black English or I can speak Standard English." However, empirical study of speakers' behavior has never justified the application of this condition; instead, we find a continuum of styles and an intimate mixing of different values of the variants (inherent variation).[23]

Condition II applies directly to the AAVE variables that we have been discussing. Finite *be, will, would, have* appear at the same level of linguistic structure as non-finite *be, been, done, be done*. They all occur as first members of the verb phrase. But the environments that govern the appearance of the AA elements have little to do with the environments that favor the appearance or non-appearance of the finite GE elements of the auxiliary. There is no evidence that the fine-grained control of finite *be* by the preceding and following environment applies to the AA elements, or that the semantics of the AA elements is reflected in the use of GE *would* or *have*.

Condition III also applies to the recognition of co-existent systems in AAVE. As noted above in the discussion of contraction and deletion of finite *be*, the presence of phonological conditioning is a critical condition for the assignment of variation to a given level of linguistic structure. It is not obvious a priori that phonological constraints could not affect the variable insertion of morphemes. But many empirical studies converge to show that phonological conditioning applies only to elements that are regularly present in underlying form, while variable insertion of a morpheme does not show such conditioning (Labov

22 Extensive variation in the pronunciation of *Volkswagen* in English fails to show the same kind of strict co-occurrence. While some combinations such as [foksvægən] may be ruled out, it is difficult to find two sets of pronunciations that must co-occur, and the best one can establish is an implicational scale. This may be the product of the fact that the rules of German pronunciation are not generally available to the English-speaking population in the way that the rules of French pronunciation are available in Quebec.

23 We can recognize a tendency to segregate the AA component according to the audience. Except for habitual *be*, the AA tense and aspect forms are rarely heard in public discourse, mass media, situation comedies, and the like. But even when the AA component is used most freely, among vernacular speakers and vernacular audiences, the AA elements are interspersed with GE elements, since they do not form a complete linguistic system in themselves.

1987).[24] As far as we know, the AA elements in AAVE show no phonological conditioning.[25]

Condition IV is the principal basis for the present proposal for the recognition of two parallel systems in AAVE, which depends upon rules of strict co-occurrence between the AA and GE components.

In the preceding section, evidence was presented that in the AA component, there is no semantic feature of tense: no reference to location in time. But it is not simply the semantic feature of tense that is absent from the AA component. Sentences with these particles do not have the syntactic behavior that is characteristic of GE auxiliaries. The four elements of non-finite syntax mentioned above can be enlarged to a list of six. AA elements are not involved in:

- auxiliary inversion
- tag question formation
- negative placement
- cliticization on the subject
- subject–verb agreement
- verb phrase deletion.

The absence of these syntactic behaviors from all clauses with AA auxiliary elements contrasts with the clauses that have finite tense markers and follow the patterns of GE syntax. One could attach each of these sets of properties to the dictionary entries for the individual AA elements. But it seems more efficient and realistic to create an AA *category* and attribute this behavior to membership in this category. The recognition of co-existent systems is equivalent to recognizing a new lexical category in the grammar with associated syntactic and phonological properties. It is not therefore different in kind from the recognition of a category of factive or stative verbs. The crucial difference is that the insertion of this category into the AAVE grammar makes it qualitatively different from the grammars of OAD, where there are no elements that behave

---

24 The phonological conditioning of variables like English (t,d), (r), (l), French (l) and (*que*), Spanish and Portuguese (s) and (n) is associated with other properties that indicate the presence of a constant underlying form. In contrast, we find no phonological conditioning for the variation of the English relative pronoun and complementizer (*which/that/ø*]), nor of (*ing*), nor of AAVE third singular -*s* or *be*. This statement applies to the variable insertion of morphemes, but not of course to the variable insertion of phonemes like English /t/ in *prince* [prints] or French /t/ in *a-t-il*.

25 Phonological conditioning frequently depends on the reduction processes of casual speech. Some of the AA elements like *be* and *been* have full or stressed vowels, and are not easily reduced even in the most rapid speech. Others like *done*, *be done*, and *come* can be reduced so far that they are difficult to detect in the stream of speech. But since they are all relatively infrequent marked elements whose absence cannot be consistently detected quantitatively, the study of phonological conditioning is difficult.

with this set of semantic and syntactic properties. We are therefore close to the kind of solution advocated by Mufwene (1992) that recognizes different grammatical options for AAVE from other dialects.

The nature of the strict co-occurrence in AAVE can be sketched in this way. If a speaker of AAVE selects an AA element as the first member of the auxiliary (*be, done, be done, been, been done, come*), then a wide range of syntactic options are excluded. On the other hand, if the first element of the auxiliary contains a finite tense marker, then those syntactic possibilities are activated.

One might think of this situation as a crimp in the productivity of syntactic rules comparable to the fact that auxiliaries like *can* and *will* do not show subject–verb agreement and that others like *must* do not show tense marking. But the division of AAVE into an AA component and a GE component is more general and sweeping than this, since the two components appear to have two distinct structural analyses. It is not the purpose of this chapter to resolve all the problems necessary to arrive at a formal description of the two structures involved.[26] At first glance, it appears that the AA component has fewer of the structures that would motivate the attachment of auxiliaries to nodes higher than the verb phrase itself, so that simpler structures are needed to generate sentences with AA auxiliaries. However, there are a number of issues that must be resolved before a well-motivated decision can be made in this area:[27]

- Though the AA elements may be independent of tense semantically, it is not clear whether they are independent from the syntactic framework that involves tense. Several of the AA elements are closely coupled with formal makers of tense: *be done* is frequently preceded by the contracted future marker [l] and is almost always followed by an element with the past participle marker, frequently indistinguishable from the preterit (see examples 20–35); *done* is always coupled with a following preterit form. AA elements do not occur in non-finite positions, in infinitives or gerunds (although habitual *be* and finite *be* are neutralized in those positions).

- *Done*, like *steady*, has many of the formal properties of an adverb rather than an auxiliary, except for its fixed position at the beginning of the verb phrase. Unlike *already*, it does not move into other adverbial positions. It is reasonable to ask how the other AA elements like *be* or *been* differ from adverbs.

- Although the syntactic behavior of the AA elements does not require their attachment to a higher node, their semantic content generally modifies the entire verb phrase, a situation that is normally projected from an IP node.

---

26 Just as the final version of this chapter was completed, my attention was drawn to a paper given by Green at the 1994 Chicago Linguistic Society meeting, which addressed this question.

27 I am grateful to Sabine Iatridou for raising some of these questions and indicating their potential significance for a syntactic analysis.

We need to know more about the semantic scope of the various AA elements in order to assign them their position in the syntactic structure.

• The fact that *be, done, been,* and *be done* do not occur in questions and tag questions may not be a reflection of their status in the syntax so much as their semantic character. These are highly emphatic, foregrounded elements that are incompatible with expressions of doubt or ignorance. In a scale of modality, they are opposed to irrealis as *surrealis*: they express a higher state of reality than normal. As far as negation is concerned, habitual *be* is the only one that normally occurs with negation, where it requires *do*-support: see (11), (12).[28]

In all of these considerations, it appears that habitual *be* is closer to normal auxiliary status than the others. It is the only one that is negated and receives *do*-support in negatives and tag questions. It accepts the *-s* verbal inflection, though there is not yet any clear agreement on whether the *bes* form is other than a stylistic variant of *be*.[29] It may well be identified with the invariant *be* that occurs in non-finite positions in GE. There is no reason to think, therefore, that the AA elements are homogeneous in their structural or semantic behavior. Like any grammatical system, the AA component shows prototypical members that possess all the defining properties, and marginal members that share only some of these properties. In this sense, *been* and *be done* are prototypical. While habitual *be* shares some properties with the GE auxiliary, and *done* and *steady* share some properties with the GE adverb, these two are the most easily recognized as distinctively different from any grammatical category in OAD.

Despite these differences, members of the AA component can be characterized together as invariant particles that occur as first members of the verb phrase, convey aspectual and modal meanings but no semantic information on tense, and do not enter into any movement or placement rules of the GE component. They together form a system that is distinct from but co-exists with the GE elements of the grammar. From this point on I will therefore refer to the AA *system* and the GE *system* of AAVE.

5.8 The GE system of AAVE

Let us now turn to the GE system of AAVE, which is not by any means to be identified with the GE component of OAD. The majority of the research reports on AAVE, dating from the 1960s, deal with the differences between the AAVE

---

28 When the negative *ain't* precedes *been*, it is always the unstressed equivalent of the OAD present perfect. If stressed *been* or *done* are negated, the effect is one of a meta-statement, indicating that the use of that AA element was inappropriate.

29 On the other hand, *steady* (Baugh 1984) is the only AA element that does not have a fixed position in the verb phrase, and in other respects it is the most adverbial, consistent with its etymological origin.

and OAD treatment of consonant codas, liquid vocalization, finite *be*, the possessive and verbal *-s* inflections, auxiliary inversion, negative concord, and the relative pronoun. The results of this work show that in almost every area, the AAVE version represents a difference in degree rather than in kind, that the rules are cut from the same template but in the AAVE version they are extended one or two steps further than in the OAD version.

The main interest for the present discussion is in those generalizations that can be extended across the GE and AA systems, differentiating the GE of AAVE from the GE of OAD, and indicating the mutual influence of one AAVE system on the other. We begin with the observation that many syntactic and morphological operations in the GE of OAD depend upon the location of the first member of the finite auxiliary, which contains an obligatory element with whatever tense information is available for that clause. For all speakers of English, the location of this element appears to be problematical when there is no overt expression of the past/present distinction, as with the invariant modals *must* and *ought*, and the reduced colloquial forms of *is supposed to, has got to*. In the colloquial forms of OAD, *must* and *ought* appear freely in declarative sentences. Thus *He must've/musta* [mʌstəv/mʌstə] *done it* is common, but auxiliary inversion and negative placement with these modals are confined to more elevated styles. *Must he do it?* and *He mustn't do it* are colloquially realized as *Does he hafta/gotta do it?* and *He doesn't hafta/gotta do it*. The non-standard forms *He don't/'posta do that* and *He don't gotta do that* reflect the difficulty in locating a tense marker when the *is* of *is supposed to* and the *has* of *has got to* are elided consistently in colloquial speech.

These irregularities in the location of the tense marker are shared by AAVE and OAD. But AAVE speakers show a far more extended set of syntactic phenomena that reflect the difficulty or the impossibility of locating a tense marker in the first member of the auxiliary.

Learners of AAVE therefore have a distinctly different problem than learners of OAD when faced with invariant elements of the English auxiliary, which show no surface realization of the tense marker. This can be seen prominently in the case of double modals. For Southern states English as spoken by whites, there are two modals, and the first element contains the tense marker (Boertien 1979; Di Paolo 1989). In AAVE, the first element appears to function as an adverb without a tense marker. This is shown in (75), where the *might* of *might could* is parallel to the *might* in the second clause. If *might* functions here as an adverb without a tense marker, we can understand why the negative requires separate *do*-support in the second clause.

(75) You *might could* go to the church and pray a little, but you – that still *might don't help* you. (member of the T-Birds, 12, South Harlem, 1965)

In (76), *useta* appears to be an adverb in the double modal *useta couldn't*. In the first sentence, *useta* is shifted to the front of a declarative sentence, like the adverbs *formerly* or *frequently* in formal styles, or *lots of times* in colloquial styles. Here it plainly does not carry the tense marker.[30]

> (76) Useta they looked just alike, but now you can't tell the difference. I *useta couldn't* figure out which one was Richie and which one was Eddie. (member of the Jets, 16, South Harlem, 1966)

The same difficulty in recognizing tense markers can be seen with single modals. Sentence (77) is produced by the GE system, where a tense marker is supplied for the past progressive. But the tense information, inaudible in *useta*, is placed on the second element of the auxiliary.

> (77) He *useta* was workin'. (member of the T-Birds, 11, South Harlem, 1965)

In OAD, the tense information in *useta* is implicitly recognized:

> (77a) He *useta* be workin'.

In (78–81), the same difficulty in locating the tense marker in the invariant form *might* is shown in *do*-support for the negative.

> (78) They *might* tell you sump'm and you *might don't* know. (12-year-old boy, Chicago, 1965)
> (79) I *might don't* understand all of it. (12-year-old boy, South Harlem, 1965)
> (80) She still *might don't* even like the thing. (12-year-old boy, South Harlem, 1965)

The same situation prevails for *must*. In place of *mustn't* we have *must didn't* and *must don't*.

> (81) *Father*: Didn't you read the note?
>   *Son*:   I read it.
>   *Father*: Well you *must didn't* read it too good! (conversation overheard waiting for elevator at 3784 10th Ave, 3 October 1967)
> (82) I mean – I ain't seen they wardrobe; but if they gon' walk around the street with holes in they pants, they *must don't* have too much in they

---

30 Though it should be noted that the presence of the *-ed* of the tense marker in *looked* is an inference rather than an observation, given neutralization before the initial affricate of *just*. There is no syntactic operation available in AAVE or OAD that would place the finite member of the auxiliary in this position in a declarative sentence.

wardrobe; right? (member of the Oscar Brothers, 17, South Harlem, 1966)

There is no doubt that the past/present opposition is as strong in AAVE as in OAD. The difficulty in (81–82) has nothing to do with the semantics of tense, but rather the location of the syntactic tense marker. That difficulty is not limited to the sentence types given in (75–82), but extends to all the sentences types given in (7–32) and (34–74); for these, it is not merely difficult but impossible to find a tense marker. Thus a generalization that extends across the GE and AA systems of AAVE might be stated as:

(83) The tense marker in AAVE is optional, not obligatory.

The term *tense marker* cannot be given a precise syntactic definition at present, given the unanswered questions concerning the formal structure of AAVE outlined above. But (83) captures the common characteristic of the two systems of AAVE, which must be represented in one way or another in the description of the grammar. A second common feature of (7–32) and (34–74) also extends to the GE system of AAVE. Given the invariant character of the AA aspect/mood particles, there is no possibility of subject–verb agreement. A large body of research on the GE system of AAVE indicates that subject–verb agreement is marginal. It is fairly consistent in the use of *am* and *is* with first singular and third singular subjects.[31] Elsewhere, there appears to be no special mark on the third singular, so that the *-s* which often appears is inserted variably as a morphological entry associated with superposed dialects.[32] A second common generalization across systems is therefore:

(84) AAVE shows no subject–verb agreement, except for present-tense finite *be*.

---

31 This is one respect in which AAVE appears to have converged with OAD, since forms like *they is* and *he am* are reported in earlier forms of AAVE.

32 The evidence for this statement includes the absence of phonological conditioning in the vernacular, the presence of irregular and unsystematic assignments of *-s*, inability to use the third singular *-s* for semantic interpretation (Torrey 1983), and the very low levels of *-s* use found as we approach closer and closer to vernacular speech. At the same time, it must be noted that all studies of verbal *-s* show a statistically significant preference for placement in third singular position as compared with other positions. This appears to be due to the fact that knowledge of the GE component in OAD penetrates all speakers of AAVE who have any degree of personal contact with speakers of OAD: the use of verbal *-s* in the third singular drops below 5 percent only with core members of the AAVE community who have no such contacts (Myhill and Harris 1986).

5.9 The current trajectory of AAVE

The most distinctive feature of modern AAVE is the rich development of semantic possibilities in the AA system, possibilities that are unavailable and unknown to speakers of OAD. This semantic efflorescence of the AA system appears to be connected with the fact that the main work of the grammar is done by the GE system of AAVE. The assignment and realization of tense is almost entirely handled by the GE system. This is also true of the main constituents of the aspect system: the progressive and the perfect. The optional AA component can then be said to be freed from the drudgery of every-day grammatical work, and can be specialized to develop the highly colored semantics of social interaction that we have reviewed. This process is the opposite of the semantic bleaching that is typical of grammaticalization: it may be thought of as grammatical colorization.

The social matrix in which this development has taken place is the asymmetric position of African Americans in American society. White speakers live in one linguistic world, continually illuminated and informed by borrowings and partial glimpses of African-American lexicon and idiom, but with almost no input from the AA system of AAVE.[33] African Americans live in two worlds. Even if they have no face-to-face contacts with speakers of OAD, they have inherited a GE system that is solidly rooted in the history of English, and indeed preserves many earlier features of English grammar and lexicon that have disappeared in OAD. Even among core members of the AAVE community who have the least contact with OAD, there is continual contact with African Americans who have been influenced by OAD grammar. Though this may not reduce the further divergence of the AA element, it reinforces those parts of the GE system of AAVE that are held in common with OAD.

One can observe here a parallel with the development of phonology in AAVE. As speakers of AAVE moved to the Northern and Midland cities, they dropped most features of Southern states phonology and merged the rest into a general Northern AA phonology, a phonological koine (a compromise variety from the dialects that come in contact with each other).[34] But some features of Southern states phonology have been retained as optional markers of style. Thus monophthongization of /ay/ in free position is a constant, unmarked feature of most Southern states dialects. But in Northern varieties of AAVE,

---

33 It is an extraordinary fact that until now, no observations have been reported of the use of the AA system in literature or the mass media, except for habitual *be* and conventional uses of *done*. The writers of situation comedies centered on African-American families have captured many aspects of phonological and grammatical style-shifting within the GE component, but there appears to be an unconscious barrier against the perception or recognition of the AA component.

34 This process of shift away from Southern towards Northern traits is well documented for the case of final unstressed *i* in *happy, silly*, etc. by Denning (1989).

monophthongization is affective, as in the contrast of a *high* [hai] *building*, and *getting high* [ha::].

Much of the discussion of the current trajectory of AAVE concerns the issue of divergence and convergence of AAVE with OAD (Labov and Harris 1986; G. Bailey and N. Maynor 1987, 1989; Fasold *et al.* 1987; Butters 1989; Denning 1989).[35] The major facts about convergence are well established, through studies of the use of finite *be*, the pronominal system, and derivational morphology (Vaughn-Cooke 1986). The evidence for divergent processes is accumulating at a considerable rate. Though our first evidence for this dealt with the re-interpretation of verbal -s within the GE system of AAVE in Philadelphia (Myhill and Harris 1986), this has not yet been reported elsewhere. The most important body of evidence on divergence concerns the AA system. The strongest real-time evidence concerns the development of habitual *be*. There is some reason to believe that *steady*, *come*, and *done* have long-standing parallels in the Caribbean: when their semantic use in Caribbean grammars is described with a detail comparable with that available for AAVE, we will be better able to judge how recent these developments are in AAVE. The most spectacular semantic developments are found in the prototypical AA aspect forms, *been* and *be done*. The inference that these are recent developments is based on the fact that they have not been reported earlier or elsewhere. Given their concentration in highly interactive social exchanges, it is not likely that we will obtain from past records a body of data comparable with that acquired by Baugh and Dayton, but research in Caribbean and West African communities may produce that kind of material and might well modify our current views.

There is much more to be said about the recent history of AAVE. The role of camouflage, as developed by Arthur Spears (1982), plays an important role in these developments. The relations between Gullah and other forms of AAVE must be examined more closely. The presentation here is designed simply to sketch the main lines of development that center on tense and aspect in the AA system and the creation of co-existent systems within the grammar. At present, we have no reason to believe that such co-existent systems existed in the nineteenth century. To the extent that this description of the past and present forms of AAVE is accurate, the realization of a separate AA system represents the most general form of divergence between AAVE and OAD.

The developments of the past twenty-five years of research on AAVE have not been unrelated to the original insights of Beryl Bailey, especially her observation of the family resemblance between AAVE and Jamaican Creole,

35 This issue has produced a large literature on the "divergence controversy," and even references to "divergence theory." I do not think that there is a major issue of theory involved here, but merely questions of fact. As our knowledge of the grammars spoken by African Americans in the nineteenth century grows, and our knowledge of the semantics of the tense and aspect systems of the Caribbean grows, we will have new facts to contribute to the recent history of AAVE.

and her insistence on a structural analysis of the relations between dialects. Though the picture I have given is incomplete, I believe that it follows the direction of her thinking in the concluding statement of her 1965 paper:

(85) I have been able to show that subsystems can be abstracted subsystems which are so ordered as to make it possible to ignore certain categories which are basic in English.

Thus Bailey clearly foresaw the two themes of this chapter: that there is a distinct AA system, and that this system acts on the grammar as a whole to modify certain generalizations of General English grammar.

Acknowledgments

This paper was originally given at a session of the American Anthropological Association in Chicago in the fall of 1991, organized by Marcyliena Morgan, on "Racism, linguistics, and language in Africa America: Papers in honor of Beryl Loftman Bailey." I am much indebted to the contributions to my thinking of my colleagues at that meeting and in exchanges since with Guy Bailey, Walter Edwards, Michael Montgomery, Salikoko Mufwene, John Rickford, Gillian Sankoff, and Don Winford. Many references in this chapter will show my special indebtedness to the contributions of John Baugh, and to my colleagues on the research project on "The influence of urban minorities on linguistic change," particularly Sherry Ash, John Myhill, and Wendell Harris. The support of the National Science Foundation for that project is gratefully acknowledged. It will be evident throughout this chapter that the major database used for the study of African-American tense and aspect is the result of the observations and analyses of Elizabeth Dayton, to whom I am most deeply indebted. Since much of her work remains unpublished, I have drawn primarily upon handouts of papers she has given at various meetings, but hope that in the near future the main body of her research will become generally available.

References

Ash, Sharon and John Myhill (1986) "Linguistic correlates of inter-ethnic contact." In Diversity and Diachrony, D. Sankoff (ed.). Amsterdam and Philadelphia: John Benjamins, pp. 33–44.

Bailey, Beryl (1965) "A new perspective in American Negro dialectology." American Speech 11: 171–77.

—— (1968) Jamaican Creole Syntax. Cambridge: Cambridge University Press.

Bailey, Guy (1993) "A perspective on African-American English." In American Dialect Research, Dennis Preston (ed.). Philadelphia: John Benjamins, pp. 287–318.

Bailey, Guy and Natalie Maynor (1985) "The present tense of BE in Southern black folk speech." American Speech 60: 195–213.

—— (1987) "Decreolization?" Language in Society 16: 449–473.

—— (1989) "The divergence controversy." *American Speech* 64: 12–39.

Bailey, Guy, Natalie Maynor, and Patricia Cukor-Avila (1989) "Variation in subject–verb concord in Early Modern English." *Language Variation and Change* 1989: 285–301.

Baugh, John (1979) "Linguistic style-shifting in Black English," unpublished dissertation, University of Pennsylvania.

—— (1980) "A re-examination of the Black English copula." In *Locating Language in Time and Space*, W. Labov (ed.). New York: Academic Press, pp. 83–106.

—— (1983) *Black Street Speech: Its History, Structure and Survival*. Austin: University of Texas Press.

—— (1984) "Steady: Progressive aspect in Black Vernacular English." *American Speech* 59: 3–12.

Bernstein, Cynthia (1988) "A variant of the 'invariant' BE." *American Speech* 63: 119–124.

Bickerton, Derek (1975) *Dynamics of a Creole System*. Cambridge: Cambridge University Press.

Boertien, Harron S. (1979) "The double modal construction in Texas." In *Texas Linguistic Forum* 13, Carlota Smith and Susan F. Schmerling (eds.), pp. 14–33.

Brewer, Jeutonne (1986) "Durative marker or hypercorrection? The case of -s in the WPA Ex-Slave Narratives." In *Language Variety in the South: Perspectives in Black and White*, M. Montgomery and G. Bailey (eds.). Tusacloosa: University of Alabama Press, pp. 131–148.

Burrowes, Audrey and Richard Allsop (1983) "Barbadian Creole: A note on its social history and structure." In *Studies in Caribbean Language*, L. Carrington (ed.). St. Augustine, Trinidad: Society for Caribbean Linguistics, pp. 38–47.

Butters, Ronald R. (1989) *The Death of Black English: Convergence and Divergence in Black and White Vernaculars*. Frankfurt: Peter Lang.

Cukor-Avila, Patricia (1995) "The evolution of AAVE in a rural Texas community: An ethnolinguistic study," unpublished dissertation, University of Michigan, Ann Arbor.

Dayton, Elizabeth (1996) "Grammatical categories of the verb in African-American vernacular English," unpublished dissertation, University of Pennsylvania.

Denning, Keith (1989) "Convergence with divergence: A sound change in Vernacular Black English." *Language Variation and Change* 1: 145–168.

Di Paolo, Marianna (1989) "Double modals as single lexical items." *American Speech* 64(3): 195–224.

Dillard, J. L. (1972) *Black English*. New York: Random House.

Dunlap, Howard G. (1977) "Some methodological problems in recent investigations of the Ø copula and invariant BE." In *Papers in Linguistic Variation*, D. Shores and C. Hines (eds.). Tuscaloosa: University of Alabama Press, pp. 151–160.

Edwards, Walter F. (1991) "A comparative description of Guyanese Creole and Black English preverbal aspect marker *don*." In *Verb Phrase Patterns in Black English and Creole*, Walter F. Edwards and Donald Winford (eds.). Detroit: Wayne State University Press, pp. 240–255.

Edwards, Walter F. and Donald Winford (eds.) (1991) *Verb Phrase Patterns in Black English and Creole*. Detroit: Wayne State University Press.

Fasold, Ralph (1972) *Tense Marking in Black English*. Arlington, VA.: Center for Applied Linguistics.

—— (1976) "One hundred years from syntax to phonology." Chicago Linguistic Society. Parasession on Diachronic Syntax.

Fasold, Ralph W., William Labov, Fay Boyd Vaughn-Cooke, Guy Bailey, Walt Wolfram, Arthur K. Spears, and John Rickford (1987) "Are black and white vernaculars diverging?" Papers from the NWAVE XIV Panel Discussion. *American Speech* 62: 3–80.

Feagin, Crawford (1979) *Variation and Change in Alabama English*. Washington DC: Georgetown University Press.

Fickett, Joan G. (1970) "Aspects of morphemics, syntax, and semology of an inner-city dialect," unpublished PhD dissertation, State University of New York at Buffalo.

Fries, Charles C. and Kenneth Pike (1949) "Co-existent phonemic systems." *Language* 25: 29–50.

Guy, Gregory (1981) "Syntactic and phonetic variation in Carioca Portuguese," unpublished dissertation, University of Pennsylvania.

Herzfeld, Anita (1983) "Limon Creole and Panamian Creole: comparison and contrast." In *Studies in Caribbean Language*, L. Carrington (ed.). St Augustine, Trinidad: Society for Caribbean Linguistics, pp. 13–22.

Holm, John (1984) "Variability of the copula in black English and its creole kin." *American Speech* 59: 291–309.

—— (1988) *Pidgins and Creoles. Volume 1: Theory and Structure*. Cambridge: Cambridge University Press.

Hopper, Paul (1991) "On some principles of grammaticalization." In *Approaches to Grammaticalization*, Elizabeth Trangott and Bernd Heine (eds.). Amsterdam: Benjamins, I: 17–35

Labov, William (1966) *The Social Stratification of English in New York City*. Washington DC: Center for Applied Linguistics.

—— (1971) "The notion of 'system' in creole languages." In *Pidginization and Creolization of Languages*, D. Hymes (ed.). Cambridge: Cambridge University Press, pp. 447–472.

—— (1975) "Review of R. Fasold, *Tense Marking in Black English*." *Language in Society* 4: 222–227.

—— (1982) "Objectivity and commitment in linguistic science: The case of the Black English trial in Ann Arbor." *Language in Society* 11: 165–201.

—— (1987) "The interpretation of zeroes." In *Phonologica 1984: Proceedings of the Fifth International Phonology Meeting*, W. U. Dressler *et al.* (eds.). Eisenstadt and London: Cambridge University Press, pp. 135–156.

Labov, William and Wendell A. Harris (1986) "De facto segregation of black and white vernaculars." In *Diversity and Diachrony*, D. Sankoff (ed.). Philadelphia: John Benjamins, pp. 45–58.

Labov, William, P. Cohen, C. Robins and J. Lewis (1968) "A study of the non-standard English of Negro and Puerto Rican speakers in New York City." Cooperative Research Report 3288. Vols. I and II. Philadelphia: US Regional Survey (Linguistics Laboratory, University of Pennsylvania).

Lefebvre, Claire, Hélène Magloire-Holly and Nanie Piou (eds.) (1982) *Syntaxe de l'Haitien*. Ann Arbor: Karoma.

Loman, Bengt (1967) *Conversations in a Negro American Dialect*. Washington. DC: Center for Applied Linguistics.

Montgomery, Michael B., and Guy Bailey (eds.) (1986) *Language Variety in the South: Perspectives in Black and White*. Tuscaloosa: University of Alabama Press.

Montgomery, Michael, Janet M. Fuller and Sharon Paparone (1993) "'The Black men has wives and Sweet harts [and third person plural -s] jest like the white men':

Evidence for verbal -s from written documents in 19th-century African-American speech." *Language Variation and Change* 5: 335–357.

Mufwene, Salikoko S. (1992) "Why grammars are not monolithic." In *The Joy of Grammar*, D. Brentari, G. Larson and L. MacLeod (eds.). Amsterdam/Philadelphia: John Benjamins, pp. 225–250.

Myhill, John (1988) "The rise of BE as an aspect marker in the Black English vernacular." *American Speech* 63: 304–325.

—— (1991) "The use of invariant Be with verbal predicates in BEV." In *Verb Phrase Patterns in Black English and Creole*, Walter F. Edwards and Donald Winford (eds.). Detroit: Wayne State University Press, pp. 101–113.

Myhill, John and Wendell A. Harris (1986) "The use of the verbal -s inflection in BEV." In *Diversity and Diachrony*, D. Sankoff (ed.). Amsterdam/Philadelphia: John Benjamins, pp. 25–31.

Poplack, Shana and David Sankoff (1987) "The Philadelphia story in the Spanish Caribbean." *American Speech* 62: 291–314.

Poplack, Shana and Sali Tagliamonte (1989) "There's no tense like the present: Verbal -s inflection in early Black English." *Language Variation and Change* 1: 47–84.

—— (1991) "African-American English in the diaspora: Evidence from old-line Nova Scotians." *Language Variation and Change* 3: 301–340.

Rickford, John (1973) "Carrying the new wave into syntax: The case of Black English *bin*." In *Analyzing Variation in Language*, R. Fasold and R. Shuy (eds.). Washington, DC: Georgetown University Press, pp. 162–183.

—— (1980) "How does DOZ disappear?" In *Issues in English Creoles: Papers from the 1975 Hawaii Conference*, Richard Day (ed.). Heidelberg: Julius Groos Verlag, pp. 77–96.

—— (1986) "Social contact and linguistic diffusion: Hiberno English and New World Black English." *Language* 62: 245–289.

—— (1992) "Grammatical variation and divergence in Vernacular Black English." In *Internal and External Factors in Syntactic Change*, M. Gerritsen and D. Stein (eds.). Berlin/New York: Mouton, pp. 175–200.

Rickford, John R. and Faye McNair-Knox (1994) "Addressee- and topic-influenced style shift: A quantitative sociolinguistic study." In *Perspectives on Register: Situating Register Variation within Sociolinguistics*, D. Biber and E. Finegan (eds.). Oxford: Oxford University Press, pp. 235–276.

Rickford, John R. and Christine Theberge Rafal (1996) "Preterite *had* + V-*ed* in the narratives of African American preadolescents." *American Speech* 71: 227–254.

Rickford, John R., Arnetha Ball, Renee Blake, Raina Jackson, and Nomi Martin (1991) "Rappin on the copula coffin: Theoretical and methodological issues in the analysis of copula variation in African-American Vernacular English." *Language Variation and Change* 3: 103–132.

Shepherd, Susan (1981) "Modals in Antiguan Creole, child language acquisition, and history," unpublished dissertation, Stanford University.

Singler, John (1991) "Copula variation in Liberian Settler English and American Black English." In *Verb Phrase Patterns in Black English and Creole*, Walter F. Edwards and Donald Winford (eds.). Detroit: Wayne State University Press, pp. 129–164.

Slave Narratives. "Slave narratives: a folk history of slavery in the United States from interviews with former slaves" (typewritten records prepared by the Federal Writers' Project, 1936–1938, assembled by the Library of Congress Project, Work Projects

Administration). Washington, DC. (Available on microfilm in the Van Pelt Library, Film no. 1448.)

Spears, Arthur (1982) "The Black English semi-auxiliary *come*." *Language* 58. 850–872.

—— (1990) "Haitian Creole tense, mood and aspect." In *Pidgin and Creole Tense–Mood–Aspect Systems*, J. Singler (ed.). Amsterdam/Philadelphia: John Benjamins, pp. 119–142.

Stewart, William A. (1967) "Sociolinguistic factors in the history of American Negro dialects 1967." *The Florida FL Reporter* 5.2 (Spring).

—— (1971) "Observations (1966) on the problems of defining Negro dialect." *The Florida FL Reporter* (Spring/Fall): 47–49.

Taylor, Douglas (1977) *Languages of the West Indies*. Baltimore: Johns Hopkins Press.

Torrey, Jane (1983) "Black children's knowledge of standard English." *American Educational Research Journal* 20: 627–643.

Vaughn-Cooke, Fay (1986) "Lexical diffusion: evidence from a decreolizing variety of Black English." In *Language Variety in the South: Perspectives in Black and White*, M. Montgomery and G. Bailey (eds.). Tuscaloosa: University of Alabama Press.

Viereck, Wolfgang (1988) "Invariant BE in an unnoticed source of American early Black English." *American Speech* 63: 291–303.

Winford, Donald (1992) "Back to the past: The BEV/creole connection revisited." *Language Variation and Change* 4: 311–357.

—— (1993) "Variability in the use of the perfect *have* in Trinidadian English: A problem of categorical and semantic mismatch." *Language Variation and Change* 5: 141–187.

Wolfram, Walt (1969) *A Sociolinguistic Description of Detroit Negro Speech*. Arlington, VA: Center for Applied Linguistics.

—— (1974) "The relationship of white Southern speech to vernacular Black English." *Language* 50: 498–527.

Wolfram, Walt and Donna Christian (1976) *Sociolinguistic Variables in Appalachian Dialects*. Washington, DC: Center for Applied Linguistics.

6

THE CREOLE ORIGINS OF AFRICAN-AMERICAN VERNACULAR ENGLISH: EVIDENCE FROM COPULA ABSENCE

John R. Rickford

6.1 Introduction

Two issues loom large in discussions of the development of African-American vernacular English (AAVE). The first is the "creole origins issue" – the question of whether AAVE's predecessors, two or three hundred years ago, included creole languages similar to Gullah (spoken on the islands off the coast of South Carolina and Georgia) or the English-based creoles of Jamaica, Trinidad, Guyana, Hawaii, or Sierra Leone. The second is the "divergence issue" – the question of whether AAVE is currently becoming more different from white vernacular dialects in the US.

The creole origins issue is the older issue. The earliest linguists to suggest the possibility that AAVE had pidgin or creole roots were Schuchardt (1914), Bloomfield (1933: 474), Wise (1933), and Pardoe (1937).[1] The case was articulated in more detail by Bailey (1965) and repeated in Hall (1966: 15). It was vigorously championed by Stewart (1967, 1968, 1969) and Dillard (1972, 1992), and it was subsequently endorsed by Baugh (1979, 1980, 1983), Holm (1976, 1984), Rickford (1974, 1977), Fasold (1976, 1981), Smitherman (1977), Edwards (1980, 1991), Labov (1982), Mufwene (1983), Singler (1989, 1991a, 1991b, to appear), Traugott (1976), and Winford (1992a, 1992b, 1997), among others. Arguing against the creole hypothesis, and asserting instead that the speech of African Americans derives primarily from the dialects spoken by

---

1 See Reinecke *et al.* (1975: 482) and Holm (1988: 32–33, 55) for discussion of the early contributions of these pioneers on the creole origins issue. And for discussion of a previously unpublished manuscript by Schuchardt which bears on this topic, see Gilbert (1985).

British and other white immigrants in earlier times (hence the label "dialectologist") were Krapp (1924, 1925), Kurath (1928), Johnson (1930), Brooks
(1935, 1985: 9–13), McDavid and McDavid (1951), McDavid (1965), Davis
(1969, 1970), D'Eloia (1973), Schneider (1982, 1983, 1989, 1993b), Poplack
and Sankoff (1987), Poplack and Tagliamonte (1989, 1991, 1994), Montgomery
(1991), Tagliamonte and Poplack (1988, 1993), Montgomery et al. (1993), and
Ewers (1996), among others. It should be added that positions are not always as
polarized as these lists of creole proponents and opponents might suggest. For
instance, while McDavid and McDavid (1951) felt that most AAVE features
came from white speech, they recognized creole influence in the case of Gullah,
and urged careful study of African and creole languages to see whether AAVE
features in other areas might be traced to these. Similarly, Winford's (1997)
paper is self-described as written from "a creolist perspective" – but it is one
which allows for considerably more influence from British and other white
dialects than creolists like Stewart and Dillard would concede. And Mufwene
(1992: 158) argues that "neither the dialectologist nor the creolist positions
accounts adequately for all the facts of AAE" and that new intermediate
positions are necessary.

The divergence issue is more recent, first advanced in a 1983 conference paper
by Labov and Harris (published as Labov and Harris 1986) on the basis of data
from Philadelphia, and supported by other researchers from the University of
Pennsylvania – Ash and Myhill (1986), Graff et al. (1986), Myhill and Harris
(1986) – with data from the same city. Data from the Brazos Valley, Texas, and
from elsewhere in the South were also introduced in support of this claim by
Bailey and Maynor (1985, 1987, 1989). The issue was debated by Ralph Fasold,
William Labov, Fay Boyd Vaughn-Cooke, Guy Bailey, Walt Wolfram, Arthur
Spears, and myself in a panel discussion at the fourteenth annual conference on
New Ways of Analyzing Variation (NWAV 14), held at Georgetown University
in 1985 (Fasold et al. 1987). Butters (1989) is a critical book-length review of
the divergence literature. Other contributions to this issue, several recognizing
convergence as well as divergence in the recent history of AAVE, include
G. Bailey (1993), Denning (1989), Butters (1987, 1988, 1991), Rickford
(1991b) and Edwards (1992).

I will concentrate now on the creole origins issue since it is the older and
better investigated one and the one which continues to inspire more controversy
and new research.

6.2 Some definitions

To understand the "creole origins issue," we need to have some idea of what
pidgins and creoles are, and for this, I will draw on Rickford and McWhorter
(1997: 238):

Pidgins and creoles are new varieties of language generated in situations of language contact. A *pidgin* is sharply restricted in social role, used for limited communication between speakers or two or more languages who have repeated or extended contacts with each other, for instance through trade, enslavement, or migration. A pidgin usually combines elements of the native languages of its users and is typically simpler than those native languages insofar as it has fewer words, less morphology, and a more restricted range of phonological and syntactic options (Rickford 1992a: 224). A *creole*, in the classical sense of Hall (1966), is a pidgin that has acquired native speakers, usually, the descendants of pidgin speakers who grow up using the pidgin as their first language. In keeping with their extended social role, creoles typically have a larger vocabulary and more complicated grammatical resources than pidgins. However, some extended pidgins which serve as the primary language of their speakers (e.g. Tok Pisin in New Guinea, Sango in the Central African Republic) are already quite complex, and seem relatively unaffected by the acquisition of native speakers.

Although it was assumed for a long time that creoles evolved from pidgins, Thomason and Kaufman (1988: 147–166) and others have argued that many creoles, particularly those in the Caribbean and in the Indian Ocean, represent "abrupt creolization," having come into use as primary or native contact languages before a fully crystallized pidgin had had time to establish itself.

We also need to take into account *creole continuum* situations, like those in Guyana, Jamaica, and Hawaii, where, in between the deepest creole (the basilect) and the most standard variety of English (the acrolect), there exists a spectrum of intermediate varieties (the mesolects). In the pioneering work of DeCamp (1971) and many of his successors, it was assumed that such continua developed from earlier bilingual creole/standard situations through a process of *decreolization* in which the creole variety was gradually leveled in the direction of the standard. However, Alleyne (1971) suggested that in Jamaica, a continuum-like situation may have existed from the very beginnings of black/white contact, depending on the degree and nature of the contacts which house slaves, field slaves, and other segments of the slave community (e.g. old hands vs. the newly arrived) had with metropolitan English speakers. Subsequently, Baker (1982, 1991: 277), Bickerton (1986) and Mufwene (1996a) suggested that, given the lower proportions of blacks to whites in the founding phase of most colonies, creole continua may actually have formed "backwards," with the first generations of Africans acquiring something closer to metropolitan English, and later generations acquiring successively "restructured" or creolized varieties as they had less access to white norms and learned increasingly from each other.

The reason this issue is relevant to us is that early creolists like Dillard and Stewart tended to assume that the earliest variety of AAVE was a relatively uniform and basilectal creole which subsequently decreolized into mesolectal forms increasingly closer to English. However, more recent discussions of the creole issue, for instance by Rickford (1997) and Winford (1997), provide more explicitly for variation across a continuum of varieties from very early on, although I (for one) contend that creole varieties were a significant part of the mix of the early contact situation, particularly in the South, and that a gradual process of quantitative decreolization must have been taking place in the USA over time, with fewer speakers using creole varieties, and more speakers using varieties closer to Standard English.

6.3 Relevant questions and evidence in relation to AAVE

From the point of view of the creolist/dialectologist debate, the fundamental question is whether a significant number of the Africans who came to the United States between the seventeenth and nineteenth centuries went through processes of pidginization, creolization, and (maybe) decreolization in acquiring English (the creolists' position), or whether they learned the English of British and other immigrants fairly rapidly and directly, without an intervening pidgin or creole stage (the dialectologists' position).

Although linguists who address the creole issue typically concentrate on one kind of evidence, or at most two, there are at least *seven* different kinds of evidence which could be brought to bear on the primary question of whether AAVE was once a creole, each of them involving secondary questions of their own.

6.3.1 Sociohistorical conditions

One could ask, first of all, whether the sociohistorical conditions under which Africans came to and settled in the United States might have facilitated the importation or development of pidgins or creoles. With respect to importation, Stewart (1967), Dillard (1972), and Hancock (1986) favor the hypothesis that many slaves arrived in the American colonies and the Caribbean already speaking some variety of West African Pidgin English (WAPE) or Guinea Coast Creole English (GCCE). Rickford (1987a: 46–55) and Schneider (1989: 30–33), among others, feel that such slaves were probably not very numerous. However, the case for significant creole importation from the Caribbean in the founding period has been bolstered by recent evidence that "*slaves brought in from Caribbean colonies where creole English is spoken were the predominant segments of the early Black population in so many American colonies*, including Massachussetts, New York, South Carolina, Georgia, Virginia and Maryland in particular" (Rickford 1997: 331).

With respect to conditions for the creation or development of contact varieties on American soil, low proportions of target language (English) speakers relative to those learning it as a second language favor pidginization and creolization. The frequency of small US slave holdings and the relatively high proportion of whites to blacks in the US – in contrast with Jamaica and other

British colonies in the Caribbean (Parish 1979: 9; Rickford 1986: 254) – are thought by some to make it less likely that these processes took place in the US, particularly in the founding period (Schneider 1989: 35; Mufwene 1996: 96–99; Winford 1997). However, as Schneider (ibid.) points out, "just because a majority of plantations was small does not necessarily imply that a majority of the slaves lived on small plantations"; he cites Parish's (1979: 13) observation that "the large-scale ownership of a small minority meant that more than half the slaves [in the mid-nineteenth-century US] lived on plantations with more than twenty slaves."

Moreover, there were striking differences from one region to another. A creole is much more likely to have developed in South Carolina, where "blacks constituted over 60% of the total population within fifty years of initial settlement by the British" (Rickford 1986: 255) than in New York, where blacks constituted "only 16% of the population as late as the 1750s, one hundred years after British settlement" (ibid). When one considers that from 1750 to 1900, 85–90 percent of the black population lived in the South, and that African Americans in other parts of the country are primarily the descendants of people who emigrated from the South in waves beginning with World War I (G. Bailey and N. Maynor 1987: 466), it is clearly the demographics of the *South* rather than the *North* or *Middle* colonies which are relevant in assessing the chances of prior creolization (Rickford 1997).

To variation by region must be added considerations of variation by time period. For instance, both Mufwene (1996a) and Winford (1997) are more sanguine about the possibilities of creole-like restructuring in Southern colonies in the eighteenth and early nineteenth centuries than in the seventeenth century, as the proportions of blacks to whites increased. Finally, as Rickford (1977: 193) has noted, "Questions of motivation and attitude must also be added to data on numbers and apparent opporunities for black/white contact." We have striking contemporary examples of white individuals in overwhelmingly black communities (Rickford 1985) and black individuals in overwhelmingly white communities (Wolfram *et al.* 1997) who have not assimilated to the majority pattern because of powerful cultural and social constraints. This is likely to have been equally if not even more the case two or three hundred years ago, when the constraints against assimilation were more powerful. Constraints like these might have been sufficient to provide the "distance from a norm" which Hymes (1971: 66–67) associates with the emergence of pidgin/creole varieties.

Although sociolinguists have recently begun to do substantive research on the sociohistorical conditions under which Africans came to and settled in the American colonies, and the possibility that they imported or developed pidgin/creole speech in the process, there is still need for more research at the levels of individual colonies or states, counties and districts, and plantations or households.

6.3.2 *Textual attestations of* AAVE *from earlier times*

The second kind of evidence one might consider is textual attestations of AAVE from earlier times, or "historical attestations" for short. The known evidence of this type can be divided into two broad categories: (a) literary texts, including examples from fiction, drama, and poetry as well as those from travellers' accounts, records of court trials, and other non-fictional works (Brasch 1981); and (b) interviews with former slaves and other African Americans – many born in the mid-nineteenth century – from the 1930s onward, including the two subcategories distinguished by Schneider (1993b: 2): "the so-called ex-slave narratives" published by Rawick (1972–79), and the tape recordings made for the Archive of Folk Songs (AFS), published and analyzed by Bailey *et al.* (1991). A third source of early-twentieth-century data can be found in the interviews with 1,605 African Americans concerning "hoodoo" which were recorded by Harry Hyatt between 1936 and 1942 on Ediphone and Telediphone cylinders and subsequently published (Hyatt 1970–78) and analyzed (Viereck 1988, Ewers 1996).

In general, the literary texts – the primary data sources for Stewart (1967) and Dillard (1972) – take us back much further in time, to the early eighteenth century, at least; but they tend to be relatively brief and open to serious questions of authenticity (Viereck 1988: 301, fn 1; Schneider 1993b: 1–2). Of the early-twentieth-century interviews, the AFS materials – the data source for the analyses by various researchers in Bailey *at al.* (1991) – are generally considered the most reliable, but the audible recordings consist of only a few hours of speech from a dozen former slaves, and like the other nineteenth-century materials, these represent a relatively late or recent period in African-American history (cf. Rickford 1991a: 192; Wald 1995). Moreover, as Bailey *et al.* note, in their introduction (pp. 18–19), "the recordings and transcripts often lend themselves to a variety of interpretations" and their representativeness is limited both in terms of speaker type and time period (cf. also Rickford 1991a). The reliability of the ex-slave narrative materials – the primary data sources for the studies by Brewer (1974) and Schneider (1989), among others – has recently been questioned by Maynor (1988), Wolfram (1990), and Montgomery (1991) on the grounds that errors were introduced by field-workers who set down the texts by hand and by editors who subsequently over-represented certain stereo-typical dialect features. However, Schneider (1993b) has made a spirited defense of these materials, arguing that their errors and distortions are detectable from comparisons with the AFS materials and by other means. The reliability of the Hyatt recordings – especially the early Ediphone recordings which required the interviewer to "repeat into a speaking-tube every word or phrase spoken by the informant" (Hyatt 1970–78: 1, xx) – is open to question. But the later Telediphone recordings (made with a microphone) and tape recordings are better, and Ewers (1996: 27) assumes that despite drawbacks, "the Hoodoo material is in principle a sufficiently reliable basis for carrying out morphological and syntactic studies."[2]

6.3.3 Modern-day recordings from the African-American diaspora

The third source of evidence is modern-day recordings from the African-American diaspora or "diaspora recordings" for short. These consist of audio recordings with descendants of African Americans who left the United States for other countries in the late eighteenth or early nineteenth century, and who, because of their relative isolation in their new countries, are thought to represent an approximation to the African-American speech of their emigrating foreparents. The first diaspora data to be examined in relation to the creole issue came from the Samaná region in the Dominican Republic, where the descendants of African Americans who emigrated there in the 1820s constitute an English-speaking enclave in a Spanish-speaking nation (Poplack and Sankoff 1987; Poplack and Tagliamonte 1989; Tagliamonte and Poplack 1988; DeBose 1988, 1994). The second source of diaspora data was Liberian Settler English, the variety spoken by the descendants of African Americans who were transported to Liberia by the American Colonization Society between 1822 and 1910 (Singler 1991a: 249–250). The third and most recent source of diaspora data is African Nova Scotian English, the English spoken by the descendants of African Americans who migrated to Nova Scotia, Canada, in the late eighteenth and early nineteenth centuries (Poplack and Tagliamonte 1991). Attractive though these diaspora varieties are as sources of extensive tape-recorded data on which quantitative analysis of selected variables can be performed, the significant question which they leave unanswered is whether they can indeed be taken as reflecting late-eighteenth or early-nineteenth century English, unaffected or only minimally affected by internally or externally motivated change (e.g. from contact with neighboring varieties of English or Spanish), and also unaffected by the Observer's Paradox.[3]

6.3.4 Similarities between AAVE and established creoles

The fourth type of evidence is similarities between AAVE and established creoles, or "creole similarities" for short. The theoretical justification for

---

2 While Ewers' study is substantive and very valuable, her assumption that morphological and syntactic textual analysis is not as seriously affected by poor recording quality as phonetic and phonological analysis represents a common error (cf. Schneider 1989: 49, whom she quotes). Labov's (1972b: 190, fn 9) view is the exact opposite, and corresponds more closely to my own experience: "In phonology, we can wait for the clear, stressed forms to emerge from the background noise. But many grammatical particles are reduced to minimal consonants or even features of tenseness or voicing which are difficult to hear in less than the best conditions, and many are so rare that we cannot afford to let one escape us."

3 The Observer's Paradox (Labov 1972b: 209): "the aim of linguistic research in the community must be to find out how people talk when they are not being systematically observed; yet we can only obtain these data by systematic observation."

considering this type of evidence, which has been widely applied to other cases, is provided in Rickford (1977: 198): "If a certain set of clear cases are agreed upon by everyone to constitute pidgins and creoles in terms of the standard theoretical parameters, and these cases display certain characteristic linguistic features, then other cases that also display these characteristics can be assumed to belong to the same type or class, unless evidence to the contrary is shown." The primary creole varieties with which AAVE has been compared are the English-based varieties spoken in Barbados (Rickford and Blake 1990; Rickford 1992b), Guyana (Bickerton 1975; Rickford 1974; Edwards 1991), Jamaica (B. Bailey 1965; Baugh 1980; Holm 1984; Rickford 1991c), Trinidad (Winford 1992a, 1992b), and the South Carolina Sea Islands ("Gullah" – Stewart 1967; Dillard 1972; Rickford 1980; Mufwene 1983) and Liberian Settler English (LSE, Singler 1991a, 1993). The importance of attending to intermediate or meso-lectal creole varieties rather than basilectal ones has been stressed by several researchers (Rickford 1974; Bickerton 1975; Winford 1992a), and quantitative analysis of selected features has, for the last two decades at least, become the standard comparative method. Mufwene (p.c.) has suggested that connections between AAVE and Caribbean mesolectal varieties might be informative typologically, but not historically, since "there has been no historical connection established between those varieties and AAVE." But recent sociohistorical evidence indicating the importance of Caribbean slaves in the early settlement of many American colonies (Rickford 1997) helps to provide precisely this connection.

6.3.5 Similarities between AAVE and West African languages

The fifth type of evidence is similarities between AAVE and West African languages or "African language similarities" for short. Although the existence of lexical Africanisms might be considered of little significance, no matter how extensive, the demonstration that contemporary AAVE parallels West African languages in key aspects of its grammar might be taken as evidence of the kind of admixture or substrate influence which is fundamental to pidginization and creolization (Rickford 1977: 196). Alleyne (1980), Holm (1984), and DeBose and Faraclas (1993) have provided such evidence for copula absence in AAVE, a variable to which we return in more detail below.

6.3.6 Differences from other English dialects

The sixth type of evidence is differences from other English dialects, especially those spoken by whites, which we might refer to as "English dialect differences" for short. As Rickford (1977: 197) notes, "The question of prior creolization [of AAVE] has been frequently defined in terms of how different it now is from other English dialects and how different we can presume it to have been in the past." The theoretical assumption for this is that dialects involve linguistic continuity with earlier stages or other varieties of the language, while pidgins and creoles involve "a sharp break in transmission and the creation of a new code" (Southworth 1971: 255). The principal dialects with which AAVE has been compared with respect to this criterion is white vernacular dialects in the US (Davis 1969; Labov 1972a; Wolfram 1974; G. Bailey and N. Maynor 1985), although British varieties thought to have influenced AAVE through contact in the US (Schneider 1983) have also received some attention. As we will see below, this type of evidence has been more fundamental in discussions of the divergence issue than in discussions of the creole issue, with Fasold (1981) and others warning that contemporary difference might mask earlier similarities, or vice versa. Nevertheless it is still of relevance to the creole issue.

6.3.7 Comparisons across different age groups of African-American speakers

The seventh and final type of evidence is that which is potentially available from comparisons across different age groups of African-American speakers, or "age-group comparisons" for short. Such evidence could provide fundamental indications of decreolizing change in apparent time (Labov 1972), but it has virtually never been invoked in relation to the creole issue. Indeed, Stewart (1970) and Dillard (1972), the principal proponents of the creole hypothesis, have argued that because of age-graded avoidance of creole forms by adults, African-American children in fact use the significant creole forms more often, the exact opposite of what a theory of prior creolization and ongoing decreolization would predict. Age-group data have, however, been considered more often in relation to the divergence hypothesis.

Table 6.1 provides a summary of the different kinds of evidence which bear on the creole hypothesis. In order to review this hypothesis further, I will now go on to survey one linguistic feature using all but the first and the last kinds of evidence (the ones which are least frequently used). Several different features have been examined in relation to the creole issue – including third person present tense and plural s-marking, perfect and past tense marking, habitual be, and completive done – but the one that has been considered most often, using

Table 6.1 Possible types of evidence bearing on the issue of creole origins of AAVE

1 Sociohistorical conditions (suitable for pidginization and/or creolization)
2 Historical attestations (literary texts, ex-slave narratives and recordings)
3 Diaspora recordings (Samaná, Liberian Settler English, African Nova Scotian English)
4 Creole similarities (between AAVE and Caribbean creoles, Gullah, Hawaiian, etc.)
5 African language similarities (between AAVE and West African varieties)
6 English dialect differences (between AAVE and British/white American dialects)
7 Age-group comparisons (across different generations of AAVE speakers)

the widest variety of evidence, is the absence of present tense forms of the copula *be* (e.g., "He Ø tall," "They Ø going") and I will accordingly survey the data on this feature.

6.4 Copula absence in AAVE with respect to different types of evidence

6.4.1 Historical attestations (literary texts, ex-slave narratives and recordings)

Let us begin first with the evidence of *historical attestations*. Although Stewart and Dillard depend more heavily on *literary texts* than anyone else, their texts include only a few examples of copula absence (e.g. Stewart 1967 cites "Me massa Ø name Cunney Tomsee"[4] from the speech of Cudjo in John Leacock's 1776 play, *The Fall of British Tyranny*), and they provide no extended analysis of this variable. For the latter, we need to turn to Repka and Evans (1986), who examined potential copula tokens in the speech of black characters in ten American literary works (six dramas, three novels, and one short story) written by white authors between 1767 and 1843.[5] Their results, shown separately for the eighteenth and nineteenth centuries, and presented in terms of the person/ number of the subject, are shown in Table 6.2. Note that in the eighteenth century, zero was the most common variant of the copula. Moreover, if the nine invariant *be2* forms in the eighteenth-century data are excluded (as they are by most researchers on the grounds that *be2* is typically habitual while zero and the conjugated forms are not), the rate of copula absence in the first person, third singular, and plural and second person categories rises to 100%, 100%, and 77% respectively. Categorical copula absence of this kind is virtually unheard of in modern US samples, so on the face of it, these data support the creolist position, particularly since first person copula absence does not occur in modern AAVE although it does in Barbadian, Jamaican, Trinidadian, and other Caribbean creoles (see Rickford and Blake 1990).

Repka and Evans' nineteenth-century data show considerably lower rates of copula absence, which they attribute to "convergence . . . with the speech of a dominant white society" (p. 10). This inference may be correct, but the fact that copula forms with plural and second person subjects show no copula absence whatsoever is troubling, since such forms typically show higher rates of copula

---

4 This is not a great example, because as Beryl Bailey (1966) has noted, *niem* ("name") is a special naming verb in Jamaican (and other creoles) which requires no predicating copula.
5 The sources include John Leacock (1776) *The Fall of British tyranny*, John Murdock (1795) *The Triumphs of Love*, James Fenimore Cooper (1821) *The Spy*, and Edgar Allan Poe (1843) "The gold bug." These are admittedly late in the evolution of African-American dialects, but they still take us further back than the ex-slave narrative recordings and Hoodoo texts, as well as diaspora data from Samaná.

Table 6.2 Black characters' copula absence in eighteenth- and nineteenth-century American literary sources

	1st singular	*3rd singular*	*Plural & 2nd singular*
18th-century sources	78% (7/9)	89% (24/27)	54% (7/13)
19th-century sources	60% (6/10)	33% (25/75)	0% (0/6)

Source: adapted from Tables 1 and 3 in Repka and Evans (1986).

absence than other subjects in early-twentieth-century and modern AAVE,[6] as well as in contemporary Trinidadian English (Winford 1992a: 34).[7] This anomalous result may be an artifact of limited data (Repka and Evans found only six copula tokens with plural and second person subjects, or four if their two tokens of *be2* are excluded). Alternatively, it may reflect a genuine change in the linguistic conditioning of copula absence over time, or it may simply confirm people's fears that literary data of this type are conventionalizations rather than trustworty reflections of contemporary speech. This issue is one that could bear further examination, with an even more substantial data set of literary texts than Repka and Evans examined, and taking into account the social statuses of the characters depicted in each.[8]

Brewer (1974) presents some interesting evidence on copula absence in the ex-slave narratives, including the observation (pp. 96–98) that such narratives include several attestations of copula absence in the past tense, as in (1) and (2):

6 The early-twentieth-century evidence is in Repka and Evans (1986). In their analysis of four works written by African-American authors (Chestnutt, Toomer, Hughes, and Hurston) between 1899 and 1937, copula absence is 20% (61/310) with plural and second person subjects, 3% with first singular subjects, and 3% (20/720) with third singular subjects. For evidence on modern AAVE, see Rickford *et al.* (1991: 117), who report a .67 variable rule feature weight for copula absence with second person and plural subjects in the East Palo Alto data (as computed by the "Labov deletion" formula in which deletions are computed as a proportion of deleted and contracted forms, with full forms excluded from consideration), but a much lower feature weight (.33) for third person singular subjects.

7 The evidence of Barbadian and Jamaican is somewhat more ambiguous. Rickford and Blake (1990: 267, Table 2) found that plural and second person subjects did favor copula absence in Barbadian speech more than first singular or third singular subjects did (variable rule feature weights of .58, .47, and .45 respectively), but the difference was not statistically significant. Rickford (1991c) found that plural and second person subjects were slightly *less* favorable to copula absence in Jamaican Creole than third singular subjects, and slightly *more* favorable than first singular subjects (variable rule feature weights of .50, .54, and .46 respectively), but the differences were, again, not statistically significant.

8 Since AAVE is primarily a lower- and working-class phenomenon, fictional characters from other socioeconomic strata should not be expected to show the same frequencies of copula absence, although we might perhaps expect them to show the same kinds of conditioning if they show sufficient copula absence for conditioning to be evident.

(1) De only child I ever had died when he Ø just a baby. (Tex 72: 255)
(2) A'ter freedom Ø declare, I go to school. (SC 51: 223)

Past tense copula absence does occur in Caribbean creoles (Rickford 1991c, 1996: 369) but rarely or not at all in present-day AAVE (Wolfram 1969: 166), so on the face of it, Brewer's evidence is another potential plus for the creolist hypothesis. However, Schneider (1997) has suggested that the zero copula is among the non-standard features whose frequency was exaggerated (by field-workers and/or editors) in these narratives, and this again makes the validity of the evidence open to question.

In order to get better historical evidence on copula absence in AAVE, let us turn now to Bailey (1987: 35), who analyzes copula absence in the AFS recordings of the ex-slaves born in the mid to late nineteenth century. The first row of Table 6.3 shows the relative frequency of zero copula which Bailey found in that data set for third person singular, plural and second person subjects combined (a total of 275 tokens, including 4 tokens of be2) according to following grammatical environment. The hierarchical ordering of these environments certainly corresponds to the dominant pattern in modern-day samples of AAVE (see W. Labov 1972a: 86; Rickford et al. 1991: 121), and the fact that __gonna shows categorical copula absence is striking (because this is not the case in any of the ten modern US samples summarized in Rickford et al., ibid.). But we also need data on the number of tokens for each subcategory and the over-all percentage of copula absence, and the article does not provide either.

Poplack and Tagliamonte (1991: 319) do provide an overall percentage of copula absence for an overlapping AFS data set, designated in their paper as "Ex-Slave Recordings." (Their "Ex-Slave Recordings" came from the AFS data set, but they included Quarterman's recording, which Guy Bailey omitted, and they did not have access to the data of an additional informant – identified as "Colored Fellow" which Bailey included.) The fact that their overall percentage of copula absence is so low (16%) would certainly argue against the creole hypothesis. But unless the numbers of tokens in Bailey's subcategories with low percentages (__NP and __Loc) overwhelmingly outnumber the numbers of tokens in the subcategories with high percentages (__V+ing and __gonna), it is difficult to see how Poplack and Tagliamonte arrive at such a low overall rate.

Table 6.3 Copula absence in the AFS ex-slave recordings by following grammatical environment

	__NP	__Locative	__Adjective	__Verb+ing	__gonna
G. Bailey (1987)	12%	15%	29%	71%	100%
Poplack and Tagliamonte (1991)	.39	.69	.27	.72	.78

Source: adapted from G. Bailey (1987: 35) and Poplack and Tagliamonte (1991: 321).

Further signs that the Bailey and the Poplack and Tagliamonte analyses do not agree are the different hierarchies of following grammatical constraints which they report for this variable, depicted in Table 6.3. While they agree in showing the auxiliary environments as most favorable to copula absence (with __gonna in the lead), they disagree on the relative ordering of __NP, __Adj, and __Loc, with (among other things) Bailey reporting __NP as least favorable and Poplack and Tagliamonte reporting __Adj as least favorable. The incommensurability of these analyses of what is a substantially overlapping data set may be due to the fact that Poplack and Tagliamonte's analysis is based on a sample of 209 tokens, while Bailey's is based on 275 tokens; with the overall token count so low, a difference of sixty-six tokens can crucially affect the analysis. Bailey's sample includes six tokens of invariant be2, while Poplack and Tagliamonte's does not; but these are too few to account for the differences in their analysis. More significant, perhaps, is the fact that Poplack and Tagliamonte's figures represent variable rule feature weights or probabilities, while Bailey's represent percentages.

Moreover, Poplack and Tagliamonte compute copula absence as "Labov deletion" (Rickford *et al.* 1991: 106–107) – counting tokens of zero as a proportion of tokens of zero and contraction only, while Bailey computes copula absence as "Straight deletion," counting tokens of zero out of tokens of zero, contraction, and full forms combined.[9] Some variationists regard "Straight deletion" as more valid because it remains closer to observed data and filters it through fewer assumptions and operations. Perhaps we will need more general agreement on how to reconcile or arbitrate between these two methods before we can reliably interpret the different views of the ex-slave recordings which these two studies provide.

6.4.2 *Diaspora recordings (Samaná, African Nova Scotian English, Liberian Settler English)*

For evidence from diaspora recordings we will consider first the data on copula absence in Samaná English. Without making any connection whatsoever to the creolist hypothesis, Poplack and Sankoff (1987: 302) report that, in contrast with urban AAVE where first person *am* is absent less than 1% of the time, such absence occurs 10% of the time in Samaná English. This is in fact a plus for the creolists' side of the issue, because, as noted above, copula absence with first person subjects is characteristic of the Caribbean creoles (see footnote 7 above for relevant data) and in American literary texts from earlier periods (see Table

---

9 In Rickford *et al.*'s (1991: 117) study of copula absence in East Palo Alto, California, the relative positions of __Loc and __Adj in the feature weight hierarchy were reversed when the same data were analyzed as Labov deletion (__Loc: .42; __Adj: .47) and Straight deletion (__Adj: .45; __Loc: .47).

6.2 above). But what Poplack and Sankoff emphasize instead is their very different (and often-cited) conclusion that "at least insofar as its copula usage is concerned it [Samaná] bore no more resemblance to English-based West Indian creoles than modern ABE [AAVE], and indeed less." This conclusion rests, however, on two types of evidence, both of which are are subject to reinterpretation.

The first is the low overall *rate* of copula absence which Poplack and Sankoff (1987: 304, Table 3) report for Samaná English – 20% with pronoun subjects, which is slightly more than the comparable figures of 16% for Harlem adults in formal speech, 10% for Middle Class Detroit adults, and 18% for Lower Class Texas adults, which they list in the same table, but less than the figures of 51% for Working Class Detroit adults and 27% for Harlem adults in group style, which they also report. (The Detroit, Harlem, and Texas data are from Labov 1972a, Wolfram 1969, and G. Bailey and N. Maynor 1985 respectively.) However, the 20% figure for Samaná is heavily influenced by data from the first person subject category (80 tokens) and by the cases of *it*, *what*, and *that* as subjects (162 tokens). In the AAVE data with which Samaná is compared, these categories are excluded on the grounds that contraction is virtually categorical therein. If, for the sake of comparability (and because contraction in these categories in Samaná is around 80%), these categories are excluded from the Samaná data, the rate of copula deletion with pronoun subjects in Samaná doubles to 40% (71/176).[10] And since it is known that overall rates of copula absence can vary significantly by style – Poplack and Sankoff themselves (1987: 304) report an 11% difference between Labov's Harlem adults in "formal" and "informal" style; Winford (1980: 57) reports differences of 49% and 69% respectively between the careful individual and peer group styles of his Working Class and Lower Middle Class Trinidadian informants; Rickford and Blake (1990: 262) report a 74% difference in a Barbadian's speech to his peers versus the interviewer; and Rickford and McNair Knox (1994: 247) report a 30% difference between a California teenager's speech to a white versus a black interviewer – it is possible that Poplack and Sankoff's speakers have an even more creole-like and copula-free vernacular than the one they elicited. This is of course a possibility for all sociolinguists. All of our attempts to elicit vernacular varieties are subject to the methodological axioms (including Style-Shifting: "there are no single style speakers") and the Observer's Paradox adumbrated by William Labov (1972b: 208–209), and it is only through complementary methods like peer group recordings, rapid and anoymous observations (W. Labov 1972b: 210), and repeated recordings with different interlocutors (Rickford 1987b) that we can be confident that we have tapped into the

10 If Samaná subjects with *there*, *where*, *here*, *these*, *those*, *this*, and *them* are also excluded – on the grounds that some or all of these were excluded in the AAVE studies as well (see Winford 1992a: 55, fn 6) – the overall deletion rate would remain at 40% (57/144).

vernacular. In this regard, it is interesting that in more recent recordings of Samaná speakers made by Stanford graduate student Dawn Hannah (see Hannah 1996, Table 3), the percentage of copula absence with pronoun subjects (including WIT subjects, i.e. tokens of *What's*, *It's*, and *That's*) was 48%, more than twice that reported by Poplack and Sankoff in 1987.

The second kind of evidence on which Poplack and Sankoff base their conclusion is the fact that the *constraint ranking* for copula absence in their Samaná data, particularly by following grammatical environment (see the first row of Table 6.4), is "similar to those attested" for urban AAVE "in Harlem, Detroit and rural Texas" but "quite different from the few creoles which have been studied quantitatively" (p. 310). Note, however, that Poplack and Sankoff's Samaná data differ quite sharply from previous AAVE data sets in showing __NP as more favorable to copula absence than both __Loc and __Adj (see Rickford et al. 1991: 121 for a comparison of several AAVE data sets with respect to following grammatical environment), so the "similarity to AAVE" evinced by these data is not perfect. Moreover, the copula absence pattern which Poplack and Sankoff took as their baseline creole pattern – a higher Ø rate before adjectives than before V+*ing*, for instance (based on Jamaican and Gullah data in Holm 1984) – has been shown to be spurious, the result of analytical errors in Holm 1984 (see Rickford and Blake 1990: 261; Rickford 1996: 359) and the result of reliance on copula patterns in Caribbean creole basilects rather than its mesolects or intermediate varieties, which are more similar to those of AAVE synchronically and in terms of possible diachronic derivation (Rickford 1974: 93; Winford 1992a: 23). When the errors in Holm's data are corrected, Poplack and Sankoff's (1987: 307) Samaná hierarchy of following grammatical constraints on copula absence is much more similar to that reported for Barbadian, Jamaican, and Trinidadian – especially insofar as the positions of __V+*ing* and __*gonna* at the top of the hierarchy are concerned (Rickford and Blake 1990: 268).[11] (See Figure 6.1.) Finally, when we compare the constraint hierarchy for Samaná reported by Hannah (1996) – see the second row of Table 6.4 – __NP ranks as the least favorable environment and __V+*ing* and __*gonna* as the most favorable environments, precisely as found for other sets of AAVE and Caribbean creole data.[12]

Let us consider now the diaspora data from African Nova Scotian English (ANSE), introduced by Poplack and Tagliamonte (1991). The overall rate of copula absence which they report (p. 319) for the descendants of nineteenth-century refugeee and fugitive field-slaves whom they recorded in North Preston,

---

11 One anomaly is the fact that a following *adjective* remains the least favorable following environment for copula absence in Samaná, but this is not the case in Hannah's more recent Samaná data (row two, Table 6.4).

12 The statistics from Hannah (1996) cited here are for "Labov deletion" (cf. Rickford et al. 1991), the same method used by Poplack and Sankoff (1987). Her "Straight deletion" VARBRUL weights for copula absence are: .14 __NP; .43 __Adj; .47 __Loc; .88 V+*ing*; .97 __*gon*.

Table 6.4 Copula absence (Labov deletion) in Samaná English by following grammatical environment

	_NP	_Adjective	_Locative	_Verb+ing	_gon(na)
Poplack and Sankoff (1987)	.41	.19	.23	.46	.59
Hannah (1996)	.12	.44	.42	.89	.93

Source: adapted from Poplack and Sankoff (1987: 307) and Hannah (1996: Table 4).

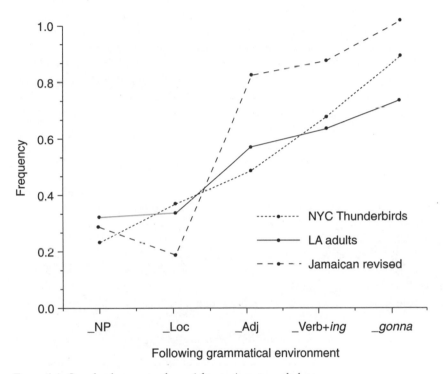

Figure 6.1 Copula absence in three African-American dialects
Source: Rickford (1996: 368). Jamaican statistics based on De Camp's (1960) data, revised.

Nova Scotia (Canada), is 20%, identical to the rate found by Poplack and Sankoff (1987) for Samaná English, and equally inimical to the creole hypothesis. However, the ANSE data set similarly includes tokens of the copula with first person subjects and with *it*, *what*, and *that* as subjects – and it is just as likely that the overall rate of copula absence would rise if these were excluded, as they were in most earlier studies of AAVE. One point worth noting – though it is not commented on by the authors – is that copula absence with first person subjects in the ANSE data set appears to be relatively substantial (feature weight of .29); in fact ANSE is more similar in this respect to Barbadian (feature weight of .47; Rickford and Blake 1990: 267) than to Samaná English (feature weight of .06; Poplack and Sankoff 1987: 307), and certainly more so than to urban AAVE (less than 1 percent for AAVE in East Palo Alto, California; Blake 1997: 64, Table 3).

The effect of following grammatical environment which Poplack and Tagliamonte (1991) found in ANSE is shown in Table 6.5.[13] Discussing these results, the authors observe that they are similar to the findings of W. Labov (1969) for peer groups in Harlem, and "to many other studies of this variable in AAVE," and that they are "quite different from the ranking found by Holm (1984) for Jamaican Creole and Gullah" (p. 319). The counter-arguments to this claim which we expressed in discussing the Samaná data in Table 6.4 apply equally to these data, however. Poplack and Tagliamonte do mention (pp. 320–321) the evidence in Rickford and Blake that Holm's "creole" data should not be taken as archetypical, but they go on to suggest (following Holm's theoretical argumentation) that if a prior creole origin were to leave its vestiges in a decreolizing or decreolized variety, we would expect to find the following patterns of copula absence:[14]

(3) __gonna > __V+ing > __Adj > __Loc > __NP

The authors then go on to ask, *inter alia*, why the expected ordering of adjective and locative does not obtain in the ANSE and other putatively decreolized data sets (like Samaná and Barbadian). This is a valid question, and one of several about the AAVE constraint hierarchy which Mufwene (1992) has challenged creolists to explain; we shall return to it below.

For the final set of diaspora evidence, let us turn now to Liberian Settler English (LSE). Singler (1991b: 132) reports the following rates of non-past copula absence for three Settlers from different parts of Liberia: Carolina 78%

Table 6.5 Copula absence in African Nova Scotian English (ANSE) by following grammatical environment

	__NP	__Adjective	__Locative	__Verb+ing	__gonna
Poplack and Tagliamonte (1991)	.31	.46	.49	.69	.73

Source: adapted from Poplack and Tagliamonte (1991: 321).

13 Omitted from this table, as it is also from Tables 6.3 (second row) and 6.4 (first row), is the feature weight reported by the authors for a following *Wh*-clause; in all three cases it is higher than the feature weight for __gonna.

14 The hypothesis is also stated alternatively by the authors as follows: categorical or high frequency of copula *absence* before gonna, V+ing, and adjective, and categorical or high frequency of copula *presence* before locative and NP.

(n=138), Albert 58% (n=173), and Slim 54% (n=223). These rates are all high, and argue in favor of the creolist position. Another pro-creolist feature of LSE speech is the fact that copula absence occurs there in the past tense as well (compare Barbadian, Jamaican). This is particularly true of the speech of Carolina, who comes from Sinoe County, a region in Liberia which had a heavy influx of Mississippi Settlers, and is very isolated (Singler 1991b: 150).[15] An example follows:

(4) When it [Ø was] good flour, twelve cent a pound. (Carolina, Singler 1991b: 131)

In non-past environments (that is, the environments on which copula analyses in AAVE and creoles normally focus), copula absence is also common in LSE with first person subjects, occurring 64% of the time (n=53) in the speech of the three speakers examined in Singler (1991b: 134), and 54% of the time (n=150) in the speech of the fourteen Sinoe County speakers discussed in Singler (1993). As noted above, first person copula absence is common in the Caribbean creoles but not in contemporary AAVE, and its frequency in LSE suggests that the English of the African-American Settlers who set out for Liberia in the nineteenth century may have been more creole-like than contemporary AAVE is.

The effects of following grammatical environment on the copula absence of Singler's three LSE speakers is shown in Table 6.6.[16] While the LSE hierarchy follows the AAVE (and creole) copula absence hierarchy insofar as a following NP is least favorable to copula absence and a following ___gon most favorable to

Table 6.6 Copula absence in Liberian Settler English (LSE) by following grammatical environment

	___NP	___Adjective	___Verb+ing	___Locative	___gon
Carolina	43%	93%	97%	100%	100%
Albert	32%	65%	85%	94%	100%
Slim	36%	43%	79%	91%	100%

Source: adapted from Singler (1991b: 146).

15 Singler (1993) reports data on fourteen Sinoe Settlers, including Carolina. Of these, six have overall rates of non-past copula absence between 71% and 83%, indicating that Carolina's high zero copula rate is not atypical; four others have rates between 55% and 67%; and the remaining four have rates between 33% and 40%.
16 The hierarchy of following environments holds even when a multivariate, variable rule analysis is performed (on Albert and Slim's speech only, not Carolina's, since hers is too categorical), with feature weights for copula absence (Singler 1991b: 144, Table 15) as follows: ___gon 1.00; ___Loc .86; ___V+ing .72; ___Adj .35; ___NP .29; ___Det-NP .13.

copula absence,[17] Carolina's pattern differs from the others', and the rates and relative orderings of the intermediate categories differ from those of AAVE in a way that deserves comment. Carolina clearly has a bifurcated pattern – some copula presence with a following NP, and (near)-categorical copula absence everywhere else. This is clearly the pattern of the LSE *basilect*, and it is similar to the one which Winford (1992) reports for Trinidadian Creole, particularly for the group sessions (p. 34) and for *are* (p. 37).[18] Albert and Slim represent points further along the continuum to Standard English, showing near-categorical copula absence only with __V+*ing*, __Loc and __*gon*,[19] and somewhat greater variability with a following adjective (65%, 43%). It is their data which establish, more firmly than Carolina's, the relative LSE ordering of __Loc as the second most favorable environment for copula absence (after __*gon*), __V+*ing* as the third, and __Adj as the fourth. Poplack and Tagliamonte (1991: 322–323) suggest that the locative > adjective copula absence ordering in Samaná and ANSE runs contrary to the adjective > locative creole pattern reported by Holm (1984). The LSE data provide additional evidence – along with that established by others for Barbadian and Trinidadian (Rickford and Blake 1990; Winford 1992) – that precisely this ordering obtains in some creole communities.[20] Why __V+*ing* should be less favorable to copula absence than __Loc is in LSE is not clear, however. This is certainly not the case in Trinidadian and other Caribbean data sets, and it would be interesting to see if the pattern is replicated with other LSE speakers.

Overall, the LSE copula absence data provide fairly strong support for the creolist position. One caveat, however, is that the high rate of copula absence in LSE may reflect the destandardizing influence of contact with pidginized Non-Settler Pidgin English (NSPE) over the years, just as the low rate of copula absence in ANSE might reflect the standardizing influence of contact with

17 Singler (1991: 143) argues, in fact, that *gon* has achieved auxiliary status in LSE and no longer co-occurs with non-past forms of the copula. This same argument could be made for __*gwine* in Jamaican Creole (it shows 100% "copula absence" in DeCamp's JC texts (see Rickford, 1996: 369, Table 6), and has already been made for creoles more genreally by Holm (1984: 298): "creole *go* was a calque for a protocreole preverbal marker indicating irrealis which was never preceded by any copula-like particle."

18 One difference is that in the Trinidadian data, copula absence with a following NP is not only low, but almost non-existent; the copula is almost always retained. See Winford (1992a: 35–37) for further discussion.

19 Following C. J. Bailey (1973), we adopt 80% as the cut-off point for (near) categoricality.

20 At the same time, pidgin/creole communities show variation with respect to the relative ordering of these environments, as do AAVE communities and data sets (Poplack and Tagliamonte 1991: 323; Rickford *et al.* 199: 121, Table 7); for Jamaican and Gullah, the ordering is indeed adjective > locative (Holm 1984; Rickford 1991c, 1996), perhaps in line with Singler's (1991b: 156–157) argument for *Non*-Settler Liberian English that *basilectal* varieties tend to show the high adjective copula absence pattern. (Jamaican and Gullah are arguably more basilectal than Barbadian and Trinidadian.)

Canadian English over the years. With respect to the LSE case, Singler (1991b: 153) argues that "while the general absence of nonsettler influence points to the conclusion that LSE's high rate of copula deletion is not a result of nonsettler influence, one cannot be certain of that."

6.4.3 Creole similarities

The earliest discussion of creole/AAVE similarities with respect to copula absence was that of B. Bailey (1965), who schematically compared the systems of non-verbal predication in Standard English (SE), Jamaican Creole (JC, through her native intuitions), and AAVE (as exemplified by Duke, the narrator in *The Cool World*), and concluded (p. 46) that there was a "deep structural relationship" between JC and AAVE, although not "an identical development of the systems." In particular, while SE requires an inflected form of *be* in all non-verbal predications, in AAVE such predicates are used without any copula, and JC "has a more complicated system, with zero before adjectives, an obligatory *a* before nominals, and a *de* which is often deleted before locatives" (ibid.). Although Bailey's claim that AAVE had *no* underlying copula was an idealization – as every quantitative study of spoken AAVE has shown – her paper was valuable for demonstrating that the nature of the following grammatical environment critically determined the realization of the copula in creoles, and for suggesting that comparisons between AAVE and creoles on this dimension might be important for the creole hypothesis.

Stewart (1969) extended Bailey's argument by postulating a hypothesis about the development of copula absence in Gullah, spoken off the coasts of South Carolina and Georgia, based on diachronic evidence. Earlier recorded forms of Gullah showed *da* as an obligatory copula both before predicate nominals (parallel to *a* in JC), and before unmarked verbs, so that *Dem da fish* meant both "They are fish" and "They are fishing" (p. 244). However, *da* + V then decreolized to Ø V*ing*, while *da* + NP was retained for equation, and later relexified to *iz* + NP. Subsequently, as Stewart went on to argue (although not in precisely these terms), *iz* was variably introduced in __V+*ing* environments, and zero was variably introduced in __NP environments. But the fact that zero was diachronically introduced in continuative verbal (__V+*ing*) environments earlier than it was in nominal (__NP) environments explained why copula absence was today more common in the verbal than in the nominal environments, both in mesolectal Gullah and – if the same decreolizing process were assumed – in AAVE.[21]

---

21 Stewart's (1969) account predates but essentially presumes the "more=earlier, less=later" principle which C. J. Bailey (1973) articulated. Stewart's exact words (p. 244) for the final stage in his hypothetical chain of events are as follows: "Finally, with the introduction of an optional dummy /iz/ in V-ing phrases, and a partial collapse of verbal /iz/ = Ø with equative /iz/ = Ø, one

This line of argument – that decreolizing changes happen in a certain order, keyed to environment, and that the order of those changes could explain synchronic variability – was to become a mainstay of research involving comparisons between AAVE and pidgins or creoles. Fasold (1976: 80–81) extended Stewart's stages, and Bickerton (1971, 1972) unearthed evidence of similar decreolizing processes in Guyanese Creole (GC), noting that such processes could have produced the synchronic copula absence statistics in AAVE:

> There are three Guyanese copula-type verbs: *a* (equative), *de* (locative), Ø (attributive). These are now replaced by inflected *be*, the first two in that order, and fairly completely, the third much more slowly and spasmodically . . . It follows that, in the mesolect, deleted copula is found oftenest with *gon*, not quite so often with *-ing* forms, less often with predicate adjectives, yet more infrequently with locatives, and least of all with predicate NPs – which corresponds exactly with Labov's [1969] findings for Black English [AAVE]! Indeed, these findings are quite explicable on our assumption that rule changes in Black English have, in the past, followed the same course and sequence as have those in Guyanese speech; if *be* insertion took place first in __NP environments, it would by now be mandatory or almost so for some speakers, while for some, *be* insertion before __*gonna* might not yet have even begun.
>
> (Bickerton 1971: 491)

Despite the quantitativist wording of this extract, Bickerton relied on qualitative implicational patterns for his conclusions rather than quantitative data like Labov's. Moreover, Bickerton's subsequent (1986: 226) argumentation that creole continua form "backwards," beginning with the acrolect, then the mesolect and basilect, suggests that he may no longer subscribe to the kind of decreolizing scenario sketched above.

Edwards (1980: 301) did have quantitative data, which showed that in mesolectal GC, copula absence was higher before a following adjective (93%, 14/15) than before NP (0%, 0/8), as in AAVE. But the data were from a short sample from one speaker, and the sample sizes were small. The locative environment, for instance, contained only one token, so it could not be considered in the variation analysis.

The first substantive quantitative data on copula absence in a creole was provided in Day's (1973) study of Hawaiian Creole English (HCE). Day's results – shown in Table 6.7 – are rarely if ever cited in discussions of the creole origin

can see the historical process – entirely documentable – which could easily have given rise to the statistical difference in copula deletion discovered by Labov [1969]."

Table 6.7 Copula absence in Hawaiian Creole English (HCE) by following grammatical environment

	__NP	__Locative	__Adjective	__Verb(+ing)
HCE	63% (321)	62% (130)	72% (235)	94% (372)

Source: adapted from Day (1973: 111, Table 9); number of tokens in parentheses.

of AAVE, but curiously so, since, apart from the equivalence of __NP and __Loc and a relatively high __NP absence rate, the relative frequency of copula absence by following grammatical environment in HCE matches that found for AAVE in data from New York (the Thunderbirds, Labove 1972a: 86, Table 3.2), and Los Angeles (Baugh 1979).[22]

Holm's (1976, 1984) analyses of Jamaican Creole (JC) and Gullah data in DeCamp (1960) and Turner (1948) respectively provided the first substantive statistics on copula absence in the Caribbean creoles. As Table 6.8 shows, copula absence was lower in both varieties before __NP or __Loc than before __Adj (this is referred to as the "high adj" creole pattern). Baugh's (1979, 1980) separation of the __Loc and __Adj environments in his LA data and in Labov *et al.*'s (1968) NYC Cobras data allowed us to see how strikingly JC and Gullah paralleled AAVE with respect to the ordering of these three environments.

However, as Holm himself observed (1976: 5; 1984: 293–294), the low __V+*ing* percentage of copula absence in Gullah and the low __V+*ing* and __*gon*(*na*) percentages in Jamaican ran counter to the copula absence pattern of AAVE, which was typically NP < Loc < Adj < V+*ing* < *gon*(*na*). Holm attributed the disparity to the fact that non-equivalent continuum levels were being compared. This is certainly relevant, but, as Rickford and Blake (1990: 261) argued, it was also because tokens of JC *de* and *a* were being included in the counts for __V+*ing* and __*gonna* in the creole data when they should not have

Table 6.8 Copula absence in Gullah and Jamaican Creole (JC) by following grammatical environment

	__NP	__Locative	__Adjective	__Verb(+ing)	__gon(na)
Gullah	11%	22%	62%	28%	88%
Jamaican	22%	17%	66%	17%	32%

Source: adapted from Holm (1984: 293, Table 2).

22 Day (1973) also provided a qualitative implicational analysis, and, interestingly enough, that suggested a different relative ordering of __Adj and __Loc (see his Tables 4 and 5, pp. 89–99), one which he was apparently unable to explain to his own satisfaction (see p. 111). As we have noted, the position of these two environments – relative to each other – is extremely variable in studies of AAVE.

been, since they are not feasible alternants of zero and inflected *be* in those environments (**dem de/a waakin* and **dem de gon waak*). When such variants were eliminated, the percentages of copula absence in both environments climbed to the relative positions they occupy (at the top of the following environment hierarchy) in AAVE. This was true both in the DeCamp data set originally examined by Holm (Rickford 1990), shown as "Jamaican, revised" in Figure 6.1 above, and in a new data set, from two old Jamaicans, examined by Rickford (1991c).[23] The copula percentages for both JC data sets are given in Table 6.9.[24]

Copula absence data for two different sets of Barbadian speakers were also provided by Rickford and Blake (1990) and Rickford (1992b), and while these differed from each other in the relative orderings of __Loc and __Adj (see Table 6.10), they both exemplified the basic copula absence pattern of AAVE. As noted elsewhere (Rickford *et al.* 1991: 121, Table 7), copula absence is higher in __Loc environments than in __Adj environments in some AAVE data sets, but lower in others. Of all the following grammatical environments for copula absence, these two environments show the greatest variability in their relative ordering.

Table 6.9 Copula absence in two JC data sets by following grammatical environment

	__NP	__Locative	__Adjective	__Verb(+ing)	__gwain
JC (1960)	28% (68)	18% (40)	81% (48)	86% (21)	100% (25)
JC (1991)	4% (48)	28% (32)	59% (58)	58% (43)	93% (14)

Source: adapted from Rickford (1996: 363, Table 3) and Rickford (1991c: Table 4); number of tokens in parentheses.

Table 6.10 Copula absence in two Barbadian data sets by following grammatical environment

	__NP	__Locative	__Adjective	__Verb(+ing)	__gwain
1980s (n=522)	.08	.54	.42	.65	.77
1991 data	.07 (94)	.52 (45)	.71 (104)	.89 (86)	1.00 (44)

Source: adapted from Rickford and Blake (1990: Table 3) and Rickford (1992b: table 3); number of tokens in parentheses.

23 One disparity in the case of the (1960) JC data is the fact that __Loc is lower than __NP; one disparity in the case of the (1991) data is that __Adj and __V+*ing* are equivalent. Without additional data, it is difficult to know how substantive these apparent disparities are, or to pursue explanations for their occurrence.

24 The corresponding variable rule feature weights are: __NP .23, __Loc .12; __Adj .75; __V+*ing* .79; __*gwain* 1.00 (Rickford 1996: 369, Table 7); and __NP .00; __Loc .19; __Adj .52; __V+*ing* .45; __*gwain* .83 (Rickford 1991c). Both the percentages and the feature weights were computed by the "Straight deletion" method, in which deletions are computed as a proportion of all possible forms – full forms, contractions, and deletions (Rickford *et al.* 1991: 106).

Singler's (1991b, 1993) work on Non-Settler Liberian English (NSLE), a continuum ranging from a highly pidginized basilect to a Liberian Standard English acrolect, was important not only for providing the first quantitative data on copula absence in an African pidgin or creole, but also for suggesting (1991b: 155) that the basilectal copulas (locative *de*, nominal invariant *be*) were not replaced directly by *is* in decreolization (as in Model A, Figure 6.2),[25] but through an intermediate zero stage (Model B, Figure 6.2). Guyanese mesolectal data in Bickerton (1973: 652–655) had provided similar indications.

Whereas Model A predicts higher rates of mesolectal copula absence before adjectives than before locatives and nominals, Model B predicts comparable (high) rates for all three environments in the mesolect. Another way of stating it (Singler 1991b: 156) is that preadjectival copula absence should be high in the basilect and mesolect and low in the acrolect, while prenominal and prelocative copula absence should be low in both the basilect and acrolect (although the copula is instantiated by different forms at each pole) and high in the mesolect. This is illustrated by the outputs of individual NSLE speakers in Table 6.11. If we apply this prediction to the kinds of Caribbean data sets considered in this paper, it also appears to hold true, especially with respect to the orderings of __Loc and __Adj: in more basilectal data sets, like the Gullah and Jamaican data in Tables 6.8 and 6.9, copula absence is higher before __Adj than __Loc; but in more mesolectal data sets, like the Barbadian and Trinidadian data in Tables 6.10 and 6.12 (the latter below), copula absence is higher before __Loc than __Adj.[26]

MODEL A			MODEL B			
	Basilect	Mesolect		Basilect	Mesolect	Acrolect
Loc	*de* ⟶	*is*	Loc	*de* ⟶	∅ ⟶	*is*
NP	*be* ⟶	*is*	NP	*be* ⟶	∅ ⟶	*is*
Adj	∅ ⟶	*is*	Adj	∅ ⟶	∅ ⟶	*is*

Figure 6.2 Two models of decreolization and copular distribution in Non-Settler Liberian English
Source: adapted from Singler (1991b: 155).

25 This model is represented by the quote from Bickerton (1971) on page 174
26 Of course, the prediction does not hold for the 1991 Barbadian data in Table 6.10, where __Adj shows more copula absence than __Loc, but it can be argued that the two octogenarians who are the source of these data are more basilectal than the six younger speakers who are the source of the 1980s data.

Table 6.11 Copula absence among basilectal, mesolectal, and acrolectal speakers of Non-Settler Liberian English by following grammatical environment (%)

	__Adjective	__Locative	__NP
Basilect (Gedeh Goldminer, n=100)	92	23	20
Mesolect (Charlie, n=100)	100	100	93
Acrolect (Richard, n=60)	13	0	5

Source: adapted from Singler (1991b: 156, Table 19).

Another creole data set for which quantitative data on copula absence have recently become available is Trinidadian Creole (TC, Winford 1992a), which, like Barbadian, has the advantage of being a mesolectal variety well-suited to comparisons with AAVE (ibid., p. 29). Winford first provides vernacular data from peer-group recordings (some surreptitious) with Working Class (WC) and Lower Middle Class (LMC) subjects. Copula absence in such data is very high (see top row of Table 6.12) – suggesting that the copula is underlyingly absent in all but nominal environments – but it still resembles the AAVE pattern, this time with __Loc higher than __Adj:[27] Copula absence in the individual interviews (Table 6.12, second row) is much lower overall, and much more similar in its absolute values to the frequencies reported by W. Labov *et al.* (1968) for the NYC Jets; and with the exception of an anomalous __goin percentage which may be attributed to limited data, the relative values are also more similar to those of AAVE.[28] On the basis of this and other evidence, Winford concludes (p. 49): "In view of the startling similarity of all these patterns of use, there would appear to be little reason to reject the view that the BEV [AAVE] copula system owes its origin to a process of decreolization similar to that observable in

Table 6.12 Copula (*am*, *is*, *are*) absence in Trinidadian Creole (TC) by following grammatical environment

	__NP	__Adjective	__Locative	__Verb+ing	__goin
Group sessions	1% (489)	79% (208)	90% (108)	94% (678)	97% (39)
Interviews	1% (280)	30% (175)	53% (66)	70% (275)	50% (14)

Source: adapted from Winford (1992a: 34, Table 6); number of tokens in parentheses.

27 The group data in this table are summed from Winford's (1992a: 34) Table 5 data on first person singular, third person singular, and plural and second person forms. In Table 6 (ibid.), Winford provides the corresponding VARBRUL feature weights for copula absence: __NP .00; __Adj .64; __Loc .80; __V+*ing* .85; __*goin* .88.
28 The interview data in this table are summed from Winford's (1992a: 41) Table 7 data on first person singular, third person singular, and plural and second person forms. Winford does not provide VARBRUL feature weights for these data.

the creole continua of the Caribbean." That process is sketched by him, in an expansion of Singler's Model B, as in Figure 6.3.[29]

Overall, if one simply compares the quantitative patterns of copula absence by following environment in the creole varieties and in AAVE, one is struck by the parallels between them (with one or two exceptions), and it is this parallelism which has provided one of the main planks for the hypothesis that AAVE might have been the diachronic outcome of a decreolization or variation process similar to that synchronically evidenced in the Caribbean, the Sea Islands, and Liberia.[30] But there are two sorts of challenges which one might pose to these comparisons between creole (primarily Caribbean) varieties and AAVE.

The first are general, theoretical challenges. Mufwene (p.c.) has suggested, for instance, that the comparisons might be typologically insightful but diachronically inconclusive because of the absence of a demonstrated sociohistorical connection between the Caribbean varieties and AAVE. However, recent evidence (see Rickford 1997) that Caribbean slaves constituted a substantial portion of the founding black populations in several American colonies helps to provide the missing link. Mufwene (ibid.) has also suggested that one must first prove that the continuum variability in Trinidadian, Guyanese, and other Caribbean varieties can be attributed to decreolization (here meaning the replacement and loss of basilectal creole features over time) before suggesting that the parallels between these and AAVE argue for prior decreolization in AAVE. But even if one assumes that mesolectal variability of the current

	Basilect	Lower mesolect	Upper mesolect	Acrolect
NP	*a* ⟶	Invariant *is* ⟶	*is*/forms of *be* ⟶	Inflect. *be*
Adj	∅ ⟶	∅ ⟶	∅/forms of *be* ⟶	Inflect. *be*
Loc	*de* ⟶	∅ ⟶	∅/forms of *be* ⟶	Inflect. *be*
Progressive	*a* V ⟶	∅ V+*in* ⟶	(be) V+*in* ⟶	*be* V+*in*
Future	*a go* V ⟶	∅ *goin* +V ⟶	*(be) goin to* V ⟶	*be goin to* V

Figure 6.3 Model of decreolization in the Caribbean English Creole copula system
Source: adapted from Winford (1992a: 48, Figure 6).

29 Note that while the nominal copula is replaced by zero in Singler's NSLE model, it is replaced by invariant *is* in Winford's Caribbean English Creole (CEC) model, in line with evidence that the CEC mesolect shows very low rates of prenominal copula absence.

30 As W. Labov (1982: 198) notes, this parallelism was said by James Sledd (p.c.) to constitute "the first serious evidence for the Creole hypothesis."

Caribbean type was present from the earliest periods of black/white contact (Alleyne 1971) and was *not* the product of (qualitative) decreolization, the similarities between the Caribbean and African-American speech communities in the United States would still support the possibility that the latter were subject to creole influences. One reason for this is that the mesolects, even if present from the start, are still creole-related. Another is that the extent and patterning of copula absence in African-American speech communities are unparalleled among the British populations from which Africans acquired their English, so that we cannot assume the direct transmission and smooth acquisition process which the alternative dialectologist position requires. A final theoretical issue, raised by Don Winford (p.c.), is whether we can treat copula absence as a uniquely creole feature rather than a general feature of untutored second language learning or substratal influence in language shift. Winford (forthcoming) cities Mesthrie (1992: 67–70) and points to the incidence of copula absence in South African Indian English and other New Englishes. However, the patterns of non-phonological copula absence by following grammatical environment in South African Indian English (SAIE) are quite different from those in AAVE and the creoles. In the SAIE basilect, copula absence is highest (33%) before __NP, and lower before __Adj (15%) and __PP (11%); in the mesolect and acrolect it is non-existent (Meshtrie 1992: 50, Table 2.6). Whether similar differences would show up in other ESL varieites, and the extent to which we can draw a firm line between second language acquisition/shift and pidginization/creolization (cf. Andersen 1983) remains to be determined. At present, the typological similarities and sociohistorical links between AAVE and the Caribbean/West African creoles suggests strongly to me that they were subject to similar creolizing (if not decreolizing) influences.

The second set of challenges to creole/AAVE comparisons has to do with queries about details. If one asks, for instance, *why* the AAVE patterns should be as they are, given the creole patterns, or *why* the mesolectal creole patterns are as they are, given the basilectal creole system, the answers are not always clear-cut.[31] In particular Mufwene (1992) has raised the following challenges to the creole similarities evidence:

(a) Why does AAVE typically show non-negligible percentages of copula absence before nominals (e.g. 23% *is* absence for NYC Thunderbirds), given that the creoles typically have a copula (*a* in GC and JC, *da* in Gullah) rather than zero before __NP?

(b) Why is copula absence in AAVE lower before adjectival predicates than in progressive and future constructions, given that none of these contexts requires a copula in the creoles?[32]

---

31 This is part of a larger problem in variation studies (both quantitativist and implicational) – the tendency to be satisfied with describing rather than explaining the patterns.

(c) Why is copula absence in AAVE not consistently or significantly higher before __Adj than before __Loc, given that, in the creoles, adjectives are like stative verbs and never require a copula, while locatives (optionally) take a copula (*de*)? This question was raised as well by Poplack and Tagliamonte (1991: 322–323).

Winford (1992: 48–49) dismisses these questions by noting that Mufwene and Poplack and Tagliamonte presuppose direct influence from the basilect, while it is the mesolectal copula systems which provide the "proper reference points" for AAVE. This response is certainly valid, particularly in regards to (c), where, as suggested by Singler (1991), the creole locative copula (*de*) is replaced by zero in the mesolect en route to the acrolectal use of *is*. This means that in the stage immediately prior to the upper mesolect or near acrolect represented by modern AAVE, adjectival and locative predicates are *not* distinguished in terms of the copula they require, and one would not therefore expect consistent or significant differences between them in terms of copula absence. It is significant that, as noted in this chapter, mesolectal samples that are closer to the basilect – like the Jamaican Creole samples analyzed by Holm (1984) and Rickford (1991c, 1996) – do show the "high adj" zero copula pattern (relative to __Loc) which Mufwene and Poplack and Tagliamonte all expect. These are the varieties which could be expected to show the influence of the creole basilect distinction along the lines Holm (1984: 298) hypothesized.[33] As we go further away from the basilect, however, into mid-mesolectal varieties like TC, or upper mesolectal/near acrolectal varieties like Samaná, ANSE, and AAVE, we find minimal copula absence differences between __Adj and __Loc, and more fluctuation in their relative ordering, suggesting that the "high adj" pattern of the basilect is not a major influence.

There are some cases in which copula absence for __Loc is significantly higher (20% or more) than it is for __Adj, for instance, by .42 in the cases of the ex-slaves in the second row of Table 6.3 above, by 29% and 48% in the case of Albert and Slim in the LSE data of Table 6.6, by 23% in the case of the individual TC data in Table 6.12, and by .34 in the case of Baugh's (1979: 189) data for *are* absence in Los Angeles. But in general, when copula absence for

---

32 It is not true that progressives and futures require no "copula" or auxiliary in the creoles. The basilectal progressive is (*d*)*a* or *de* V, with a clear preverbal marker or auxiliary; the basilectal future is either *go* V or *a go* V (see discussion below), the former never requiring a copula at higher levels of the continuum (where it surfaces as *gon* in some varieties), the other sometimes doing so (where it surfaces as *gwain/goin tu*).

33 "Copulas preceding *adjectives* and those preceding *locatives* could be expected to delete at substantially different rates in BEV [AAVE] were they to be calculated separately, since in the protocreole there was a copula for location (*de*) whereas adjectives were a subclass of verbs requiring no copula. The deletion rate for copulas preceding adjectives could be expected to be several times greater than that of copulas preceding locatives."

__Loc is higher than it is for __Adj, it is minimally so, for instance, by .04 in the Samaná data in the top row of Table 6.4; by .03 in ANSE, Table 6.5; by .12 in the 1980s Barbadian data, Table 6.10; by 11% in the TC group data, Table 6.12; by 3% in the Detroit WC data (Wolfram 1969: 172); by .01 and .06 in the Texas adult and child data respectively (G. Bailey and N. Maynor 1987: 457); by .02 and .05 in the East Palo Alto data, depending on whether one uses Straight deletion or Labov deletion methods respectively (Rickford et al. 1991: 117).

At the same time, appealing to the mesolect does not answer all the relevant questions, partly because our understanding of the variation paths and processes in copula variability is not complete. With respect to question (a), for instance, it certainly seems to be the case that the Caribbean creoles abhor copula absence in nominal environments to an extent that AAVE and its immediate congeners do not; compare the prenominal copula absence statistics for TC (1%, Table 6.12 above) and Barbadian (.07, .08, Table 6.10) with those for Samaná (.41, top row, Table 6.4), ANSE (.31, Table 6.5) and AAVE in NYC (.23 Thunderbirds, .32 Jets) and East Palo Alto (.27 or .29, Rickford et al. 1991: 117). Although we do find comparably high prenominal copula absence figures for some of the Creole data sets (28% JC, Table 6.9; 32–43% LSE, Table 6.6; 20–93% NSLE, Table 6.11), it must be admitted that we simply do not know why these differences exist. Some of them may be due to statistical fluctuations due to limited data, particularly in analyses based on the speech of one individual, but we need more study to determine in which varieties and why a basilectal copula goes to zero before being replaced by inflected forms of be (as in Singler's Model B, Figure 6.2 above), and in which varieties and why a basilectal copula is directly replaced by a non-basilectal copula (as in Winford's model, Figure 6.3). At present we cannot say definitively which of these de-creolization paths AAVE followed, although the LSE-based Model B seems more promising.[34]

It should also be admitted that we don't have a watertight answer to Mufwene's question (b), about why __V+ing and __gon(na) consistently show higher copula absence rates than __Adj. Winford's (1992a: 56, fn 17) answer to this is that the former two are actually auxiliary environments, subject to stronger constraints against copula insertion than copulative __Adj, since "suffixal -ing and future gon(na) are tense aspect markers which require no be support." This raises some interesting issues, but essentially restates the question. For in the basilect, adjectival, progressive, and future environments are all

---

34 One problem with Model B is that it posits simultaneous replacement of the basilect forms in all environments by zero, something which Singler himself admits (1991b: 155) may need refining. Differential timing of decreolization processes by environment – as in Winford's model, and in the empirical work of other continuum scholars (Day 1973; Bickerton 1973; Rickford 1979) – seems theoretically more plausible.

auxiliary environments (to the extent that adjectives behave like stative verbs in the basilect), and the question of how decreolization proceeds in each of these environments and ends up distinguishing them, is, in my opinion, far from settled. Considering only the future environment, for instance, is the starting point indeed *a go* + V, as Winford's model (Figure 6.3 above) suggests? What of basilectal *go* + V, whose alternation with *a go* + V (paralleling SE variation between non-prospective *will* V and prospective *is going to* V) has never been systematically studied by anyone? For Holm (1984: 298), AAVE *gonna* is a descendant of creole *go*, itself "a calque for a protocreole preverbal marker indicating irrealis [go? sa?] which was never preceded by any copula-like particle." But *go* as a strictly copula-less auxiliary varies in the continuum with forms like *gon* and *will*, which never require a copula. If AAVE *gonna* is the product of decreolization, it is likely indeed to have come from *a go* + V, as Winford hypothesizes, but it is likely to have had some influence from the copula-free *go* + V and *gon* + V, because of their phonological and semantic similarities, and this might explain the very high rates of copula absence before __*gon(na)* in AAVE and __*gwine* or __*goin tu* in the mesolectal creole varieties.[35]

In any case, the relationship between *go* and *gon* on the one hand, and *gwain* and *goin to* in the creoles deserves further study, much as the relationship between *gon* and *gonna* in AAVE does. Rickford and Blake (1990: 261) report preliminary evidence that *gon* as in "He gon tell" shows a higher proportion of copula absence than *gonna*, as in "He's gonna tell," and Winford (1992: 55, fn 8) asks whether these two forms are equally accommodating of auxiliary *be*, given that *go* in TC and *gon* in GC never take *be*, while *gwain* and *goin to* in both varieties do take *be*. When we have a clearer idea of the synchronic variation and diachronic evolution of these future markers in the creoles and in AAVE, we will have, I believe, a surer answer to Mufwene's question.

One other demurral which must be raised in relation to the creole similarities evidence is that if we consider *preceding grammatical environment* – in particular, the effect of an NP vs pronoun subject – there is not as much parallelism between the creoles and AAVE. Fewer studies of creoles report data on this environment than for following grammatical environment, but Table 6.13 summarizes the available evidence from Barbadian, Jamaican, and Trinidadian, compared with several varieties of AAVE, and with Samaná and ANSE. The first thing to note is that the relation between an NP and a personal pronoun subject is absolutely regular in AAVE: the latter favors copula absence more than the former does, by substantial margins (20–43%). By contrast, in three of the creole data sets (Barbadian 1980s, Jamaican, and plural NPs vs pronouns in

---

35 For further discussion of the relationship between the future tense markers in creoles, see Mufwene (1996b: 8–11).

Table 6.13 Copula absence by preceding grammatical environment in Caribbean creoles, AAVE, and other varieties of New World Black English

	NP__	Personal Pro__	Other Pro__
Barbadian, 1980s data (Rickford and Blake 1990: 267)[a]	.84	.19	.45
Barbadian, 1991 data (Rickford 1992b: 192)	.48	.52	
Jamaican (Rickford 1996: 369)[a]	.70	.60	.23
Trinidadian group sessions (Winford 1992a: 34)[b]	.42 / .46	.49 / .60 / .64	.39
Liberian Settler English, Albert and Slim (Singler 1991b: 145)[a, f]	.43 / .89	.24 / .51 / .51	. 22 / – / .63
AAVE, NYC Thunderbirds, zero *is* (Labov 1972a: 84)[c]	12% / 42%	51% / 60%	
AAVE, NYC Cobras, zero *is* (Labov 1972a: 84)[c]	18% / 42%	51% / 60%	
AAVE, NYC Jets, zero *is* (Labov 1972a: 84)[c]	18% / 27%	61% / 58%	
AAVE, Detroit WC (Wolfram 1969: 170)[d]	30% / 18%	63% / 41%	
AAVE, East Palo Alto (Rickford et al. 1991)[a, e]	.42 / (.54)	.62 / (.51)	.46 / (.44)
Samaná (Poplack and Sankoff 1987: 307)[f]	.81	.06 / .28 / .90	.06 / .43 / .53
ANSE (Poplack and Tagliamonte 1991: 321)[f]	.89	.16 / .52 / .91	.29 / – / .37

Notes

a "Other pronouns" includes forms like *this, there,* and *somebody.*

b NP figures are for Sing NP/Plural NP respectively; Personal Pro figures are for *I / he, she / we, you, they* respectively; Other Pro figures are for *it, what, that* subjects.

c First figure in each column = single or individual style; second figure is for group style.

d First figure in each column = Lower Working Class; second figure = Upper Working Class.

e First figure in each column = Straight deletion; second figure = Labov deletion (parentheses indicate Labov deletion results were insignificant for this factor group).

f Personal Pro figures are for *I / he, she / we, you, they* respectively; Other Pro figures are for *it, what, that / them, those, these, this / here, there, where* respectively.

LSE), the ordering is reversed, with a nominal subject favoring copula absence more than a pronoun subject; in the case of the LSE and Barbadian 1980s data sets, the margins are substantial (.38, .65). In the other creole data sets, the Pro > NP ordering does hold, but the margins are smaller than in the AAVE data sets, and in the case of the Barbadian 1991 data, virtually non-existent. This is bad news for the creole hypothesis, but the data for Samaná and ANSE provide little comfort for the dialectologist position either, since in these varieties an NP subject favors copula absence more strongly than most personal pronoun subjects, and a lot more than comparable NP subjects in AAVE.[36] I don't think we have worked enough on this aspect of copula absence to be able to say why the subject effect obtains and why it seems to vary so significantly in varieties other than AAVE,[37] but the data in Table 6.13 do help to restrain the enthusiasm which creolists and dialectologists usually express about creole/ AAVE similarities and differences on the basis of evidence from following grammatical environment alone.

6.4.4. African language similarities

The case for African substratum influence on AAVE copula usage – via an intermediate creole stage – is most strongly associated with Holm (1976, 1984), although it must be acknowledged that both Berdan (1975) and Dennis and Scott (1975) had presented similar arguments and evidence earlier, and that Alleyne (1980) and DeBose and Faraclas (1993) have presented other relevant data. The starting point for all arguments of this type is that AAVE copula absence statistically distinguishes between nominal, adjectival, locative, and verbal predicates (in terms of the different frequencies of zero in each, attested above). Standard and vernacular varieties of English provide little or no basis for this distinction (see section 6.3.5), insofar as they use the same form (an inflected form of be) regardless of following grammatical environment. But English-based creoles and a number of West African languages do, insofar as they employ different copula forms (including zero) in these different environments. Holm (1984: 297), drawing on Rowlands (1969), sketched the relevant facts for Yoruba, a language which was a part of the African-American substratum:

___V: Yoruba ń is a preverbal marker of the progressive aspect corre-
sponding roughly to English IS going, WERE going (Rowlands 1969: 60).
___Adj: Most Yoruba adjectives are a subclass of verbs which require no copula; however some "phonoaesthetic" adjectives require the copula rí . . . (Rowlands 1969: 122, 155).
___Loc: Yoruba wà (with stylistic variant mbe) expresses existence or location, as does sí after the negative (Rowlands 1969: 154).
___NP: Both jẹ́ and ṣe are used before nouns, but jẹ́ is used when we are thinking of natural, in-born, permanent characteristics while ṣe is used of what is accidental, acquired or temporary (Rowlands 1969: p. 152).

---

36 This is not the case in Hannah's (1996) analysis of more recent Samaná data, however. The VARBRUL weight for copula absence (Labov deletion) is .038 for an NP subject, and .239 to .806 for various pronoun subjects.
37 Don Winford (p.c.) suggests that it may involve phonological constraints peculiar to AAVE. However, as the data in W. Labov (1972a: 104) and other studies indicate, the pronoun effect cannot simply be attributed to the fact that most personal pronouns end in vowels, since Pro___ has a consistently favoring effect on copula absence, while a noun ending in a vowel does not (except in the case of the NYC Thunderbirds). Beyond this, no one has given any explanation, much less a convincing explanation, as to why pronoun subjects should favor copula absence more than full NP subjects.

Figure 6.4 (adapted from Holm's 1984: 305, Figure 1) shows how some of these Yoruba distinctions were merged in the Caribbean English creoles and AAVE, although the four broad categories were still separated (via different forms or percentages of copula absence).[38]

While the distinction between these four primary copula environments in West African languages seems likely to have influenced the development of the creole copula system, and, ultimately the patterns of AAVE copula absence, there are, as in virtually every other kind of evidence we have considered so far, considerations which argue against attaching *too* much influence to this distinction. One is the fact that the match between the African language categories and the creole/AAVE categories is not perfect: the different kinds of adjectival and nominal predicates distinguished in Yoruba are not distinguished in the creoles nor in AAVE, while the creole/AAVE distinction between progressives and futures does not seem to come from Yoruba and other African languages. Furthermore, Yoruba may have had little to do with the emergence of Sranan or Jamaican. Mufwene (1992: 157) and others have also argued that substratist arguments of this type do not account for variation among African languages, and would need to be supplemented by "universal selective principles" which "would explain why the features of some West African languages would have been selected over those of other languages." Holm himself (1984: 296) acknowledged that copula absence in AAVE and the creoles did correspond to some of the universals of simplification (or second language acquisition) identified by Ferguson (1971), although he felt that the African substratum was more important.[39] Finally, if McWhorter (1995)

	Yoruba	Sranan	Jamaican	BEV	Standard English
____V	ń	e	de		
	Ø }	Ø	Ø	(ɪ)z ~ •	(ɪ)z
____Adj	ri }				
____Loc	wà }	de	de		
	sɪ }				
____NP	ṣe	de }			
	jẹ́	a }	a ~ ɪz		
Emph	ni	a	a ~ ɪz	ɪz	(it's)

Figure 6.4 Merger of copular categories
Source: adapted from Holm (1984: 305).

38 Salikoko Mufwene (p.c.) argues that *rí*, *ṣe*, and *jẹ́* are the only real copulas in this list, since Yoruba *ń* is really the counterpart of English progressive *-ing* as the future marker.
39 From the point of view of the creole hypothesis, of course, universals of simplification and

is right in his suggestion that the earliest (pidgin) forms of New World Black English lacked copulas altogether, this would also reduce the likelihood of African influence (admixture) in the development of copula forms and categories in the Caribbean creoles as well as AAVE.

6.4.5 English dialect differences

The available evidence from English dialects provides support for the creolist hypothesis insofar as most English dialects outside of AAVE or creole-speaking areas do *not* show copula absence. This is particularly true of the British dialects which, according to the dialectologist hypothesis, are assumed to have influenced AAVE. Wolfram (1974: 522) reports that he was unable to find evidence of copula absence in a selective search of the available records of British varieties,[40] and to the best of my knowledge, no such evidence has yet come to light. Moreover, studies of the copula in white American dialects outside of the South – for instance in New York City (W. Labov 1969) and in California (McElhinny 1993) – have similarly found no evidence of copula absence. Of course such dialects do show copula contraction, and Labov (1969) has argued that copula absence in AAVE is an extension of copula contraction in white vernaculars and Standard English and shows similar conditioning. However, this has been challenged on empirical and theoretical grounds (Rickford *et al.* 1991; Mufwene 1992; McElhinny 1993).

For Southern dialects of American English, the picture is less clear. Williamson (1972) pointed to examples of copula absence in spoken and written samples of Southern white English, although she provided no quantitative evidence of their occurrence relative to contracted and full forms. Of the white Atlanta fifth graders studied by Dunlap (1974: 77–79), the Upper Middle Class and Lower Middle Class *never* deleted the copula, while the Lower Class deleted it only 1% of the time;[41] corresponding zero copula percentages for black Atlanta fifth graders were 1% (Upper Middle Class Black), 9% (Lower Middle Class Black), and 27% (Lower Class Black), so the difference between the two ethnic groups on this feature was qualitative, as it was also with respect to invariant habitual *be* (used by blacks but not whites). The whites from rural Franklin County, Mississippi, studied by Wolfram (1974) – primarily children and

---

substrate influence are not necessarily in conflict, since both could be elements in the prior pidginization and creolization of AAVE.

40 As Wolfram (1974: 522) goes on to note: "Of course, it must be admitted that the inability to find copula deletion in British varieties does not necessarily mean that it doesn't occur; but since copula deletion is a rather noticeable phenomenon, one would suspect that if it had occurred, there would be some report of its existence in the major sources."

41 Of the 8 instances of zero copula which comprise this 1%, 7 are with plural or second person subjects – that is, they are instances of *are*-deletion rather than *is*-deletion, as reported for other Southern dialects (Alabama, Mississippi, Texas).

teenagers – showed considerably more *are*-absence (58%), but fairly limited *is*-absence (6.5% overall). In fact, 30 of the 45 white informants whose speech was analyzed by Wolfram showed no *is*-absence at all, and those who did delete *is* did not show the same grammatical conditioning evidenced in studies of *is*-absence in AAVE. For instance, although a subject pronoun did favor copula absence slightly more than a preceding NP (15.6% vs 12.6% respectively), the difference was negligible, and in terms of following grammatical environment, the distinction was essentially a binary one, between nominal (8%) and non-nominal (16–18%) environments (see Table 6.14.) At the same time, the conditioning for *are*-absence was quite similar to that reported for copula absence in AAVE, both in terms of a robust pronoun versus NP subject effect (64% vs 33% respectively) and in terms of the role of following grammatical environment (see Table 6.14). In terms of *is*-absence, then, the difference between the white Mississippi pattern and that of AAVE was sharp, and qualitative; the *are*-absence pattern was essentially similar, or only quantitatively different.

This is also the case in Feagin's (1979) study of Anniston, Alabama. Feagin does not provide data on the conditioning of copula absence among her white speakers, but their overall patterns resemble those of Wolfram's Mississippi informants. For *is*-absence, the percentages are low: 1.7% for the Upper Class, 5.8% for the Urban Working Class, and 6.8% for the Rural Working Class. For *are*-absence, however, the figures are higher: 17.9% for the Upper Class, 35.3% for the Urban Working Class, and 56.3% for the Rural Working Class.

Finally, we have data on copula absence in the speech of white folk-speakers (over seventy-five years old, with a grade school education or less) from East-Central Texas, as reported in G. Bailey and N. Maynor (1985), and compared with the data of black folk-speakers. The white folk-speakers do show considerably more *are*-absence (36%, 148/411) than *is*-absence (2%, 26/1311), but data from black folk-speakers from the area show a similar discrimination between the two forms, although copula absence higher in both cases: *is*-absence = 6%, 46/734; *are*-absence = 58%, 159/274. The effect of following grammatical environment is similar for the whites and the blacks, too, who primarily distinguish auxiliary (__V+*ing* and __*gonna*) and non-auxiliary environments, as shown in Table 6.15.

Table 6.14 Copula (*is*, *are*) absence in rural white Mississippi English by following grammatical environment

	__NP	__Adj/Loc	__Verb+ing	__gonna
Are-absence	31% (35)	49% (218)	66% (140)	86% (69)
Is-absence	8% (65)	16% (115)	18% (40)	18% (22)

Source: adapted from Wolfram (1974: 507, 514, Tables 3 and 7); number of tokens in parentheses.

Table 6.15 Copula (*is*, *are*) absence among folk-speakers from East-Central Texas by following grammatical environment

	__NP	__Adjective	__Locative	__Verb+ing	__gonna
Whites	2% (861)	10% (339)	8% (99)	34% (159)	54% (79)
Blacks	9% (436)	14% (209)	15% (85)	73% (92)	68% (14)

Source: G. Bailey and N. Maynor (1985: 210, Table 5); number of tokens in parentheses.

In sum, we find no copula absence outside of the South, but of the four Southern varieties for which we have quantitative data, at least three show copula absence patterns comparable in their rates and conditioning with those of AAVE, particularly insofar as *are*-absence is concerned. The fact that the British dialects whose historical antecedents were the source of Southern white dialects show no copula absence makes it extremely unlikely that this feature was inherited from them. Although it is possible that this feature was independently innovated in white Southern speech, it is more likely that, as suggested by Wolfram (1974: 524), "copula absence in white Southern speech may have been assimilated from decreolizing black speech." Thus the similarities between Southern white dialects and AAVE with respect to this feature do not work against the creolist and for the dialectologist hypothesis, as one might have assumed from the general principles outlined in the introductory section.

6.5 Summary, concluding remarks, directions for research

Table 6.16 summarizes the quantitative data on copula absence by following grammatical environment which have been the mainstay of our discussions of the evidence provided by historical attestations, diaspora recordings, creole similarities, and English dialect differences with respect to the creole origins of AAVE. What it excludes, of course, is the pros and cons raised by each piece of evidence and the questions which remain, topics pursued in more detail above.

It is impossible to conclude with a balance sheet of pluses and minuses which would add up to a final decision on the creole origins issue. To my mind, there is enough persuasive evidence in these data to suggest that AAVE did have some creole roots. The very fact that copula absence is widespread both in AAVE and in mesolectal creoles, but not in white Englishes outside of the American South (where it can be argued that whites adopted the speech patterns of blacks) strongly suggests that at least some of the predecessors of modern AAVE arose from a restructuring process similar to that which produced the English-based creoles. The fact that the constraint hierarchy for following grammatical environment is so similar across the varieties shown in Table 6.16 further reinforces

Table 6.16 Summary of copula absence rates by following grammatical environment in historical attestations, diaspora recordings, creole varieties, white American English, and AAVE

	__NP	__Adj	__Loc	__V+ing	__gon
Historical attestations					
Ex-slaves (G. Bailey 1987)	12%	29%	15%	71%	100%
Ex-slaves (Poplack and Tagliamonte 1991)	.39	.27	.67	.72	.78
Diaspora recordings					
Samaná (Poplack and Sankoff 1987)	.41	.19	.23	.46	.59
Samaná (Hannah 1996)	.12	.44	.42	.89	.93
ANSE (Poplack and Tagliamonte 1991)	.31	.46	.49	.69	.73
LSE (Singler 1991b) Carolina	43%	93%	100%	97%	100%
LSE (Singler 1991b) Albert	32%	65%	94%	85%	100%
LSE (Singler 1991b) Slim	36%	43%	91%	79%	100%
Creole varieties					
Hawaiian Creole (Day 1973)	63%	72%	62%	94%	[No data]
JC 1960 (Rickford 1996)	28%	81%	18%	86%	100%
JC 1991 (Rickford 1991c)	4%	59%	28%	58%	93%
Bajan 1980s (Rickford and Blake 1990)	.08	.42	.54	.65	.77
Bajan 1991 (Rickford 1992b)	.07	.71	.52	.89	1.00
NSLE (Singler 1991b) basilect	20%	92%	23%		
NSLE (Singler 1991b) mesolect	93%	100%	100%		
NSLE (Singler 1991b) acrolect	5%	13%	0%		
Trinidadian groups (Winford 1992a)	1%	79%	90%	94%	97%
Trinidadian individuals. (Winford 1992a)	1%	30%	53%	70%	50%
White American English					
White Mississippi *are* (Wolfram 1974)	31%	49% (__Adj/Loc)		66%	86%
White Mississippi *is* (Wolfram 1974)	8%	16% (__Adj/Loc)		18%	18%
White East-Texas (G. Bailey and N. Maynor 1985)	2%	10%	8%	34%	54%
African-American vernacular English					
is, NYC Thunderbirds (Labov 1969)	.2	.48	.36	.66	.88
is, NYC Jets (Labov 1969)	.32	.36	.52	.74	.93
is NYC Cobras (Baugh 1979)	.14	.72	.31	.59	.78
is+are, Detroit WC (Wolfram 1969)	37%	47%	44%	50%	79%
is, Los Angeles (Baugh 1979)	.32	.56	.29	.66	.69
are. Los Angeles (Baugh 1979)	.25	.35	.69	.62	.64
is+are, Texas kids (G. Bailey and N. Maynor 1987)	.12	.25	.19	.41	.89
is+are, Texas adults (G. Bailey and N. Maynor 1987)	.09	.14	.15	.73	.68
is+are, East Palo Alto (Rickford et al. 1991)	.29	.47	.42	.66	.77

this conclusion.[42] The fact that AAVE varieties which might be considered closer to their creole origins on historical grounds (eighteenth-century varieties, Samaná) also behave more like creole varieties in some respects (for instance in permitting some deletion of first person *am* and/or in permitting some degree of past tense copula absence) is also a plus for the creole origins hypothesis.

At the same time, our review of the available evidence with respect to copula absence has turned up various challenges to the creole hypothesis, which can be broadly characterized as being of two types. The first is inconsistencies in data from two or more sources, for instance, the difference between analyses of the ex-slave recording data provided by Guy Bailey (1987) and Poplack and Tagliamonte (1991), or the difference between analyses of Samaná as analyzed by Poplack and Sankoff (1987) and Hannah (1996). More serious is the absence of convincing explanations for certain recurrent effects, like the differences between pronoun versus NP subjects on copula absence in AAVE and the creoles, or the reason why the following grammatical constraint hierarchy should pattern as it does, and future work should be dedicated to the pursuit of such explanations.

There is also the issue of intermediate positions on the creole origins issue, like those of Winford (1992b: 350–351), who is now willing to accept that a "creole substratum" did play some role in the history of AAVE, but not that it was once a fully fledged creole like Gullah. Similarly Holm (1988, 1992) is willing to see early AAVE as a "semi-Creole" and Mufwene (1992: 144) to recognize it as having been a separate language variety, derived from neither a creole nor any white American non-standard language variety, although structurally related to both. These are interesting new positions, but they are not inconsistent with the kinds of evidence reviewed in this chapter, and they agree

---

42 Guy Bailey (p.c.) offered the following helpful remarks after this chapter was written, and it seems most relevant to insert them here: "First, the exact order of the constraints of the following predicate on copula deletion is not really crucial to the creole hypothesis. The fact that the following environment matters at all is sufficient to prove that this comes from something other than English. In English the form of the verb always depends on the subject. Even in those dialects that do not have subject–verb concord, the form of the verb is determined by whether the subject is an NP or PRO. It is not surprising that there should be some discrepancies among AAVE and various creoles in regard to the exact effects of the following environment. After all, they've had several centuries of independent development. Second, I think the differing effects of a preceding NP or PRO on zero copula has a simple explanation: it reflects the grafting of an English constraint onto a creole process. This constraint manifests itself in a number of ways in earlier AAVE, and with several centuries of contact, it is only reasonable to assume that other dialects of English affected AAVE just as AAVE affected them. Third, I'm convinced that African and Creole influence not only extended throughout the entire period of slavery but that the period from 1790–1840 saw a real reinfusion of these element. More than half of the slaves imported to the US were imported after 1790 (most of these after 1793 and the invention of the cotton gin). With the westward expansion of the cotton kingdom, this was the most dynamic period of slavery."

at least in denying the validity of the pure dialectologist's argument – that AAVE simply represents the transfer and acquisition by Africans and African Americans of English dialects spoken by British and other white immigrants to America in earlier times.

Acknowledgments

This chapter has benefited from the comments of several colleagues since it was first written in 1994. I am particularly indebted to Guy Bailey, Michael Montgomery, Salikoko Mufwene, and Don Winford for feedback on earlier verions. Since I have not always heeded their wise counsel, however, I alone bear responsibility for the final version of this chapter. I am also indebted to Angela E. Rickford for facilitating the writing of this chapter in innumerable ways.

References

Alleyne, Mervyn (1971) "Acculturation and the cultural matrix of creolization." In *Pidginization and Creolization of Languages*, Dell Hymes (ed.). Cambridge: Cambridge University Press, pp. 169–186.

—— (1980) *Comparative Afro-American: An Historical-Comparative Study of English-Based Afro-American Dialects*. Ann Arbor: University of Michigan Press.

Andersen, Roger (1983) *Pidginization and Creolization as Language Acquisition*. Rowley, MA: Newbury House.

Ash, Sharon and John Myhill (1986) "Linguistic correlates of inter-ethnic contact." In *Diversity and Diachrony*, David Sankoff (ed.). Amsterdam and Philadelphia: John Benjamins, pp. 32–42.

Bailey, Beryl Loftman (1965) "Toward a new perspective in Negro English dialectology." *American Speech* 40.3: 171–177.

—— (1966) *Jamaican Creole Syntax*. Cambridge: Cambridge University Press.

Bailey, Charles-James N. (1973) *Variation and Linguistic Theory*. Washington, DC: Center for Applied Linguistics.

Bailey, Guy (1987) Contribution to panel discussion on "Are black and white vernaculars diverging?" *American Speech* 62: 32–40.

—— (1993) "A perspective on African-American English." In *American Dialect Research*, Dennis R. Preston (ed.). Amsterdam and Philadelphia: John Benjamins, pp. 287–318.

Bailey, Guy and Natalie Maynor (1985) "The present tense of *be* in White folk speech of the Southern United States." *English World-Wide* 6: 199–216.

—— (1987) "Decreolization?" *Language in Society* 16: 449–473.

—— (1989) "The divergence controversy." *American Speech* 64.1: 12–39.

Bailey, Guy, Natalie Maynor, and Patricia Cukor-Avila (eds.) (1991) *The Emergence of Black English: Text and Commentary*. Amsterdam and Philadelphia: John Benjamins.

Baker, Philip (1982) "The contributions of non-Francophone immigrants to the lexicon of Mauritian Creole." unpublished PhD dissertation, School of Oriental and African Languages, University of London.

—— (1991) "Column: Causes and effects." *Journal of Pidgin and Creole Languages* 6.2: 267–278.

Baugh, John (1979) "Linguistic style shifting in Black English." unpublished PhD dissertation, University of Pennsylvania.

—— (1980) "A re-examination of the Black English copula." In *Locating Language in Time and Space*, William Labov (ed.). New York: Academic Press, pp. 83–106.

—— (1983) *Black Street Speech: Its History, Structure and Survival*. Austin, Texas: University of Texas Press.

Berdan, Robert (1975) "Sufficiency conditions for a prior creolization of Black English." Paper presented at the International Conference on Pidgins and Creoles, Hawaii, 6–11 January.

Bickerton, Derek (1971) "Inherent variability and variable rules." *Foundations of Language* 7: 457–492.

—— (1972) "The structure of polylectal grammars." In *Twenty-Third Annual Round Table: Sociolinguistics: Current Trends and Prospects*, Roger W. Shuy (ed.). Washington, DC: Georgetown University Press, pp. 17–42.

—— (1973) "The nature of a creole continuum." *Language* 49: 640–669.

—— (1975) *Dynamics of a Creole System*. Cambridge: Cambridge University Press.

—— (1986) Column: Beyond Roots: The five year test. *Journal of Pidgin and Creole Languages* 1.2: 225–232.

Blake, Renee (1997) "Defining the envelope of linguistic variation: The case of 'don't count' forms in the copula analysis of African American Vernacular English." *Language Variation and Change* 9: 57–79.

Bloomfield, Leonard (1933) *Language*. London: Allen and Unwin.

Brasch, Walter M. (1981) *Black English and the Mass Media*. Amherst: University of Massachusetts Press.

Brewer, Jeutonne P. (1974) "The verb be in Early Black English: A study based on the WPA ex-slave narratives." unpublished PhD dissertation, University of North Carolina.

Brooks, Cleanth (1935) *The Relation of the Alabama-Georgia Dialect to the Provincial Dialects of Great Britain*. Baton Rouge: Louisiana State University.

—— (1985) *The Language of the American South*. Athens: University of Georgia Press.

Butters, Ronald R. (1987) "Linguistic convergence in a North Carolina community." In *Variation in language: NWAV-XV at Stanford*, Keith M. Denning, Sharon Inkelas, Faye McNair-Knox, and John R. Rickford (eds.) Stanford: Department of Linguistics, Stanford University.

—— (1988) "The historical present as evidence of Black/White convergence/ divergence." In *Proceedings of the Sixth International Conference in Dialectology, 3–7 August 1987, University College of North Wales*, Alan R. Thomas (ed.). Avon, England: Multilingual Matters, pp. 637–649.

—— (1989) *The Death of Black English: Divergence and Controversy in Black and White Vernaculars*. Frankfurt: Peter Lang.

Davis, Lawrence M. (1969) "Dialect research: Mythology and reality." *Orbis* 18: 332–337. Reprinted in 1971 in *Black–White Speech Relationships*, Walt Wolfram and Nona H. Clarke (eds.). Washington, DC: Center for Applied Linguistics, pp. 90–98.

—— (1970) "Social dialectology in America: A critical survey." *Journal of English Linguistics* 4: 46–56.

Day, Richard R. (1973) "Patterns of variation in copula and tense in the Hawaiian post-creole continuum. "*Working Papers in Linguistics* 5.2. Department of Linguistics, University of Hawaii. (Published version of Day's 1972 University of Hawaii dissertation.)

DeBose, Charles. E. (1988) Be *in Samaná English*. Occasional Paper no. 21. Society for Caribbean Linguistics.

—— (1994) "Samaná English and the creolist hypothesis." Paper presented at NWAV 23, Stanford University.

DeBose, Charles and Nicholas Faraclas (1993) "An Africanist approach to the linguistic study of Black English: Getting to the roots of the tense–modality–aspect and copula systems in Afro-American." In *Africanisms in Afro-American Language Varieties*, Salikoko S. Mufwene (ed.). Athens: University of Georgia Press, pp. 364–387.

DeCamp, David (1960) "Four Jamaican Creole texts with an introduction, phonemic transcriptions and glosses." In *Jamaican Creole*, Robert B. Le Page and David DeCamp (eds.). London: Macmillan, pp. 128–179.

—— (1971) "Toward a generative analysis of a post-creole continuum." In *Pidginization and Creolization of Languages*, Dell Hymes (ed.). Cambridge: Cambridge University Press, pp. 349–370.

D'Eloia, Sarah G. (1973) "Issues in the analysis of Nonstandard Negro English: A review of J. L. Dillard's Black English." *Journal of English Linguistics* 7: 87–106.

Denning, Keith M. (1989) "A sound change in Vernacular Black English." *Language Variation and Change* 1: 145–167.

Dennis, Jamie and Jerrie Scott (1975) "Creole formation and reorganization." Paper presented at the International Conference on Pidgins and Creoles, Hawaii, 6–11 January.

Dillard, J. L. (1972) *Black English: Its History and Usage in the United States*. New York: Random House.

—— (1992) *A History of American English*. New York City: Longman.

Dunlap, Howard G. (1974) "Social aspects of a verb form." *Publications of the American Dialect Society* 61.2.

Edwards, Walter F. (1980) "Varieties of English in Guyana: Some comparisons with BEV." *Linguistics* 18: 289–309.

—— (1991) "A comparative description of Guyanese creole and Black English preverbal marker *don*." In *Verb Phrase Patterns in Black English and Caribbean Creoles*, Walter F. Edwards and Don Winford (eds.). Detroit: Wayne State University Press, pp. 240–255.

—— (1992) "Sociolinguistic behavior in a Detroit inner-city." *Language in Society* 21: 93–115.

Ewers, Traute (1996) *The origin of American Black English: Be-Forms in the HOODOO Texts*. Berlin and New York: Mouton.

Fasold, Ralph W. (1976) "One hundred years from syntax to phonology." In *Papers from the Parasession on Diachronic Syntax*, Sanford Steever, Salikoko S. Mufwene, and Carol C. Walker (eds.). Chicago: Chicago Linguistic Society, pp. 79–87.

—— (1981) "The relation between black and white speech in the South." *American Speech* 56: 163–189.

—— (1990) *The Sociolinguistics of Language*. Oxford: Basil Blackwell.

Fasold, Ralph W., William Labov, Fay Boy Vaughn-Cooke, Guy Bailey, Walt Wolfram, Arthur K. Spears, and John R. Rickford (1987) "Are black and white vernacular diverging?" Papers from the NWAVE-16 panel discussion. *American Speech* 62.1: 3–80.

Feagin, Crawford (1979) *Variation and Change in Alabama English*. Washington: Georgetown University Press.

Ferguson, Charles A (1971) "Absence of copula and the notion of simplicity: A study of normal speech, baby talk, foreigner talk, and pidgins." In *Pidginization and Creolization*

194

of Languages, Dell Hymes (ed.). Cambridge: Cambridge: Cambridge University Press, pp. 141–150.

Gilbert, Glenn G. (1985) "Hugo Schuchardt and the Atlantic Creoles: A newly discovered manuscript 'On the Negro English of West Africa.'" *American Speech* 60: 31–63.

Graff, David, William Labov, and Wendell Harris (1986) "Testing listeners' reactions to markers of ethnic identity: A new method for sociolinguistic research." In *Diversity and Diachrony*, David Sankoff (ed.). Amsterdam and Philadelphia: John Benjamins, pp. 45–58.

Hall, Robert A. (1966) *Pidgin and Creole Languages*. Ithaca: Cornell University Press.

Hancock, Ian F. (1986) "The domestic hypothesis, diffusion, and componentiality: An account of Atlantic Anglophone Creole origins." In *Substrata Versus Universals in Creole Genesis*, Pieter Muysken and Norval Smith (eds.). Amsterdam: John Benjamins, pp. 71–102.

Hannah, Dawn (1996) "Copula absence in Samaná English." PhD qualifying paper, Department of Linguistics, Stanford University. Revised version to appear in *American Speech*.

Holm, John (1976) "Copula variability on the Afro-American continuum." In *Conference Preprints, First Annual Meeting of the Society for Caribbean Linguistics*, compiled by George Cave. Turkeyen: University of Guyana.

—— (1984) "Variability of the copula in Black English and its creole kin." *American Speech* 59: 291–309.

—— (1988) *Pidgins and Creoles*, vol. 1. Cambridge: Cambridge University Press.

—— (1992) "A theoretical model for semi-creolization." Paper presented at the Ninth Biennial Conference of the Society for Caribbean Linguistics, University of the West Indies, Barbados.

Hyatt, Harry Middleton (ed.) (1970–78) *Hoodoo – Conjuration – Witchcraft – Rootwork*. 5 vols. Hannibal, MO: Western Publishing Inc.

Hymes, Dell (1971) Introduction to part 3, "General conceptions of process." In *Pidginization and Creolization of Languages*, Dell Hymes (ed.). Cambridge: Cambridge University Press, pp. 65–90.

Johnson, Guy B. (1930) "The speech of the Negro." In *Folk-Say: A Regional Miscellany*. Norman: University of Oklahoma Press, pp. 346–358.

Krapp, G. (1924) "The English of the Negro." *American Mercury* 2: 190–195.

—— (1925) *The English Language in America*. New York: Century.

Kurath, Hans (1928) "The origin of dialectal differences in spoken American English." *Modern Philology* 25: 285–295.

Labov, William (1969) "Contraction, deleletion, and inherent variability of the English copula." *Language* 45: 725–762.

—— (1972a) *Language in the Inner City: Studies in the Black English Vernacular*. Philadelphia: University of Pennsylvania Press.

—— (1972b) *Sociolinguistic Patterns*. Philadelphia: University of Pennsylvania Press.

—— (1982) "Objectivity and commitment in linguistic science: The case of the Black English trial in Ann Arbor." *Language in Society* 11: 165–201.

Labov, William and Wendell A. Harris (1986) "De facto segregation of black and white vernaculars." In *Diversity and Diachrony*, David Sankoff (ed.). Amsterdam: John Benjamins, pp. 1–24.

Labov, William, Paul Cohen, Clarence Robbins, and John Lewis (1968) *A Study of the*

Non-Standard English of Negro and Puerto Rican Speakers in New York City. 2 vols. Philadelphia: US Regional Survey.

Maynor, Natalie (1988) "Written records of spoken language: How reliable are they?" In *Methods in Dialectology*, Alan R. Thomas (ed.). Clevedon and Philadelphia: Multilingual Matters, pp. 109–120.

McDavid, Raven I. (1965) "American social dialects." *College English* 26: 254–259.

McDavid, Raven I. and Virginia G. McDavid (1951) "The relationship of the speech of negroes to the speech of whites." *American Speech* 26: 3–17. Reprinted in 1971 in *Black–White Speech Relationships*, Walt Wolfram and Nona H. Clarke (eds.). Washington, DC: Center for Applied Linguistics, pp. 16–40.

McElhinny, Bonnie (1993) "Copula and auxiliary contraction in the speech of White Americans." *American Speech* 68: 371–399.

McWhorter, John (1995) "Sisters under the skin: A case for genetic relationship between the Atlantic English-based creoles." *Journal of Pidgin and Creole Languages* 10.2: 289–333.

Mesthri, Rajend (1992) "English in language shift: The history, structure and sociolinguistics of South African Indian English. Cambridge: Cambridge University Press.

Montgomery, Michael (1991) "The linguistic value of the ex-slave recordings." In *The Emergence of Black English: Text and Commentary*, Guy Bailey, Natalie Maynor, and Patricia Cukor-Avila (eds.). Amsterdam and Philadelphia: John Benjamins, pp. 173–189.

Montgomery, Michael, Janet M. Fuller, and Sharon Paparone (1993) "The black men has wives and Sweet harts [and third person plural -*s*] jest like the white men: Evidence for verbal -*s* from written documents on 19th-century African American speech." *Language Variation and Change* 5: 335–357.

Mufwene, Salikoko (1983) *Some Observations on the Verb in Black English Vernacular.* Austin: African and Afro-American Studies and Research Center, University of Texas at Austin.

—— (1992) "Ideology and facts on African American Vernacular English." *Pragmatics* 2(2): 141–166.

—— (1996a) "The Founder Principle in creole genesis." *Diachronica* XIII: 83–134.

—— (1996b) "Creolization and grammaticization: What creolists could contribute to research on grammaticization." In *Changing Functions, Changing Meanings*, Philip Baker and Anand Syea (eds.). London: University of Westminster Press.

—— (in press) "African American English." In *The Cambridge History of the English Language*, vol. 6, J. Algeo (ed.). *History of American English*. Cambridge: Cambridge University Press.

Myhill, John and Wendell A. Harris (1986) "The use of the verbal -*s* inflection in BEV." In *Diversity and Diachrony*, David Sankoff (ed.). Amsterdam and Philadelphia: John Benjamins, pp. 25–31.

Pardoe, T. Earl (1937) "An historical and phonetic study of the Negro dialect." PhD dissertation, Louisiana State University.

Parish, Peter J. (1979) *Slavery: The Many Faces of a Southern Institution.* Durham: British Association for American Studies.

Poplack, Shana and David Sankoff (1987) "The Philadelphia story in the Spanish Caribbean." *American Speech* 62: 291–314.

Poplack, Shana and Sali Tagliamonte (1989) "There's no tense like the present: Verbal -*s* inflection in early Black English." *Language Variation and Change* 1: 47–89.

Reprinted 1991 in *The Emergence of Black English: Text and Commentary*, Guy Bailey, Natalie Maynor, and Patricia Cukor-Avila (eds.). Amsterdam and Philadelphia: John Benjamins, pp. 275–324.

—— (1991) "African American English in the diaspora: Evidence from old-line Nova Scotians." *Language Variation and Change* 3: 301–339.

—— (1994) "*-S* or nothing: Marking the plural in the African American diaspora." *American Speech* 69: 227–259.

Rawick, George P. (ed.) (1972–79) *The American Slave: A Composite Autobiography*. 10 vols., 1972. Supplement series I, 12 vols., 1977. Supplement series II, 10 vols., 1979. Westport, CT: Greenwood Press.

Reinecke, John E., Stanley M. Tsuzaki, David DeCamp, Ian F. Hancock, and Richard E. Wood (eds.) (1975) *A Bibliography of Pidgin and Creole Languages*. Honolulu: University Press of Hawaii.

Repka, Patricia L. and Rick Evans (1986) "The evolution of the present tense of the verb *to Be*: Evidence from literary discourse." Paper presented at the Sixth Biennial Conference of the Society for Caribbean Linguistics, St. Augustine, Trinidad.

Rickford, John R. (1974) "The insights of the mesolect." In *Pidgins and Creoles: Current Trends and Prospects*, David DeCamp and Ian F. Hancock (eds.). Washington, DC: Georgetown University Press.

—— (1977) "The question of prior creolization in Black English." In *Pidgin and Creole Linguistics*, Albert Valdman (ed.). Bloomington: Indiana University Press, pp. 190–221.

—— (1979) "Variation in a creole continuum: Quantitative and implicational approaches." unpublished PhD dissertation, University of Pennsylvania.

—— (1980) "How does DOZ disappear?" In *Issues in English Creoles: Papers from the 1975 Hawaii Conference*, Richard Day (ed.). Heidelberg: Julius Groos, pp. 77–96.

—— (1985) "Ethnicity as a sociolinguistic boundary." *American Speech* 60: 90–125.

—— (1986) "Social contact and linguistic diffusion: Hiberno-English and New World Black English." *Language* 62.1: 245–89.

—— (1987a) *Dimensions of a Creole Continuum: History, Texts and Linguistic Analysis of Guyanese Creole*. Stanford: Stanford University Press.

—— (1987b) "The haves and have nots: Sociolinguistic surveys and the assessment of speaker competence." *Language in Society* 16.2: 149–177.

—— (1991a) "Representativeness and reliability of the ex-slave materials, with special reference to Wallace Quarterman's recording and transcript." In *The Emergence of Black English: Text and Commentary*, Guy Bailey, Natalie Maynor, and Patricia Cukor-Avila (eds.). Amsterdam and Philadelphia: John Benjamins, pp. 191–212.

—— (1991b) "Grammatical variation and divergence in Vernacular Black English." In *Internal and External Factors in Syntactic Change*, Marinel Gerritsen and Dieter Stein (eds.). Berlin and New York: Mouton, pp. 175–200.

—— (1991c) "Variation in the Jamaican Creole copula: New data and analysis." Paper presented at the Beryl Bailey Symposium, American Anthropology Association meeting, Chicago, November.

—— (1992a) "Pidgins and creoles." In *International Encyclopedia of Linguistics*, William Bright (ed.). Oxford: Oxford University Press, vol III, pp. 224–232.

—— (1992b) "The creole residue in Barbados." In *Old English and New: Studies in Honor of Frederic G. Cassidy*, Joan H. Hall, Nick Doane, and Dick Ringler (eds.). New York and London: Garland, pp. 183–201.

—— (1996) "Copula variability in Jamaican Creole and African American Vernacular English: A reanalysis of DeCamp's texts." In *Towards a Social Science of Language.* vol. 1: *Variation and Change in Language and Society,* Gregory R. Guy, Crawford Feagin, Deborah Schiffrin, and John Baugh (eds.). Amsterdam and Philadelphia: John Benjamins, pp. 357–372.

—— (1997) "Prior creolization of AAVE? Sociohistorical and textual evidence from the 17th and 18th centuries." *Journal of Sociolinguistics* 1: 315–336.

Rickford, John R., Arnetha Ball, Renee Blake, Raina Jackson, and Nomi Martin (1991) "Rappin on the copula coffin: Theoretical and methodological issues in the analysis of copula variation in African American Vernacular English." *Language Variation and Change* 3.1: 103–132.

Rickford, John R., and Renee Blake (1990) "Copula contraction and absence in Barbadian English, Samaná English and Vernacular Black English." In *Proceedings of the Sixteenth Annual Meeting of the Berkeley Linguistics Society,* 16–19 February 1990, Kira Hall, Jean-Pierre Koenig, Michael Meacham, Sondra Reinman, and Laurel A. Sutton (eds.). Berkeley, CA: Berkeley Linguistics Society, pp. 257–268.

Rickford, John R. and Faye McNair-Knox (1994) "Addressee- and topic-influenced style shift: A quantitative sociolinguistic study." In *Perspectives on Register: Situating Register Variation within Sociolinguistics,* Douglas Biber and Edward Finegan (eds.). Oxford: Oxford University Press, pp. 235–276.

Rickford, John R. and John McWhorter (1997) "Language contact and language generation: Pidgins and creoles." In *The Handbook of Sociolinguistics,* Florian Coulmas (ed.). Oxford: Blackwell, pp. 238–256.

Rowlands, E. C. (1969) *Teach Yourself Yoruba.* London: The English Universities Press.

Schneider, Edgar W. (1982) "On the history of Black English in the USA: Some new evidence." *English World Wide* 3: 18–46.

—— (1983) "The origin of the verbal -s in Black English." *American Speech* 58: 99–113.

—— (1989) *American Earlier Black English.* Tuscaloosa: University of Alabama Press.

—— (1993) "Africanisms in the grammar of Afro-American English: Weighing the evidence." In *Africanisms in Afro-American Language Varieties,* Salikoko S. Mufwene (ed.). Athens: University of Georgia Press, pp. 192–208.

—— (1997) "Earlier Black English revisited." In *Language Variety in the South Revisited,* Cynthia Bernstein, Thomas Nunnally, and Robin Sabino (eds.). Tuscaloosa: University of Alabama Press, pp. 35–50.

Schuchardt, Hugo (1914) *Die Sprache der Saramakkaneger in Surinam.* Amsterdam: Johannes Müller. (For English translation of preface, see Schuchardt 1980: 89–126).

—— (1980) *Pidgin and Creole Languages: Selected Essays,* Glenn G. Gilbert (ed. and trans.). Cambridge: Cambridge University Press.

Singler, John (1989) "Plural marking in Liberian Settler English, 1820–1980." *American Speech* 64: 40–64.

—— (1991a) "Liberian Settler English and the ex-slave recordings: A comparative study." In *The Emergence of Black English: Text and Commentary,* Guy Bailey, Natalie Maynor, and Patricia Cukor-Avila (eds.). Amsterdam and Philadelphia: John Benjamins, pp. 249–274.

—— (1991b) "Copula variation in Liberian Settler English and American Black English." In *Verb Phrase Patterns in Black English and Creoles,* Walter F. Edwards and Donald Winford (eds.). Detroit: Wayne State University Press, pp. 129–164.

—— (1993) "The Liberian Settler English copula revisited." Paper presented at NWAV 22, The University of Ottawa.

—— (to appear) "What's not new in AAVE." *American Speech.*

Smitherman, Geneva (1977) *Talkin and Testifyin: The Language of Black America.* Boston: Houghton Mifflin.

Southworth, Franklin (1971) "Detecting prior creolization: An analysis of the historical origins of Marathi." In *Pidginization and Creolization of Languages*, Dell Hymes (ed.). Cambridge: Cambridge University Press, pp. 255–274.

Stewart, William A. (1967) "Sociolinguistic factors in the history of American Negro dialects." *Florida FL Reporter* 5: 11.

—— (1968) "Continuity and change in American Negro dialects." *Florida FL Reporter* 6: 3–4, 14–16. 18.

—— (1969) "Historical and structural bases for the recognition of Negro dialect." In *Georgetown University Round Table on Languages and Linguistics 1969*, James E. Alatis (ed.). Washington, DC: Georgetown University Press, pp. 239–247.

—— (1970) (Includes 1967 & 1968.) "Toward a history of American negro dialect." *Language and Poverty*, Frederick Williams (ed.). Chicago: Markham, pp. 351–379.

Tagliamonte, Sali and Shana Poplack (1988) "How Black English *Past* got to the present." *Language in Society* 17.4: 513–533.

—— (1993) "The zero-marked verb: testing the creole hypothesis." *Journal of Pidgin and Creole Linguistics* 8: 171–206.

Thomason, Sarah G. and Terrence Kaufman (1988) *Language Contact, Creolization, and Genetic Linguistics.* Berkeley: University of California Press.

Traugott, Elizabeth Closs (1976) "Pidgins, creoles, and the origins of Vernacular Black English." In *Black English: A seminar*, Deborah Sears Harrison and Tom Trabassso (eds.). Hillsdale, NJ: Lawrence Erlbaum, pp. 57–93.

Turner, Lorenzo Dow (1949) *Africanisms in the Gullah Dialect.* Chicago: University of Chicago Press.

Viereck, Wolfgang (1988) "Invariant *be* in an unnoticed source of American Early Black English." *American Speech* 63: 291–303.

Wald, Benjamin (1995) "The problem of scholarly disposition G. Bailey, N. Maynor and P. Cukor-Avila (eds) *The Emergence of Black English*: Text and commentary." *Language in Society* 24.2: 245–257.

Williamson, Juanita (1972) "Selected features of speech: Black and White." *College Language Association* XIII: 420–433.

Winford, Donald (1980) "The creole situation in the context of sociolinguistic studies." In *Issues in English Creoles: Papers from the 1975 Hawaii Conference*, Richard R. Day (ed.). Heidelberg: Julius Groos, pp. 51–76.

—— (1992a) "Another look at the copula in Black English and Caribbean creoles." *American Speech* 67.1: 21–60.

—— (1992b) "Back to the past: The BEV/creole connection revisited." *Language Variation and Change* 4.3: 311–357.

—— (1997) "On the origins of African American Vernacular English – A creolist perspective. Part 1: The sociohistorical background." *Diachronica* XIV.

—— (forthcoming) "On the origins of African American Vernacular English – A creolist perspective. Part II: Structural features." *Diachronica* XV.

Wise, Claude Merton (1933) "Negro dialect." *The Quarterly Journal of Speech* 19: 523–528.

Wolfram, Walt (1969) *A Sociolinguistic Description of Detroit Negro Speech*. Washington, DC: Center for Applied Linguisics.

—— (1974) "The relationship of White Southern Speech to Vernacular Black English." *Language* 50.3: 498–527.

—— (1990) "Re-examining Vernacular Black English: Review article of Schneider 1989 and Butters 1989." *Language* 66: 121–133.

Wolfram, Walt, Kirk Hazen, and Jennifer Ruff Tamburro (1997) "Isolation within isolation: A solitary century of African American Vernacular English." *Journal of Sociolinguistics* 1: 7–38.

Part III

USE

7

WORD FROM THE HOOD:
THE LEXICON OF
AFRICAN-AMERICAN
VERNACULAR ENGLISH

Geneva Smitherman

7.1 Introduction

Hey, dog, whass hapnin?
> (Middle-aged lawyer greeting an old fraternity buddy)

I don't have no time for no "Wham bam, thank you, Mam!"
Gas me up, get me drunk, hit the skins, and scram.
> (Singer/rapper Mary J. Blige, from her 1992 album, *What's the 4 1 1?*)

When they tell you yo cancer in remission, all that mean is that bad
boy layin in the cut waitin for yo ass!
> (Middle-aged female nurse)

I-own know what dem white folk talkin bout – we never did git our
forty acres!
> (Senior female, retired domestic worker)

What red, black and green Afrikan B-boy wouldn't want to go over to
this twentysomething, Brooklyn flygirl's crib?
> (Louis Romain, "A rose grows in Brooklyn," *The Source*, July, 1993)

The Spirit got holt to him, he went to hollin and moanin and goin on,
next thang I know he talkin in tongue!
> (Senior male, church deacon, retired blue collar worker)

Crack or smack-uh take you to a sho end
You don't need it, jes throw that stuff away
You wonna git high, let the record play.
> (Rapper Ice-T, from his 1988 *Power* album)

The African-American vernacular English (AAVE) lexicon[1] reflects the dynamic, colorful span of language used by African Americans from all walks of life. There are unique English words and expressions among all segments of the community – from the young to the old; from Baptists to members of the Nation of Islam; from political activists to street people. When it comes to AAVE, the "boyz in the hood" do not have a corner on the market. To be sure, the urban Black youth culture that embraces Rap Music, graffiti, "Def Comedy Jam," "MTV," and baggy pants, i.e., *Hip Hop*, has contributed unique idioms and terms like *def* and *dope* to refer to something that is superb. But it was the senior Black women (aged 65+) in our research who had us all dying laughing when we finally understood what membership in the *Packer's Club* means: "a reference to older men who can't maintain an erection" and thus try, as one of the women put it, to "pack it in like chitlins." (*Chitlins* are 'the intestines of the hog, a delicacy that requires extensive cleaning and long hours of cooking before they can be eaten'.) Through the explosion of African-American comedy into contemporary mass culture, we made the acquaintance of *BeBe's kids* 'badly misbehaved kids', and gangs like Los Angeles' *Crips* and *Bloods* have taught us more than we ever wanted to know about powerful weapons called *AKs* 'AK-47 assault rifle' and *Nines* 'a nine-millimeter semi-automatic pistol'. But the 1960s Black Freedom Struggle,[2] reflected in the life and progressive ideas of Malcolm X, is the source of the Hip Hop fashion of wearing caps with a large

1   I have used the term "African-American vernacular English" to be consistent with the terminology chosen by the editors of this volume. However, it, like many of the labels linguists have used to refer to this speech phenomenon, is problematic, particularly when employed in the broader public arena, where the term "vernacular" is taken to refer to something of lowly status. The challenge is to formulate terminology that speaks to the African linguistic heritage, that covers the broad range of linguistic and rhetorical styles prevalent in the Black community, that is free of pejorative popular nuances, and that provides a linguistic guidepost for the development and empowerment of Africans in America – that is, terminology that is free of the "old paradigm ... based on the idea of European domination and the various critiques of that domination" (Blackshire-Belay 1996: 6). For over two decades now, African-American linguists, scholars, and activists have struggled with the problem of naming the language of the Black community. Even during the 1960s and 1970s, when the term "Black English" prevailed, most African-American intellectuals found that terminology problematic. Thus, in the 1973 conference on "Black English" convened by Black psychologist Robert Williams, the term "Ebonics" was put forth (*ebony* for Black people, *phonics* for sounds). Subsequently, Williams, who was one of the founders of the Association of Black Psychologists, published the conference proceedings under the title *Ebonics: The True Language of Black Folks* (Williams 1975). For a fuller treatment of this issue, see Mufwene (1992), Morgan (1994), Blackshire-Belay (1996).

2   The term *Black Freedom Struggle* characterizes the mass organized movement for Black empowerment that began with Mrs. Rosa Parks' now famous refusal to surrender her bus seat to a white man in Montgomery, Alabama, on 1 December 1955. Southern custom required that Blacks sitting in the "Colored" section of a bus give up their seats if the white section was filled. Mrs. Parks' unwillingness to do this led to her arrest and set in motion the Movement that would lead to the eradication of laws supporting racial segregation. The Black Freedom Struggle includes the Civil Rights Movement, led by Dr. Martin Luther King, Jr., and the Black Power Movement,

"X" emblazoned on them, appropriately deemed X *caps* in Hip Hop lingo. And many of the linguistic rituals in today's neighborhood basketball games, such as *trash talkin* 'boasting and negative talking about one's opponents so as to unnerve them', owe their genesis to *alley ball* 'basketball' players from the *Old School* (the 1960s and 1970s).

As the above examples demonstrate, the lexicon of the Black speech community crosses boundaries – sex, age, religion, social class, region. That is, the Black lexicon is comprised of idioms, phrases, terms, and other linguistic contributions from various sub-communities within the larger African-American community. The language and culture of these various sub-groups reflect the African-American experience. Thus, while it is the case that on one level, great diversity exists among African Americans today, on a deeper level, race continues to be the defining core of the Black Experience. It is quite a logical development, then, for Hip Hop culture to reintroduce race-conscious language from previous generations even as it contributes its own special lingo unrelated to race. For example, contemporary film-maker Spike Lee named his production company *Forty Acres and a Mule*, a Black expression that goes all the way back to the nineteenth century and the unfulfilled promise of emancipation. At least three decades before Spike Lee, the goal of land, expressed in the Black lexicon as *five states*,[3] had been placed on the nation's twentieth-century racial agenda. Both *forty acres* and *five states* recall the post-Civil War era and the bill passed by Congress in 1866. This legislation was designed to strengthen the Freedmen's Bureau (the Federal agency set up to resettle ex-slaves). The most interesting part of the bill, and the most controversial, stipulated that each ex-slave household should receive an allotment of "forty acres" of the land confiscated from the Confederacy, plus some start-up resources, captured in the Black lexical expression *forty acres, fifty dollars and a mule*. This payment for 246 years of free African labor in the Confederate states

spearheaded by Malcolm X. The terms *Black Liberation Movement* and *Black Movement* are also used to describe this era in the African-American experience. The decline of the Black Freedom Struggle by 1980 is generally attributed to attacks against Black leaders and activists in the form of assasinations (Martin Luther King, Jr., Malcolm X, Medgar Evers, Fred Hampton, Mark Clark, and others); imprisonment (Angela Davis, Ron Karenga, Benjamin Chavis, and others); and forced exile (Assata Shakur, Eldridge Cleaver, and others).

3 The Republic of New Africa (RNA), an organization founded during the early years of the Black Freedom Struggle, developed the concept of "five states" as reparations to Africans in America for over two centuries of free labor under enslavement. The five states were Alabama, Georgia, Louisiana, Mississippi, and South Carolina. The concept was derived from the areas of the South that constituted the *Black Belt*, where there had historically been the greatest concentration of Blacks (counties with 40 percent or more Black population). In the *Black Belt* South, Blacks had lived and worked the land continuously since enslavement. Although the idea was attacked and labeled "absurd" by the mainstream, it was merely an updating of the *forty acres* provision which the US Congress itself had attempted to make the law of the land in 1866. The RNA vision was that the five states would constitute a sovereign nation that African Americans could call their own.

not only would have provided reparations for enslavement, but it also would have established a base for self-sufficiency and initiated the economic development of the newly freed Black community. President Andrew Johnson, taking over after President Abraham Lincoln's assasination, vetoed the bill, and Congress was either unable, or unwilling, to override the veto. The Nation's 1866 failure to right the wrong of enslavement continues to haunt Blacks, particularly in this period of severe economic crises and of devastating social effects that result from an underdeveloped community.

A similar example exists in the concept of *cool*, although at first glance it might not seem to be a race-conscious idea. However, a disempowered group daily forced to face the possibility of its destruction can ill-afford to be "hot." Lynch mobs in the old days, police brutality in this new day – any heat generated by rage and anger could literally be dangerous to a Black person's health. Hence the value of calmness, suppressing one's rage and anger, that is, maintaining one's *cool* as a survival strategy. 1990s African-American youth talk about *chillin*, their middle-aged parents still refer to it as *keepin yo cool*, and an eighty-five-year-old Black man recently used the term *copasetic* to refer to the state of being *cool*.

In order to understand the AAVE lexicon, one needs to understand how and why this nation within a nation developed its unique way of using the English language. Which brings us to history and the importance of the past in understanding – and moving beyond – the present.

7.2 "What is Africa to me?"

What is Africa to me
Copper sun or scarlet sea,
Jungle star or jungle track,
Strong bronzed men, or regal black,
Women from whose loins I sprang
When the birds of Eden sang?
One three centuries removed
From the scenes his fathers loved,
Spicy grove, cinnamon tree,
What is Africa to me?
(Countee Cullen, "Heritage," 1925)

Down through the years, and especially in the decades since the Civil War, generations of African Americans have asked themselves the question posed by Harlem Renaissance[4] writer Countee Cullen. Long since removed from their native land, many Black Americans feel the same as some Blacks in my 1989 opinion poll[5] on the name change from *Black* to *African American*: "We are more American than African; we have been here too long," and "What do they mean about African American? By now we have no African in us." On the other hand, there are also many Black Americans who acknowledge a connection to Africa, what one of the people in the opinion poll called "our origin and cultural identity" (Smitherman 1991).

As far as historians, linguists, and other scholars go, during the first half of this century it was widely believed that enslavement had wiped out all traces of African languages and cultures, and that Black "differences" resulted from imperfect and inadequate imitations of European-American language and culture. For instance, Krapp (1925) presents this view about the speech of Africans in America. In the 1960s, these opinions came under close scrutiny and were soundly challenged by a number of experts, such as the linguist Dillard (1972), and the historian Blassingame (1979). Today, scholars generally agree that the African heritage was not totally wiped out, and that both African-American language and African-American culture have roots in African patterns. (This view had also been advanced by Herskovits (1941) and Turner (1949), but they were a distinct minority in those days.) Over time, and after prolonged contact with European Americans, Africans in America adopted some Eurocentric patterns, and their African patterns of language and culture were modified – but they were not erased. African-American language and culture, then, reflect a dual heritage. As DuBois (1990 [1903]) put it, "One ever feels his two-ness – an American, a Negro."

The uniqueness of AAVE is evident in three areas: (1) patterns of grammar and pronunciation; (2) verbal rituals from the oral tradition and the continued importance of the word as in African cultures; and (3) the lexicon, developed by giving special meanings to English words, a practice that goes back to enslavement and to the need for a system of communication that only those in the slave community could understand. Although here we are concerned only with the lexicon itself, there are correct ways of saying these words, of talking Black, which depend on knowledge of the rules of AAVE grammar and pronunciation. Like a popular radio DJ said to a man who phoned in a request for him to play D. J. Jazzy Jeff & The Fresh Prince's *Summertime*: "Okay, man, I'll play it for you, but see, it ain't summertime, it's summahtime." Or consider Rap Music's frequently used, if controversial, word *ho*, which comes from the AAVE

---

4 The Harlem Renaissance is considered to be an era of great flowering of Black talent in literature, music, and the arts. Also known as the *Negro Renaissance* and the era of *The New Negro*, the
Harlem Renaissance years were the 1920s. Whites flocked to uptown New York clubs and cabarets
to soak up Black culture, and Harlem was viewed as a cultural mecca. One white writer even
celebrated this uptown "paradise" with a book entitled *Nigger Heaven*. Many whites also finan-
cially supported struggling Black artists. However, the impact of this era on the masses of African
Americans was summed up by writer Langston Hughes, himself a member of the Renaissance
literati, who indicated that ordinary Harlemites hadn't even heard of the Renaissance, and if they
had, it hadn't "raised their wages any."
5 The survey was conducted between May and September 1989 in five cities with large African-
American populations: Atlanta, Chicago, Cincinnati, Philadelphia, and Detroit.

pronunciation of *whore*, not to be confused with *hoe*, as the white teacher in the film *House Party* did when she asked her Black male student why he called another Black male student's mother a "garden tool." Other examples include *def* (from the AAVE pronunciation of *death*), *wit*, from *with*, and *thang* from *thing* (as in *It's a Black thang*, 'reference to any cultural or social practice, behavior, or attitude associated with Blacks and the Black experience'). A more elaborate inventory and analysis of AAVE syntax and phonology can be found in other articles in this volume. For our purposes here, suffice it to say that a good deal of the lexicon depends on an Africanized way of speaking the English language.

The African-American oral tradition is rooted in a belief in the power of the word. The African concept of "Nommo" 'the word' is believed to be the force of life itself. To speak is to make something come into being; thus senior Black Americans will often use the cautionary statement "Don't speak on it" in the face of some negative possibility *goin down* 'occurring'. On the other hand, once something is given the force of speech, it is binding – hence the familiar Black expression *Yo word is yo bond*, which in today's Hip Hop culture has become *word is born*. The Hip Hop expressions *word, word up, word to the mother*, which are used as positive, reinforcing conversational responses to something that is said or done, all stem from the value placed on speech. Creative, highly verbal talkers are valued; skillful use of African-American verbal traditions (such as *trash talkin*) will earn a person respect and recognition, that is, *props*. Which is not at all to state that African Americans *dis* 'disrespect, discount' the written word. However, like other groups with a surviving oral tradition, such as Native Americans, *book learning* and written documents are believed to be limited in what they can convey and teach. *Check out* 'observe' the *educated fool* 'a person with book learning but no common sense'.

The act of two people engaged in conversation is referred to as an *A and B conversation*, because communication in Black requires dialogue between "A" and "B," not "A" lecturing to "B." Constant exchange is necessary for real communication to take place. Scholars refer to this style of talk as "Call–Response." It has been ritualized in the traditional Black church, particularly in the back-and-forth exchange between the preacher and the congregation during the sermon. But even outside the church, whenever African Americans communicate, Call–Response abounds. Often the verbal responses are punctuated by different styles of *giving five* 'a non-verbal way of agreeing with what someone has said by connecting the palm(s) of your hand or your fist(s) with theirs in a variety of positions', e.g., the now-popular *high five* 'palms slapped in mid-air'. The only wrong thing you can do in a Black conversation is not respond at all because it suggests that one *ain wit* the conversation 'i.e., disengaged, distant, emotionally disconnected with the speaker or speakers'. *Bet* and *word* are Hip Hop responses used to affirm what is being said, as does the older expression, *Show, you right* 'Yes, I agree with you; you are speaking truth'. *Scared of you* is a response that acknowledges and celebrates some special achievement or unique action or statement made by another person, while *Shut the noise!*, as well as the older variation, *Shut up!*, means the exact opposite, that is, 'Keep on with what you are saying; Talk on; I'm with you.'

The Traditional Black Church[6] has been the single most significant force in nurturing the surviving African linguistic and cultural traditions of African America. Over the centuries, the church has stood as a rich reservoir of terms and expressions in Black lingo. Straight out of the church have come expressions like *on time* (acknowledging that something occurred at the appropriate psychological moment), and *Brotha/Sista* (generic terms for any African American); proverbs such as *God don't like ugly* (used as chastisement of negative behavior or talk, particularly when directed against another person), and *What go round come round* 'whatever has happened before will occur again, even if in a different form'; rituals such as *shoutin* (verbalized cries of ecstasy, shouts of joy) and *gittin the spirit* (evidencing intense emotional excitement and feelings of happiness by shouting, spontaneous dancing, clapping or waving the hands during musical performances at concerts, clubs, cabarets, and other places of entertainment). In the spirit-getting, tongue-speaking, vision-receiving,

---

6 The Traditional Black Church (TBC) refers to the Protestant denomination, dating back to enslavement, that fused African styles of worship and beliefs with European-American tenets of Christianity. The denominations are the African Methodist Episcopal (AME) church; the African Methodist Episcopal Zion (AMEZ) church; the Christian Methodist Episcopal (CME) church; the Baptists (the three groups being the National Baptist Convention (NBC) USA, Incorporated; the National Baptist Convention of America (NBCA) Unincorporated; and the Progressive National Baptist Convention (PNBC)); the Church of God in Christ (COGIC); the Pentecostal church; the Holiness church; and the Sanctified church. The worship forms of the TBC include a belief in spirit-possession, that is, that a person's body can be taken over by a divine force (the Holy Spirit), expressed by *talkin' in tongue, holy dancing, shouting, moaning*; the use of uptempo, passionate music, songs, and musical instruments (such as the drum, organ, guitar); Call–Response/interaction between preacher and congregation, as well as between members of the congregation during the service.

Historically and down to the present day, the church has been a critical institutional force in the liberation, survival, and day-to-day life of Black people. Many slave rebellions were planned in the church, and there is a history of activist leadership among preachers, dating from preacher Nat Turner, who, in 1831, led what has been deemed the greatest slave rebellion, to Reverend Dr Martin Luther King, leader in the Black Freedom Struggle of the 1960s. Further, the church has served as an important social unit where there is some kind of activity almost every day of the week, and where everyday Black people have opportunities to develop and exercise their abilities in speaking, teaching, singing, organizing, planning, etc. In their *The Black Church in the African American Experience*, Drs C. Eric Lincoln and Lawrence H. Mamiya (1990) sum it up this way:

> The Black church has no challenger as the cultural womb of the black community. Not only did it give birth to new institutions such as schools, banks, insurance companies, and low income housing, it also provided an academy and an arena for political activities, and it nurtured young talent for musical, dramatic, and artistic development . . . multifarious levels of community involvement [are] found in the Black church, in addition to the traditional concerns of worship, moral nurture, education, and social control. Much of black culture is heavily indebted to the black religious tradition, including most forms of black music, drama, literature, storytelling, and even humor.

Amen-saying, sing-song preaching, holy-dancing Traditional Black Church, the oral tradition is *live!* 'exciting, lively, high-spirited'. This is so because the church has not been pressured to take on Eurocentric culture and language. As the only independent African-American institution, the Black church does not have to answer to white folk!

Paramount in the African-American experience, the church is a religious as well as a social unit in the community. True enough, the church adopted EuroAmerican Christianity, but it Africanized this Christianity. The church maintained the African concept of the unity of the sacred and secular worlds. That is, all of life is viewed as holy. No wonder, then, that many popular singers came out of the church and comfortably shift back and forth between the church and the world. *Diva* 'a superbly talented, accomplished woman' Aretha Franklin comes immediately to mind. Such entertainers incorporate elements of the communication style of the church into their musical style. James Brown, to whom so many Hip Hop artists owe a great musical debt, is another excellent example. Rappers *sample* 'borrow' richly and freely from James Brown, which is to say that they are actually reflecting the Africanized communication style of the church through this borrowing.

What is Africa to the lingo of today's *hoods* (neighborhoods, communities)? It is the source of *Nommo* and the *Bloods'* 'Black people's' respect for and celebration of the power of the word, as can be witnessed today in Rap. It made possible the development of the African-American oral tradition. It provided the basis for the integrity of AAVE grammar and the Black lexicon. Africa is the mothership. And while not all of African-American language and culture can be traced to African language patterns, a lot of it can. As ex-enslaved Cato Carter put it back in the 1930s: "Everythang I tells you am the truth, but they's plenty I cain't tell you."

7.3 From *African* to *African American*

> ... just as we were called colored, but were not that ... and then Negro, but not that ... to be called Black is just as baseless ... Black tells you about skin color and what side of town you live on. African American evokes discussion of the world.
>
> Reverend Jesse Jackson (quoted in Page 1989 and Wilkerson 1989)

Names for the race have been a continuing issue since 1619, when the first slave ship landed at Jamestown. From *African* to *Colored*, to *negro*, to *Negro* (with the capital), to *Black*, to *African American*, with side trips to *AfroAmerican*, *AfriAmerican*, *AfraAmerican*, and *Afrikan* ... What are we Africans in America, today 35-million strong, "we people who are darker than blue," as Curtis Mayfield once sang, to call ourselves?

Debates rage. The topic is discussed at conferences. Among leaders and intellectuals, as well as among everyday people, the issue is sometimes argued so hotly that folk stop speaking to each other! In 1904, the AME *Church Review* sponsored a symposium of Black leaders to debate whether the "n" of *negro* should be capitalized. However, participants of that symposium went beyond the mere question of capitalization to debate whether *negro* was even the right name for the race in the first place. In 1967, during the shift from *Negro* to *Black*, and again in 1989, during the shift from *Black* to *African American*, *Ebony Magazine* devoted several pages to the question, "What's in a Name?"

. . . And the beat goes on. Because the status of Blacks remains unsettled. Name changes and debates over names reflect our uncertain status and come to the forefront during crises and upheavals in the Black condition.

Although African Americans are linked to Africans on the *Continent* and in the *Diaspora*, the Black American, as the late writer James Baldwin once put it, is a unique creation. For one thing, other Diasporic Africans claim citizenship in countries that are virtually all-Black – Jamaicans, Bajans, Nigerians, Ghanains, etc. are not minorities in their native lands. For another, not only are Blacks a distinct minority in America, our status as first-class citizens is debatable, even at this late hour of US history. As a *Sista* 'Black woman' said about Rodney King's beating in Los Angeles, the torching of a Black man by whites in Florida, and Malice Green's death at the hands of two white Detroit policemen: "After all we done been through, here it is the 1990s, and we still ain free." Some activists have coined the phrase *neo-slavery* to capture the view that the present Black condition, with whites still powerful and Blacks still powerless, is still enslavement – it's just in a new form.

Blacks are a minority amidst a population who look distinctly different physically, and who promote race supremacist standards of physical attractiveness. This state of affairs has created a set of negative attitudes about skin color, hair, and other physical features that are reflected in the AAVE lexicon – terms such as *good hair* 'straight hair, like that of whites' vs. *bad hair* 'kinky, that is, tightly curled hair, like that of Blacks'; *high yellow* (very light-complexioned Black person); *liver lips* 'dark lips, reddish or purplish color'. Because black skin color was so devalued at one time, to call an African person "black" was perceived and labelled as *callin* that person *outa they name* 'insulting someone by use of a negative label or an implicit accusation'. It was "If you white, you all right, if you brown, stick around, if you black, git back." Thus the necessity, during the Black Freedom Struggle of the 1960s and 1970s, of purging the racial label *Black* and subsequently adopting it as a name for the race in symbolic celebration of the changed status of Africans in America.

But back to the *Rip* 'the beginning, or the point before a verbal digression'. The British Colonists, who would become Americans in 1776, called the Africans "free" (a few were, but most were not), "slave," or, following fifteenth-century Portuguese slave traders, *negro* (Portuguese adjective, meaning 'black'). But the Africans called themselves *African* and so designated their churches and organizations – such as the names African Educational and Benevolent Society, African Episcopal Church, and African Masonic Lodge No. 459. In those early years, the thought was Africa on my mind and in my *mind's eye* 'the inner eye of the brain, the source of insight and foresight'. Enslaved Africans kept thinking and hoping, all the way up until the nineteenth century, that they would one day return to Mother Africa. Some hummed the tune "I'll fly away," believing that, like the legendary hero Solomon, they would be able to fly back to Africa. And especially after fighting at Lexington, Concord, and Bunker Hill in America's Revolutionary War, they *thought* they would be free to return home. Instead, the thirteen British colonies that became the United States tightened the reins on their African slaves, passing laws abolishing temporary enslavement and indentured servitude for Africans, and making them slaves for life.

By 1800, several generations of Africans had been born on American soil, thousands had been transported from Africa, and the Black population numbered over one million. Both the vision and the possibility of returning to Africa had become impractical and remote. Further, a movement had begun to abolish slavery and to make the Africans citizens. And both free and enslaved Africans were becoming critically aware of their contributions to the development of American wealth. In light of this new reality and in preparation for citizenship and for what they thought would be opportunities to enjoy the national wealth they had helped create through two hundred years of free labor, enslaved Africans began to call themselves *Colored* (often spelled *coloured* in those days), and the designation *African* declined in use.

Colored was used throughout much of the nineteenth century until the white backlash began. The year 1877 marked the end of Reconstruction and set the stage for "the Coloreds" to be put back in their "place." The political deal cut in *DC*[7] 'Washington, DC' led to the withdrawal of the Federal/Union troops, which had been stationed in the South to insure justice for the ex-enslaved Africans. Power and home rule were returned to the Old Confederacy. The "freedmen" (as they were called by the Federal Government and whites) lost the small gains in education, citizenship, and political power that the Civil War and the Emancipation Proclamation had made possible. New forms of repression and torture began – lynch mobs, Ku Klux Klan, loss of voting rights, and the

---

7 Although Rutherford B. Hayes had won the Presidency by popular vote, the Presidential race of 1876 came down to a count of the electoral votes in order to make Hayes' election official. Southern Democrats in the House of Representatives instituted a filibuster, preventing the electoral votes from being counted; their intent was to create chaos by filibustering until Inauguration Day. Hayes and his boys, however, wanted the Presidency badly, and so in back rooms of the capital, a deal was cut. In return for the South's calling off the filibuster and permitting the Electoral College to cast its votes so Hayes could be named President, the Federal Government would withdraw the Union troops from the South, it would begin a nineteenth-century form of "benign neglect" of the Negro, and finally, the Federal Government would return home rule to the South.

beginning of separate and (*un*)equal. By 1900, the quest was on for a new name to capture the new reality of being neither "slave nor free," as one ex-enslaved African put it.

Although some *Colored* had begun using and rallying for the label *negro*, when the National Association for the Advancement of Colored People (NAACP) was founded in 1909, the community had not yet reached group consensus. The push for *negro* and for its capitalization hit its full stride during the period between the two World Wars. The vision was that with the US campaign to "make the world safe for democracy," and with *Colored* soldiers shedding their blood for America, surely the yet-unsettled contradictory situation of Africans in America would be resolved on the side of first-class citizenship and economic equity. Leaders such as Dr. W. E. B. DuBois, editor of the NAACP journal, *Crisis*, launched a massive nationwide effort to capitalize and to elevate the Portuguese adjective *negro* to a level of dignity and respect. The NAACP mailed out over 700 letters to publishers and editors. Community newsletters addressed the issue, debates were held, and the name issue was addressed in talks and sermons in the Traditional Black Church. By 1930, the major European-American media were using and capitalizing *Negro*. (The two glaring exceptions were *Forum* Magazine and the US Government Printing Office, which continued for some time to use the lower case of *negro*.) *The New York Times* put it this way: "[This is] not merely a typographical change ... [but] an act in recognition of racial self-respect for those who have been for generations in the 'lower case'."

Negro was the name until the 1960s, when Africans in America struggled to throw off the shackles of Jim Crow and embraced Black culture, the Black experience – and black skin color. Again, conferences were held, many under the rubric of "Black Power," debates ensued, and yes, folk had hot arguments and *fell out with* one another 'severed their relationship' about abandoning the name *Negro* for *Black*, which was "only an adjective," as it was often put. However, the motion of history could not be stopped. The name change to *Black* and the profound significance of this change in the language and life of Blacks was captured in a 1968 popular hit song by James Brown: "Say it loud: I'm Black, and I'm proud."

The final period in the name debate (for now at least) began in late 1988 with a proposal from Dr. Ramona Edelin, President of the National Urban Coalition, to call the upcoming 1989 summit the *African American*, rather than the *Black*, Summit. She asserted that this name change "would establish a cultural context for the new agenda." Her vision was that present-day Africans in America were facing a new reality: the erosion of hard-won progress since the late 1970s, high unemployment, the rise of racism, the growth of urban youth violence, the proliferation of crack (introduced, it was widely argued, by the CIA), and the general deterioration of the community. The situation called for a reassessment within the framework of a global identity, linking Africans in North America with those on the Continent and throughout the Diaspora.

As in previous eras, the name issue, this time around involving the shift from *Black* to *African American*, has been debated at community forums and conferences. It has been the topic of conversation and heated arguments at family reunions, social gatherings, church events, the barber shop, and the *beauty shop* (a gathering place where Black women not only get their hair done but also, through verbal interaction, engage in social bonding). The change has not been as cataclysmic, though, as the shift from *Negro* to *Black* was in the 1960s, since *African American* lacks the negative history of *Black*. Further, *African American* returns us to the source – the *African* of early years, but with a significant dimension added: "American." This addition calls attention to four hundred years of building wealth in America and legitimates the demand for political and economic equity. This argument was put forth as long ago as 1829 by David Walker, one of the first *red, black and green Brothers*, in his *Appeal*, which was published during the era of *Colored*.[8] Calling for open rebellion against enslavement, and opposing the American Colonization Society's plan to resettle enslaved Africans in Africa, Walker stated:

> Men who are resolved to keep us in eternal wretchedness are also bent on sending us to Liberia . . . America is more our country than it is the whites' – we have enriched it with our BLOOD AND TEARS.
> (Appeal, in four Articles: Together with a Preamble to the Coloured Citizens of the World, but in particular, and very Expressly to those in the United States of America (Walker 1829))

To date, *African American* appears to have caught on throughout the community although *Black* continues to be used also (and, to a lesser extent, the name *African*, spelled as *African* or *Afrikan*). In opinion polls about the name issue, Black youth are the strongest supporters of *African American*, which is not surprising, given Hip Hop culture's *African-centered* consciousness which relocates Africa from the margins to the center of Black American life, and views Blacks as subjects, rather than as objects, of history. However, there are those – generally the parents and older siblings of the youth – who, like Black women in our Detroit sample (Smitherman 1991) still favor *Black*, because this name generated an intense, long-overdue struggle over old, past scripts of racial self-hatred, and because the eventual adoption of the name *Black* symbolized a victorious shift to the positive in the African-American psyche.

8 "Historically, red, black and green are the colors of the flag of the 'Black Nation'; currently the color combination suggests strong identification with Blackness and the Black Experience".

7.4 "They done taken my blues and gone": Black talk crosses over

A 16-year-old white Pennsylvanian says his high school is full of "wiggers," whites . . . desperate to adopt black modes of dress and conduct . . . Call 'em wanna-bes, call 'em rip-offs, call 'em suckers, but they're everywhere – white folks who think they're black . . . whites have been riffing off (or ripping off) black cultural forms for more than a century and making a lot more money from them . . . [whites] cavalierly adopt . . . the black mantle without having to experience life-long racism, restricted economic opportunity, or any of the thousand insults that characterize black American life . . . It's a curious spectacle . . .

(White journalist, James Ledbetter, staff writer for the *Village Voice*, in "Imitation of Life," from the Fall 1992 preview issue of *Vibe Magazine*)

In the 1990s USA, the "curious spectacle" is everywhere. White males *hoop* 'play basketball' on courts in Great Falls, Montana, in Oak Park, Illinois, in Orange County, California, and in Brownsville, Tennessee, *high-fivin* it and *talkin trash*, often without the slightest inkling that they are doing a *Black thang*. And they think nothing of donning X *caps* (symbolizing Malcolm X, 1960s Black leader), wearing them sideways or backwards as is fashionable in the *hood*. White females *sport* 'display' *tudes* 'attitudes; oppositional, arrogant, defiant posture' of twenty-first-century assertive womanhood as they rap "Fly Girl" from Queen Latifah's 1991 album, *Nature of A Sista*:

I always hear "Yo, Baby" . . .
No, my name ain't "Yo,"
And I ain't got yo "baby."

Coming into their own, White girls issue ultimatums to their *wiggas* 'Whites who act Black, White niggas', *dropping science* 'enlightening, informing' from Mary J. Blige's 1991 title cut, "What's the 4 1 1?":

The same ol shit you pulled last week on Kim,
I'm not havin that . . .
So come correct with some respect. . . .

A 1993 article by a European American used the title "A new way to talk that talk" to describe a new talk show (*talk that talk*, 'to use the forms of the AAVE verbal tradition; speaking in a powerful, convincing manner'). Webster's tenth edition of its *Collegiate Dictionary* listed *boom box* 'large, portable stereo' as just a plain old word, with no label indicating "slang," "sub-standard," or "Black." A lengthy 1993 article in the *New York Times Magazine*, entitled "Talking trash," discussed this old Black verbal tradition as the "art of conversation in the NBA." And in his first year in office, Clinton, the Nation's "baby boomer" President, was taken to task for "terminal hipness." (*Hip* is the adjective for 'sophisticated, aware; excellent, superb'.) The absorption of AAVE into Eurocentric culture masks its true origin and reason for being. It is a language born from a culture of struggle; a way of talking that has taken surviving African language elements as the base for the creation of self-expression in an alien tongue. Through various processes such as "Semantic Inversion" (taking words and turning them into their opposites), African Americans stake our claim to the English language, and at the same time, reflect distinct Black values that are often at odds with Eurocentric standards. "Fat," spelled *phat* in Hip Hop, refers to a person or thing that is excellent and desirable; reflecting the traditional African value that human body weight is a good thing, and implicitly rejecting the Euro-American mainstream, where skinny, not fat, is valued and everybody is on a diet. Senior Blacks convey the same value with the expression, *Don't nobody want no bone* 'No one wants a person who is just skin and bones'. By the same process of turning words into their opposites, *bad* means 'good', *stupid* means 'excellent', and even the word *dope* becomes positive when used to refer to someone or something considered 'very good, superb'.

The blunt, coded language of enslavement *sigged* on Christian slaveholders with the expression, *Everybody talkin' 'bout Heaven ain' goin' there*. To *sig* or *signify* 'to criticize or insult, either seriously or just for fun, with a clever, indirect statement that means more, or is deeper than, what's simply stated'. In this instance, enslaved Africans were commenting on the hypocrisy of European Americans who professed Christianity but practiced slavery. Hip Hop language, too, is bold and confrontational. It uses obscenities, graphic depictions of the sex act, oral and otherwise, and it adheres to the pronunciation and grammar of AAVE. Thus Hip Hop's *fly girls* and *fly guys* 'hip, street-wise, savvy, sophisticated' snub their noses at the European American world as well as the *European Negro* world, that of 'Blacks who identify with, act, and think like European Americans'. On the former, European American journalist Upski, writing from the "front lines of the White Struggle," says:

> . . . even lifetime rap fans . . . usually discount a crucial reason rap was invented: white America's economic and psychological terrorism against Black people – reduced in the White mind to "prejudice" and "stereotypes," concepts more within its cultural experience.
>
> (*The Source*, May 1993)

On the latter, Armond White, reviewing the 1993 film *CB4* states:

216

CB4 offers an unenlightened view of rap . . . It panders to . . . the black bourgeois fear that only "proper" language and "civilized" attitudes are acceptable means of addressing politics or articulating personal feelings.

(*Emerge*, May 1993)

But "back to the lecture at hand" (to borrow a quote from Rapper Dr. Dre): the crossover of African-American language and culture was bemoaned by Black writer Langston Hughes ("they done taken my blues and gone"), as he reflected on the out-migration of Black culture during the Harlem Renaissance era of the 1920s when the "Negro was in vogue;" it was analyzed by White writer Norman Mailer in his 1957 discussion of the "language of Hip" and "White Negroes;" it is resented, even as I write, by *boo-coos* 'a lot' of African Americans, like twenty-two-year-old Jamal, in my survey of Black opinion on the *wigga* phenomenon:

White folk kill me tryin to talk and be like us; they just want the good part. But it don't go like that; you got to take the bitter with the sweet.

(Smitherman, research-in-progress)

Actually, as I said to the *Brotha* 'Black man', there's plenty of bitter to go around. Contrary to popular Black stereotype, White folks' lives are not all sweetness and light. Despite European Americans' higher material circumstances, it really is true that neither man nor woman can live by bread alone. European Americans live "lives of quiet desperation" too; it's just a different kind of desperation. Which is exactly why Black talk continues to cross over, doing so today on an unprecedented scale because of the power of post-modern technology.

The dynamism and creativity in the lexicon revitalizes and re-energizes bland Euro-talk. There's electricity and excitement in *playas* 'flamboyant, flashy, highly desirable men or women, with the power to have multiple relationships'. The metaphors, images, and poetry in Black talk make the ordinary *all that, and then some* 'excellent, fantastic, superb'. AAVE is a dramatic, potent counterforce to verbal deadness and emptiness. One is not simply accepted by a group, she is *in like Flin*. Fraternities and sororities don't merely march; they perform a *step show* 'intricate marching patterns and steps performed in a group formation'. And when folk get *amp* 'stirred up, in a heightened emotional state', they don't fight the feeling, they *testify* 'give testimony to, speak about the power of something or someone in a high-spirited, emotional way'. For Whites, there is a certain magnetism in the African-American use of English because it seems to make the impossible possible. *I bet you a fat man against the hole in a doughnut . . .*

For *wiggas* and other White folk latching onto Black talk, that's the good news. The bad news is that there's a reality check in AAVE. Its terms and expressions keep you grounded, catch you just as you are taking flight and bring you right back down to the *nitty gritty* 'fundamental essence' of life. Words like *nigga* reinforce Blackness since, whether used positively, generically, or negatively (and all three nuances are possible), it can only refer to people of African descent. *Devil*, a negative reference to the White man, reminds Blacks to be on the look-out for deception. *Run and tell that!*, a historical reference to Blacks who snitched to White folks about Black business, is a cultural caution to those planning Black affairs to be wary of the Judases among them. Such words in the Black lexicon are constant reminders of race and the Black Struggle. And when you use African-American verbal traditions, i.e., when you *talk that talk*, you must pay homage to the Black experience, or as Rapper Ice Cube would say, be "true to the game."

Both in Rap Music and in reality, the words *b* (bitch) and *ho* (whore) are used as generic references to Black women. There are other sexually nuanced words and expressions like *two minute Brotha* 'a man who completes the sex act in a few seconds, and it's all over for the woman' and (*got your*) *nose open* to describe a male or female so deeply in love that he or she is ripe for exploitation. Terms like these in the AAVE lexicon are continuing reminders that, despite all the talk about Black passion and "soul," despite all the *sixty-minute-man* myths 'male ability to sustain sexual intercourse for a solid hour', despite all the *woofin* and *shit-talkin* 'boasting, projecting omnipotence, using strong, arrogant, talk', at bottom, the man–woman *thang* among African Americans is just as problematic as it is among other groups.

Some African Americans see crossover as positive, because it may reduce racial tension. Asserting that she is "optimistic about wiggers," fashion journalist Robin D. Givhan, states:

> Appreciating someone else's culture is good. An increased level of interest among whites in what makes some African Americans groove can only be helpful to improved race relations.
>
> (*Detroit Free Press*, 21 June 1993)

Yet the reality of race and personal conflicts (which are often intensified by racism) does make crossover problematic. Whites pay no dues, but reap the psychological, social, and economic benefits of a language and culture born out of struggle and hard times. In his "We use words like 'mackadocious'", Upski (*The Source*, May 1993) characterizes the "White rap audience" thus: "When they say they like rap, they usually have in mind a *certain* kind of rap, one that spits back what they already believe or lends an escape from their limited lives." And Ledbetter (1993) yields this conclusion: "By listening to rap and tapping into its extramusical expressions, then, whites are attempting to bear witness to – even correct – their own often sterile, oppressive culture." Yet it is also the case that not only Rap, but other forms of Black language and culture, are attractive because of the dynamism, creativity, and excitement in these forms. However one accounts for the crossover phenomenon, one thing is certain: today we are witnessing a multi-billion-dollar industry based on this linguistic and cultural phenomenon while there is continued material underdevelopment and deterioration in the *hood* that produces it. In Ralph Wiley's (1992) collection of essays, *Why Black People Tend to Shout*, which contains his *signifyin*[9] piece, "Why Black people have no culture," he states: "Black people have no culture because most of it is out on loan to white people. With no interest."

7.5 From *home* to *homey*

You're the kind of girl I wanna get closer to
Become the most to you
Like lovers suppose to do
Cause I fell straight into your trap
And since they say love is blind
I'm the Ray Charles of rap
And I'm waitin for you to put me in ya mix
Because you got my nose open like a jar of Vicks.
        ("Very special," by rapper Big Daddy Kane, from his 1993 album
                               Looks Like A Job For . . .)

Here, the Rapper's allusion to blind singer and musician Ray Charles is a metaphorical acknowledgement of Ray's genius. Born in 1932 and blind since the age of six, Ray Charles released his first LP in 1957 and was at the height of his popularity during the 1960s (the *Old School era*). His creative, soulful style blends gospel, jazz, blues, and funk. Thus Big Daddy Kane and other Hip Hop artists pay tribute to their musical elders and seek to root themselves in the Tradition.

The Mary J. Blige *tip* 'the essence of a person or thing' is a soulful blend of Rhythm 'n' Blues, Hip Hop, and 1960s Motown era sounds. This twenty-one-year-old *diva* says that her work "brings people back to those good Old School music days . . . Otis Redding, Gladys Knight, Al Green, Donny Hathaway, the Staple Singers." *Guru* 'gifted/unlimited/rhymes/universal' of the Rap group Gang Starr had long wanted to *jam* 'sing, play music, perform with high intensity' with the "old cats." His 1993 album *Jazzmatazz*, which he calls "an experimental fusion of Hip Hop and live jazz," featured Donald Byrd, Roy Ayers, Branford Marsalis, and other jazz greats. Guru *kicks the ballistics* 'present the facts, inform, enlighten':

9 "Signifyin is the verbal art of ritualized insult, in which the speaker puts down . . . talks about . . . someone, to make a point or sometimes just for fun" (Smitherman 1994: 206).

This is fusion we're doing here. But it's some gangsta shit. These old cats, they all made records reflecting street life. That's why rappers sample their shit.

("Cool Like Us," in *Details*, July 1993)

Ice Cube's popular *jam* 'song or recording' "It was a good day" (from his 1992 album *The Predator*), samples the Isley Brothers' "Footsteps in the dark," from their 1977 album *Go For Your Guns*. *Divas* En Vogue went gold with their single "Something he can feel," a Curtis Mayfield *jam* recorded by Aretha Franklin in the 1970s. Rapper Ice-T paid homage to history when he sold "dope beats and lyrics, no beepers needed" in his "I'm your pusher" *jam* based on Mayfield's 1972 *Superfly* movie soundtrack. P.E. (Public Enemy), always political, protested Arizona's refusal to honor Dr. Martin Luther King's holiday in "By the time I get to Arizona," on their 1991 album *Apocalypse 91: The Enemy Strikes Black*, a Rap that recalls Isaac Hayes' talk-singing *jam*, "By the time I get to Phoenix," from his 1969 *Hot Buttered Soul* album.

Signifyin, trash talkin, playin the dozens (verbal ritual of talking negatively about someone's mother for fun and humorous effect) – these and other African-American verbal traditions are all over the place today, from Rapper Schooly D's early *jam*, "Signifyin rapper," to the rhymes of Mary J. Blige's "4 1 1" duet with Rapper Grand Puba. Reaching back to Blackness untainted by the crossover explosion that the 1960s set in motion . . . coming correct, with all due respect . . . engaged in a conscious return to the Source . . . making their way toward an African identity for the twenty-first century – these *homiez* (Black people) are in search of home.

Nor is today's generation the first to look for home. Forcibly removed from their native land, homeless Africans in America have been on a continual quest for home since 1619. After Emancipation, they thought they could make home the rich, fertile land of the South. But Reconstruction ended, and the Federal/Union Government abandoned them, forcing them to survive amidst lynch mobs and the Ku Klux Klan, and leaving them to fend for themselves as sharecroppers trapped in a new form of enslavement. African Americans began to leave their Southern homes in droves, migrating to urban metropolises during and after World Wars I and II. Senior *Bloods* and their children of the 1950s and 1960s searched for home in the *Promised Land* (any place in the Northern US, from a comparison of the Black plight to that of the Hebrews who sought escape "out of Egypt" to the Biblical Promised Land). However, what they found was urban blight, poor housing, inadequate schools, police brutality, and other social problems of the "inner city." What Langston Hughes called the "dream deferred" exploded in the *rebellions* 'riots' of the 1960s. The source of much of Hip Hop's language and many of its cultural forms is the generation that produced these *rebellions* during the Black Freedom Struggle of the 1960s and 1970s. TLC, the name of a popular female Rap group, is the abbreviation for *tender loving care* (as well as the initials for the first names of these three *divas*); both the phrase and the abbreviation date back at least to the 1960s and can still be heard in the conversations of those who came of age during that time. Phrases from the 1960s and 1970s, such as *git it on wit yo bad self* 'begin your plan or action because you are powerful enough to do it' are frequently heard when rappers like P.E. are *in the house* 'conspicuously present on the scene'. Words like *jam* and *funky* 'fundamental, soulful essence, the raw sound' are as common in Hip Hop as they were during the 1950s. And when *b-ball* 'basketball' star "Sir Charles" (Barkley) and film-maker Spike Lee are proudly characterized as "90s niggaz" (a phrase Barkley himself coined), we are reaching way back to enslavement when the *bad nigga* was born. *Bad niggaz* were fearless, powerful slaves. They dared to buck *Ol Massa* 'the slave master', they didn't take no shit from Blacks or Whites, and some of them even lived to tell about it.

Bridging generations, a good deal of Hip Hop lingo recycles either the same word or a variation of an older term. Words like *pad* (house), *ig* (insult someone by deliberately ignoring them), *fry* (straightening kinky hair with a heated comb), and *salty* (angry) appeared in Cab Calloway's 1938 *Hepster's Dictionary* and are still in current use today.

Would you refer to *big-time it* (1960s/1970s) or to *live large* (1990s)? Answer: either, since both refer to lavish material possessions and living the Good Life. But neither the 1960s nor the 1990s generation has anything on seniors who convey the same meaning with their colorful expression *living high off the hog*, that is, living as though you're eating the upper parts of the hog, such as ribs or pork chops, rather than the lower part, the pig feet or chitlins. The *pimp walk* of the 1960s/1970s, the male strutting style of walking with a slight dip in the stride, is essentially the same as the *gangsta limp* of the 1990s; both expressions can be heard today. Though neither style of *strutting* is identical to the *cat walk* of earlier years, what is important in all of this is the concept of a style of walking that projects a self-assured, confident, even cocky, man-image. Like walking with *attitude*, conveying the message *I got it goin on* 'being highly successful, accomplished'.

Basic in the AAVE lexicon, then, is the commonality that takes us across boundaries. Regardless of job or social position, most African Americans experience some degree of participation in the life of the community. They get their hair done in African-American *beauty shops*, they worship in Black churches, they attend African-American social events, and they generally *par-tay* 'party' with Blacks. This creates in-group crossover lingo that is understood and shared by various social groups within the race. They use words like *kinky* and *nappy* to describe the tight, intricately curled texture of African-American hair and they understand readily the different ranges of meaning – from positive to neutral to negative – in the word *nigga*. As stated, the closest connection in Black talk, as in today's music, is between Hip Hop and the 1960s/1970s. In addition to the terms given above, other examples include *cool/cool out* (1960s/1970s) and *chill* (1990s), *doin it to def* (1960s/1970s) 'doing something to the very ultimate, for

221

maximum effect' and *def* (1990s) 'superb, excellent', *run it down* (1960s/1970s) or *break it down* (1990s) 'explain or simplify something, make it plain', *block boy* (1960s/1970s) and *banjy boy* (1990s) 'a gay male who dresses like straight males', *all the way live* (1960s/1970s) and *live* (1990s) 'an exciting, desirable event, person, place, or experience', and *ace boon coon* (1960s/1970s) and *ace kool* (1990s) 'your best friend'.

Another feature of Black talk is the coining of phrases that capture unique characteristics of people. The older term *bogard* 'to aggressively take over something' was based on the style of film star Humphrey Bogart, who typically played strong-arm, tough-guy roles. Today's generation has contributed *Oprah* to the lexicon, after-talk show personality Oprah Winfrey, to refer to 'the art of getting someone to reveal intimate facts about her/himself' as Oprah skillfully manages to do on national television.

AAVE had its genesis in enslavement, where it was necessary to have a style that would mean one thing to Africans but another to Europeans. Forced to use the English of *Ol Massa*, enslaved Africans had to devise a system of talking to each other about Black affairs, and about *The Man* (the White man) right in front of his face. Because of continued segregation and racism, this necessity for a coded form of English persisted even after emancipation, and it underlies the evolution of Black talk. The still-unresolved status of Africans in America accounts for the constant changes in its lexicon. When a term crosses over into the White world, it becomes suspect and is no longer considered *dope* in the Black world. A new term must be generated to take its place. There is a certain irony in this aspect of the lexicon because in this cultural circumstance, imitation is not considered flattery. The same lingo generated by the creative juices of the community and considered *def* today can tomorrow become *wack* 'undesirable, unhip' and suitable only for *lames* 'not up to date, unhip, out-of-step' if it gets picked up by Whites. Of course a lot of African-American talk does get picked up by European Americans, in this post-modern 1990s era, with "MTV," "BET," "Def Comedy Jam," and other television programs, and especially given the power of the media to spread culture and language rapidly throughout the nation. Nonetheless, the pattern persists: once phrases and terms are adopted by Whites, Blacks scramble to come up with something new.

On the other hand, language that does not cross over, regardless of how old it is, continues to be used in the community. Examples include most of the vocabulary of the Traditional Black Church and many of the terms referring to male–female relationships. For example, *got my nose open* is at least half a century old and was used (as pointed out earlier) in Big Daddy Kane's 1993 "Very special" *jam*. Another example is *Wham bam, thank you Mam!* (also *Bip bam, thank you Mam!*), used especially by women to refer to a male who completes the sex act in a matter of seconds; this *signifyin* expression is also at least fifty years old and was used by Mary J. Blige in her 1992 "4 1 1" *jam*. Other terms that don't cross over are some pejorative words for Whites, such as *Ann* 'White woman', *Charlie* 'White man', *honky* 'White person', terms referring to Black hair and other physical features, such as *ashy* 'whitish appearance of Black person's skin, due to exposure to wind, rain, or cold', *light-skin* 'light complexioned', *dark-skin* 'dark complexioned', *kitchen* 'hair at the neckline, generally the most African part of Black hair, the most *kinky*', and other words that describe Blacks only, such as *Oreo* 'a Black person who identifies with Whites, like the cookie, black on the outside, white on the inside', *colorstruck* 'African American obsessed with and preferring only those Blacks with a light complexion', and *Tom* 'Black person who identifies with whiteness, caters to Whites, exhibits lack of loyalty to Blacks'.

Though often misunderstood (and even damned) for their *nitty gritty* language, especially the *muthafuckas*, *ho's*, and *niggaz*, the Hip Hop generation is coming straight out of the oral tradition. In that tradition, language is double-voiced, common English words are given unique Black meanings, and a *muthafucka* is never a person with an Oedipus complex. (Depending on context, *muthafucka* may have a neutral, negative, or positive reference to a person, place, or thing.) Rather than breaking with the Black past, as some members of the previous generation have tried to do, Hip Hoppers seek to connect with past verbal traditions and to extend the semantic space of Black lingo by adding a contemporary flavor. They are not merely imitating and reproducing the past, but grounding themselves in it as they seek to stamp their imprint upon the Black tradition. Any time one ventures beyond the tried and true, errors *big-time* 'very much', painful distortions, and horrific extremes are likely to result. Experimentation breeds successes as well as failures. The violent antagonism toward and brutalization of women by male Rap groups, such as Los Angeles' NWA (Niggaz With Attitudes), is a case in point. But it was also NWA who, early on, in their 1989 *jam* "Fuck the police," hipped us to the brutality of the Los Angeles Police Department and should have prepared us for the Rodney King tragedy had we listened.

This is a historical moment in which Rap and other forms of Black language and culture are used to sell everything from Coca-Cola and Gatorade to snow blowers and shampoo for White people's hair. When you factor in profits from music, television programming, sports, clothing, and advertising, it is clear that America's corporate economy is capitalizing on Hip Hop, making it a booming multi-billion-dollar industry. However, while Black talk has crossed over, Black *people* have not, as is excruciatingly evident by the staggering unemployment and economic deterioration of the *hood*, re-emerging racism (even on college campuses), and open physical attacks on African-American males by the police as well as by ordinary White citizens. Recognizing *what time it is* 'the real deal, the truth', *homiez* are in search of authentic Black language and culture, an unapologetic African-American self, and a way to resolve the unfinished business of being African in America. Their quest has led them to the ruins of the 1960s. There, *homeboys* and *homegirls* 'African-American males and females' found folk like Rudy Ray Moore's "Dolemite," with his hilarious, pornographic talk and, yes, his put-downs of women. But there they also found the "do-rag lover and revolutionary pimp"[10] Malcolm X.

References

Blackshire-Belay, Carole A. (1996) "The location of Ebonics within the framework of the africological paradigm." *Journal of Black Studies* 27: 5–23.

Blassingame, John (1979) *The Slave Community: Plantation Life in the Antebellum South.* New York: Oxford University Press.

Dillard, J. L. (1972) *Black English.* New York: Random House.

DuBois, W. E. B. (1990) *Souls of Black Folk.* 2nd edn. New York: Vintage Books/Library of America. First published in 1903.

Herskovits, Melville (1941) *Myth of the Negro Past.* Boston: Beacon Press.

Krapp, George Philip (1925) *The English Language in America.* New York: Modern Language Association.

Ledbetter, James (1992) "In imitation of life," *Vibe Magazine.*

Lincoln, C. Eric and Lawrence H. Mamiya (1990) *The Black Church in the African American Experience.* Durham: Duke University Press.

Morgan, Marcyliena (1994) "The African-American speech community: reality and sociolinguists." In *Language and the Social Construction of Identity in Creole Situations*, Marcyliena Morgan (ed.). University of California-Los Angeles: Center for Afro-American Studies.

Mufwene, Salikoko (1992) "Ideology and facts on African American English." *Pragmatics* 2 (2): 141–68.

Page, Clarence (1989) "African American or Black? It's debatable." *Detroit Free Press,* 1 January, 1989, A1, A12.

Smitherman, Geneva (1986) *Talkin and Testifyin: The Language of Black America.* Detroit: Wayne State University Press.

—— (1991) "'What is Africa to me?': Language ideology and African American." *American Speech* 66: 115–32. Reprinted in *Word: A Black Culture Journal,* Winter, 1993, and in *African American Communications: A Reader in Traditional and Contemporary Studies,* James W. Ward (ed.), Kendall Hunt, 1992.

—— (1994) *Black Talk: Words and Phrases from the Hood to the Amen Corner.* Boston: Houghton Mifflin.

—— (research-in-progress) "Survey of African American opinion on the use of *nigga* and *wigga.*"

Turner, Lorenzo (1949) *Africanisms in the Gullah Dialect.* Chicago: University of Chicago Press.

Wiley, Ralph (1992) *Why Black People Tend to Shout.* New York: Penguin Books.

10 From the poem "Malcolm spoke/who listened? (this poem is for my consciousness too)," by Haki Madhubuti, from his collection *Don't Cry, Scream,* published in 1969, under the name Don L. Lee.

Wilkerson, Isabel (1989) "Many who are Black favor new term for who they are." *New York Times*, 31 January 1989, l, 8.

Williams, Robert L. (ed.) (1975) *Ebonics: The True Language of Black Folks*. St Louis: Institute of Black Studies.

8

AFRICAN-AMERICAN LANGUAGE USE: IDEOLOGY AND SO-CALLED OBSCENITY

Arthur K. Spears

8.1 Background

This chapter is about what has been perceived as obscene language. As I indicate below, I prefer to use the term *uncensored speech* in order not to prejudge the actions of the users of such speech. My wish not to prejudge is not the result of unreflexive liberal humanism; rather, it reflects one of the major conclusions presented below, namely, in many cases, rigorous analysis of form, meaning, and communicative behavior is required before one can pass judgment on the speech of members of communities other than one's own, where the term *community membership* is determined by age, socioeconomic class, ethnicity, gender, and other variables.

Those who are invariably offended even by mentions, let alone uses, of "obscenity" should not read further. At the outset, I should make some clarifications and disclaimers since it seems that many people wish, and indeed insist upon, forcing the discussions below into the judgmental framework of their own personal norms of propriety.

Like most social science writers, I have tried to be objective; but it goes without saying that it is possible that some biases based on my own position and personal history in society have inadvertently influenced my discussions. I should also point out that well over a hundred people, students and others, the great majority of whom are African Americans[1] who are culturally African American, have read and discussed with me various versions of this chapter, and that it currently incorporates information they have given me. My goal has been to analyze a type of speech behavior which is certainly controversial but has

---

1 I will use *African American* and *Black* interchangeably, capitalizing the latter when it is used in the sense of the former. Similarly, when used in the sense of European American, *White* is capitalized.

This article focuses on the historically English-speaking segment of African Americans whose descent is primarily from United States-dwelling citizens.

important implications for understanding some sectors of the African-American community – and even of the White community and of other American communities. The type of speech behavior discussed below is indeed present throughout the United States and no doubt present to some extent in all societies.

The examples that I use sometimes represent to varying extents misogynist and other oppressive views, but at the same time they represent behavior that is important to understand. Such behavior cannot be understood without examination, which in turn requires exemplification. I should also point out that the use of specific terms in specific utterances does not necessarily imply anything concerning misogyny or other oppressive orientations. For example, the use of *bitch* and *ho'* (which, by the way, can be used for males as well as females, but usually for the latter) does not necessarily imply that an utterance is misogynist. Thus, some females use *bitch* generically to refer to other females – as do some males. Geneva Smitherman (p.c. 1997) provides the example of a well-known male (African-American) gangsta rap artist who said to a prominent (African-American) female economist, as they shared a limousine on the way to a program they were going to do together, something along the lines of, "Wow, I don't think I've ever met a bitch economist before." The rapper was positively impressed and had no intention of insulting the economist. He was not aware of her rules of speech use and evaluation. She was not aware of his and rebuked him with uncommon severity – all the way to their destination.

Likewise, the use of *nigga*[2] in an utterance does not necessarily mean that it is racist or reflective of self-hate. Terms such as these are used sometimes simply to refer to individuals without any evaluative implications. Sometimes they are even used in positive evaluative contexts. This is a major point of the discussion below. It is also important to remember that racism, sexism, and other oppressive views can be communicated in utterances with no censored expressions. Geneva Smitherman (p.c.) provides the telling example of a male preacher who refers to all the women pastors in the audience as "Sista so-and-so," rather than "Reverend so-and-so." The same preacher refers to male preachers as "reverend."

Like most studies, this one is part of a larger project. I have begun my study of uncensored speech with some of the most controversial items because these seem the best point of entry into the general phenomenon. I am aware that the examples will make some people feel uncomfortable, as I would be for example in reading an article on racist Ku Klux Klan speech behavior sprinkled with

---

2 I use non-standard spelling for some words to reflect their pronunciation and to emphasize their use by African-American speakers as opposed to others. In some cases such distinctions are important, e.g., that between *nigga* and *nigger*, which in much African-American discourse on language are two different words. The second belongs to White varieties of English and carries its own semantic and pragmatic properties.

words such as *nigger*. However, realizing that the article was oriented toward understanding that speech behavior in an attempt to figure out what should or could be done about it, if anything, I, personally, would put my discomfiture aside. Others might react differently. In any case, I recommend that readers approach the material herein intellectually.

Although the examples below do not represent my speech or attitudes, they are part of my world, so to speak, since I hear this kind of speech daily in the African-American community in which I have lived for over a decade and in the one in which I grew up. When the weather is not too harsh, I can sit on my front stoop and collect examples. I hear daily similarly "obscene" speech throughout the city I live in – from Whites and virtually every other group of English speakers. African Americans are not the only group that uses uncensored speech.[3]

The kind of speech described below is used by only some African Americans. It is *not* true that all African Americans use uncensored speech. Some do not. It is not true that all Whites use uncensored speech. Empirical research alone will tell us how many African Americans – and Whites as well as others – do or do not use uncensored speech. Such speech is found in all of the major social groupings, e.g., male and female as well as all classes. There are also people in all of these groupings who do not use it. Most important to remember is that it is not confined to rappers or working-class or un(der)employed males, the group with whom such behavior is often popularly associated. In all age and class groups, some males and some females regularly use uncensored speech. This statement can be corroborated by anyone living in the African-American communities I live and have lived in, and the same is surely true of those living in many other African-American communities, and undoubtedly also those living in many non-African-American communities.

This is a crucial point because many people, linguists included, believe that people who use uncensored speech can be categorized socially in a neat way. The major social groupings that social scientists usually employ are inadequate for this purpose. I believe that religious values along with family upbringing and mores are among the key determinants of the use or non-use of uncensored

3 When I was in college at Kansas University, White male friends informed me that for most White males at the university – students and some faculty and staff – *nigger* was the normal term of reference for African Americans when no African Americans were present and outside of censored contexts. Among those so using *nigger* were student body presidents. During the year that I lived in a college dormitory, I overheard uses of *nigger* as I went along the hallways.

Given the usage of *nigger* in the college community, it is not surprising that an African-American college friend who later became a judge in Kansas City reported that White judges not infrequently slipped and used *nigger* in his presence and sometimes with pejorative accompanying lexical material, e.g., "big burly black nigger."

In high school, a female White friend informed me that many in her group of friends normally used *nigger* – including herself, but they didn't necessarily "mean anything by it," i.e., it was not necessarily used in a negative evaluative context.

speech; and, I might add, it will be easier to characterize those who do not use such speech rather than those who do.

This writing is not about Asian Americans, Whites, and others, whether they do or do not use uncensored speech. It is focused on those African Americans who do use it regularly. It is not about African Americans who do not use uncensored speech regularly. It does not trivialize or marginalize this last group: it is simply not about them.

So, what are we to make of the following phrase?

(1) muthafuckin bitch-ass nigga

Several questions come to mind, and I will attempt to provide answers in the discussions below.

1 Is such language acceptable or should it be classified as obscenity? Should this and similar expressions[4] be forbidden, if indeed that is possible?
2 Is such language abnormal in any sense?
3 Do the frequency and function of this and similar expressions indicate anything about the character of some African-American communities in the United States? More specifically, do this and similar expressions indicate a degeneration in social life, in ethics and values?
4 Do such expressions tell us something fundamental about language use in at least some African-American communities?

I will return to the question of what speech tells us about community life and values and enter some comments here on debates concerning acceptability.

A number of recent events have raised fundamental questions concerning what type of speech is acceptable and whether certain types of speech should be prohibited. One set of events relates to the racist language to which students of color (mostly African American) have been subjected on college campuses, calling forth organized protests by the victimized groups along with their allies and the installation of speech codes, whose appropriateness, effectiveness, and legality are still under debate.

Another event I will discuss in more detail since it bears closely on the issues of primary concern for discussions below, is related to the furor raised by the lyrics of songs on an album of the African-American rap group 2 Live Crew, *As Nasty as They Wanna Be*. Outrage over the obscenity and explicitly sexual and misogynist subject matter came to a boil in 1990. (Here, I speak in the voice of those who condemned these songs. Nevertheless, I do not want to prejudge. What is obscene and what is verbally sexual or misogynist is ultimately a matter of interpretation.) Media coverage of the debate initiated by that outrage

---

4 I use *expression* as a cover term for words, phrases, sentences, etc.

included writings in *The New York Times* by Michele M. Moody-Adams, "Don't confuse 2 Live Crew with Black culture" (25 June 1990, p. A16) and Henry Louis Gates, Jr, "2 Live Crew, decoded" (19 June 1990, p. A23) among others.

These writers and others who entered the debate were dealing with lyrics talking about placing a "bitch" on a bed, lying on her back with her legs in the air making her "pussy splats." Moreover, the lyrics go on to speak of trying "to abuse it," a "big stinkin' pussy" ("Put her in the buck" by 2 Live Crew). This example is provided to give readers a clear idea of what the furor was about.

As several social commentators have noted, the content represented in 2 Live Crew's music has been present in urban African-American communities for a long time, and in non-African-American communities also. For most of that time, however, it did not go outside of those communities, although popular comics such as Moms Mabley, Redd Foxx, and Richard Pryor, in particular, opened the door to the outside so that groups such as 2 Live Crew could come through.

The content and style of 2 Live Crew's rap, however, most certainly do not represent the only strain in verbal forms of African-American popular culture. Indeed, even among rappers, the style of 2 Live Crew represents a minority. Many rappers infuse their music with social critique, strategies for community self-help, and sociohistorical remembrances seeking to instill group pride and initiative. It is disgraceful yet expectable that so much media attention in the United States has focused on one corner of the rap industry to the almost whole-sale exclusion of mainstream media coverage of what is on the whole – in terms of uplift, business acumen, grassroots orientation, and critical depth – among the most progressive institutions in the African-American community (Dyson 1993; Rose 1994).

2 Live Crew's lyrics incorporate ideas, discourse strategies, and verbal styles which have long been present in toasts (rhyming epic celebrating African-American culture), playing the dozens, and signifying (as Gates noted in his editorial). The lyrics, then, are certainly within the African-American cultural tradition. However, there are several African-American cultures, just as there are several AAEs,[5] related yet different, separated by socioeconomic class in addition to other social factors. We must keep in mind that prose versions of 2 Live Crew's lyrics are heard daily in urban African-American communities

---

5 I use the term *African-American English* (AAE) as a cover term for Standard African-American Englishes (SAAE) and African-American vernacular Englishes (AAVE), both of which are in turn the cover terms for the collection of standard and non-standard varieties of AAE respectively. In doing this, I am making two claims: (1) AAE comprises not one but a number of related standard and non-standard varieties, and (2) varieties of AAE may have distinctively African-American traits while having none of the features widely agreed upon as being non-standard, e.g., the use of *ain't* and multiple negatives within a sentence. The distinctively African-American features of SAAE have to do primarily, but not solely, with prosody and language use. See Spears (1988) for more discussion.

and not thought worthy of special attention. I hear them regularly in my neighborhood. Moreover, the girls and women to whom this kind of explicit language might in some circumstances actually be directed are perfectly capable of providing just the response it deserves.

With regard to rap specifically, it must be mentioned that most types of rap have a caustic turn, one that touches all the topics it considers. Rap comments and discourses on women, people of same-sex orientation, government social policy, the police, capitalism, rival rap groups, and alienation tend all to be equally caustic. Noteworthy exceptions to this caustic turn are gospel, educational, and what some call "bubble-gum" rap, exemplified by Will Smith, who later became the star of the television situation-comedy "The Fresh Prince of Bel Air."

To return to our original question of what is acceptable, it should be emphasized that only a proper linguistic (in the broad sense including the social and the grammatical) understanding of expressions such as that in example (1) can provide the foundation for an answer.

8.2 The framework

Language norms and interpretation are the subject matter of the broad sociocultural study of language referred to as the ethnography of communication. As originally developed by Hymes and Gumperz, and subsequently students who joined them, it has been concerned with a deeper understanding of language in its social context than had been provided by studies preceding it. The focus was not only on (1) linguistic repertoires (the range of language varieties one uses in speaking) but also (2) non-verbal communication, (3) the speech community (which shares at least one speech variety – dialect, language, jargon, etc. – and rules for language use, interpretation, and evaluation), (4) speech genres (preaching, joking, etc.), and (5) the rules themselves for speech interpretation and evaluation. For examples of the early classic studies in the ethnography of communication, see Gumperz and Hymes (1964, 1972).

Interpretation is related to important notions such as key (other terms are also used), which refers to manner of speech or trope, whether an utterance should be taken literally, figuratively, or ironically, for example. Speech evaluation is along several conceptual lines: positive/negative, profane/sacred, obscene/decent, high/low (with regard to formality of context and socioeconomic stratum), and so forth.

Outside *Maledicta: The International Journal of Verbal Aggression* and a few studies such as Zwicky *et al.* (1971), Halliday (1976), Davis (1989), Andersson and Trudgill (1990), Hughes (1992), Jay (1992 – primarily psychological), and Bolton and Hutton (1995), relatively little theoretical attention has been given to "bad" language. By "bad" language, I refer to language that is evaluated as negative by important, power-wielding segments of a community, if not the entire community, but that is, of course, sometimes used nevertheless.

231

Although much attention has been devoted to variation in speech according to social context (church, school, pool hall, etc., with peers, parents, or strangers), next to nothing has dealt with major shifts in language evaluation across social contexts and historically. To facilitate discussion, I introduce the term *mode*, meaning a context- or participant-based style of speech characterized by high distinctiveness in the rules of speech evaluation on a positive/negative scale. Of central concern for this writing is *uncensored mode*. In this mode, expressions that in censored contexts are considered obscene or evaluatively negative are used in an almost or completely evaluatively neutral way. Among *censored contexts*, I include church services and other contexts in which persons of high, mainstream-supported respect[6] are present, e.g. ministers, elderly relatives, etc. Thus, we could say that in locker rooms, almost invariably uncensored mode (hereafter UM) speech is used, whereas in church we would expect censored speech.

In sum, some types of language can go anywhere. Some cannot. The study of modes would be concerned with what speech can go where and when, with what exceptions, and more generally how we can characterize the speech of particular contexts in mode terms.

Uncensored speech is found in virtually every community; it is by no means limited to the African-American community. It is also found in a wide range of segments of the community. Thus, it is certainly not limited to younger age groups, even though we might hypothesize that, other things being equal, it will be found more among younger groups. Nor is it limited to males or lower-income groups.

The increase in the sheer amount of uncensored speech and its use in a wider range of contexts than previously, not only among Anglo-African Americans and Latino-African Americans but also among Whites and others as well, has been noted by many. It is clear that there has been a shift over this century in the use of uncensored speech in the United States and in all similar modern, highly industrialized societies. Practically anyone over forty (perhaps even younger) in such a society can confirm this by considering changes that have occurred in the classroom, television, and movies.

What is new and what occasions this writing is the presence of uncensored speech in the mass media in much greater quantities than before and its *normalization*, the use of uncensored expressions by some types of people in most social settings in an evaluatively neutral way, i.e., the expressions are not inherently negative or positive. That is, they are neutralized: they are negative, positive, or neutral in force depending on how they are used. Many people who function exclusively or primarily in mainstream settings are not aware of this. In

---

6 Obviously, some individuals enjoy high respect in uncensored mode social situations, but not outside, e.g., some people with a high level of charisma and verbal agility, and high-income individuals whose revenue comes from illegal activities.

brief, neutralization across a wide range of social contexts, if not almost all, results in normalization.

Some of the types of semantic change that have accompanied neutralization and normalization are noteworthy also, particularly generalization of meaning, evident in the case of *nigga*. In the case of this lexical item, one of its principal semantic features (to look at the issue in this way) has been deleted: [+ of African descent]. Neither ethnicity nor lineage determines its use anymore (see below). Instead of being a consequence of neutralization and normalization, generalization appears strongly to be a consequence of the higher level of adoption by the general American community of aspects of African-American culture today than in the past.

The term *uncensored mode* has been coined in recognition that individuals operate effectively within different evaluative language norm contexts – which is true of language users worldwide. My focus, however, is on certain African-American groups, among whom there is normalization in a broad range of social situations. (Normalization has also increased among other groups, indicating that the change is a by-product of American culture, or, perhaps, the post-modern, postindustrial, capitalist state.)

8.3 An analysis of two expressions

8.3.1 *Introduction*

In this section, I will present analyses and discussions of two features in example (1): *-ass*, exemplified in *bitch-ass*, and *nigga*. These items are among those seen as the main offenders by many who would prohibit or limit uncensored language. I will concentrate mainly on these two items but will also provide some comments on a few related words and a basic semantic interpretation of the phrase itself.

Often it is assumed that writings on the structure and use of AAE are contrastive with White language varieties since indeed many of them have been concerned with where differences lie. My concern in this writing is not contrastive. I am interested in presenting aspects of AAE grammar and use, and in some cases one finds the same phenomenon with White varieties. Nevertheless, it should be remembered that with respect to all of the features discussed below, there are significant quantitative or qualitative differences between AAE and White vernaculars.

This analysis is based on (1) papers, personal communications, and speech tape recordings of students who have lived in African-American communities (principally in New York City) and who have direct and regular contact with African-American groups using UM speech as their main mode or certainly one of their important modes of speech, (2) my own knowledge based on living in several African-American communities, and (3) interviews with various individuals who have lived in African-American communities across the nation.

233

(The main source is 1.) I also refer to a few brief writings in the popular press on the subject.

8.3.2 The grammar of -ass words

My concern in this section will be with the grammar (specifically, morphology, syntax, and semantics) and pragmatics of what I refer to as -ass words (hereafter AWs), so termed because of the special type of compounding involved in words such as *bitch-ass*. A number of the following examples with negative import refer to females (although an expression such as *bitch-ass* can be said of males too). This occurs because of the dynamics of the kind of discourse being examined, a discourse, one might add, which reflects the sexism in American society in general and in the African-American community specifically. (See, among the many works in a African-American feminist tradition, Hooks 1990.) In a number of cases, examples which have negative import referring to males and which are pragmatically authentic are not available, or the author, being male and middle-class, has less access to the full range of uncensored discourse than others, who might be able to provide additional, appropriate, male-oriented examples to expand the data set already collected.

The grammar and use of these compounds is more complex than what is presented below, which is intended to serve solely as an introductory treatment. AWs are closely related in semantics and pragmatics to *-time* words, such as *jive-time* (acting or talking in an unserious or a deceptive way), *hippy-time* (acting or talking like a hippy [i.e., flower child of the 1960s and 1970s] or pseudo-hip person), *country-time* (unsophisticated, naive), *punk-time* (behaving like a male homosexual or in an unmanly way), and *Jew-time* (behaving in a way, often stereotypically, associated with Jews) (as distinct from *Jew-town*,[7] which may be used as a verb, adverb, adjective, or noun).

The first element of AWs need not be a noun; one also finds adjectives, e.g., *jive-ass* (insincere, insignificant), *stank-ass* (smelly, nasty); participles, e.g., *cock-suckin'-ass*, *muthafuckin'-ass*; and various other types of complex formatives, e.g., *pussy-whipped-ass* (female-dominated), *no-dancin'-ass*, *cock-diesel-ass* (impressively muscular) (allomorphs: *cock-diese*, *cock-dee*); and occasionally full VPs, e.g., *ain't-got-no-rap-ass* (unable to speak persuasively, especially to desirable females). I have singled out AWs for attention because they reflect a productive

---

7 *Jew-town* denotes – variously according to its syntactic category status – traits and behaviors (commercial only, it appears) stereotypically associated with Jews. I have not heard it outside the Chicago area, though it may well be used in other areas. When not a noun, it may be freely used in reference to non-Jews. Thus, in a way somewhat similar to *nigga* (see below), its application has been generalized, i.e., in terms of the ethnicity of the individuals of whom it is predicated. Additionally, it, like *Jew-time*, appears to be neutralized, used in positive, negative, and neutral evaluative contexts.

morphological process that is central to UM and because they illustrate and elaborate on the point made concerning neutralization: not only is neutralization contextual, it also has grammatical dimensions that require linguistic analysis for full understanding.

Before making the first point about AWs, I point out that hyphens will be used to link ass to the preceding lexical material in AWs, as opposed to other kinds of expressions with *ass*. *Ass* in AWs does not denote 'buttocks' literally. Of course, *ass* is used in the sense 'buttocks', so there arises a question as to whether the grammar of African-American English distinguishes two *asses*. I will refer to the *ass* that occurs in AWs as "discourse *-ass*." I will refer to the noun *ass* denoting 'buttocks' as "anatomical *ass*." There is also a third usage of *ass*, occurring in expressions in which it is preceded by a possessive pronoun, usually used as the equivalent of the reflexive *self*, as in example (2), but also used as a substitute for other pronouns, e.g., *him*, as in example (3a), and *he* in (3b):

(2)　　Get your triflin' *ass* out of here. (= Get your triflin' *self* out of here.)
(3)　a.　I saw his *ass* yesterday. (= I saw *him* yesterday.)
　　　b.　His *ass* is gonna get fried. (= *He* is gonna get fried [reprimanded, punished].)

I refer to this third type of expression in which *ass* occurs as a "metonymic pseudo-pronoun" (MPP), "metonymic" because *ass* in its anatomical sense has been metonymically extended to stand for the whole person. I note in passing that speakers of probably all varieties of American English use some types of MPPs, for instance, *Get your butt out of bed!* In other varieties, though, there are not as many of them nor do they have anything approaching the broad range of use found in AAE varieties.

In some cases, the type of *ass* (anatomical, discourse, or metonymic) being used is not clear, as in (4):

(4)　Look at his fat ass.

The use of *ass* in this example might literally refer to buttocks (anatomical *ass*) or metonymically to the entire person, in which case the sentence would be the equivalent of *Look at his fat self*. In some cases, however, the specific modifier of *ass* allows for only one interpretation. For example, the phrase *satchel ass* (used mainly by older African Americans) can be interpreted only as anatomical since *satchel* (in my vernacular at least) can refer only to buttocks, not the whole person, unlike an adjective such as *fat*. Thus, if someone said *Look at that satchel ass muthafucka*, he or she would necessarily be referring to the buttocks of the "muthafucka."

An important question is how one can tell when there is an AW, with discourse *-ass*. In some cases, access to the mind of the speaker or social context is necessary, e.g., with *fat(-)ass idiot*. In other instances, the linguistic context suffices, e.g., *satchel ass idiot* or *shelf-butt-ass Joe*. In the former, *ass* is necessarily anatomical, while in the latter it is necessarily discourse *-ass*, i.e., an AW. Anatomical and discourse *ass* cannot occur next to one another, thus the unacceptability of **Look at that fat ass-ass idiot*, where, were this string permissible, the first *ass* would be the anatomical one, the second the discourse *-ass*. Interestingly, discourse *-ass* can occur, however, with *butt*, another word for *ass*, as in the just-cited example *shelf butt-ass Joe*.

The meaning of *-ass* in AWs is to be found on the level of discourse and expressive meaning. That is, what *-ass* in AWs communicates invariably is something about the communicative situation. The basic meaning, then, is social and abstract. AWs mark a discourse as being in UM. It may in specific utterances have the force of an intensifier, as Smitherman (1994: 94) observes; but this is not always the case.

AWs are a type of compound. They are written hyphenated to indicate that they receive stress as compounds do, e.g., *blackbird*, which has primary-secondary stress (1–2 stress). With AWs, secondary stress falls on *-ass*, and primary stress falls on one of the syllables of the first element. Like other compounds, and nouns in general, AWs can serve a modifying function, namely, to modify other nouns, e.g., *crazy-ass muthafucka* 'a crazy (i.e., funny, mentally ill, bold) male' (as opposed to the other interpretation, *fat ass muthafucka* 'a male with fat buttocks'.)

AWs are unlike the typical compound, but like a grammatical morpheme, in that the meaning of *-ass*, as noted, has been semantically bleached: it no longer denotes literally; rather, its meaning resides on the discourse-expressive level, marking UM. It has gone from denoting a body part to identifying a discourse mode. (As an MPP, *ass* has been generalized to refer to the entire person.)

There are several morphological and syntactic constraints on AWs. A morphological constraint is that *-ass* is not inflected. Note that normally expressions referring to certain kinds of body parts possessed by an individual have the *-ed* suffix, e.g., *pidgeon-toed*, *slew-footed*, *left-handed*, *cross-eyed*, etc. (In my vernacular, anatomical *ass* is variably inflected; thus *fat assed idiot* and *fat ass idiot*, but not **triflin'-assed idiot*, though *triflin'-ass idiot* is fine. (Again, the hyphen indicates an AW.) Notice that *smart-ass*, uninflected, appears frequently in *The Village Voice*, apparently from the pens of White writers. Uninflectability is an expected result of grammaticalization. Anatomical *ass* is only variably uninflected. This is possibly the result of its association through homophony and diachrony with discourse *-ass*. It is clear that, historically, discourse *-ass* arose from anatomical *ass*. (The reverse is highly implausible.)

One syntactic constraint on AWs is that they must be followed by a noun.

(5) a. * He's jive-ass (insincere).
   b. * He's triflin'-ass.
   c. * He's bitch-ass.

    d. * He's a jive-ass.

    e. * He's a triflin'-ass.

    f. * He's a bitch-ass.

(Some people accept (5a) and (5b) with AWs containing adjectives, but not (5c) containing an AW with a noun.) Other types of sentences with an AW followed by a noun are also unacceptable, e.g., *I saw that jive-ass, *I saw that bitch-ass. The sentences in (6) are acceptable.

    (6) a.   She's a triflin'-ass woman.

          b.   He's a jive-ass fool.

It is not obvious how this restriction might be explained.

To return to questions of meaning, it should be observed that AWs do not consistently signal "hard" semantic content; indeed, in most cases, they do not. So, frequently one AW may be easily substituted for another.[8] AWs most often occur with slang expressions that come in sets of semantically interchangeable items, e.g., the set of generalized positive evaluation *fly, phat, fresh, dope*.

AWs are more about poetics, ways of positioning oneself in the world and emotive reactions and attitudes toward other entities. However, AWs *do* carry some lexical, as opposed to discourse, meaning, but that meaning is always carried by the formative to which -*ass* is attached. This is in accord with the claim that the -*ass* in AWs is semantically bleached and evaluatively neutral. The fact is that whatever hard information is carried by the first element accounts for selecting particular items to combine with, e.g., *bitch* as opposed to *tired* or *funky*.

AWs are often used by the speaker simply because of their rhythmic utility. As with *playing the dozens, snapping*,[9] *reciting toasts*, denotative meaning and

---

8 This is especially true in abusive modes of speech such as *playing the dozens* and *reading*, where the goal is to be as verbally "abusive" as possible or to be relentlessly "abusive" in a creative way. The quotation marks indicate that such speech may or may not be truly abusive since in abusive mode what is normally abusive becomes normal and is thus not necessarily abusive. *Playing the dozens* is one well-known speech event that unfolds in abusive mode, where verbal dexterity is of utmost importance. *Reading* is a speech activity in which degradation or reprimand is the most important goal, though creativity is important also. Reading is often associated with male African-American homosexuals (for lack of a better term – some in this group reject *gay* as White-oriented), but females and males of all sexual orientations engage in reading. I remember my grandmother, born shortly after the Civil War, reading the boyfriends of an aunt of mine as "cotton-pickers" and "ink-spitters," i.e., 'very dark-skinned person.' What Whatley (1981) observes for *fussing* (not abusive necessarily) holds true for reading also: higher status and older individuals have more leeway to do so with impunity.

9 *Playing the dozens* and *snapping* are not quite the same for all participants in African-American culture. For some, snaps (wisecracks, quick retorts) may figure in playing the dozens, but for a communicative situation to be characterized as playing the dozens, there must be an exchange between at least two interlocutors and the verbal exchanges may go beyond the grammatical

economy of expression are not the issue. Rather, expressive ingenuity and social effect are. In sum, AWs may express significant lexical content (with the word[s] accompanying -*ass*), but more often than not, their primary function is to be found at the poetic-expressive-discourse level.

This last point is true for a number of items typical of UM, e.g., *muthafuckin*, which has little or no referential meaning, as opposed to discourse-expressive, meaning. Observe that, while *muthafucka* generally refers to any male person, like the word *guy*, *muthafuckin* is more general and can be used to refer even to inanimate beings, e.g., *Get all that muthafuckin-ass, funky shit out of here*. It can be used for female referents too, e.g., *Bitch, I'll kick your muthafuckin ass*.

AWs reflect a highly productive compounding process. There are, however, some very clear exceptions, some variably so, e.g., **butter-ass* (accepted by a few people), **dope-ass*, **phat-ass*, and **nigga-ass*. (The first element in the first three is a general term of positive evaluation like *cool* and *fly*.) There appear to be no grammatical or sociocultural explanations for these exceptions as a group. Some may have plausible explanations within the scope of our current knowledge of uncensored mode speech, but I will not pursue the matter.

That AWs are not inherently negative or positive can be easily shown by the fact that, in addition to occurring with negative expressions such as *triflin'* and *fucked-up*, they also occur with positive ones such as *fly*, *fine* (good-looking), and *cock-diese*,[10] e.g., *fine-ass muthafucka* (good-looking male), *fine-ass bitch* (good-looking female). Many people are simply unwilling to believe that AWs have uses with positive evaluation, but these and equivalent sentences can actually be heard. (An example, with context, of such a "difficult-to-believe" utterance would be *Hey, muthafucka* as a perfectly friendly greeting. I was greeted that way on a number of occasions during my junior high school through college years – by middle- and working-class peers, males in these cases.[11])

8.3.3 Nigga

Most Americans know that *nigga* (hereafter N except in examples) is used among African Americans (and other blacks in the US), but African Americans (and blacks in general) take grave offense at whites calling them N. In what follows, I will concentrate on African Americans, since non-African-American

---

formulas found in snaps, e.g., *Yo' mama's so (ugly, fat,* etc.) X, where X is a degree-specifying string. An example of a snap is *Yo' mama's so ugly she has to sneak up on a glass to get a drink of water*.

10 Quantitatively, there is a tendency for AWs to occur in negative sentential contexts; and there is a reason for this based on highly generalized communicative practices – not on word meaning. See above on *abusive mode*.

11 A female French friend has reported that it was common for close female university-student friends to greet each other, in a totally positive way, with [name], *putain!* (whore). This way of talking is apparently not limited to African-American or American communities.

blacks in the US are a varied group and I do not know much about their attitudes specifically. What is not widely known is that usage of the word is much more subtle (see Smitherman, this volume). It is currently used by younger African Americans (roughly under 30) and some non-African Americans to mean 'male'; it applies to males of any ethnicity in much the same way as does *guy*. (It may also refer to females included in a group with males.) The meaning of *nigga* does not change in any consistent way when applied to persons of different ethnicities.

The problem has historically been with Whites calling African-Americans N. It is not fully clear, but apparently sometime during the immediate post-Vietnam War era, or perhaps during the war itself, N began to be applied to non-African Americans, by African Americans, Whites and others. So, perhaps the first issue to be dealt with is specifically when whites can call African Americans N.

The important features of situations in which this is possible without offense, assume a certain type of relationship among the interlocutors, are African-American cultural dominance (and perhaps numerical dominance) and inter-personal relationships involving Whites who are able to function in a culturally African-American way and who have established solid, trusting relationships with African Americans. One context where one definitely finds at least some Whites permitted N-use would be urban basketball courts (Curbelo 1994). It would appear that only among younger African Americans, say those under thirty, does one find appreciable numbers who accept, under stipulation, N-use by Whites.

Certainly, the great majority of African Americans, male and female, use N when among other African Americans, and do so regardless of their attitudes about N-use. In other words, some may be against N-use, but use it nevertheless. N-use attitudes are mostly of two types: positive and negative. The negative view is presented well by a twenty-eight-year-old college student (who uses an AW):

> There is a real danger when we ourselves have accepted the use of a word that was imposed on us by our oppressors to degrade and humiliate our ancestors. By us allowing this word to permeate our communities, our minds and our vocabulary, is like we're saying to the white man-slaveholder, "Yeah, you're right we ain't nothing but a stinky-ass nigger anyway." So we need to raise our consciousness and stop this annihilation.
>
> (quoted in Curbelo 1994)

The positive view has quite eloquently been expressed thus:

> Look, we have the power to determine how and what we say. We can't let no white man determine that for us. It's like, if we ain't gonna use it because white people have misused it, that's bullshit. We need to take

the power back and have control over our own lives and that includes how we talk and the words we use. . . . I mean great black poems have been written about "nigger" by great "niggas" for "niggas". . . . It can be an empowering word, and it can show black pride. In the '70s, you saw a lot of that, people in Afros calling each other "nigger," making music about it, writing poems, making films. . . . I just saw a documentary recently on Malcolm X, made in the '70s, and the opening is this whole thing showing black people in Afros on the street, and there was some kind of tune through this whole thing saying, "Nigger, nigger, nigger" . . . . It was deep, real powerful stuff . . .

(quoted in Curbelo 1994)

My data and understanding of N-use indicate that the use of the word itself is a marker of UM since most speakers would censor it in what I have termed censored contexts (see above).

N has definitely been neutralized, and I sense that it is used positively as much as negatively. We might also distinguish neutral uses, whereby N simply means 'guy, dude, homeboy, homie, brotha' (brother), or 'partna' (partner). These uses appear to be quantitatively predominant.

The following are examples.

(7) a. Da's a funny nigga, he be tellin' jokes all-la time and be havin' us rollin'. (*neutral*) (Birdsong 1994)
   b. (Ready to fight) Wussup (what's up), nigga! (*negative*) (Gibbs 1994)
   c. (Greeting a friend, followed by a hug) Wussup (what's up), nigga! (*positive*) (Gibbs 1994)
   d. my nigga (said of boyfriend or husband)

Apposite to issues revolving around N-use is a short writing by Gloria Naylor, the well-known African-American author of the novels *The Women of Brewster Place and Mama Day*.[12] She makes the crucial point that the meaning of words does not inhere in the sequence of sounds they are made of.

As linguists must repeatedly emphasize, the meanings of words is for the most part conventional, assigned by society in the process of use. Words are what people make of them. The meanings of those sound sequences we call words change over time, through linguistic drift below the level of consciousness, and sometimes by means of conscious, political activism. Witness what happened

12 Unfortunately, an exact reference cannot be provided. The copy of this writing that I have does not identify the publication but does state that the article first appeared in *The New York Times* in 1986. A search of *Times* indexes did not turn up the article, however. Nor did searches of a number of indexes and other references. No response has been received from queries sent to the author. It seems that the writing that came into my hands may be an excerpt of a longer piece.

with the apotheosis of the word *black* during the Black is Beautiful Movement of the 1960s and 1970s. (Of course, in some segments of the African-American community there has been a marked recidivism, as *black* regains ground as a term of abuse.[13])

Naylor describes how she had actually heard N used in her home and neighborhood environment many times before N was hurled at her by a White person. She reacted that time, knowing something was wrong but not sure of what it was. She learned from that incident that N was a word that can be used to humiliate. Of course, what she heard was what some African Americans consider a different word, one with a distinctive pronunciation and intent (which I spell *n-i-g-g-e-r*). In her view, the African Americans she knew had taken a term of degradation in the mouths of Whites and defanged it. N was used by African Americans to refer to the "varied and complex human beings they knew themselves to be."

Naylor adds to the list the following types of examples (not verbatim):

(8) a. *triflin niggas* (said of neglectful parent, public drunks, the contentedly unemployed, poor housekeepers, etc.) (*negative*)
   b. I'm telling you, that *nigga* kicked ass! (admiration) (*positive*)

N has long had a neutralized use among African Americans, probably since the earliest days of Anglophone North America. This is nothing new. What is new, however, is generalized reference, i.e., using N to refer to anyone of any race or ethnicity. Thus, White public school teachers hear themselves referred to as "that White nigga" or simply "nigga," and Asian Americans in San Francisco can be heard, as they navigate high school hallways, to call one another *niggas*; and the same is true of White students (Grant Venerable, p.c.). This is also the usage across the San Francisco Bay in Oakland, where, too, N is not racially or ethnically specific (Richard Wright V, p.c.). N still, however, prototypically refers to blacks since it is not normally qualified by *African American, Black*, or any other term that denotes African Americans, though qualifiers referring to other ethnicities are not unusual. Nevertheless, it should be stressed that N is used for non-blacks without ethnic modification.[14]

---

13 I have always found it curious that not only *black* but also *yella* (cf. *yellow*) and *high yella* (almost or as light-skinned as a white person) can be terms of abuse. Thus, one would hear the following negative statements,

Look at that black bitch/muthafucka.
Look at that yella/high yella bitch/muthafucka.

but *Look at that brown(-skinned) bitch/muthafucka* doesn't work if intended as an insult.

14 Of course, *nigger* has been used in figures of speech to refer to groups today considered white, e.g., *nigger turned inside out*, said of the Irish in the nineteenth century, and sometimes used by African Americans (and no doubt Whites) today in reference to light-skinned Hispanics.

N used with generalized reference among African Americans and others is most probably a result of the near hegemony of African-American popular culture among youth. Generalized reference is limited to youth and continues to stun older (roughly, over thirty-five) African Americans and non-African Americans when they hear it so used.

As noted already, N most often means 'guy', or 'dude', to use an older term. It is almost never used to refer to females unless they are referred to as part of a collective including males. It has also, to repeat, been ethnically and racially generalized.

It is interesting that the same thing has happened with N cognates in other languages, e.g., Haitian Creole *nèg* and Brazilian Portuguese *nego*. Consequently, this development should not be taken as exceptional. Why does this happen? There is no definite answer. It probably happens in contexts where Blacks, or people of color, are in certain respects culturally dominant, and generalized usage among them spreads to the wider population. Ethnically generalized reference in the United States can almost certainly be attributed to African-American popular culture hegemony and notably rap music. The Haitian historical facts surely fit. The Brazilian case, however, is more complex; and, while this is a reasonable explanation, it requires further research for firmer support.

To return to example (1), we are now in a better position to provide a translation. N would normally refer to a male, and of course not necessarily a black one. *Bitch-ass*, which would typically refer to a female, can also refer to males, but in the sense of 'male who has qualities stereotypically linked to females,' i.e., someone not manly, lacking in courage, weak. This particular phrase refers to males, of course, since N normally refers to males. *Muthafuckin* here functions principally as a marker of UM, i.e., its function is primarily expressive-discursive. Thus, possible translations of *muthafuckin bitch-ass nigga*, with no censored words, are 'wimp', 'unmanly guy', 'chicken' (in the sense of coward), 'sissy', and so forth.

8.4 Discussion

We are now in a better position to return to the four questions raised at the beginning of this chapter:

Question 1 It is impossible to forbid the use of any expression, at least not in any broad range of contexts, so the question of prohibition is a non-starter. This is not theoretically but practically so since the resources for the level of social engineering required would never be allocated in a society such as ours. Obscenity, in the final analysis, is in the ears of the hearer. The labeling of expressions as obscene varies socially, regionally, and temporally. Thinking on words as well as actions and images to be censored varies with respect to social context, region, and time.[15]

If obscenity is considered with regard to its essence, we are really talking about what is considered, by some people on some occasions, as unacceptable speech, which covers not only expressions, but also topics, tropes, and aspects of grammar (in the broad, socially adequate sense, including pronunciation, morphology, syntax, semantics, and pragmatics). Unacceptable speech, then, is the appropriate unit of analysis, especially if we aim for a socioculturally viable theory of "bad" language, which accords due attention to relations of power and dominance. Speech is deemed unacceptable for a variety of reasons, ranging from prohibitions against "using the Lord's name in vain" to those against using language considered abusive or supportive of inequalities (related to sexism, heterosexism, classism, and white supremacy). Non-standard language is seen as unacceptable for reasons ranging from a perceived need for standardization in the service of capitalist-based technology and enterprise to the creation and maintenance of cultural capital. Some expressions, for example, are eschewed simply because they bring us, species chauvinists that we tend to be, too closely face to face with our animal biology, e.g., *shit*, *fuck*, and others denoting basic biological functions.

Thus seen, one can assume that unacceptable or "bad" speech is an ever-present feature of human social life. We have reason to hypothesize that the complexity and volume of speech labeled unacceptable has increased historically as sociocultural complexity itself has increased, especially in respect to socio-cultural stratification, which ranks groups and the cultural particulars associated with them in terms of their unequal access to resources. The existence of unacceptable speech assumes the desire to censor speech, but in class-stratified societies it also reflects the power to do so. Hence, with regard to the normal-ized expressions of concern, one could suppose that they might well have been decensored by now were it not for the normative pressures of the hegemonic institutions with which normalizing speakers must negotiate, if only infrequently.

Question 2 Obscenity and other unacceptable language is certainly normal, in the sense that it has always been with us. Normal/abnormal distinctions are the product of social convention and consequently hinge fundamentally on culture- and class-based value judgments. If certain social groups have normalized language called unacceptable by others, then that language is normal for the former.

There are at least three real issues, the first two related to the social distribution of power and influence: Who has the power to judge? Who has the power to censor? Both powers exist all along the social scale, but toward the bottom censorship fades into mere censure, buttressed by ridicule, loss of status, and ostracism. The issue that sociolinguists should do more to broadcast

---

15 Consider for example the Irish text of biblical and other Christian writings, the *Book of Kells* (approximately AD 800), whose illustrations include among things a masturbating soldier (Scott Jaschik, "Notes from academe: Ireland – inside the Irish imagination: the medieval Book of Kells seen through modern eyes," *The Chronicle of Higher Education*, 28 February 1997, p. B2).

concerns the communicative competence underlying what are actually value judgments. This issue, adumbrated above, is particularly relevant for middle- and upper-middle-class African Americans and Whites who have the economic and cultural capital to pass judgments in this society. The problem is that critics and social commentators in these two categories *typically* lack the communicative competence necessary, but assume they possess it. With African Americans, this is because they may indeed be competent in some African-American groups in some African-American communities and take for granted that they are competent in all African-American cultural spheres.

In some ways, such African Americans are victims of not realizing how fast cultural change has occurred in Black America since the 1960s, whose events and movements unleashed the significant cultural divergence within the African-American world that we see today. Under segregation, upper-status African Americans did have a clearer picture of the range of behaviors throughout the social continuum. Those who have reached the age and position to see their writing published in major outlets of hegemonic discourse such as the largest-circulation newsweeklies and *The New York Times* are too old and too removed by class and cultural change to retain any authority they may once have had.

There has been an increasing sociocultural and geographical separation between lower-income and higher-income African Americans, due primarily to the creation of African-American middle- and upper-middle-class suburbs and the increasing entry of upper-status African Americans into higher-paying occupations, both results of the Civil Rights Movement.

Whites apparently assume competence on the basis that they are Anglophone Americans, but the assumption itself rests on a cultural presumptuousness. So it is, for example, that Janet Maslin, the head film critic at *The New York Times*, confused the issue in her review of the 1994 Boaz Yakin film *Fresh*, wherein the main character, a twelve-year-old African-American boy called Fresh, is supposedly "so numb to racial epithets that he often uses 'nigger' when address-ing his white friend" ("Black, 12 and complex: more than role models," *The New York Times*, 1 April 1994, C6). Most African Americans would not consider the friend white, but that is another issue. As already pointed out, *nigga* has been neutralized, normalized, and generalized in reference. The fact that the Fresh character used it as he did cannot, consequently, be employed in this way as a launching pad to social commentary. It is to Yakin's credit that he was tuned in enough, even though non-African American, to Fresh's poverty-stricken, drug-infested milieu to present a level of linguistic realism going beyond general knowledge. (Ms Maslin, I should note, figures among the most thoughtful of film critics. The example merely illustrates a feature of our social ecology, and she is willy-nilly a product of her times and milieu.)

Question 3 As to whether the kind of speech discussed above indicates a degeneration in social life, much can be said. However, I will limit myself to a discussion that leads to the principal point I wish to present in this chapter, namely, that the meaning and function of all speech is a matter of interpretation, in the sense that what speech means is not always apparent in any direct way. This is so, for one thing, because language is used both literally and figuratively. Much speech is full of tropes, and even layers of tropes, which to varying degrees remove tokens from the sphere of literal, direct interpretation. By *token*, I mean specific instances of speech said in specific social situations by and to specific interlocutors with specific social identities, histories, motivations, and goals. In other words, tokens are necessarily linked to a social environment and the performance of social work, e.g., joking, oath-taking, informing, engaging in small talk, and so forth. Consequently, speech does not always reflect beliefs, attitudes, and behavior in a direct way. Etiquette, humor, and norms for the interpretation of speech vary from community to community. The ability to interpret and thereby have the basis for evaluating the speech of one's peers and others is necessary for functioning successfully in one's community. Indeed, some arrogance is implied when a person outside of the community in which a cultural form originates steps forward, prior to rigorous analysis, to interpret and evaluate it.

The major point to consider is that just because we "speak the same language," it does not mean that we use that language the same way in communicating. Different social groups have their own rules for language use and the evaluation of speech. This applies to different subgroups within the same ethnic group or "race." Keep in mind also that different social groups speak different dialects, so in some cases we are confronted with words which sound and seem to be the same or similar but are not.[16]

Obviously, the language of low-income, urban African-American youth is not completely divorced from that of middle-class White or African-American parents. However, it would be unwise in the extreme for these people to assume that they know what, to take one example, rap songs mean – linguistically and socially. The literature devoted to language study reveals many examples of people assuming they have completely understood each other, when in reality serious miscommunication has occurred. Speaking a language variety closely related to the other's often falsely lulls us into assuming that we are competent to judge what the other says.

This said, there is still room in some cases for criticism. What the foregoing comments imply is not that we should not judge, but that we should do so with

---

16 Major differences in language use are largely responsible, for example, for the continuing conflicts between certain African Americans and Jewish Americans. The tension is especially exacerbated when African Americans speak to other African Americans in "hearing distance" of others, or when others "listen in on" speech intended for African Americans solely. Upper-caste Anglophones typically refuse to believe they are not competent to interpret a wide range of lower-caste Anglophone, i.e. African-American, speech. As happens commonly, bidirection-ality in communicative competence breaks down most descending the social scale. See Kochman (1981) for excellent examples.

the appropriate knowledge and caution. In other words, cultural critique is always in order, e.g., the cultural critique that occurred during the Black is Beautiful Movement within the Civil Rights Movement. We should also be aware that what is, is not always what should be. We might expect that, even when properly interpreted by those fully competent to do so, 2 Live Crew's lyrics, to take one example, do show signs of sexism, among other things. But, then again, 2 Live Crew are males in a sexist society. We should not forget that sexism and other social ills are the problem. The lyrics of this group as well as the verbal output of any individuals are useful diagnostics of social ills only to the extent that they are interpreted in their proper sociocultural context.

Question 4 To the extent that we are required to provide a theory of uncensored speech in order to account for its grammar and use, we will learn something fundamental not only about language in the African-American community, but also in all communities, given that uncensored speech can be assumed to be present in all sociocultural settings. An adequate understanding of uncensored speech will certainly assist in analyzing and perhaps dissolving problems arising from intergroup communication. These problems can go significantly beyond misunderstandings, which we often find in film and book reviews.

Some examples will help to illustrate this point. It is interesting that the expressions *Hymie* and *Hymietown* are not normally used by African Americans in the Chicago area, although they are current among Whites. It is ironic, then, that Jesse Jackson, the African-American politician and long-time Chicago resident who used the latter and was severely criticized for doing so, used an expression atypical in the African-American speech of that area, regardless of wherever he may have actually picked the expression up. These expressions are, however, normalized in the speech of some sectors of the White Chicago community. A very interesting sociolinguistic, psychological, and political question is whether Jackson, trying to fit into the mainstream, White culture of informal settings, innocently used a term that he was not communicatively competent to use. The notions of uncensored mode, neutralization, and normalization provide us with a framework to pose more sophisticated questions regarding instances of verbal offense.

Another example: Where I grew up, *bastard* was normalized (and therefore neutralized), particularly among young African-American, male peer groups. I once used the French equivalent, *bâtard*, in addressing (in Paris, at a student residence) a young, male French friend, who became extremely upset. Fortunately, I was able to metacommunicate (in language available to me at the time) the relevant cultural differences in terms of neutralization and normalization and thereby to diffuse the situation.

246

8.5 Conclusion

My main concern in writing this has been the African-American middle and upper classes, within whose ranks are found those with the most network resources, education, skills, assets, and entrepreneurial know-how. This is the segment of the African-American community that most needs to have an over-all understanding of African-American culture. Often, in these two groups, understanding of African-American culture is limited to those aspects that pertain narrowly to these classes. While it is also positive for people of other ethnic groups to understand African-American culture and the African-American community – as well as those of non-AfricanAmericans – it is the African-American middle and upper classes who will have the most concern and motivation for using knowledge gained of the whole of African-American culture in a constructive way.

More affluent African Americans' scorn for aspects of mass African-American culture (those traits of African-American culture[17] that are concentrated in lower-income groups and that most distinguish it from those of White culture) has a long history. This is certainly not the only response to mass African-American culture, but it is a prominent one. It is neither surprising nor inevitable and is a reflex of misinformation and/or the internalized oppression typical of all groups that have been long oppressed (Fanon 1968 [1961]; Spears 1991, 1992). It is not surprising because such negative attitudes are inculcated and supported by powerful, White-elite-controlled institutions. That such scorn continues is testimony to the relative weakness of African-American mass media, and the poor (and hindered) distribution of African-American intellectual output. Very few non-scholarly African-American publications present sophisticated cultural and specifically political/economic debate with any regularity. *Crisis*, founded by the venerable W. E. B. DuBois; *Emerge*, the newsmonthly; and New York City's *Amsterdam News* are notable among the exceptions. The more successful African-American popular periodicals slavishly promote American-style electoral politics and capitalism, as they are lavishly supported by advertisers benefiting from those institutions. Sharp critique, even with tacit acceptance of the American political and economic system, is typically punished by no advertising from major White corporations. Witness the demise of *The National Leader* during the 1980s, unable to continue with only the advertising of a few relatively progressive African-American corporations (and, of course, some liquor and cigarette advertising).

African-American popular culture is one of the primary engines of American popular culture, and it springs, as is typical of the main currents of popular culture, from lower-income sectors of the community. The cultural prejudices of

---

17 This is not to imply that African-American culture is monolithic; indeed, there are many cultures but they can be seen as having a shared core.

many entrepreneurial middle-class African Americans have prevented them from recognizing prime business opportunities in popular African-American culture. Observe how two of the most important musical movements in the post-Civil Rights era, reggae and rap, were long shunned by the most important African-American media enterprises, allowing White companies to move in to commercialize these musical forms without competition from African Americans, who were better positioned to do so.

Uncensored speech cannot be profitably discussed without emphasizing the twoness of African-American consciousness in the United States, first exposed by DuBois (1961 [1903]). Twoness is basically the dual personality caused by the cohabitation of two consciousnesses or cultural systems within one mind, the White and the African-American, the hegemonic and the subaltern. African-American middle- and upper-class negative attitudes towards mass African-American culture are all the more ironic because many, perhaps most, of these African Americans on occasion use the same type of uncensored speech that is probably more widespread among lower-income African Americans. Their White counterparts behave similarly in regard to the speech of their lower-income counterparts.[18] It is almost as though, while operating within the hegemonic framework, African Americans (like members of other ethnic groups throughout the world who have their own versions of dual consciousness) sometimes criticize what they themselves do when operating out of their alternate consciousness. Observe the following example (Geneva Smitherman, p.c.), uttered by an African-American woman church member in a discussion during which she expressed her firm opposition to the use of *nigga*: "Well . . . just tell me one thing: why niggas always got to be using the word *nigga* so much?"

Acknowledgments

The research presented in this chapter was supported in part by the the CUNY Institute for Research on the African Diaspora and the Caribbean (IRADAC). I want to thank especially Darrell Dillon and Dale Burts, among many others, for the information they provided.

18 I make the distinction between the amount of uncensored speech used by upper- and lower-income groups on the basis of the fact that in the lower-income groups there is greater unemployment but more employment where censored speech is not required. This is not to claim that there is no uncensored speech in upper-income occupational settings – far from it – only that within those settings, there is a higher number of subsettings requiring censored speech.

References

Andersson, Lars and Peter Trudgill (1990) *Bad Language*. Cambridge, MA: Blackwell.

Birdsong, Michael D. (1994) "The question of the 'N' word: The when, the why, the who, and the what." The City College, The City University of New York term paper for course on African-American English.

Bolton, Kingsley and Christopher Hutton (1995) "Bad and banned language: Triad secret societies, the censorship of the Cantonese vernacular, and colonial language policy in Hong Kong." *Language in Society* 24.2: 159–186.

Curbelo, Evelyn (1994) "Paper on 'Nigger.'" The City College, The City University of New York term paper for course on African-American English.

Davis, Hayley (1989) "What makes bad language bad?" *Language and Communication* 9: 1–9.

DuBois, W. E. B. (1961 [1903]) *The Souls of Black Folk*. Greenwich, CT: Fawcett Publications, Inc.

Dyson, Michael Eric. 1993. *Reflecting Black: African-American cultural criticism*. Minneapolis: University of Minnesota Press.

Fanon, Frantz (1968 [1961]) *The Wretched of the Earth*, C. Farrington (trans.). New York: Grove.

Gibbs, Jonathan W. (1994) "The use of words: How so-called foul words can have many meanings." The City College, The City University of New York term paper for course on African-American English.

Gumperz, John J. and Dell Hymes (eds.) (1964) "The ethnography of communication." *American Anthropologist* 66.6, pt II: 1–34.

—— (1972) *Directions in Sociolinguistics: The Ethnography of Communication*. New York: Holt, Rinehart, and Winston.

Halliday, Michael (1976) "Anti-languages." *American Anthropologist* 78: 570–584.

Hooks, Bell (1990) *Yearning: Race, Gender, and Cultural Politics*. Boston: South End Press.

Hughes, Geoffrey (1992) *Swearing: A Social History of Foul Language, Oaths and Profanity in English*. Cambridge, MA: Blackwell.

Jay, Timothy (1992) *Cursing in America: A Psycholinguistic Study of Dirty Language in the Courts, in the Movies, in the Schoolyards and on the Streets*. Amsterdam: John Benjamins.

Kochman, Thomas (1981) *Black and White: Styles in Conflict*. Chicago: University of Chicago Press.

Rose, Tricia (1994) *Black Noise: Rap Music and Black Culture in Contemporary America*. Hanover, NH: Wesleyan University Press / University Press of New England.

Smitherman, Geneva (1994) *Black Talk: Words and Phrases from the Hood to the Amen Corner*. Boston: Houghton Mifflin.

Spears, Arthur K. (1988) "Black American English." In *Anthropology for the Nineties*, Johnnetta B. Cole (ed.). New York: The Free Press, pp. 96–113.

—— (1991) "Teaching race, racism, and ideology." In *Transforming Anthropology* (special issue, *Teaching as Praxis: Race and Ideologies of Power*, Pem Davidson Buck and Deborah D'Amico [eds.]) 2.1: 16–21.

—— (1992) "Culture critique and colorstruction: Black-produced media images of Blacks." In *Transforming Anthropology* (special issue, *Teaching as Praxis: Decolonizing Media Representations of Race, Ethnicity, and Gender in the New World Order*, Andrew A. Maxwell and Pem Davidson Buck [eds.]) 3.1: 24–29.

Whatley, Elizabeth (1981) "Language among Black Americans." In *Language in the USA*,

Charles A. Ferguson and Shirley Brice Heath (eds.). Cambridge: Cambridge University Press, pp. 92–107.

Zwicky, Arnold M., P. H. Salus, Robert I. Binnick, and A. L. Vanek (1971) *Studies Out in Left Field: Defamatory Essays Presented to James D. McCawley*. Edmonton: Linguistic Research, Inc.

9

MORE THAN A MOOD OR AN ATTITUDE: DISCOURSE AND VERBAL GENRES IN AFRICAN-AMERICAN CULTURE

Marcyliena Morgan

9.1 Introduction

Research on African-American discourse, verbal genres, and interactions has been voluminous, covering the fields of linguistics, folklore, anthropology, sociology, psychology, education, and literary criticism. The way African Americans talk to each other not only reveals how languages are socially constructed (e.g., Volosinov 1973; Bakhtin 1981), but that speech events, activities, participants, and context affect language in complex and often unpredictable ways (cf. Goffman 1974; Hymes 1974; Gumperz 1982; Ochs 1992). An analysis of how language has contributed to the social construction of the African-American experience is especially illuminating since omnificent African-American verbal styles and repertoires continue to flourish, in spite of American middle-class values which both criticize and fetishize the culture and language. The concrete result of this dualism is a dominant culture which describes African-American speech as bad, uneducated, unintelligible, etc., while wantonly imitating and celebrating its wit, creative vitality, and resilience.

This chapter explores many of the verbal and discourse genres and practices which constitute the African-American speech community. In the discussion that follows, *discourse genres* refer to language and communication styles which commonly occur in socially, culturally, and politically defined contexts. In contrast, *verbal genres* refer to speaker's use of culturally significant varieties and styles which mediate, constitute, and construct contexts. Thus, while both discourse and verbal genres may co-construct various contexts, verbal genres can collide with strongly framed discourse norms eroding or disrupting well-defined social contexts. The following analysis locates various speech genres within a system of social face that is partially constructed through directed and indirect discourse. This system includes: *signifying* or *sounding*, adolescent *instigating*, adult *conversational signifying*, *reading a person*, and *reading dialect*. These styles and practices combine to mark the African-American speech community as distinct across generation, gender, and class.

9.2 Social face and forms of speech

Scholarly discussions of verbal performance and discourse are often explorations into how power or status is expressed and negotiated in society (Brenneis and Meyers 1984; Fabian 1990; Kuipers 1990; Yankah 1995). This is also true in African-American communities, where social standing and cultural membership are constructed according to how a speaker interacts when among members of the dominant culture, and within all social strata of the African-American community. The cultural value attached to how one negotiates both interactive domains provides an exegesis of how individuals communicate culture, identity, and citizen rights. In this sense one's social *face* is partially determined by the ability to construct (or co-construct) social relationships and deconstruct the power/truth dynamics of social interaction. Thus language is viewed as a mediated social act and, as argued earlier by Volosinov (1973: 68): "what is important for a speaker about a linguistic form is not that it is a stable and always self-equivalent sign, but that it is an always changeable and adaptable sign." Accordingly, from the speech community's perspective, language and interaction are constituted through stabilized norms and the control and power speakers may exercise over those norms. Within this particular framework, words, phrases, and the existence of dominant grammatical and phonological norms are resources which reinforce, highlight, exploit, and critique social and cultural roles. This is especially true of African-American urban youth, for whom the interminable invention and re-invention of African-American terms, e.g., *frontin'* (being deceptive), *dissin'* (being disrespectful), and *readin'* (exposing someone's interactive deception), actually serve to unravel the relation of verbal skill and social and political power (cf. Foucault 1973, 1980, 1981).[1] As the popular "old school" music rapper Big Daddy Kane demonstrates:

> I'll damage ya, I'm not an amateur
> But a professional, unquestionable, without a doubt superb
> So full of action, my name should be a verb
> > (Harding [p.k.a. Big Daddy Kane] 1988)

While there are many African-American terms which describe various forms of social face, perhaps the most widespread cultural concept which both critiques and symbolizes its construction is the notion of being *cool* (current and trend

---

1 All of these terms have been in use for over two decades (Major 1970, 1977, 1994; Smitherman 1994) though their meanings have shifted over time. The definitions included here are those of urban youth and rap fans (Braithwaite 1992; Jones 1994).

setting, calm, detached, yet in control) in any situation (cf. Major 1994; Smitherman 1994). Gwaltney (1981: 143) pays tribute to the cultural value of this social stance in his description of one of his community contributors, Nancy White: "She is the exemplar par excellence of the highest status that core black culture can accord – that of the cool, dealing individual." Rapper Kool Moe Dee, in his 1991 hit "How kool can one black man be?", also provides insight into this cultural concept:

> But cool ain't a mood/ It's an attitude dude/ It's a tone/ It's a tempo/ A mind set/ A rhythm/ Lifestyle/ Religion/ It's just how ya' livin'/ I'm righteously cool/ While here and hereafter/ I'm so cool/ That I have to ask ya'/ How cool?/ How cool?/ How cool can one black man be?/
>
> (Dewese 1991)

In a cultural sense, a cool face is the ability to act on symbolic incidents and subtle varieties of cultural practice with eloquence, skill, wit, patience, and precise timing. Though some scholars and artists have tied African Americans' reverence of a cool social face to racism and/or male coping skills (Abrahams 1962; Grier & Cobbs 1968; Horton 1972; Kunjufu 1986; George 1992; Majors and Billson 1992), it is clear that *coolness* is mainly a cultural practice (cf. Smitherman 1977; Gwaltney 1981) used by both men and women and having counterparts in all parts of the African Diaspora and Africa (Alleyne 1980, 1989; Yankah 1995).[2] It exists in contrast to *fools* or *acting a fool*, a cultural insult which both denigrates and dismisses a person as a cultural member. Mabel Lincoln describes this type of outcast:

> To black people like me, a fool is funny – you know, people who love to break bad, people you can't tell anything to, folks that will take a shotgun to a roach. (. . .) But most of us try to be cool. That is what we respect the most in ourselves and look for in other people. That means being a person of sober, quiet judgement.
>
> (Gwaltney 1981: 68–69)

Being cool is important, especially in interactions, because indirect discourse requires that all participants (including hearers) constantly assess and address potential meanings within and across contexts. Coolness then, is one of the symbolic *goods* which has exchange value and can be used to accrue linguistic and pragmatic capital. One can *lose their cool* or social face in interactions where participants may be culturally challenged (e.g., not know current lexical terms

---

2 For example, African-American coolness is similar to the Akan notion of "dry" speech as clear, precise, witty, and having integrity. This contrasts with Akan "wet" or "un-cool" speech, which is viewed as immature, dull, and slurred (cf. Yankah 1995).

or meanings), or when the dominant culture (e.g., the police, legal system, school) argues that a particular form of interaction (e.g., *baited indirection* below) is not understood.

The way in which African-American verbal style constitutes social face can be attributed to three discernible factors: (1) the retention and adaptation of African styles of interaction, (2) face-to-face rules for Black/White interactions which were enforced from slavery until the end of segregation, and (3) urbanization and popular culture's role in the coalescence of a national Black youth identity. These factors are examined through a discussion of the role and construction of audience(s) in interaction and the importance of indirect discourse and direct speech.

9.2.1 Audience and interaction

African-American interaction intricately entwines multiple norms and levels of language and style. The speech community greatly values and celebrates the ability to manipulate and mediate varieties and genres. African-American *heteroglossia* (Bakhtin 1981; Duranti 1994) refers to the simultaneous existence and use of multiple norms and forms of language and communication style which comprise a coherent yet contrasting system of language and discourse rules and norms. This type of interaction is not unique to the United States, and has been widely reported in Africa and throughout the African Diaspora (e.g., Reisman 1974; Fisher 1976; Irvine 1974, 1982, 1993; Hunter 1982; Saah 1984; M. Morgan 1989, 1993; Yankah 1995). Though there are many similarities between the language and communication norms in other Diaspora situations, African-American heteroglossia developed under the added element of repressive segregationist laws.

It is important to remember that until the 1970s, Southern segregationists attempted to control and regulate verbal interactions of Blacks, and especially interactions between Blacks and Whites. These policies, which were protected by the legal system, considered certain forms of direct talk by African Americans to constitute claims regarding rights and status (K. Morgan 1980; Gwaltney 1981; M. Morgan 1994a). Thus *talk* and *interaction* were constitutive elements of a system of inequity, and participants' social roles were partially constructed through conversation. The resulting unwritten, but enforced, policy meant that in order to participate in the average Black/White interaction, a Black person minimally had to abide by language and communicative rules which functioned to mark a presumed belief in the superiority of a White audience/hearer. Some rules of how Blacks were to communicate with Whites included: (1) talking only when permission was granted; (2) never having direct eye contact; (3) never using educated speech (unless told to perform); (4) determining and then saying whatever the person wanted to hear, etc. (M. Morgan 1994b).

The harsh consequences that might result when the communicative dictums described above were ignored have been brilliantly illustrated in many slave narratives and literature about segregation and Black cultural life (e.g., Brent 1973; Gwaltney 1981; Johnson 1982; Walker 1982; Simonsen 1986; Williams 1986; Morrison 1987; Whitfield 1992). In one particularly wrenching account of how these conversational dictums operated in the segregated South, John Henry Martin, a tenant farmer, recalls verbally challenging a White landowner who had cheated him out of his payment for the tobacco harvest.

> I said, "Mr Lewis, what about my check? I ain't got none, and I had tobacco." He said, "John Henry, I just don't know what the problem is." And the devil flew in me! I said, "You got that damn check!" He said, "Naw, I don't know nothing about it." I wanted to hit the old man. But I thought to myself, "Naw, it ain't no need of hitting him. You done enough, done talked to him so." . . . I told my wife 'bout it, and she said, "Lord, we gonna have to move!"
>
> (James 1993: 29)

Though Mr Martin clearly and directly articulates that he thought Mr Lewis kept his money, he also considers the voicing of his thoughts equivalent to physically attacking Mr Lewis. He recognizes that he has broken the rules of Black/White interaction by directly accusing Mr Lewis of keeping his profits, and his wife corroborates his dire assessment of the interaction with her statement "Lord, we gonna have to move!" Thus Mr Martin's use of a statement which revealed that Mr Lewis cheated him was enough to jeopardize his and his family's economic survival and life.

The situation described above includes many of the conditions for the development of antisocieties as described by Goffman (1961) and Halliday (1978). *Antisocieties* typically emerge when those who dominate individuals require that the subjugated reaffirm or co-construct, in public, the dominator/ dominated relationship by verbal or physical confirmation (e.g., bowing heads or saying "Yes sir/mam"). However, antisocieties should not be viewed solely as underground institutions. They are in response to control from those with power and are only underground in the sense that disempowered or marginalized groups participate in them. Consequently, from the perspective of the non-dominant group, they are very much above the ground and a significant aspect of everyday speech.

In response to the demand that they have the *attitude* of someone who should be oppressed, African-American culture and antisociety undermined the values, attitudes, and beliefs that the dominant society held toward them (Bryce-Laporte 1971) through the use of existing African systems of indirectness (M. Morgan 1989, 1991, 1993). Once the phenomenology of indirectness became pervasive within African-American culture and social encounters, interactions, words, or phrases could have contradictory or multiple meanings beyond traditional English interpretations. Thus the *counterlanguage* functioned to signal the antisociety (e.g., Black audience) and provided a means for a speaker to reveal a social face which resisted and contested the practice of racial repression.

As part of the counterlanguage, and in stark contrast to the cross-racial rules of interaction outlined earlier, Black interactions embodied and highlighted an exacting sense of speaker agency (M. Morgan 1993). This intense focus on speaker agency was co-constructed with a Black audience for whom language forms and styles signal that content or speaker intent is being camouflaged. In other words, within the system of repression, the counterlanguage provided a vehicle for face-work (Goffman 1967) and protected and confirmed the existence of the antisociety. It constituted speaker agency so that the act of talking was potentially political and highly symbolic.

Within the above framework, the basic concept of audience included all Black hearers and potential hearers, as well as the likelihood that there were spies and overhearers/reporters. Thus the audience and hearer, whether immediately present or presumed present through gossip, spies, etc., were socially and culturally constructed entities. As a result, speakers were also expected to exhibit their interactional prowess and manage to direct what was said to a Black audience who, in turn, held him or her responsible for what was said as well as possible interpretations. Thus in many profound ways, a speaker's social face, status, and standing – or *cool* – was always at stake (Smitherman 1977; M. Morgan 1991).[3]

This discussion has explored how African Americans resisted rules which governed how they talked in public by adapting indirect language and communication system(s) inherited from Africa – a system that most non-African Americans were unaware existed. This system encompassed multiple audiences, layers of understanding, and concomitant multiple subjectivities. It may not have survived and been adapted, were it not for dominant Southern society's insistent communication and language monitoring of African Americans. Irrespective of the reason for its present significance in African-American interactions, it is the foundation of all African-American discourse.

9.2.2 Indirectness

The social contexts in which African Americans interact include a complex system of indirectness, co-constructed intentionality, and speaker responsibility (Smitherman 1977; Kochman 1981; M. Morgan 1991). These features demonstrate the coalescence and adaptation of several African language practices. Two practices in particular shape African-American language use. One is the use of intermediaries in conversation and the other is the tension between indirect and direct speech.

---

3 Speakers, therefore, were rarely viewed as innocent in terms of intent; and what a speaker may argue is a *misunderstanding* is largely viewed as the hearers' *understanding* of what the speaker really means (M. Morgan 1989, 1991).

Intermediate or instrumental agents have been reported to be central in interactions and formal talk throughout Africa and the Diaspora (Irvine 1974, 1982; Reisman 1974; Fisher 1976; Hunter 1982; Saah 1984; Yankah 1995; M. Morgan 1989, 1993).

In fact Yankah (1995) reports that numerous African societies practice social and verbal indirection through intermediaries who protect the public "face" of chiefs. For example, in many African societies where audiences must confirm the leader's right to lead, those in power often use a spokesperson to deliver a message and mediate for them in case the audience finds fault in the message. In this instance the sender, who never addresses the audience, has some protection (Irvine 1974, 1982; Hunter 1982; Saah 1984; M. Morgan 1989, 1993). Yankah goes on to explain that verbal genres can also serve the function of mediators in interaction.

> In some parts of Africa and the Diaspora folk tale, libation, and epic performances adopt various modes of mediation, such as integrated responses, that are intended to minimize the hazards of performance. These verbal genres, by their very norms of performance are thus partly conditioned to save face.
>
> (1991b: 3)

Within the African-American community in the United States, verbal acts also function to save face as they address multiple audiences, some aware and some unaware, through camouflaging. For example, in the Americas, those of African descent often argue that musical performers cannot be held responsible for any inappropriate interpretation of the meanings of lyrics by unintended audiences who do not understand that the music has a mediating function.[4] As a result, intentionality and responsibility are viewed as both socially situated and constituted so that speakers and audience collaborate in determining what is meant by what is said (Duranti 1993). Thus speakers who use indirectness mean to target certain individuals and mean to do so indirectly.

While African-American indirectness can take many forms in discourse, there are essentially two forms which seem to be indicative:

1   *Pointed indirectness* (a) when a speaker means to say something to a mock receiver that is intended for someone else and is so recognized; and (b) when a speaker refers to local knowledge to target someone else.

---

4 This should not be confused with those cases where targeted audiences make literal interpretations that artists insist were not intended. This argument has been widely reported in popular culture when Jamaican dance hall and hip hop artists defend interpretations of their words and lyrics (e.g., the complementary hip hop adjective *phat* 'fat') which results in a positive interpretation from hip hop audiences and a negative interpretation from ones representing the dominant culture.

2   *Baited indirectness* When a speaker attributes a feature to a target that is true.[5]

Pointed and baited indirectness are not mutually exclusive and one type of indirectness can quickly lead to another. Pointed indirectness requires local knowledge to understand what a speaker means and is seldom recognized by non-African Americans when it occurs. In contrast, baited indirectness is often noticed, yet misunderstood by most non-African Americans (see below). This is largely because in baited indirectness attributes and features mediate speakers and targets, and they are therefore only directed to appropriate targets (Yankah 1995). That is, for many African Americans, it is not logical that a person would respond to something attributed to him or her unless it were true (Kochman 1981). The use of these forms of indirectness requires knowledge of elaborate norms of interaction and assumes that members of the African-American speech community consider speaker intentionality to be socially constructed and corroborated by audiences and hearers.

9.2.3 Pointed indirectness

Speakers who employ pointed indirectness focus on the context and plausibility of a surrogate as the intended target. This type of indirectness is only successful if recognized by hearers who share prior knowledge about events, or where the context has been established in such a way that the addressed target and those around can determine the identity of the intended target. It is used by all social classes (cf. Fisher 1976), especially to key signifying (see below) and, in contexts that include non-members, it can function to enact identity, solidarity, and/or resistance, among speech community members participating in the interaction (M. Morgan 1989, 1993, 1994). Typically, neither the surrogate nor the intended target respond since, for this form of indirection, any response corroborates what the speaker says. In the few cases that I have witnessed where the intended target has responded to the speaker, the target was direct and argumentative (M. Morgan 1994).

If the surrogate responds to the speaker (e.g., does not perform the role of mock receiver) and does not recognize that it is implausible that he or she is the target, the surrogate runs the risk of embarrassment, especially if the comment is complimentary and the speaker and/or hearers believe that what is said is only true for the intended target. For example, at a middle-class social gathering I heard a woman say to a man who was not smiling and did not have dimples: "I like a man with a warm smile and deep dimples." Unfortunately, the man (surrogate) responded with a flattered and beaming dimple-less smile and said "Thank you," which caused everyone, including the intended target to laugh at the surrogate.

5 These definitions are an expansion of M. Morgan (1989, 1993).

Pointed indirectness can also occur when information is conveyed through cultural/local knowledge which, in turn, becomes the mediator of the message (cf. Yankah 1995). An example of this practice is provided by Mary Walker, a folk artist in Los Angeles, who was eighty-one years old when she told the story about how she met her late husband, whose large portrait dominated her living room. She began her detailed narrative with a description of the 1927 Mississippi River flood and then returned to the meeting of her husband. In the transcript, a period within parentheses indicates a one-second pause and a number within parentheses indicates a pause of the stated number of seconds. Text within double parentheses describes an extralinguistic action.

1	Mary Walker:	I was coming to 17
2	I:	Whew!
3	Mary Walker:	And so here comes Daddy Dickson – the Dickson (.) the lawn mower man.
5	I:	Uh huh
6	Mary Walker:	And he came, and uh, I went and I said, and I paid him.
7		I was always home with the children. And uh we hadn't
8		got sent up to Monroe, cause everything was so distressed.
9		The water was rising just over night. Every time they
10		knock it was higher and higher. But we was sorta on the highest place.
11	I:	MmmmHmm
12	Mary Walker:	And uh, and here comes the yard man. And he come to
13		mow the yard. And it wasn't like old mens today – if he
14		see a young girl he would try to get her for himself. He
15		says, "My wife has a son from (3) St. Louis, Missouri."
16		And says " He's visiting us, and I would like for you to
17		meet him." And oh I was: (3) flip, like most young
18		girls. I was wanting to see what was happening. And I said
19		"Oh sure! Well send him over."
20	I:	MmmmHmmm
21	Mary Walker:	And that's the man up there ((points to a large portrait))
22		He was curly headed in the front. Been like your baby.
23	I:	MmmmHmmm
23	Mary Walker:	And so when ah, the day he was suppose to come, I was
24		mopping the floor – just making strokes, you know, (2)
25		like that, (2) cleanin' up?
26	I:	MmmmHmmm
27	Mary Walker:	And I said to myself (2) should I tell him the truth? I
28 →		says something close to **this peckerwood walking**
29		laughs
30	I:	MmmmHmmm
31	Mary Walker:	And when I got there he says are you

32 →   **Miss Mary Cooper?** And then I knew it was him, you
33   know. (laughs) And he says yes. And uh, he says, my
34   father-in-law told me, my step-father told rather, uh, that
35   you were here, that you gonna be here for a while.

Mary Walker's story, which was recorded by a White female friend of hers, focuses on audience and presumed cultural/social knowledge in a way which is seldom reported for "American Stories" (Bauman 1986; Polanyi 1989) in that she uses pointed indirectness to tell the listener a very important fact. When she first saw her husband, Mary Walker thought he was White. Her confusion about his race is conveyed through culturally significant information and symbols. It is first conveyed in line 22, where Mrs Walker compares her husband's hair to her friend's (the interviewer) daughter's blond curly hair – "He was curly headed in the front. Been like your baby." This information was ignored by the interviewer who thought that Mrs Walker might be signifying that her child is really Black since both her husband and her friend's baby have hair that is not completely straight. However, it becomes clear that Mrs Walker intends to say that her husband could pass for White in line 28, when she uses "peckerwood," a pejorative Southern term for Whites, to refer to her husband when she first sees him. That he was not White, but Black, is further revealed in line 32, where her future husband uses the respect address form "Miss Mary Cooper." In Louisiana in 1927, White men did not refer to young Black women as "Miss." The information in this narrative is culturally constructed and indirect and can be interpreted as follows.

Cultural information	Interpretation
He was curly headed in the front. Been like your baby.	We know that your baby is White.
peckerwood	I thought of a negative term for a White man when I saw him.
Miss Mary Cooper	He showed me respect, so I knew he was black.

Mrs Walker skillfully uses cultural respect / formal address terms, which reveal that her husband could pass for White. She refers to cultural symbols (e.g., hair, insult term [*peckerwood*]) that signify on both her husband and the listener (see *signifying*, Section 9.3.1 below). But once Mr Walker delivers the respectful and formal greeting, it is clear that he is Black (see also M. Morgan 1994b).[6]

---

6 Her friend did not recognize these cultural signs and did not understand that the story was about how Mr Walker could pass for white.

9.2.4 Baited indirectness

In contrast to pointed indirectness, baited indirectness occurs when a speaker means to talk about someone by targeting possible attributes or features. If a hearer responds at all, whether protesting or affirming the allegation that he or she possess these attributes, the audience considers what is said to be true for the hearer. Baited indirectness, which often appears as circumlocution, can employ collective nouns and indefinite personal pronouns, e.g., *something* or *someone*, which highlight that the attribute being discussed is distant from the specific hearers (M. Morgan 1994a). Its function is to disambiguate participant beliefs and attitudes by provoking a response from those who fit the description. An example of baited indirection, which resulted in controversy, occurred when a rapper, Ice T, recorded a rap song entitled "Cop Killer." It seems that the police did not first determine whether they fit Ice T's description of brutal cops before criticizing his rap song. Instead, they seemed to believe that Ice T referred to them. Ice T explains his position:

> At the very beginning of "Cop Killer," I dedicate it to the LAPD and to police chief Daryl Gates. The lyrics are blatant and very specific: the chorus explains what the record's about:
>
> COP KILLER, it's better you than me.
> COP KILLER, fuck police brutality!
> COP KILLER, I know you family's grievin'
> Fuck 'em!
> COP KILLER, but tonight we get even.
>
> Better you than me. If it's gonna be me, then better you. My anger is clearly aimed at *brutal* police. The song was created to be a protest record – a warning, not a threat – to authority that says, "Yo, police: We're human beings. Treat us accordingly."
>
> (Ice T and Siegmund 1994: 168–169)

In the above quote, Ice T argues that by naming the Los Angeles police department and its chief, Daryl Gates, he had explicitly stated that he is *only* talking about corrupt and brutal police – not all police. However, if the aggressive and massive attack on "Cop Killer" by many police departments in the United States is any indication, dominant American culture is not prepared to accept the rules of baited indirection, especially when they are presented by Ice T. That is, either there is no such person as a cop who is not brutal, or only a few police officers for whom the statements did not apply were willing, or able, to distinguish that they were not the target of Ice T's comments.[7]

---

7 As a result of the way Warner Brothers handled the controversy, Ice T asked to be released from his recording contract and Warner Brothers granted his request.

9.2.5 Direct and directed discourse

The system of indirection outlined above reveals that African-American audiences are co-authors (Duranti 1984, 1993) who, along with speakers, contribute to and determine the intent of what is said. In this sense, speaker intent is constituted through collaboration and is not considered complete without it. In contrast, direct discourse is marked by the absence of collaboration and the sense that speakers and audiences rely on each other for meaning. There are two main types of direct discourse. The first instance occurs in institutional settings (e.g., school, work) where the event or context prescribe speaker intent. The other case I call *directed discourse* (M. Morgan 1989). It is marked by the absence of indirection, audience collaboration, and a disregard for social context. Directed discourse is often used to disambiguate a situation, determine truth, etc.

African-American attitudes toward direct discourse have been discussed in educational, work, and legal contexts where formal communication is defined in relation to tasks and individual activities and where power relationships are extreme. Some researchers have called this communication style "work" or "school" language (e.g., Kochman 1981; Dandy 1991) because how one speaks is often considered part of a job rather than a reflection of the attributes or attitudes of speakers. Consequently, this form of discourse is considered to be functional rather than truthful or dishonest. Because direct discourse is void of intent which can be co-constructed, it is often viewed suspiciously outside of institutional contexts. This is especially true for direct questions, which many African-Americans view as "confrontational, intrusive, and presumptuous" (Kochman 1981: 99) and potentially harmful (Jones 1988).

Within the framework outlined above, direct questions are institutional ways of knowing which are not based on the truth (intentionality) of the questioner or respondent. The black expression *Talking like a man with a paper in his hand* (Gwaltney 1981: xxiv) refers to those who ask questions without recognizing or understanding that both listening and hearing are culturally constituted. For many African Americans, the statement *I hear you* is either an affirmation or an insult, depending on the context. Thus from a Black perspective, questions should appear in social contexts which incorporate their reasoning, rather than to simply satisfy institutional or intellectual curiosity and need. Author Gloria Naylor (1988) captures this notion in her novel *Mamma Day* when she writes of a doctoral student who returns home to his rural community to interview residents about, among other things, the significance of the symbolic expression *18 & 23*, much to the disbelief and horror of his relatives, friends, and neighbors who thought they had raised him to "know better."

> And then he went around asking us about 18 & 23, there wasn't nothing to do but take pity on him as he rattled on about "ethnography," "unique speech patterns," "cultural preservation," and whatever else he seemed

to be getting so much pleasure out of while talking into a little gray machine . . . And we all told him the God-honest-truth: it was just our way of saying something.

(Naylor 1988: 7)

Though the young, lost scholar never discovered the meaning of the expression *18 & 23*, he believed he was successful because his home community eventually answered his question. They simply conspired to provide the kind of explanation he "needed" or "wanted" to hear in order to satisfy his thesis.

While direct discourse is considered formulaic and does not focus on participants' role or intentions, directed discourse focuses on a clear target and is unpredictable regarding language variety and discourse style. Directed discourse evolves from the notion that speakers are advocates and there is no such thing as an impersonal position (Kochman 1981, 1983). During conversation, it can occur in response to direct discourse when hearers believe that speakers should possess or should demonstrate their own beliefs and intentions. It can also occur within indirect discourse when hearers believe that speakers are misrepresenting themselves in some way (e.g., John Henry Martin above).

9.2.6 Reading

One cultural enactment of directed discourse is called *reading*.[8] This form of interaction occurs whenever a speaker denigrates another to his or her face (Goffman 1967) in an unsubtle and unambiguous manner. Though there may be self-reporting of reading having taken place without witnesses (e.g., in a story, the narrator may simply report "*I READ her!*"), reading is legitimate only when it is accomplished in the presence of other witnesses who corroborate that it, in fact, occurred.[9] It is directed speech to the point that it is often accusatory. When a target gets read, he or she is verbally attacked for inappropriate or offensive statements or for what is perceived, by the reader, as a false representation of his or her beliefs, personal values, etc. It is not unusual to get read for acting out class privileges, failing to greet friends, pretending to have beliefs that are not actually held, etc. (M. Morgan 1995). The point here is not that a reader is correct or incorrect, but that the reader is willing to jeopardize his or her own face (as well as that of the target) by disclosing what the reader believes is the target's attempt to camouflage his or her beliefs, attitudes, etc. regardless of setting or context.[10]

---

8 This form of directed discourse is also called *throwing shade*.

9 Some people will use the term *reading* to mean 'telling someone off'. Since this cannot be confirmed (no audience), it is not always considered proof that reading occurred.

10 Recent examples of direct discourse can be found within the hip hop genre where artists "diss" opponents who fail to "come correct," "represent," or "give props." This form of directed discourse is especially severe as audiences wait for artists to do battle (e.g., Tim Dog and Dr Dre; Dr Dre and Eazy E; Kool Moe Dee and LL Cool J; MC Lyte and Antoinette; etc.)

A modern example of public reading is the use of *the diss* in rap and hip hop culture. The style of dissin' or criticizing another artist was once a hip hop trope. It essentially involves scathing personalized critiques of rap lyrics, images, the ability to represent the essence of urban life, physical appearance, reputation, authenticity, and so on. Artists diss each other when one believes that someone did not *come correct* either in terms of representing hip hop's sense of fairness and truth or not being supportive to another group member. One of the most aggressive dissing sequences occurred between 1989 and 1995 around the break up of the rap group NWA (Dr Dre vs. Ice Cube; Ice Cube vs. Dr Dre; Ice Cube vs. Easy E; Dr Dre and Eazy E). Apart from the dissing war which erupted in recordings and in interviews, an East Coast rapper launched an additional attack on Dr Dre. The diss occurred when Tim Dog, a rapper from the Bronx, criticized Dr Dre for physically attacking a female video jockey (Dee Barnes) of a popular hip hop television program "Pump up the volume."

> I crush Ice Cube, I'm cool with Ice T
> But NWA ain't shit to me
> Dre beatin' on Dee from Pump It Up
> Step to the dog and get fucked up
> I'm simplistic, imperialistic, idealistic
> And I'm kickin' the ballistics
> Havin' that gang war
> We want to know what you're fighting for
> Fighting over colors?
> All that gang shit is for dumb motherfuckers
> Come to New York and we'll see who gets robbed
> Take your jeri curls, take your black hats
> Take your wack lyrics and your bullshit tracks
> Now you're mad and you're thinking about stompin'
> Well I'm from the South Bronx
> Fuck Compton!
> (Tim Dog 1991: "Fuck Compton")

In his rhymes, Tim Dog refers to ex-NWA member Ice Cube, rapper Ice T, and Dee Barnes. He *signifies* (discussed in Section 9.3.1 below) on both NWA and the entire West Coast urban youth culture by referring to their dress and hair styles as reactionary and lame. The word *colors* refers to street gang colors that are often the source of conflict in the Los Angeles area. A *jeri curl* is an African-American hairstyle once worn by some members of NWA. Men who have long hair in this style are often thought to have self-hate. The word *wack* means 'unbelievably stupid'.

As the preceding section suggests, perhaps the most outstanding quality of African-American interaction is the way in which speaker agency and audience instantiation combine to shape and evaluate both the choice of styles across interactions and the choice of varieties within each style. While African-American discourse is based on a system of indirectness, the use of directed and direct discourse styles are viewed as choices. The use of indirect discourse requires knowledge of African-American English (AAE) and, in most cases, American English (AE) norms.

9.2.7 Reading dialect

The African-American notion of reading as an interpretive practice also occurs at the level of linguistic analysis through a process I call *reading dialect*. Reading dialect occurs when members of the African-American community contrast or otherwise highlight obvious features of AAE and AE in an unsubtle and unambiguous manner to make a point.[11] The point itself may or may not be a negative one. These lexical and grammatical structures are very well known in the community and are often the focus of verbal play, humor, and irony. For example, to stress a point members might say: "It's not simply that I am cool. I be cool. In fact, I been cool (a very long time)." In the African-American community, not only the two dialects of AAE and AE but also varieties within those dialects are consistently read by interlocutors.[12]

Within the framework proposed here, reading dialect involves dialect opposition: highlighting and exploiting AE and AAE forms which members consider to be different (M. Morgan 1994). When speakers employ dialect reading in interactions, they immediately signal to members that some indirect form of opposition is in play. Since many features of AE and AAE are shared or structurally similar, it isn't always clear to members of the African-American community when other members are using AE and when AAE. What reading dialect accomplishes is to transform the status of a lexical, prosodic, grammatical, or discourse structure that could be either AAE or AE into a framework which exploits the congruities and incongruities of each system and how they impact each other. This is achieved by the use of features or rules of AAE which are generally known and culturally marked. One of the most common forms of reading dialect concerns AAE lexical usage (see Smitherman, this volume).[13]

Another significant aspect of reading dialect involves a prosodic system which prescribes specific responses from speakers, targets, and hearers. This prosodic system includes: *loud-talking, marking, high pitch,* and *timing/rhythm.*

---

11 I will use African-American English (AAE) to refer to the range of language varieties used by people in the United States whose major socialization has been with US residents of African descent. I will use American English (AE) to refer to the general discussion of varieties that are not considered socially marked or marked by class, region, gender, etc. Situations which refer to varieties of AE will be so designated. According to this definition, members of the African-American community may speak either AE or AAE.

12 When reading occurs in formal contexts, it is usually considered inappropriate.

13 The lexical terms included here represent those widely used by urban youth at the time of writing.

Loud-talking occurs in the presence of an audience or overhearers when someone talks about someone else at a volume which is either louder than necessary
for the addressed target to hear or markedly different in volume (louder or
quieter) from utterances which precede or follow. It can occur on a word or an
entire segment. According to Mitchell-Kernan,

> Loud-talking often has the effect of unequivocally signalling the intent
> of the speaker from the perspective of the addressee. That is to say, it
> assures that intent will be imputed beyond the surface function of the
> utterance, which might be to seek information, make a request, make
> an observation, or furnish a reply to any of these.
>
> (Mitchell-Kernan 1972: 329)

The target of loud-talking is always directly addressed and hearers generally
make an effort to pretend that they are not aware of the speech event under-
way. In contrast to loud-talking, *marking* is a mode of characterization where
mannerisms are mimicked. When marking, a speaker *copies* a language variety
out of context. This is done in such a way that the marking is attributable to a
type of person who is different from the speaker and/or intended hearers.
As Mitchell-Kernan (1972: 333) explains: "Rather than introducing personality
or character traits in some summary form, such information is conveyed by
producing or sometimes inserting aspects of speech ranging from phonological
features to particular content which carry expressive value." Thus, marking is a
side remark about a subject which is constituted through language.

Pitch and *timing* are also important resources in interaction. Members of the
African-American community associate high pitch with dishonest, authoritative
discourse and low pitch with honest or true discourse and AAE. Pitch contrast
can occur across words or expressions and often co-occurs with other linguistic
features involved in dialect opposition. Its appearance often reflects the attitude
of the speaker toward the interlocutor or topic.

Timing also signals speaker attitude in that *rhythm* is viewed as an important
aspect of what is said. As in other communities (Sacks *et al.* 1974; Levinson
1983; Pomerantz 1984), skipping a beat (or two) suggests that a speaker has a
view or an attitude which does not align with the other interlocutors. In contrast, speaking rhythmically (often with regularized intervals between talks and
pauses) signals that the interaction is highly marked as African-American and
likely to lead to conversational signifying.

Finally, laughter and other vocalic expressions like sucking teeth (Rickford
and Rickford 1976) often signify disapproval and the opposite meaning of what
is being said. Laughter, when used by women, is often the *fool's laugh*, which
instantiates that what is occurring or being talked about is foolish. Women also
use laughter when they think someone thinks that they are the fools, and are
mistaken in their assumption.

Indirectness and the function of direct and directed discourse are learned from adults and as younger children are socialized through play with older children. One of the ways African-American children learn how to be cool in interactions is through language play and play language, especially the ritual games of *signifying* and *instigating*.

9.3 Language play and play language

Children and young adults explore the complexities, intricacies, and hazards of an interaction system based on directed and indirect discourse through games which often implode on speakers and explode on targets and hearers. Children's *play language*, which includes teasing, bossing friends, etc. can quickly move to *language play*, where verbal prowess can be honed, old scores can be settled, and the play day can be brought to a proper close. Both males and females participate in most forms of verbal play (Goodwin 1990), though depending on context and adolescent social standing, each gender tends to favor some activities more than others.[14] Two widely known forms of language play are *signifying* (see below) and *instigating* (see Section 9.3.4).

9.3.1 Signifying

Signifying is a verbal game of indirection also known by the following regional names: *sounding, the dozens, joning, snapping, busting, capping, bagging,* and *ranking* (Abrahams 1962; Kochman 1972a; Labov 1972a; Mitchell-Kernan 1972, 1973; Smitherman 1977; Garner 1983; Gates 1988; Percelay *et al.* 1994). Mitchell-Kernan describes signifying as "the recognition and attribution of some implicit content or function which is obscured by the surface content or function" (1972: 317–318). Signifying is a form of play for adolescents which can serve indirect functions in verbal interactions among adults (e.g., conversational signifying). Many (e.g., Dollard 1973 [1939]; Abrahams 1962; Kochman 1972b; Percelay *et al.* 1994) have suggested that signifying started as an outlet from racial oppression. However, for youth who must learn both the verbal and social face rules of being Black in America the community skills developed from signifying turn to a bonus.

The notion of *play* involved in signifying differentiates the real from the serious (Abrahams 1970, 1976; Goffman 1974; Kochman 1983, 1986) by focusing on that which is socially and/or culturally significant (e.g., relatives, sexuality, physical appearance, political figures, class, and economic status) and placing it in implausible contexts. Whether a context is plausible or implausible is culturally determined. For example, a signifying episode which includes a

---

14 It is important to consider context and social standing, especially in the 1900s where some young women appropriate what they report to be male language styles during play to demonstrate their notion of hard core cultural membership.

police officer who "serves and protects" the Black community would be considered an implausible context. Once the implausible or unreal state is established, these cultural signs interact with the context through irony, sarcasm, wit, and humor in order to *play* with the serious signifier. For example, one commonly heard signifying turn regarding appearance is: *You're so ugly, you went into a haunted house and came out with a job application.* If it is plausible that the sign fits the context (e.g., "you *are* ugly"), the interaction is considered to be an insult rather than play.[15]

Gates (1988: 48) has referred to signifying as the "the trope of tropes" of African-American discourse and believes that it functions as a stylish critique of African-American rhetorical and cultural styles. Gate's definition is a far cry from earlier and recurring assessments that signifying functions as a way for adolescent males to cope with overbearing Black women (Dollard 1973 [1939]; Kunjufu 1986; Dandy 1991; Majors and Billson 1992). As Percelay *et al.* (1994: 22) clarifies:

> Ironically, the focus on "your mother" in so many snaps points to a reverence most contestants share for their mothers. In the dozens, this reverence is used as an emotional weapon.

While some folklorists and anthropologists (especially Kochman 1972a, 1972b; Abrahams 1976) successfully placed signifying within verbal performance genres, they focused on the place where they saw these performances – the street – as the locus of men's cultural and social activity. Generally, everyday life stories are not the focus of discussion in the street, where fantastic, fantasized, and improbable tales of heroism, strength, wit, and virility function as semiotic or symbolic capital (Rossi-Landi 1983; Bourdieu 1991). This is especially evident today when signifying is a standard part of televized American comedy routines, advertising for sporting events, clothing, fast food, and friendship- and family-oriented public service announcements.[16]

In its form as verbal play, signifying or snapping is mainly performed by adolescent males, though it also occurs among adult males and females involved in competitive activities (e.g., sports, stock trading). Percelay *et al.* (1994) introduce seventeen adjectival categories of snaps, including: fat, stupid, sex, and ugly.[17] *Playing the dozens* is the term often used for signifying sequences which include the noun phrase *Your mother* or *Yo mama*. While playing the

---

15 Of course I'm representing adolescent notions. As such, I'm clueless regarding criteria for most of these insults.

16 In fact, this is becoming a recurring issue within African-American culture because when signifying occurs without any cultural context, especially when performed by adults, it appears perverse, and a form of self-loathing.

17 The seemingly obsessive interest in these categories seems to reflect the extent and limitation of adolescent male humor and imagination.

dozens may be an important part of adolescent male activity, members also recognize it as a language socialization activity (Goodwin 1988, 1990), especially for conversational signifying (discussed below in Section 9.4).

9.3.2 Playing the dozens: Yo mama

As Percelay et al. (1994) suggest, *your mother* (or *yo mama*) statements both highlight and subvert the notion that mothers are sacred (Smitherman 1977). These statements should not be misunderstood to relate specifically to someone's particular mother since that is not a requirement to participate. *Your mother* statements are a device to practice and perform verbal skill and this practice often occurs in the presence of family members, including mothers, who help judge their effectiveness and comment on the wit or irony in the statements, often offering other examples which they deem more impressive.

Along with being constituted through African-American cultural contexts, *your mother* statements are also grammatically constituted. They are usually marked by both AAE and AE norms, which are juxtaposed in terms of both the linguistic level and the system of indirection being employed. That is, there is a tendency to use AAE and AE categorically within linguistic levels but not across levels. This tendency is apparent in what Hutcherson (1993), a stand-up comic and comedy writer, argues is the anatomy of a *mother* joke. He describes it as beginning with *Your mother so* followed by an adjective that will be the straight line of the joke. He argues that it is also acceptable to begin with *That's why, your mother* even if what follows is not an explanation (p. 52). Derrick Fox (1992: 20) provides two examples.

> That's why your mother is so dumb: she was filling out a job application and it said, "Sign here." And she put "Aquarius."

> That's why your mother's so bald headed: every time she gets in the shower, she gets brainwashed.

Hutcherson (1993) suggests that one can never use *This is why* or *This is the reason* your mother. There may be restrictions on this form because deictic constructions using *this* make the referent specific, immediate, and possible in the future while *that* suggests that the descriptive adjective and following clause (usually describing a physical deformity) which follows is in the distant past, and possibly not a real depiction of the past. In this sense, *that* serves an existential function (Quirk et al. 1972).

The cases of *the dozens* under discussion will be those coded with the structure: *Your mother (is) so adjectival* . . . *(that)* . . . where the adjectival phrase is followed by a clause. In these cases, the full form copula *is* appears with the same frequency as the phonologically assimilated (preceding *so*) or contracted *s*. While plural and verbal *s* are variable, both are seldom variable within the same clause.

269

The comparative correlative subordinator *so . . . that* adds emotive emphasis and *that* is often omitted.[18]

Thus it is possible to hear:

(1) Your mother is so fat that when she sits on a quarter she gets two dimes and a nickel.

(2) Your mother is so old that when she read(s) the Bible she reminisces.

As well as:

(1a) Your mother so fat (that) (when) she sit(s) on a quarter she get(s) two dimes and a nickel.

(2b) Your mother so old (that) (when) she reads the Bible she reminisce(s).

In the first case of signification, *so fat* and *quarter* are combined to reveal that the act of *sitting* results in the squeezing out of the component parts of the quarter coin (two ten cent coins and one five cent coin). In the second example, the age of the mother is related to when the Bible was written so that the mother is as old as the Bible and some of the events reported there may be childhood memories.

When one considers the above examples, it seems clear that with *the dozens*, grammatical norms may actually allow the audience to pay attention to the level(s) of indirection present. What makes the above cases signifying and not simply indirection, is the combination of grammatical structure and form and the level of deconstruction of the characteristics and attributes of the adjectival – the logic. Cases of signifying like *playing the dozens* or *your mother* statements are constructed through the interaction of both grammar and speech event. Moreover, this verbal genre is but one aspect of a system of African-American indirection. Similarly, African-American linguistic practices are one aspect of a multilevel grammatical system which is constructed through AAE and AE linguistic and pragmatic systems.

Once a *your mother* sequence is launched, it is usually acknowledged as *in play* within an interactive episode when another person responds with a statement

---

18 This analysis is preliminary and based on hundreds of *mother* statements, many of which have the same content. Most of the statements were produced by adolescent boys who originate them, share them, or memorize them from joke books, magazines, and records. Though this analysis focuses on the comparative nature of these constructions, the word *so* could also be interpreted mainly as a quantifier (Labov 1972c). The grammatical norms for playing *the dozens* seems to rely on copula full forms rather than contractions. With the exception of full form *is*, professional comedians tend to use AAE grammar categorically (e.g., lack of verbal or plural *s*), though this may be because they consider *mother* statements stereotypical or stylized.

and is therefore in competition with the initiator (Abrahams 1962; Labov 1972a, 1972b; Kochman 1983). The episode continues until someone delivers enough witty, acerbic, and indirect statements that the audience or interactors determine the winner. As Hutcherson (1993) explains, the true essence of *the dozens* is the relationship between choice of signs and the *logic* of the implausibility. For Hutcherson, this *logic* is culturally loaded and refers to African-American local theories (cf. Geertz 1983; Lindstrom 1992) which include knowledge of cultural celebrations as well as United States racism, bigotry, injustice, etc. One of the "logical" examples that Hutcherson (1993: 52) cites is as follows:

> Your mother is so fat they won't let her have an X jacket because helicopters keep trying to land on her back.

The local information necessary to understand the irony in the signification is that the X jacket is in reference to an emblem associated with Malcolm X, an African-American leader and activist known for his criticism of US racism and his anti-capitalist leanings. Malcolm X was assassinated in 1965 and a movie depicting his life was released in 1991. The X appeared on clothing of urban youth in the early 1990s as part of the massive commodification of Malcolm X. The helicopter is in reference to both a knowledge of landing markings and a first-hand knowledge on how helicopters (called *ghetto birds*) patrol, constantly scan, descend, and land in urban areas.

9.3.3 He-said-she-said

Unlike their male peers who play signifying games which are fast paced and considered outside of interaction, girls' language socialization often involves interactions which include several verbal styles. In particular, a girl who has been labeled an *instigator* (see next section) cannot redeem herself during the next day's play . She must undergo an elaborate *waiting game* and *make-up* session before re-establishing herself. Goodwin's (1980, 1990, 1992) analysis of *he-said-she-said* disputes among African-American girls illustrates the elaborate lengths to which they are willing to go in order to determine who said what behind someone's back. Girls focus on the content of previous and future interactions – what someone actually said, could say, or would say if given the opportunity. Consequently, the language style is not formulaic, but focuses on pragmatics and re-establishing the social order.

In children's *he-said-she-said disputes*, the role or motive of the person instigating is not generally investigated by the offended party. Rather, the offended party works to maintain and/or re-establish her social face through future stories in response to instigating stories, by retelling stories, building audiences, harvesting stories, and building future hypothetical stories (Goodwin 1992). As Goodwin explains, "The goal of the instigator's storytelling is to elicit a statement from the offended party which leads to her confronting the offending party" (1992: 187).

As girls get older, however, they shift their focus to include language variety, the intention of the instigator, and all participants in the process. Moreover, talking about someone behind her back takes on a new seriousness, so that the activity is not simply gossip, but rumor. In the African-American speech community, when a rumor achieves widespread audience discussion and assessment, it is often treated as truth, even when it is not believed to be factual (cf. Turner 1993). Because rumor also signals a loss of social face, its target must defend her honor.

9.3.4 Instigating

By the time girls have become teenagers, they have a significantly different focus on the instigator in he-said-she-said events. For young African-American women, talking behind one's back is treated with the same seriousness as a capital offense. Before the alleged offending party is confronted, the accused party must prove that the intermediary who reported the offense is not simply an instigator.

Instigating events are as much about participants and occurrences of talk as they are about what was allegedly said by whom. The focus is not only what was said but how it was said and how friends talk about their participation. For teenagers, the event is designed to expose and either acquit or convict the instigator as well as the offending party. Days or weeks may elapse as offending statements are denied and/or confirmed and analyzed by several witnesses and hearers. Though the alleged instigator is not contacted until the end, the aim of the offended party is to determine who really started the rumor about her. In the process of determining who the instigator is, friendships are tested, roles in conversations are assessed, and all involved parties become interested in identifying the alleged perpetrator of the speech event. As with young children, the person reported to be the source of the statement is the last person contacted in a rather complicated procedure.

Following is a story about instigating told by Zinzi, a twenty-year-old student. Zinzi uses instigating, directed discourse, and baited indirectness as she attempts to resolve the instigation. In the transcript, capital letters indicate some form of emphasis which may be signaled by changes in pitch or amplitude. A period indicates a stopping fall in tone, not necessarily the end of a sentence, while a comma indicates a continuing intonation, not necessarily between clauses of sentences. Colons indicate that the sound just before the colon has been lengthened. A question mark indicates a rising inflection, not necessarily a question, and an exclamation mark indicates an animated tone, not necessarily an exclamation. All overlapping utterances, including those which start simultaneously, are marked with a single left bracket and a number between parentheses indicate the duration of a pause in seconds. Text within double parentheses describes an extralinguistic action. A hyphen can indicate a short untimed pause, a halting or abrupt cutoff.

1 *Zinzi:*   And then so she thought that she was close enough to
2   Tyrone and so Tyrone wouldn't tell me. BUT? Tyrone
3   being the BEST friend that he is, he's just like, "You
4   know?, Sheila is spreading ru?mors about you. I don't know
5   if anybody else? told? you, but you know, she saying that
6   you and Barry been DOing things and duh?duh duh.dah
7   dah. dah?." And I was just like (2) "Oh? she di"d? huh?"
8   And then so I decided (2) just instead of going up in her
9   face – 'cause I didn't like her anyway – instead of going up
10   in her face, that I'd go and ask my OTHer friends and
11   things like that. So I went and asked them, and they were
12   like, "Yeah, yeah, ((high pitched, soft, voice)) she did tell
13   me about that but I didn't believe her." And I'm like –
14   Uhuh, yeah, right! That's how come you didn't TELL me,
15   because you didn't BELIEVE her. Yeah (2) O.K. And so a
16   an?yway, when I went and confro: nted? her. And then I
17   just got the satisfac?tion out of it (2) because all it took was
18   like a little? confrontation and
19 M. *Morgan:* What did you say?
20 *Zinzi:*   Well I, I asked her? – well not ACTually ASked her – but
21   I accused? her?, and I was like "Oh, so I heard that you
22   been telling ru?mors about Barry and I." And then she?
23   didn't deny? it. And she was just like "It DID? happen."
24   And I'm like "How do you know it happened then?" So, at
25   first? we were talking? lo: w? and then got kind? of lo""ud
26   and the: n? since this was like in front of the church?
27   house. And then it was like, O.K. (2) let's just take this
28   ELSEwhere. And you KNOW how when HIGH school
29   kids get – just like (2) when you TAKE stuff Elsewhere and
30   then EVERYBODY! FOLLOWS. And then it's like (2)
31   ALRIGHT (2) now I'm going to have to fight her 'cause
32   EVERYbody else is over here too. And then so she was still
33   talking her little SMACK LIP? (2) and things like that.
34   And you know (2) everybody was like "Yes you DI:: D say
35   that (2) and I HEARD IT" and she was like "Yeah I DI::D
36   say it because it IS TRUE?." And I'm just like "You
37   DON"T know NOTHING about NOTHING and
38   dah?dahdahdahdah?. And then so – ((suck teeth)) that was
39   it (2) when she just got up in my face. And I could just (2)
40   SMELL her breath? and FEEL her spit? and it was just like
41   ((claps)) tat! And it was on ((laughs)).
42 M. *Morgan:* Wait a minute. No! You fought?
43 *Zinzi:*   Of course. ((laughs)) Like, what did you WANT me to DO?:
44   "Well that's O.K. you can? go ahead and tell rumors

273

| 45 | about me? Go right ahead ((in a hypercorrect, high pitched |
| 46 | voice))" No! |

In contrast to the boy's signifying episodes described earlier, instigating episodes include conversational signifying and often lead to physical confrontations. These confrontations are not viewed as a loss of face or coolness. Rather, they are often considered a logical last resort. Zinzi confirms this in lines 9–10 where she decides to ask her friends what Sheila said "instead of going up in her face."[19] Zinzi's story is different from those reported by Goodwin in one major respect. The basic three stages of: (1) *confrontation*, (2) *instigating*, (3) *offense* (Goodwin 1990, 1992) have been expanded to include: (a) *interrogation* (of "so called" friends) and (b) *punishment*.[20]

It is clear that the social order is in jeopardy as Zinzi canvasses her friends for their role in Sheila's conversations in lines 13–18. She begins by calling Tyrone her best friend, though she fully intends to determine who her "real" friends are and whether what Tyrone said is true. She *interrogates* several friends and bystanders about whether they heard Sheila say that Zinzi was "doing something" with Barry. Zinzi then finds out exactly what her friends said when Sheila talked about her. During this time all parties (including Zinzi) focus on past, present, and possible conversations with and about Sheila.

Once she has established the truth, Zinzi decides to go up in Sheila's face (lines 8–9). She searches for, finds, and confronts the instigating Sheila. Sheila accepts responsibility for what she says (lines 27–28 and 39–40) and Zinzi denies that it is true and, eventually, Zinzi strikes Sheila. Zinzi explains her physical attack of Sheila by defending her right to protect herself against unfounded rumors.

While all of the above language activities are marked by confrontations and accusations, they illustrate the construction of social role and relationship through indirectness, cultural symbols, and audience co-construction and collaboration. Children are interested in and aware of the multilayered nature of these activities, especially how speaker intent and meaning are constructed and validated.

The level of complexity common in childhood is maintained and often expanded among adults, who often punctuate their conversations with the statement "I don't *play!*" In the black expression "know when you're *playing*" (also Gwaltney 1984: x), the word *play* refers to speaker intentionality as well as to whether one tells the truth or understands the consequences of what is said. This is an important characteristic of adult interaction where all participants have learned that intentionality is not simply a psychological state but socially constructed (Duranti 1993).

---

19 This expression means 'to confront or fight'.
20 Though this is a reported story, I have other recordings of teenagers instigating. I have also helped mediate the pre-confrontation stage of these episodes, though with only minor success.

9.4 Adult language, culture, and interaction

African-American conversation often includes *conversational signifying* (Mitchell- Kernan 1971; Labov 1972a; Smitherman 1977) where participants are indirectly targeted by speakers who attribute some personal characteristics of the target to culturally marked signs (M. Morgan 1994). While sharing many features of signifying (described above), this type of interaction includes culturally marked signs which can be objects, certain statements, significant persons, etc. It does not involve turns but occurs over an entire conversation. And finally, unlike in the case of the children described above, the words *your mother* are considered moronic and interpreted as a case of arrested development when uttered by adults. Following is a conversation between two professional African-American males in their early thirties which I heard at a middle-class social gathering.

Man 1: You can trust me.
Man 2: I know I can. (laughing)
Man 1: No, I mean you can really trust me. (serious tone)
Man 2: Yeah man, I told you, I know I can. (Man 2 and overhearers laugh)

This episode is a case of conversational signifying because in the African-American community, the statement *You can trust me* is often a cultural sign which signals situations where those in power are manipulating people or events. Children are taught that statements like *You can trust me* and *I'll watch out for you* from those with an unproven track record, and in positions of power, are often ruses.[21] Thus conversational signifying is keyed through the juxtaposition of interactional and broader, and often subtle, cultural norms and expectations.

Many occurrences of conversational signifying also include grammatical parallelism where interactors incorporate similar grammatical structures and word order while altering the meaning of the structure being copied (Labov 1972b). In these sequences, both dominant societal and African-American language values and norms are highlighted in immediate response sequences or throughout the conversation. Whether or not signifying is being attempted is also related to whether a speaker has a right to the floor; in African-American women's interactions, those rights are embedded in cultural norms and expectations concerning a speaker's right to speak or pass judgment about a topic.

---

21 During fieldwork in Chicago, I saw a man expelled from a middle-class gathering (at the host's mother's request) because he told his friend's mother that her son didn't have to worry about his job because "you can trust me." The mother became agitated and said, "I never asked him anything. If he has to say it, it isn't true."

9.4.1 African-American women in (inter)action

Active participation in discourse is often based on the extent of the participant's personal involvement in the events being discussed. A striking characteristic of African-American women's discourse is that if all major participants are not present during the telling of what happened, especially for events where what someone said is reported, the event is only marginally discussed. This is because innumerable recriminations may result when someone reports what someone said about someone else if the speaker is not there to address interpretations of what she meant. The importance adult women attach to the audience's right to determine intentionality, even when information is delivered behind the speakers' back, is vividly illustrated in instigating among young girls (see above). Being labeled either a *back stabber* or *instigator* results in social censure and public disgrace (Goodwin 1990). Within women's interactions, however, the main discourse focus is not whether someone instigates or back stabs but rather, whether the intentionality assessments made by the audience are reasonable considering the context and whether the original speaker had the opportunity to address them. Thus, instead of focusing on who said something about someone, as girls do, adult women focus on speakers' rights to express their own experience. Consequently, conversations which may appear to be about a person can easily become a conversation about something else.

The following conversation includes a short narrative about African-American life in Chicago in the 1920s. In "Riff Raff," Judy and Arthell are involved in an interaction of pointed indirectness in which Judy's signifying includes directing some of her interaction to her daughter.

The story "Riff Raff" began a five-hour taping session of two women friends in their late 50s to early 60s. Talk occurred over a day of food and socializing. During their interaction, the women acknowledged me as both audience and a representative of my generation. This was accomplished in line 4, where Judy *signifies* by establishing that the youth of today have no social status because the typical person of today has less self respect than the prostitutes of Eva's and Doris' youth.

Riff Raff

```
 1  Judy:  The neighborhood was VERY well: kept (2) at that time
 2         We had a lot of riff raff. Well (2) we wouldn't call 'em
 3         riff raff (3) In those days they were riff raff
 4         because they were like the people of today. had a woman
 5         that lives next door (2) Christi:ne and her mother
 6         (We) use to refer to her as Miss Huff (3) Christi:ne Huff
 7         and her mother Miss Huff. They were the WHORES (2) of the
 8         area. You could always see them working ((laughs)) the
 9         street.
10  Art:   But they got respect didn't they?
11  Judy:  Very much respect
```

After completing this story, the women told other instances where the *working women* of their day were better than the average woman of today (lines 3–4). They took care of their children and were good mothers and neighbors. Thus Judy uses pointed indirectness to criticize her daughter and perhaps her daughter's generation. She also establishes a clear link between the time when the Huffs were her neighbors and her own connection with that period by casting the narrative in the past in line 4 (*had a woman*) and using the present tense when describing them as neighbors in line 5. Thus they situate themselves and their generation in relation to the interviewer/audience. Even women of the streets were better mothers than the women of today. Throughout the inter-action, the women continue to refer to a younger audience, who they situate in opposition to their generation. They use indirection through signification to accomplish this task.

9.5 Conclusion

This chapter has shown how the African-American speech community is constructed by its historical, political, cultural, and social life. Whether using pitch or indirectness, semantic extension or grammatical reading, speakers imbue language with their historical, social, and cultural experience in the United States. This chapter has explored the systemic workings of verbal and discourse styles and practices of the African-American speech community, espe-cially its youth. It has contextualized and in some cases reinterpreted current and previously described speech styles, such as *signifying* or *sounding, instigating, conversational signifying, reading* a person, and *reading* dialect, within a system of social face which is partially constructed through a system of directed and indirect discourse.

Another central theme of this chapter has been to show how African-American language features and verbal repertoires occur within a cultural frame-work based on African and African-American norms and practices. These language styles and practices combine to mark the African-American speech community as distinct across generation, gender, and class. In this sense, AAE is neither simply a variety nor a style, but a bold and elusive instance of the power of human beings to cultivate language in order to ensure that they have cultural and historical memory, control over their identity, and a way to reflect on and make sense of their daily lives as they see them.

References

Abrahams, Roger (1962) "Playing the dozens." *Journal of American Folklore* 75: 209–218.
—— (1970) *Deep Down in the Jungle.* Chicago: Aldine.
—— (1976) *Talking Black.* Rowley, MA: Newbury.
Alleyne, Mervyn (1980) *Comparative Afro-American: An Historical-Comparative Study of English-Based Afro-American Dialects of the New World.* Ann Arbor: Karoma Press.

—— (1989) *Roots of Jamaican Culture*. London: Pluto Press.

Bakhtin, Mikhail (1981) In *The Dialogic imagination: Four Essays*, M. Holquist (ed.) and C. Emerson and M. Holquist (trans.). Austin: University of Texas Press.

Bauman, Richard (1986) *Story, Performance and Event: Contextual Studies of Oral Narrative*. Cambridge: Cambridge University Press.

Bourdieu, Pierre (1977) "The economics of linguistic exchanges." *Social Science Information* 16 (6): 645–668.

—— (1991) *Language & Symbolic Power*. Cambridge, MA: Harvard University Press.

Braithwaite, Fred (1992) *Fresh Fly Flavor: Words and Phrases of the Hip-Hop Generation / Fab 5 Freddy*. Stamford, CT: Longmeadow Press.

Brenneis, Donald and Fred Myers (1984) *Dangerous Words: Language and Politics in the Pacific*. Prospect Heights, IL: Waveland Press.

Brent, Linda [Harriet Jacob] (1973) *Incidents in the Life of a Slave Girl*. New York: Harcourt, Brace, Jovanovich.

Bryce-Laporte, Roy Simon (1971) "The slave plantation: Background to present conditions of urban Blacks." In *Race Change and Urban Society*, Peter Orleans and William Russell Ellis, Jr (eds.). Beverly Hills: Sage, pp. 257–284.

Dandy, Evelyn (1991) *Black Communications: Breaking Down the Barriers*. Chicago: African American Images.

Dewese, Moe (p.k.a. Kool Moe Dee] (1991) *How Kool Can One Blackman Be*. On Moe Dee: Funke Funke Wisdom. Zomba Recording Corp. BMG Music.

Dollard, John (1973 [1939]) "The dozens: Dialectic of insult." In *Mother Wit from the Laughing Barrel: Readings in the Interpretation of Afro-American Folklore*, Alan Dundes (ed.). Jackson, MS: University Press of Mississippi.

Duranti, Alessandro (1984) "The social meaning of subject pronouns in Italian conversation." *Text* 4.4: 277–311.

—— (1993) "Truth and intentionality: An ethnographic critique." *Cultural Anthropology* 8 .2: 214–245.

—— (1994) *From Grammar to Politics: Linguistic Anthropology in a Western Samoan Village*. Berkeley: University of California Press.

Fabian, Johannes (1990) *Power and Performance*. Madison: University of Wisconsin Press.

Fisher, Lawrence (1976) "Dropping remarks and the Barbadian audience." *American Ethnologist* 3.2: 277–42.

Foucault, Michel (1973) *The Order of Things: An Archaeology of Human Sciences*. New York: Vintage Books.

—— (1980) *Power/Knowledge: Selected Interviews and Other Writings 1972–1977*, Colin Gordon (ed. and trans.). New York: Pantheon.

—— (1981) *Foucault Live (Interviews 1966–84)* John Johnson (trans.). New York: Semitotext(e), Columbia University.

Fox, Derick (1992) "Punchline." *The Source* (July): 20.

Garner, Thurmon (1983) "Playing the dozens: Folklore as strategies for living." *Quarterly Journal of Speech* 69: 47–57.

Gates, Henry Louis Jr (1988) *The Signifying Monkey: A Theory of African-American Literary Criticism*. Oxford: Oxford University Press.

George, Nelson (1992) *Buppies, B-Boys, Baps & Bohos: Notes on Post-Soul Black Culture*. New York: Harper Collins.

Geertz, Clifford (1983) *Local Knowledge: Further Essays in Interpretive Anthropology*. New York: Basic Books.

Goffman, Erving (1961) *Asylums: Essays on The Social Situation of Mental Patients and Other Inmates*. New York: Anchor Books.

—— (1967) *Interaction Ritual: Essays in Face to Face Behavior*. Garden City, NY: Doubleday.

—— (1974) *Frame Analysis*. Harper Colophon: New York.

Goodwin, Marjorie Harness (1988) "Cooperation and competition across girls' play activities." In *Gender and Discourse: The Power of Talk*, S. Fisher and A. Todd (eds.). Norwood, NJ: Ablex.

—— (1990) *He-Said-She-Said: Talk as Social Organization Among Black Children*. Bloomington: Indiana University Press.

—— (1992) "Orchestrating participation in events: Powerful talk among African American girls." In *Locating Power: Proceedings of the 1992 Berkeley Women and Language Group*, K. Hall, M. Bucholtz, and B. Moonwomon (eds.). Berkeley: Berkeley Women and Language Group, Linguistics Department, pp. 182–296.

Grier, William and Price Cobbs (1968) *Black Rage*. New York: Bantam Books.

Gumperz, John (1982) *Discourse Strategies*. Cambridge: Cambridge University Press.

Gwaltney, John (1981) *Drylongso: A Self-Portrait of Black America*. New York: Vintage Books.

Halliday, M. A. K. (1978) "Antilanguages." In *Language as a Social Semiotic: The Social Interpretation of Language and Meaning*. Baltimore: University Park Press.

Harding, Antonio [p.k.a. Big Daddy Kane] (1988) *R.A.W.* On Cold Chillin' ASCAP Music Publishing.

Horton, John (1972) "Time and cool people." In *Rappin' and Stylin' Out: Communication in Urban Black America*, T. Kochman (ed.). Champaign, IL: University of Illinois Press, pp. 19–31.

Hunter, Linda (1982) "Silence is also language: Hausa attitudes about speech and language." *Anthropological Linguistics* 24.4: 389–395.

Hutcherson, Warren (1993) *Dr Hutcherson's Guide to Mother Jokes*. P.52. The Source.

Hymes, Dell (1974) *Foundations in Sociolinguistics: An Ethnographic Approach*. Philadelphia, PA: University of Pennsylvania Press.

Ice T and Heidi Siegmund (1994) *The Ice Opinion*. New York: St Martin's Press.

Irvine, Judith (1974) "Strategies of status manipulation in the Wolof greeting." In *Explorations in the Ethnography of Speaking*, R. Bauman and J. Sherzer (eds.). London: Cambridge University Press.

—— (1982) "Language and affect: Some cross-cultural issues." In *Georgetown University Round Table on Language and Linguistics*, H. Byrnes (ed.). Washington, DC: Georgetown University Press.

—— (1993) "Insult and responsibility: Verbal abuse in a Wolof village." In *Responsibility and Evidence in Oral Discourse*, Jane H. Hill and Judith T. Irvine (eds.). Cambridge: Cambridge University Press.

James, Sherman (1993) *The Narrative of John Henry Martin*. Manuscript.

Johnson, Charles (1982) *Oxherding Tales*. New York: Grove Weidenfeld.

Jones, Delmos (1988) "Towards a native anthropology." In *Anthropology for the Nineties*, Johnetta Cole (ed.). New York: The Free Press, pp. 30–41.

Jones, K. Maurice (1994) *The Story of Rap Music*. Brookfield, CT: Millbrook Press.

Kochman, Thomas (ed.) (1972a) *Rappin' and Stylin' Out: Communication in Urban Black America*. Champaign, IL: University of Illinois Press.

—— (1972b) "Toward an ethnography of Black American speech behavior." In *Rappin' and Stylin' Out: Communication in Urban Black America*, Thomas Kochman (ed.). Champaign, IL: University of Illinois Press, pp. 241–264.

—— (1981) *Black and White Styles in Conflict*. Chicago: University of Chicago Press.

—— (1983) "The boundary between play and nonplay in Black verbal dueling." *Language in Society* 12 (3): 329–337.

—— (1986) "Strategic ambiguity in Black speech genres: Cross-cultural interference in participant-observation research." *Text* 6.2: 153–170

Kuipers, Joel (1990) *Power in Performance*. Philadelphia: University of Pennsylvania Press.

Kunjufu, J. (1986) *Countering the Conspiracy to Destroy Black Boys Vols. I and II*. Chicago: African American Images.

Labov, William (1972a) "Rules for ritual insults." In *Rappin' and Stylin' Out: Communication in Urban Black America*, Thomas Kochman (ed.). Champaign, IL: University of Illinois Press.

—— (1972b) *Language in the Inner City: Studies in the Black English Vernacular*. Philadelphia: University of Pennsylvania Press.

—— (1972c) *Sociolinguistic Patterns*. Philadelphia: University of Pennsylvania Press.

Levinson, Stephen (1983) *Pragmatics*. Cambridge: Cambridge University Press.

Lindstrom, Lamont (1992) "Context contests: Debatable truth statements on Tanna (Vanuatu)." In *Rethinking Context: Language as an Interactive Phenomenon*, A. Duranti and C. Goodwin (eds.). Cambridge: Cambridge University Press, pp. 101–124.

Major, Clarence (1970) *Dictionary of Afro-American Slang*. New York: International Publishers.

—— (1977) *Black Slang: A Dictionary of Afro-American Talk*. London: Routledge & Kegan Paul.

—— (1994) *Juba to Jive: A Dictionary of African-American Slang*. New York: Penguin Books.

Majors, Richard and Janet Mancini Billson (1992) *Cool Pose: The Dilemmas of Black Manhood in America*. New York: Lexington Books.

Mitchell-Kernan, Claudia (1971) *Language Behavior in a Black Urban Community*. Monographs of the Language-Behavior Laboratory University of California, Berkeley, Number 2.

—— (1972) "Signifying, loud-talking, and marking." In *Rappin' and Stylin' Out: Communication in Urban Black America*, Thomas Kochman (ed.). Champaign, IL: University of Illinois Press, pp. 315–335.

—— (1973) "Signifying." In *Mother Wit from the Laughing Barrel*, A. Dundes (ed.). New York: Garland Publishing, pp. 310–328.

Morgan, Kathryn (1980) *Children of Strangers: The Stories of a Black Family*. Philadelphia: Temple University Press.

Morgan, Marcyliena (1989) "From down south to up south: The language behavior of three generations of Black women residing in Chicago," unpublished dissertation, University of Pennsylvania.

—— (1991) "Indirectness and interpretation in African American women's discourse." *Pragmatics* 1.4: 421–451.

—— (1993) "The Africanness of counterlanguage among Afro-Americans." In *Africanisms in Afro-American Language Varieties*, S. Mufwene (ed.). Athens: University of Georgia Press.

—— (1994a) "The African American speech community: Reality and sociolinguistics." In *Language and the Social Construction of Identity in Creole Situations*, M. Morgan (ed.). Berkeley: Center for African American Studies.

—— (1994b) "Just to have something: Camouflaged narratives of African American life." Manuscript.

Morrison, Toni (1987) *Beloved*. New York: Knopf.

Naylor, Gloria (1988) *Mamma Day*. New York: Vintage Books.

Ochs, Elinor (1992) "Indexing gender." In *Rethinking Context: Language as an Interactive Phenomenon*, Alessandro Duranti and Charles Goodwin (eds.). Cambridge: Cambridge University Press.

Percelay, James, Ivey Monteria, and Stephan Dweck (1994) *Snaps*. New York: Quill.

Polanyi, Livia (1989) *Telling the American Story*. Cambridge, MA: MIT Press.

Pomerantz, Anita (1984) "Agreeing and disagreeing with assessments: Some features of preferred/dispreferred turn shapes." In *Structures of Social Action*, J. Maxwell Atkinson and John Heritage (eds.). Cambridge: Cambridge University Press, pp. 57–101.

Quirk, Randolph, Sidney Greenbaum, Geoffrey Leech, and Jan Svartvik (1972) *A Grammar of Contemporary English*. London: Longman.

Reisman, Karl (1974) "Contrapuntal conversations in an Antiguan village." In *Explorations in the Ethnography of Speaking*, R. Bauman and J. Sherzer (eds.). London: Cambridge University Press.

Rickford, John and Angela Rickford (1976) "Cut-Eye and suck teeth: African words and gestures in New World guise." *Journal of American Folklore*, 89.353: 194–309.

Rossi-Landi, Ferruccio (1983) *Language as Work and Trade: A Semiotic Homology for Linguistics and Economics*. South Hadley, MA: Bergin & Garvey Publishers, Inc.

Saah, Kofi (1984) "Language use and attitudes in Ghana." *Anthropological Linguistics* 28.3: 367–377.

Sacks, Harvey, Emanuel Schegloff, and Gail Jefferson (1974) "A simplest systematics for the organization for turn-taking in conversation." *Language* 50.4: 696–735.

Simonsen, Thordis (1986) *You May Plow Here: The Narrative of Sara Brooks*. New York: Simon and Schuster, Inc.

Smitherman, Geneva (1977) *Talkin and Testifyin: The Language of Black America*. Boston: Houghton Mifflin.

—— (1994) *Black Talk: Words and Phrases from the Hood to the Amen Corner*. New York: Houghton Mifflin.

Spears, Arthur (1982) "The semi-auxiliary come in Black English Vernacular." *Language* 58: 850–72.

Turner, Patricia (1993) *Heard it Through the Grapevine: Rumor in African-American Culture*. Berkeley: University of California Press.

Volosinov, Valentin Nikolaevic (1973 [1930]) *Marxism and the Philosophy of Language*. Translated by Ladislav Matejka and I. R. Titunik. New York: Seminar Press.

Walker, Alice (1982) *The Color Purple*. New York: Harcourt, Brace, Jovanovich.

Whitfield, Stephen (1992) *A Death in the Delta: The Story of Emmett Till*. Baltimore: The Johns Hopkins University Press.

Williams, Sherley Anne (1986) *Dessa Rose*. New York: Berkeley Books.

Woolard, Kathryn (1992) Language Ideology: Issues and Approaches. *Pragmatics* 2.2: 235–250.

Yankah, Kwesi (1995) *Speaking for the Chief: Okyame and the Politics of Akan Royal Oratoray*. Bloomington, Indiana: Indiana University Press.

10

LINGUISTICS, EDUCATION, AND THE LAW: EDUCATIONAL REFORM FOR AFRICAN-AMERICAN LANGUAGE MINORITY STUDENTS

John Baugh

10.1 Introduction

> It is not an issue in this case that the students have been misclassified as handicapped. The procedures used in making the classification completely follow the law.
>
> (Judge Charles Joiner: cited in Smitherman 1981: 336)

The "case" referred to – the 1979 Ann Arbor case argued before Justice Joiner – has come to be known as the Black English Trial.[1] Eleven African-American plaintiffs had been placed in remedial special education classes based on pathological linguistic evaluations that failed to take into account their linguistic heritage as speakers of African-American vernacular English (AAVE). Although Judge Joiner ruled in favor of the plaintiffs, he did so based on the issue of "teacher training" and left the matter of "linguistic classification" unresolved. Should African-American children who speak standard English be considered as "language minority students," which was advocated by the Ebonics resolutions that were adopted by the Oakland School Board in their controversial resolutions of 18 December 1996 and 15 January 1997? Based on Judge Joiner's ruling one must conclude they should be.

Why? Because their native dialect represents a "language barrier" to full participation in school. Some urban educators have remarked that language

---

1 Readers who are unfamiliar with the case should consult Smitherman (1981).

development is a low academic priority for poor students of color, because of the myriad of other social problems they face in daily life. The paradox at hand lies in the fact that a good education is critical to breaking perpetual cycles of poverty, and linguistic skills are a strong indicator of the likelihood of eventual academic success. These matters came to a head during the Black English Trial, because the plaintiffs successfully argued that their school district had failed to teach them to read and write using *Standard English* (emphasis added). The practice of using speech pathology to identify African-American students as "linguistically disabled," for placement into Special Education, is challenged in this chapter.

Based on a strict legal interpretation, Judge Joiner concluded that using speech pathology in this manner was, and still is, "completely within the law."[2] Evidence at the trial showed that the plaintiffs' dialect was grammatically coherent; they speak a vernacular dialect of American English that is not standard, but which can be traced as a direct result of the linguistic consequences of the African slave trade. Rather than base his ruling on these historical and empirical facts, Judge Joiner opted to concentrate on the teachers and their training – or lack of it. He ultimately concluded that the teachers did not acknowledge sources of educational difficulty that could be traced to the linguistic heritage of the plaintiffs; again, every plaintiff spoke AAVE.

I believe this case draws attention to a neglected dimension of educational policy; the statutory exclusion of linguistic minorities whose ancestors spoke pidginized and creolized English. With the noteworthy exception of native Hawaiians, discussed briefly below (see Section 10.7), federal regulations exclude many such students. However, Judge Joiner based his ruling on Section 1703(f) of Title 20, a law that was written to bolster Title VI (which protects students' civil rights) and the *Lau v. Nichols* decision in support of limited-English-proficient (LEP) students (Crawford 1992; Hakuta *et al.* 1993). The relevant statute follows:

> No State shall deny equal educational opportunity to an individual on account of his or her race, color, sex, or national origin, by – . . .
>
> (f) the failure by an educational agency to take appropriate action to overcome language barriers that impede equal participation by its students in its instructional programs 20 U.S.C. 1703(f).

Judge Joiner interpreted this law in such a way that it applies to black students for whom Standard English is not native (SENN), based on legitimate "language

---

2 Wolfram (1983, 1993) has written extensively on this subject, and readers are encouraged to consult his work for a more thorough discussion of the role of speech pathology in the education of African-American students.

barriers." The school district in question did not appeal the ruling. As such Judge Joiner's conclusions are advisory and do not have the regulatory (or legislative) clout of rulings from higher courts. The vast majority of school districts around the US that serve SENN students do not have adequate language policies in place. Districts that have attempted to follow Judge Joiner place primary emphasis on teacher education, which is a good place to start. However, very little effort is devoted to adequate reform of policies for AAVE students as linguistic minorities.[3]

I believe that the term "language minority" is too narrowly defined under current regulations, and that a revised definition is needed in support of reforms that seek to provide high academic standards for all students; indeed, this need has been accentuated by the Ebonics controversy that was triggered in Oakland. We need language policies that will ensure that students who are not native speakers of Standard English will not fail due to linguistic neglect. The status quo is one that favors students who arrive at school speaking Standard American English (with tolerance for regional variation). Unless systemic reforms take adequate account of the dynamics of linguistic diversity among students, we are unlikely to meet our desired goal to combine high academic standards with greater educational equity for all.

The following definition for language minorities has been used operationally in the present case: students for whom Standard English is not native; this definition includes the national standard as well as regional standard dialects. Under this definition, LEP is not synonymous with "language minorities;" rather, LEP students represent a subset of other linguistic minorities who are not native speakers of Standard English.[4]

It is unclear to me why Judge Joiner did not address the role of pathology in the plaintiffs' classroom placements. There is an abundance of linguistic evidence, much of it cited in Judge Joiner's ruling, that emphatically refutes any linkage between AAVE and pathological speech impediments. Had policy makers acted previously on this discrepancy, much of the Ebonics controversy could have been avoided; that is, before it could become the object of future litigation.

---

3 On 5 January 1994, Felice Lee wrote a front page article for the *New York Times* on the issue of drifting policies for AAVE students in New York City. She points out that their educational policies, while recognizing the existence of AAVE and its historical ties to Africa, make no special provisions for the needs described by plaintiffs in the Black English Trial.

4 This definition is broad enough to include non-standard white speech from Appalachia, derived from the uneducated speech of former indentured servants, as well as deaf students (who receive federal funding under a separate categorical program). Although we maintain this broader definition throughout the chapter, the discussion at hand focuses exclusively on the African-American case unless otherwise stated.

Once students acquire Standard English they would no longer be classified as a "language minority." Students who acquire "Standard English as a second dialect" should be integrated into mainstream classes where their academic performance is comparable to that of native Standard English speakers.

10.2 A brief survey of relevant law

Under the proposed operational definition, laws pertaining to language minorities would be broader than statutes written for non-English-speaking students, although it is clear that laws regarding bilingual education are absolutely essential to the welfare of traditional LEP students. The cases that brought these matters to law and educational policy were *Plyer v. Doe*, 457 US 202 (1982) and *Lau v. Nichols*, 414 US 563 (1974). *Plyer v. Doe* resulted in a decision that required states to provide free public education to undocumented immigrant children, and *Lau v. Nichols* is the famous Supreme Court case that called for school districts to tend to the needs of LEP students through educational services that would be tailored to their linguistic needs. Both cases have been instrumental to the development of subsequent policies in support of various forms of bilingual education.

Although a great deal has been written recently regarding educational reforms for language minority students (Fix and Zimmerman 1993; Hakuta *et al.* 1993), emphasis is placed on LEP students (who are eligible for Title VII; see Section 10.3). There is little scholarly acknowledgment of the tremendous ambiguity of the legal language that defines language minority status, as discussed below in Section 10.2.1. The clearest evidence of this fact can be found in Judge Joiner's remarks. As indicated above, his ruling was based on Title 20 of the 1974 Equal Education Opportunity Act. More precisely, Section 1703(f) of Title 20 was cited; however, this statute was originally written to bolster Title VI and bilingual education.

The essential point boils down to the fact that 1703(f) was never intended to apply to non-standard English; authors of the provision felt they were serving the needs of traditional language minority students. Judge Joiner's decision, to base the entire case on "20 U.S.C. 1703(f)," has extraordinary implications for the education of African-American students, but, again, because this case was not taken to a higher court, neither educators nor legislators have been compelled to grapple with the linguistic inadequacies in categorical programs that are intended to help poor African Americans. Similar issues loom for impoverished students who speak other non-standard dialects of English.

As mentioned previously, the matter regarding the wisdom (or legality) of using speech pathology to place African-American students into Special Education was left unresolved in Judge Joiner's ruling, but the practice (which is legal) is so common across the country that litigation on these procedures could easily be forthcoming. Another misguided practice that has yet to be challenged in court has to do with the *ad hoc* placement of African-American students in LEP classes. Anecdotal evidence of this practice has emerged from our research for the Consortium of Policy Research in Education (CPRE) that examines the academic progress of language minority students in states and school districts that are devoted to systemic reform.

The general pattern that we have observed resembles the Black English Trial in the sense that educators, often at the school site, determine that some of their African-American students are unlikely to fare well in mainstream classes. However, these students (who rarely represent the entire African-American population at the school), are too few to justify separate services; placement in LEP classes is an expedient compromise, which is often influenced by economic considerations and efforts to conform to state and federal regulations. These become relevant because these black students are also likely to be those who are served by Title I programs.[5]

10.2.1 Legal summary

Current regulations exclude most AAVE speakers from funding for language minority students because English is their native language. However, some AAVE speakers confront many "language barriers" in educational contexts. They also could be included within existing definitions for LEP students, which Fix and Zimmerman (1993: 12) characterize as follows:

> LEP children have difficulty reading, writing, speaking, and under-standing English, a definition drawn from the Bilingual Education Act of 1978. Limited English proficiency is not a measure of a person's proficiency in his or her native language.

In the case of AAVE students, LEP status *does* hinge on "a person's proficiency in his or her native language." All dialects are not equal from a social or educational point of view, and speakers of non-standard English "have difficulty reading, writing, and speaking" Standard English; which is the entire point of the Black English Trial, and more recently in the form of the Ebonics resolutions that were adopted by the Oakland school board. AAVE natives are likely to understand Standard English, due to pervasive and constant exposure to it through mass media. It is on the basis of "understanding (Standard) English" that AAVE students dramatically differ from their LEP peers. But it is also clear that comprehension of Standard English, in the face of other language barriers, does not imply that AAVE students have the same academic advantages as do students who speak Standard English natively (many of whom are students of color).

Judge Joiner's ruling complicates the regulatory boundary between LEP students and their non-standard English school-mates. Prior to his ruling, laws and regulations regarding LEP students were careful to exclude African

---

5 Fix and Zimmerman (1993) provide an interesting discussion regarding the paradox associated with "serving" LEP and Title I students. Just because funds and programs are provided for categorical students, this need not imply that students are effectively served by these programs.

Americans. In the wake of his ruling, however, that separation is not so clear. Judge Joiner's observations are more in line with our operational definition for language minority students, which includes speakers of non-standard English that confront significant language barriers in educational contexts.

10.3 A survey of corresponding educational policies and proposed reforms

This discussion focuses on three categorical programs that are most relevant to language minority students:[6] Title I, Title VII, and Special Education. Title I is aimed at students in poverty. Considerable research has been devoted recently to the role of LEP students in relationship to Title I. Hakuta *et al.* (1993) and Fix and Zimmerman (1993) call for expanded service to LEP students through Title I. A significant justification for their independent observations lies in the disproportionate funding for Title I in contrast to Title VII, to which we now turn.

Title VII provides federal funding in support of bilingual education for LEP students across the US. Approximately $200,000,000 dollars a year is provided for Title VII, whereas Title I receives over 6 billion dollars annually, making it the largest source of federal funding in support of education. Advocates of bilingual education have been mindful of the fact that many LEP students, who *are* eligible for Title I, tend to be excluded from those programs because they receive Title VII support.

Fix and Zimmerman (1993) state that many school officials at the district level are often confused about relevant regulations; local education agency (LEA) officials tend to isolate Title I programs from Title VII based on the belief that students enrolled in ESL, or "sheltered English" classes, do not qualify for Title I. Since language is the presumed source of "handicap" for LEP students, some school administrators wrongly conclude that those students cannot also receive support through Title I.[7] Title I recipients, many of whom are African American, are eligible for funding based on a combination of factors that confirm student poverty. Under current regulations, language is not considered to be the source of educational "handicaps" for English-speaking students who are impoverished. Poverty and low academic achievement are the bases of Title I entitlements; again, a consideration of language barriers for native speakers of non-standard English has traditionally been absent from Title I statutes.

Census data and a host of other evidence, such as Assistance to Families with Dependent Children (AFDC), and participation in free lunch programs, are

---

6 We maintain our broader operational definition for language minority students throughout this discussion. LEP students and students who speak non-standard English are included within our operational definition.

7 Fix and Zimmerman (1993) describe these issues in far more thorough detail.

used by federal, state, and local officials to determine which students should receive services through Title I. Just as Hakuta *et al.* (1993) have observed that many LEP students should be eligible for Title I, due to poverty, so too must we recognize that many AAVE students face language barriers in schools (and in the larger society) despite their status as native English speakers. AAVE has been devalued since the inception of slavery, and those who speak with a strong non-standard dialect often face considerable difficulty mastering Standard English literacy. Indeed, it is because of this reality that Oakland educators passed their controversial Ebonics resolutions; they were seeking ways to enhance Standard English proficiency among the majority of African-American students who are enrolled in Oakland's public schools.

This linguistic reality defies the implied separation of educational problems that are supposed to be repaired by Title I, Title VII, and Special Education. Special Education, intended for students with disabilities, is the final categorical program that we consider, because it is particularly relevant to the education of AAVE students. Readers of this chapter are probably aware that far too many African-American students are found in Special Education, which is provided to overcome cognitive and physical limitations among students from any social background. Medical evidence would suggest that no more than 4 percent of the normal population would fall under any of the mental "handicaps" that call for Special Education.

Remedial education has been synonymous with Special Education throughout most of the country, and under these programs "Learning Disabled" (LD) students have been relegated to classes with watered-down curricula that were designed for students with pathological limitations. Under provisions of Special Education we have observed some school districts where as many as 47 percent of African-American students are enrolled in Special Education, a trend that certainly challenges the assumptions one would draw from medical evidence. The Black English Trial is central to the point at hand; the assumption that black plaintiffs were "linguistically handicapped" fostered their placement into programs where educators denied the existence of corresponding academic language barriers.

One of the most significant findings derived from our national CPRE survey of language minority students corresponds to the alarming number of AAVE students who are placed into Special Education based on language. There is a logical explanation for this trend: many school districts hire speech pathologists for the express purpose of helping students with genuine speech impediments. Up to now uninformed school officials have assumed that AAVE was akin to a pathological speech impediment. In much the same manner that a stutter calls attention to a speaker, so too does AAVE call attention to itself in circumstances where it represents a stigmatized minority dialect. Based on the presumption that speakers of AAVE would be "handicapped" in competitive academic environments, pathologists, legislators, English teachers, and educators in general have encouraged black students to master Standard English, but they have done so based on policies that are uninformed by relevant linguistic research, thereby restricting the likelihood of black academic success.

It is at this stage that we come to the point of law that Judge Joiner used in support of his decision. He observed that the teachers of the African-American plaintiffs were clearly aware of the students' non-standard dialect, but they (the teachers) did not acknowledge that they were asking their black students to shift between two dialects. The teachers were advocating the adoption of Standard English, but they did so without overt recognition of the sources of linguistic interference that result from AAVE. They had never received training about "black English," but they were aware of its existence; its existence justified the "linguistically handicapped" label that established the basis of the law suit; that is, based on speech evaluations that equated AAVE with other linguistic afflictions. As a result of perceived pedagogical gaps, Judge Joiner ordered the school district in question to provide training for its teachers to ensure their knowledge of the linguistic structures associated with AAVE, and how those dialect differences might interfere with developing literacy for black students who do not speak, read, or write in the dialect(s) of wider communication.[8]

10.3.1 Policy summary

Policies for AAVE students have been driven by two forces: relevant law and corresponding funding. In many cases funding constraints have determined the agenda; the misuse of funds for less fortunate students is a practice that cannot be tolerated if systemic educational reforms are to succeed. There needs to be accountability that dollars spent for categorical programs are effective, resulting in greater success for students who are served by those programs. A local California anecdote is illustrative. Title I funds are used by a suburban school district in support of minority students who attend the local high school as part of a racial desegregation plan. A linguistic researcher at the school site noticed a Spanish-speaking student whose writing showed signs of dyslexia.[9] This was brought to the attention of school officials who claimed that no program was available to help the student. As an LEP student she qualified for bilingual education, but assessment tests for students with dyslexia were available only in English. Under these policies this student is unlikely to achieve academic success, and such a result would be in opposition to the goals embodied in

8 Smitherman (1991) has used the concept of a "dialect of wider communication" instead of "Standard English" because of the inherent variation and evolutionary change that is associated with all dialects, standard or otherwise.

9 I wish to thank Norma Mendoza-Denton for sharing this episode from her research among Latinos in high schools in California. Her research demonstrates that it would be a mistake to simply withdraw categorical support from poor minority students who attend schools in wealthy school districts, particularly when there is so much evidence of racial and linguistic segregation at the schools, along with inferior classes and services for poor students.

systemic reform. (See Smith and O'Day 1991; Furhman and Massell 1992; Kirst and Carver 1993.)

10.4 Linguistic implications derived from the Black English Trial

School districts rarely hire linguists, and teacher training programs rarely include linguistics classes; even under circumstances where linguistic expertise and training are adopted, there is little likelihood that the type of information required to enhance prospects for academic success among language minority students is available. The dearth of linguistic understanding for language minority students among educators can have negative consequences for AAVE students.

A distinguished panel of linguistic and educational experts affirmed the grammatical coherence of AAVE during the Black English Trial, which was strongly reaffirmed through a 1997 resolution by the Linguistic Society of America (see Burling 1973; Dillard 1972; Baugh 1980, 1983; Rickford http://www-leland.stanford.edu/~rickford/). The school district called no expert witnesses, opting instead to indicate that plaintiffs were indeed speakers of English, and that the school district was not obligated to make special provisions for them or any other student that might speak a dialect of English other than the local regional standard.

Experts in support of the plaintiffs provided grammatical and historical evidence regarding the birth and evolution of African-American dialects. I was surprised to see little attention paid to the historical consequences of "illiteracy laws," which refer to the statutes that were written to prevent slave literacy. Slave owners feared that educated slaves would be difficult to control, and the courts went along with this overtly racist practice prior to the "Emancipation Proclamation" (Higgenbotham 1978).

Brown v. Board, in 1954, was hailed as the case that would lead to educational equity for African Americans, and other minority students of color. However, true equity has rarely been achieved, and the categorical programs that are described above were intended to bolster the Brown decision through the "War on Poverty." Because the Brown case was based on racial segregation, matters of dialect diversity – to say nothing of the social stigma that most whites felt (and still feel) toward AAVE – were never adequately addressed. Since then various efforts to foster racial integration in schools have been controversial, seldom achieving the balance of racial harmony and educational equity that were their goals.

It is against this historical and legal template that linguists offered some of the first evidence to indicate that: (1) AAVE is not pathological, and that diagnoses of black children as "linguistically handicapped" are misguided and, perhaps, unethical; and (2) language barriers to academic achievement exist for many native English speakers who do not speak Standard English.

These matters are further complicated by the fact that considerable linguistic diversity exists within every racial and ethnic group in the US. Slave descendants have a unique linguistic history, however, when compared with every other group that has migrated to the US. As forced immigrants, what Ogbu (1978, 1992) has called "involuntary caste-like" minorities, slaves did not have the linguistic luxury of a gradual transition to English. Whereas the typical European immigrant came to the US with fellow speakers of their native language, slaves were linguistically isolated upon capture; that is, whenever possible. Whereas the typical European immigrant was able to maintain a family, slaves had no such right; as chattel they were subject to immediate sale, a practice that destroyed many black families. Whereas the typical European immigrant was able to attend public schools, slaves were denied education by law, and, after emancipation, were subject to inferior education under strict policies of educational apartheid.

These circumstances collectively amplified linguistic schisms that are the direct result of long-standing racial segregation throughout the country. Although the categorical programs that were put in place during President Johnson's "War on Poverty" were designed to overcome racial barriers to equality, they failed to take adequate account of potential language barriers in education (or other social contexts), and the "completely legal" pathological assessments that have been used since then have actually served to resegregate students in the contexts of "integrated" schools.

I will not provide a list of linguistic characteristics, which is readily available elsewhere.[10] I believe the plaintiffs in the Black English Trial state the importance of educational linguistic reform:

> Plaintiffs themselves urge a simple remedy. They would require the defendant School Board to identify each student who speaks "black English" and then use the best of the knowledge available in the (sic) school system to teach standard English, after taking into account the "black English" background of the children.
>
> (Judge Charles Joiner, cited in Smitherman 1981: 346)

10 Readers who are unfamiliar with linguistic research on African Americans may wish to consult the following sources: Wolfram (1969), Dillard (1972), Fasold (1972), Labov (1972), Burling (1973), Smitherman (1977), Baugh (1983), Mufwene (1983), Montgomery and Bailey (1986), Rickford (1996), Winford (1992), Green (1993), and the other contributions to this volume.

10.5 Speech pathology and the placement of AAVE students in Special Education

The linkage between speech pathology and Special Education is well known to most educators, and is justified in numerous instances. The wisdom, ethics, and morality of using speech pathology to place African-American students into Special Education has evolved along with the maturation of corresponding African-American linguistic research. Readers who are unfamiliar with these trends may wish to consult Wolfram's (1983, 1993) research on this topic; his is the most thorough evaluation of these practices, and he offers various suggestions on how educators might cope with the language barriers confronting their AAVE students.

Here I wish to address the "perception" that is created when school policies effectively equate AAVE with pathological speech afflictions. A child from any social background or gender may "stutter" for any number of reasons, but only those of us who can trace our ancestry to former American slaves are likely to be native speakers of AAVE. Those who stutter and AAVE speakers often share the experience of being the objects of linguistic bigotry, albeit for very different reasons. Speech impediments are the result of cognitive and/or physical attributes of individuals, and they can be found among people from every social, ethnic, and racial background. Non-standard educational language barriers for black students are the result of several factors, some of which have been discussed previously; they are the linguistic consequences of slavery and corresponding laws to prevent African-American literacy.

If systemic reform truly hopes to provide all students with access to challenging curricula with high standards, then it will be necessary to take students' linguistic background into account. Up to now language support has been focused on students for whom English is not native, and in some instances African-American students have been the victims of other misguided language policies.

10.6 Local expedience: the *ad hoc* placement of AAVE students in LEP classes

Our CPRE research examines the plight of language minority students in states and school districts that are dedicated to systemic reform. States under analyses seek high academic standards through challenging curricula for all of their students.[11] Students who require special educational assistance, are often

---

11 Results from our CPRE research are being evaluated at the time of this writing. We have already gathered survey data from twelve states regarding regulations and statutes that pertain to their language minority students who received federal categorical funds. Observations cited in the text are based on survey results and telephone interviews with state education officials from across the country.

excluded from programs with high academic standards (Fuhrman and Massell 1992). To a very large extent our observations are a mirror image of Fix and Zimmerman's (1993) results, which found that LEP students are woefully underserved by Title I. We observed that most Title I recipients are rarely considered to be language minority students.

We have discovered some cases where officials within a district, or at the school site, have placed African-American students in classes for LEP students, but these decisions were not based on the needs of AAVE students. Rather, the AAVE students in question were believed to have language difficulties that precluded their participation in mainstream classes, and were subsequently placed in the programs (or classes) designed for LEP students. In most cases we have found that financial and regulatory considerations drove those decisions, rather than the educational welfare of students. According to telephone interviews with LEP program administrators, African-American students are sometimes placed in ESL (English as a Second Language, or sheltered English) classes because principals and teachers at the school site have determined that these students should participate in programs supported with categorical funds (from their state and/or the federal government), and that often the primary categorical programs at a site may be focused on LEP students.

Some major urban school districts in California have gone so far as to teach Standard English to African-American students by way of ESL methods, but there is very little evidence to suggest that this practice is wise or effective. In much the same way that pathological diagnostics have been misused with black students, so too has the adoption of ESL methods been ill-suited to African-American educational achievement.

On a brighter note, we have observed individual teachers who have made strategic in-class adjustments for their linguistically diverse students, but these "successful" models are rare and do not result from enlightened linguistic policies. For example, many of the California teachers who participate in the Standard English Proficiency Program (SEP) have devised special curricula to help AAVE students enhance their literacy and speech, and they do so in ways that preserve the cultural dignity of black students while not exacerbating linguistic stereotypes that diminish their unique linguistic heritage.

ESL teachers face different problems in various regions of the country, and corresponding pressures on schools, from a linguistic point of view, vary considerably throughout the United States. California, Florida, New York, and Texas cope with these problems far more adequately than do most other states. Local officials tend to be unsure as to the best procedure for their students of color (Fix and Zimmerman 1993; Kirst and Carver 1993).

The essential point can be stated simply: AAVE students need the services that the plaintiffs in the Black English Trial called for previously: instructional methods that will enable them to acquire Standard English literacy skills. ESL methods are unlikely to yield this result.

10.7 The Hawaiian alternative: categorical programs in support of bidialectal education

The closest linguistic parallel that we find to the African-American situation is that facing students in Hawaii, where pidginization and creolization were common, as was the eventual suppression of languages other than English. Native Hawaiians have their own categorical program that stresses the value of bidialectal education. Although there are considerable differences between African Americans and Hawaiians, they share a history of creolized English that has, at least partially, stood as a barrier to educational success.

Legislators from Hawaii were able to convince the federal government that native Hawaiians were in need of federal educational support. There are striking parallels between the justification for the linguistic emphasis in Hawaii's categorical program, and the history of non-standard English among Southern slaves and their racially isolated descendants. Both groups were "involuntary caste-like" minorities; both groups have been denied the use of the languages of their ethnic backgrounds, and both groups have performed poorly in schools – that is, once they were given the opportunity to attend schools.

The magnitude of the problems, however, differs greatly between the two groups. Because Hawaii is insular, its language difficulties are confined to the state, in physical isolation from the mainland. The linguistic legacy of slavery is far more pervasive throughout the mainland, and can be traced prior to the birth of the nation. Hawaii is a young state; from the beginning of statehood Hawaiians were able to take greater advantage of the courts to redress the historical oppression of native Hawaiians. Until recently the courts were an unreliable source of legal relief to blacks, and empirical evidence confirms that the US justice system is still far from being truly color-blind (Higgenbotham 1990).

The Hawaiian categorical program is designed to help native Hawaiians succeed in higher education. Linguistic research that bolsters their programs is grounded in studies of language in social context that identify linguistic differences between Hawaiian Pidgin English (HPE) and Standard English. At present there is a strong effort in Hawaii to revive the indigenous language, and to preserve the native culture as much as possible. Here too Hawaii differs greatly from African America. It is nearly impossible to trace the linguistic ancestry of African slaves, and it would be even more difficult to "revive" African languages on the mainland in any fashion that would be comparable to the revitalization of the Hawaiian language in Hawaii.

Despite these differences, the striking similarities hint at possible educational solutions. AAVE students speak non-standard English, and that linguistic fact calls for teacher training that provides a better understanding of the educational consequences of pidginization and creolization. The success of the Hawaiian categorical programs can be attributed, in part, to the respect that is afforded students' mother tongue, a fact that stands in sharp contrast to the Black English Trial.

The experts further testified, however, that efforts to instruct the children in standard English by teachers who failed to appreciate that the children speak a dialect which is acceptable in the home and peer community can result in the children becoming ashamed of their language, and thus impede the learning process. In this respect, the black dialect appears to be different than the usual foreign language because a foreign language is not looked down on by the teachers
(Judge Charles Joiner, cited in Smitherman 1981: 343–44)

Perhaps the most important dimension of the Hawaiian categorical program is its overt respect for the vernacular dialect. With very few exceptions, this sense of cultural respect is still missing in the education of most AAVE students.

10.7 Toward a redefinition of language minority students and the "language barriers" they confront in educational contexts

Current regulations regarding language minority students focus on English as the threshold for LEP status. LEP students are not native speakers of English, or they live in situations where English is not the dominant language, which in turn makes them eligible for Title VII funds, that is, if they reside in a community that has made successful application for those funds.

English speakers, regardless of dialect, are excluded from existing federal and state provisions for language minority students. A model of current linguistic regulations for categorical students is illustrated in Figure 10.1. I propose an alternative model, presented in Figure 10.2, which is more in line with US linguistic demographics.

Figure 10.2 provides a far more accurate linguistic division of students throughout the US. It is important to make pedagogical distinctions between all three divisions and develop programs accordingly. Let us begin with the third category first; ESL students have not been adequately served by existing regulations, and we agree with Hakuta et al. (1993) and Fix and Zimmerman (1993)

LANGUAGE HISTORY	EDUCATIONAL LINGUISTIC STATUS	RELEVANT STATUTES
Native English speakers	Language majority students	Excluded from Title VII Programs
Native speakers of languages other than English	Language minority students (a.k.a. students for whom English is not native [ENN students])	Included within Title VII Programs

Figure 10.1 Current regulatory definition of language minority students

LANGUAGE HISTORY		EDUCATIONAL LINGUISTIC STATUS	RELEVANT LAW
NATIVE ENGLISH SPEAKERS	*Category 1* Native speakers of Standard English	Language-dominant group – native speakers of national (or regional dialects of) Standard English	Excluded → Title VII and provision from 20 U.S.C. 1703(f)
	Category 2 Native speakers of non-standard English	Language minority groups – speakers of non-standard English who are SENN	Title VII exclusion but included within 20 U.S.C. 1703(f)
NATIVE SPEAKERS OF LANGUAGES OTHER THAN ENGLISH (*Category 3*)		Language minority groups – including all students currently defined as ENN	Included in Title VII and reaffirmed by 20 U.S.C. 1703(f)

Figure 10.2 Proposed reform of regulatory definitions for language minorities

in their call for educational reforms that would allow more LEP students to receive services through Title I.

A comparable, but inverse, argument holds for many AAVE students, who currently receive Title I funding, or who participate in Special Education. Many of these students encounter genuine language barriers that impede their academic progress, yet there are no adequate federal or state regulations that recognize this fact. Much like the argument put forward by defendants in the Black English Trial, existing regulations presume that native English proficiency does not warrant special programs or the funding that would be required to maintain them.

In the case of AAVE, where dialect differences have been confirmed through numerous linguistic studies, a strong case can be made in favor of considering AAVE students as members of a language minority group; that is, in much the same manner that HPE speakers are a linguistic minority in Hawaii. Such students are not traditional LEP students, but neither are they native speakers of Standard English. Therein lies the need for modified policies to enhance their educational prospects.

If AAVE students have been neglected in this process, Standard English natives have been given the least consideration of all. After all, they are the students who are most likely to succeed. Why should we spend money to support students who have inherited linguistic advantages over students in categories 2 and 3 (see Figure 10.2)? Students in the first category are in need of a different kind of linguistic training. *They must learn to be tolerant of those who do not speak Standard English.*

Although the US has always been considered to be a cultural and linguistic melting pot, linguistic ignorance abounds, even among the well educated. It is not uncommon to hear woefully uninformed comments about language minority students who appear in categories 2 and 3. Rather than merely criticize students (and citizens) that were not born into circumstances where they learned Standard English natively, we need policies to educate Standard English speakers regarding the evolution of linguistic diversity in the United States.

It is an accident of history that English survived as the dominant colonial language in the United States, in much the same manner that French is influential in Quebec, and Spanish is the dominant language in Mexico. Few citizens are aware of our linguistic history, and far too many of us act on false linguistic stereotypes that lead to the kinds of misunderstandings that led to the Black English Trial. Students in category 1 must learn that they have a linguistic heritage that places them at considerable advantage in this society, and that the long-standing attitudes of linguistic elitism among politically powerful speakers of American Standard English have restricted opportunities for less fortunate citizens from other linguistic backgrounds.

Considered collectively, we should have special language programs for all students. Standard English speakers would learn about the history of American dialects and languages, giving them a better sense of the linguistic dimensions of "the melting pot." Courses that enhance linguistic tolerance are needed to counter existing linguistic prejudice. Students who speak non-standard English would not only learn about this history, but would also receive special instruction based on their personal linguistic heritage. Moreover, this instruction would be provided in such a way that no student would be made to feel ashamed of her or his linguistic ancestry. Finally, calls to reform LEP education are, comparatively, well advanced. Students in the third category must learn English, but not at the expense of losing their mother tongue. For far too long our education policies have squandered valuable linguistic resources under a shroud of linguistic chauvinism that is in direct opposition of our need to participate fully in the global economy, where knowledge of other languages and cultures is most desirable.

10.9 Conclusion: systemic reform and language minority students

Under the current proposal school districts would be encouraged to combine funds for categorical students in search of local solutions that are tailored to the learning community of each school (Heath and McLaughlin 1993). Every principal could conduct a linguistic survey or census within his or her school, which should be up-dated annually to record and anticipate changing language (and dialect) population trends within schools and LEAs.

Every student can be identified based on linguistic background, including deaf students. We propose that educators adopt the three linguistic divisions proposed here, namely, (1) students who are native speakers of Standard English, (2) students who are native speakers of non-standard English, and (3) traditional LEP students for whom English is not native. In this way we can tailor instruction to capitalize fully on diverse resources at different school sites. For example, a school that is populated with students from categories 1 and 2 will require programs that differ from schools filled with minority students (e.g., from categories 2 and 3).

The ultimate test of funding must be made through accountable demonstrations of students' progress. If schools that receive categorical funds fail to confirm educational gains for students served with those funds then an appropriate regulatory agency should intervene to ensure that new remedies are tried, and that those new remedies are based on knowledge regarding "best practices" for the categorical students in question.

Much like Judge Joiner, I leave matters of best educational practice (including forms of assessment) to the professional judgment of local educators. Another dimension of the present CPRE research shows that, in much the same manner that Gardner (1983, 1991) describes different learning styles, teachers develop "preferred teaching styles," and each school site (i.e. every learning community) differs from one locality to another.

I hesitate to suggest that schools be compelled to make an annual linguistic census, but I would strongly encourage the practice on the grounds that such data would provide teachers and school administrators with a wonderful ethno-linguistic profile of their student body. These data, along with other local considerations, should serve as the bases of policies to ensure that every student has the opportunity to learn, with challenging curricula that reflect high academic standards.

Without a more complete understanding of linguistic diversity in schools we are unlikely to overcome the historical pattern of educational preference for upper-middle-class students who reside in homes where Standard English is the norm. By the turn of the century such children will be a minority in California and Texas. The proposed adjustment in linguistic categorization of language minority students is intended to make the categories more elastic, in support of integrated regulations between federal, state, and LEAs, that are likely to ensure efficient and effective delivery of high-quality instruction to all students. Any regulation, or layer of bureaucracy, that cannot be shown to be of direct educational benefit to the welfare of all students should be discarded in favor of reforms that are flexible enough to allow officials within districts and/or at local school sites to ensure that every student they serve has an adequate opportunity to learn. This personalized service, responsive to the linguistic needs of every student, will prove to be one of the ultimate tests of systemic reform. This discussion is provided in support of that effort, because greater linguistic awareness of students, along with greater tolerance for linguistic diversity, will be essential to the future educational welfare of all students, regardless of background.

Acknowledgments

Primary support for this research has been provided through the Consortium for Research on Policy in Education (CPRE) under the directorship of Dean Susan Fuhrman of the Graduate School of Education at the University of Pennsylvania, and the National Science Foundation (BNS87–00864). I have benefited greatly from relevant discussion with several colleagues, including my fellow co-editors of this volume: Guy Bailey, Salikoko Mufwene, and John Rickford; and Mike Kirst, Charla Larrimore Baugh, David Bloome, Kenji Hakuta, Lisa Green, Walt Wolfram, Norma Mendoza-Denton, Tempi Champion, and Peter Roos. The project could not have been completed without the timely research assistance provided by Charla Larrimore Baugh, Yuri Kuwahara, Kangmin Zeng, Howard Block, Sandy Stein, Lisa Weiner, and Liz Parker. I have not always heeded their advice, and all limitations herein are my own.

References

Baugh, John (1980) "A reexamination of the Black English Copula." In *Locating Language in Time and Space*, William Labov (ed.). Orlando: Academic Press, pp. 83–106.
—— (1983) *Black Street Speech: Its History, Structure, and Survival*. Austin: University of Texas Press.

Brown v. Board of Education, 347 U.S. 483, 493 (1954).

Burling, Robbins (1973) *English in Black and White*. New York: Holt.

Crawford, J. (1992) *Hold your Tongue: Bilingualism and the Politics of "English Only."* New York: Addison-Wesley.

Dillard, J. L. (1972) *Black English*. New York: Random House.

Fasold, Ralph (1972) *Tense and the Form be in Black English*. Washington: Center for Applied Linguistics.

Fix, M. and W. Zimmerman, (1993) *Educating Immigrant Children: Title I in the Changing City*. Washington: Urban Institute.

Fuhrman, Susan and D. Massell (1992) *Issues and Strategies in Systemic Reform*. New Brunswick, NJ: Rutgers University, Consortium for Policy Research in Education.

Gardner, H. (1983) *Frames of Mind*. New York: Basic Books.

—— (1991) *The Unschooled Mind*. New York: Basic Books.

Green, Lisa (1993) "Topics in African-American English: The Verb System Analysis," unpublished PhD dissertation, University of Massachusetts at Amherst.

Hakuta, Kenji, *et al.* (1993) *Federal Education Programs for Limited-English Proficient Students: A Blueprint for the Second Generation*. New York: Carnegie Corporation.

Heath, S. and M. McLaughlin (eds.) (1993) *Identity and Inner-City Youth*. New York: Teachers College Press.

Higgenbotham, L. (1978) *In the Matter of Color: Race and the American Legal Process*. Oxford: Oxford University Press.

—— (1990) "Racism in American and South African courts: Similarities and differences." *New York University Law Review* 65.3: 479–588.

Joiner, C. (1981) "Memorandum opinion and order." In *Black English and the Education of Black Children and Youth: Proceedings of the National Invitational Symposium on the 'King' Decision*, Geneva Smitherman (ed.). Detroit: Wayne State University, Center for Black Studies, pp. 336–358.

Kirst, M. and R. Carver (1993) "School reform in Florida: A decade of change from 1983–1993". Manuscript.

Labov, William (1972) *Language in the Inner-City: Studies in the Black English Vernacular*. Philadelphia: University of Pennsylvania Press.

Lau v. Nichols, 414 U.S. 563 (1974).

Lee, F. (1994) 4 January *New York Times*.

Montgomery, Michael and Guy Bailey (eds.) (1986) *Language Varieties in the South: Perspectives in Black and White*. Tuscaloosa: University of Alabama Press.

Mufwene, Salikoko (1983) "Some observations on the verb in Black English Vernacular." African and Afro-American Studies and Research Center. Austin: University of Texas.

Ogbu, J. (1978) *Minority Education and Caste*. New York: Academic Press.

—— (1992) "Understanding multicultural education." *Educational Researcher* 5.14: 24.

Plyer v. Doe, 457 U.S. 202 (1982).

Rickford, John R. (1996) "Regional and social variation." In *Sociolinguistics and Language Teaching*, Sandra Lee McKay and Nancy Hornberger (eds.). Cambridge: Cambridge University Press, pp. 151–194.

—— (1997) Web-site: http: //www-leland.stanford.edu/~rickford/

Smith, M.S. and J. O'Day (1991) "Systemic school reform." In *The Politics of Curriculum and Testing*, S. Fuhrman and B. Malen (eds.). New York: Falmer Press.

Smitherman, Geneva *Talkin' and Testifyin'*. Boston: Houghton-Mifflin.

—— (1977) (ed.) (1981) "Black English and the education of Black children and youth." *Proceedings of the National Invitational Center for Black Studies.*

—— (1991) "'What is Africa to me?': Language ideology and African American." *American Speech* 66: 115–32.

Winford, Donald (1992) "Another look at the copula in Black English and Caribbean Creoles." *American Speech* 67.1: 21–60.

Wolfram, Walt (1969) *A Sociolinguistic Description of Detroit Negro English*. Washington: Center for Applied Linguistics.

—— (1983) "Test interpretation and sociolinguistic differences." *Topics in Language Disorders*. 3.3: 21–34.

—— (1993) "Research to practice: A proactive role for speech-language pathologists in sociolinguistic education." *Language Speech and Hearing Services in Schools* 24: 181–85.

SUBJECT INDEX

NAME INDEX

311